The Colonizing Self

A Theory in Forms Book   Series Editors Nancy Rose Hunt and Achille Mbembe

Duke University Press / *Durham and London* / 2020

The Colonizing Self

OR, HOME AND HOMELESSNESS IN

ISRAEL/PALESTINE Hagar Kotef

Printed in the United States of America on acid-free paper ∞
Designed by Courtney Leigh Richardson and typeset in
Portrait by Westchester Publishing Services

Library of Congress Cataloging-in-Publication Data
Names: Kotef, Hagar, [date] author.
Title: The colonizing self : or, home and homelessness in Israel/Palestine / Hagar Kotef.
Other titles: Theory in forms.
Description: Durham : Duke University Press, 2020. | Series: Theory in forms | Includes biblio-
graphical references and index.
Identifiers: LCCN 2020017127 (print) | LCCN 2020017128 (ebook)
ISBN 9781478010289 (hardcover)
ISBN 9781478011330 (paperback)
ISBN 9781478012863 (ebook)
Subjects: LCSH: Land settlement—West Bank. | Land settlement—Social aspects—West Bank. |
Israelis—Colonization—West Bank. | Israelis—Homes and haunts—Social aspects—West Bank. |
Israelis—West Bank—Social conditions.
Classification: LCC DS110.W47 K684 2020 (print) | LCC DS110.W47 (ebook)
DDC 333.3/156942089924—dc23
LC record available at https://lccn.loc.gov/2020017127
LC ebook record available at https://lccn.loc.gov/2020017128

Cover art: © Marjan Teeuwen, courtesy Bruce Silverstein Gallery, NY. The cover image by
the Dutch artist Marjan Teeuwen, from a series titled *Destroyed House*, is of a destroyed house
in Gaza, which Teeuwen reassembled and photographed. This form of reclaiming debris and
rubble is in conversation with many themes this book foregrounds—from the effort to render
destruction visible as a critique of violence to the appropriation of someone else's home and
its destruction as part of one's identity, national revival, or (as in the case of this image) a
professional art exhibition.

TO MY DAD—SO MUCH OF WHAT IS WRITTEN HERE IS A PROLONGED CONVER-
SATION WITH HIM; AND TO MAYA AND NOA, WHOM I HAVE MOVED AWAY FROM
HOME, BUT FOR WHOM I'M TRYING, ENDLESSLY, TO BUILD ANOTHER

Contents

Preface

I think Israelis should be aware that their presence in many places in the country entails the loss of a Palestinian family, the demolition of a house, the destruction of a village. . . . Many Israelis resist this because they think the consequence would be to leave. Not at all. . . . The last thing I want to do is to perpetuate this process by which one distortion leads to another. I have a horror of that. I saw it happen too many times. I don't want to see more people leave.—EDWARD W. SAID

"The Nakba is the history of anyone living on this land and/or anyone who cherishes it," states Eitan Bronstein Aparicio, director of the organization Zochrot and founder of De-Colonizer. And yet, it seems that making it, indeed, part of his own history is a struggle for Bronstein Aparicio—a struggle that manifests itself as a movement between two poles: On the one hand, Bronstein Aparicio is part of an ongoing endeavor to make the Palestinian Nakba visible and legible to the Jewish Israeli public. On the other hand, he reports grappling with the risk of colonizing Palestinian memory itself in and through this endeavor. As a result, he states, he can "never feel at home."[1] Throughout this book we shall reencounter this sentiment: a sense of Jewish Israeli home that becomes impossible, or at least unstable, when home is entwined with the present or past of the Palestinian disaster. Yet we

Epigraph: Edward W. Said, "Interview with Ari Shavit," *Ha'aretz*, August 18, 2000, republished in *Power, Politics, and Culture: Interviews with Edward W. Said*, by Edward W. Said, ed. Gauri Viswanathan (New York: Vintage Books, 2001). An English version can also be found at "Edward Said Interviewed by Ari Shavit for *Ha'aretz*," MiddleEast.org, August 26, 2000, http://www.middleeast .org/archives/8-00-31.htm.

1 Eitan Bronstein Aparicio, "Finding Home in a New Memory: A Journey to the Golan," *+972 magazin*, June 4, 2016, https://972mag.com/finding-home-in-a-new-memory-a-journey-to-the -golan/119816#_ftnref1.

shall find that just as prevalent is a sound sense of home that emerges despite, besides, and even through this disaster. The negotiations of a sense of belonging against the reality of this disaster give rise to the type of "self" this book seeks to identify. For the sake of brevity, I call it "the colonizing self."

In narrating his struggle, which so accurately captures the impasses of many activists working to undo the evils their own societies generate, Bronstein Aparicio takes us to the ruins of his wife's village, Mansura. Situated in the Golan Heights, Mansura is a Syrian village that was demolished in 1967. With his wife's family and others, Bronstein Aparicio returned to this site of destruction to tell the stories of the ruined village and to rebuild it—if only very partially—as a symbolic gesture. It is through this project, he writes, that he was finally able to construct his own sense of home. Through this experience, "it became clear to me that the story of Mansura had become my own—not exclusively mine but also my own."[2] In Bronstein Aparicio's description, the story of expulsion, expropriation, and demolition became "his own" when he participated in reconstructing both the oral history and the concrete space of the village; it is therefore "his" story *as a storyteller*, or as a *participant in reconstructing* both stories and traces. But what Bronstein Aparicio recognizes, and yet refuses to assert, is that the stories of the ruins were always also his stories; not as stories he comes to inhabit through Palestinian narratives or through his own embodied effort to create counternarratives, but as stories he inhabits through Israeli narratives and embodied projects that were always part of the Israeli project of settling the land. These stories were his own as the agent of these homes' destruction, rather than as the agent of their reconstruction and narration.

Akin to the Palestinian memories, these stories of settlement are passed on through generations (from my grandparents' generation, which was directly involved in the Nakba, to us, who still live in its aftermath and keep generating other catastrophes); and akin to the Palestinian memories, they come to shape Israeli identity. Yet they are often told differently, through gaps and silences that nonetheless carry with them acts of ruination. Stories of triumphs alongside stories of wartime anxiety and a fear of war that so many of us grew up with—that so many of us inhabit directly, having lived through wars and violence of various kinds—are inlaid with the physical remnants of Palestinian destruction. To recognize ourselves in these stories is to refuse a gap between "the state" and its people, between what "it" has done and who "we" are. For Bronstein Aparicio, or for me and

2 Bronstein Aparicio, "Finding Home."

many others, it is to refuse a gap between the Left in Israel and Israeli violence, between some progressive "us" and all those forces standing between "us" and "peace." This refusal is not an act of erasing those distinctions; it is a form of taking responsibility—for what we have done, or for what was and is done in our name, or for all the destruction and violence whose fruits we still enjoy. This sense of responsibility can then become a first step toward reconstituting these distinctions in a way that is more politically productive.

I recall trips with my father along an abandoned railway to the ruins of Na'ane, which was close to the kibbutz where he was born and where my grandparents still lived. I recall bathing on hot summer days in a pool in the Golan Heights that was built by the Syrian army for its officers. We knew it was called "the officers' pool," we always passed through the traces of war on our way to it, and yet this was "our" pool, a site of beauty amid fig trees, whose freezing water became our challenge—who would be brave enough to jump? My childhood memories, my home, cannot be detached from the violence of 1948 and 1967. When I miss my home, this is part of what I miss. In this regard, my point here and one of the main arguments of this book is that the construction of Jewish attachment to the landscape of Israel, the establishment of belonging to the land, the founding of home as well as homeland, includes a certain longing for and belonging to a past violence that becomes integral to Israelis' self-identity. It is this identity I seek to understand here.

Many Israelis who write about the occupation or the wider colonial facets of Israel's control over Palestinians—including myself—often focus on the mechanisms and technologies of power and domination, the structure of the law, or the logics of violence and governance. I seek here to turn the gaze toward the subject positions within the wider networks of occupation and settlement: the settler or colonizing self. How, then, can a critique be formulated when its material conditions are the object of critique? One can criticize one's state, to be sure—its violence, its wars. But how can one question the legitimacy of their own home; how can one point to the wrongs that are embedded in the very nature of their political existence? What would it mean for a Jewish Israeli to not simply write against "the occupation," but to recognize that her home is historically conditioned on the destruction of Palestinians' homes; that her attachment to this place is founded on a history—not such a distant history—of violence and is conditioned, at least to some extent, on the perpetuation of this violence? (And since Israel has become a paradigm of a certain kind of leftist critique, it is worth noting that the primary difference between Israel and other settler colonies such as the United States or Australia in this regard is temporal density). Once we move to engage in such a critique, there is no more separation between the "I" who writes and her object of critique, that is, the state and its doings: military and police violence, planning policies, legal discrimination. The I itself becomes the object of critique and her voice—the place from which she speaks, her language, the dialogues available to her—can no longer pretend to assume a position that is simply and clearly oppositional to injustice. From this perspective, this book was impossible to write, an act of hitting an ethical and political wall wherever I turned. It is a book about these impasses.

Ultimately, at stake here is not the possibility to settle this mode of being-at-an-impasse, but to find ways of presence in the land (Israel in my case) that fracture and then undo it. I am not interested, in other words, in lamenting the tragedy of this subject position, but in offering a critique of this form of subjectivity. And yet to understand the mechanisms by which the colonizing self can be decolonized and a territory—a home—can be inhabited in noncolonial ways despite a history of colonization, we first need to understand what Manu Samnotra refers to as "the objective conditions of colonialism."[3] In particular, we need to understand the mechanism of the colonizing self's entrenchment in both space and senses of justice. This is the main object of the book.

3 Manu Samnotra, "'Poor in World': Hannah Arendt's Critique of Imperialism," *Contemporary Political Theory* 18, no. 4 (2018): 562–82.

Acknowledgments

This book is strangely personal, and yet was conceived with the help, support, thoughts, and investment of so many others. I have had the rare opportunity and sheer luck of working with the most brilliant colleagues, who have engaged with this manuscript in thorough, critical, and committed ways beyond what I could have ever hoped for. I really cannot thank them enough. Their thoughts and comments have shaped this book and so many of its arguments. At SOAS, my new home, Laleh Khalili, Ruba Salih, Rahul Rao, Charles Tripp, Rafeef Ziadah, and Carlo Bonura have read the manuscript or significant parts of it. The insights and thoughts they provided, their critique and their questions, have been essential to the process of writing it and thinking through its many predicaments. I have been overwhelmed, in the most positive way possible, by their thoughtfulness, kindness, and ways of seeing.

Over one brunch in London, Neve Gordon shifted much of the ethnographic work for this book, and helped me disentangle so many of my questions. On many other occasions he offered ideas, suggestions, and at times skepticism. These, and the comments he provided on the full draft, are woven throughout the final outcome. Over the years, our paths crossed in several continents, and now in London he has become not only a treasured colleague but also a friend. Noam Leshem and Keally McBride read the full manuscript as well. They did this thoroughly and carefully and with rare attentiveness. In Keally's hand it became a jigsaw puzzle, and as I worked through her comments—always as generous as they are astute—so many of its pieces fell into place. Noam has been significant in adding some of the missing pieces to the puzzle, rendering the picture somewhat more complete.

Merav Amir seems to have become a person without whom I find it difficult to think. Much of the ideas herein were formed in a constant dialogue with her, endless phone conversations, and exchange of drafts. She was also kind enough to join me on the trip to Giv'ot Olam, during which significant parts of the ethnographic work for chapter 3 took place. Murad Idris has become an interlocutor and a friend during the long course of writing this book. At numerous junctures he has thought with me or pushed me to think differently, often shedding so much light on a problem with just one quick, almost incidental comment.

Kobi Snitz kindly traveled with me to the West Bank several times. He accompanied me when I went to take pictures or to check the accuracy of maps marking fences around settlements; he organized the visit to Yanun and facilitated the conversations I had there; he put me in touch with others, who provided crucial information. I am grateful for his time, for the indispensable information he provided following years of activism, and for his company. Hagit Ofran from Peace Now, Dror Etkes from Kerem Navot, Ziv Stahl from Yesh Din, and John Brown from many places have all provided vital support in the process of writing this book. I am not merely indebted for their time and help; I am in awe and admiration of their work, for which the adjective "important" seems like an understatement. They are some of the few people who demonstrate in their daily doings that the space between the sea and the river can be made into a different, less destructive one.

Throughout the years, segments of the work herein have been presented in quite a few workshops, seminars, and conferences, and this book has benefited from so many such interactions. I have had the privilege of thinking out loud alongside some of the brightest critical thinkers in the world, and I thank those who gave me the opportunity to do so and those who engaged in the conversation. These have included two installments of Association for Political Theory (APT) (and I am especially thankful to Libby Anker and Adom Getachew for their comments as discussants), one Western Political Science Association (WPSA) (with special thanks to Jeanne Morefield for her comments as a discussant), an American Political Science Association (APSA), as well as many workshops and colloquiums. I thank Shai Gortler for the invitation to present at the Minnesota Political Theory Colloquium; Monica Brito Vieira for inviting me to the Political Theory Workshop at York; Sorana Jude for the invitation to the Politics Seminar in Newcastle; Merav Amir (again) for inviting me to the Lexicon Workshop at Queen's University, Belfast; Yair Wallach and Moriel Ram for the invitation to the "After Oslo" Lecture Series, as well as the "Turning to Matter and Space in Israel-Palestine" Workshop, both at SOAS; Jason Edwards for the invitation to the Birkbeck Political Theory Colloquium; Miriam Ticktin and Alexandra Delano for the invitation to the Zolberg Institute on Migration and Mobility at the New School for Social Research; María González Pendás and Whitney Laemmli, for the invitations to present at the Crisis of Democracy

Workshop at Paris's Institute for Ideas and Imagination; and Teresa Bejan for the invitation to present at the Oxford Political Thought Seminar.

Jack Halberstam and Lisa Lowe have offered me the rare honor of presenting a chapter as part of a Modern Language Association presidential panel, and I am grateful for this and for their support of my scholarship at large. David Joselit generously organized a public lecture at the Committee on Globalization and Social Change, CUNY Graduate Center, where I also had the opportunity of meeting the brilliant Audra Simpson, who has since become a dear interlocutor. Kristina Hagström-Ståhl has given me several exceptional opportunities to present bits and pieces of this project at Gothenburg—I thank her for the conversations she facilitated, her own unique insights, and her generosity. Catharina Bergil's inspiring invitation to Gothenburg's Dance and Theatre Festival began this exchange and, in a way, gave me the opportunity to think with others on this work for the very first time. There were also the intense and productive workshops organized by Jo McDonagh and Jonathan Sachs at the Clark Library, University of California, Los Angeles; by Adam Stern at Yale; by Murad Idris and Lawrie Balfour at the University of Virginia; and by Irus Braverman at SUNY Buffalo. Finally, again with Murad Idris, there was the Empire by Its Other Names Workshop we both assembled at Columbia University. The people I met through these scholarly encounters, and those whom I already knew and saw again, the intensity of discussion, and the thoughtful suggestions they made have been critical to the formation of the pages herein, and will stay with me much beyond.

The Politics Seminar at SOAS and the workshops organized by the Centre for Comparative Political Thought are other venues in which I have had the opportunity to present, listen, share thoughts, and work through critiques. And I thank Charles Tripp (again and again) for cultivating these spaces. Further, the ideas herein have been shaped through engagements with colleagues at SOAS's Politics and International Studies Department, as well as through less formal conversations and exchanges. Many of them have been acknowledged above as readers of the manuscript. I express my deep appreciation also to Meera Sabaratnam; Kerem Nisancioglu; Salwa Ismail, to whom I am especially grateful, as she facilitated my arrival at the department; Manjeet Ramgotra; and Mark Laffey, whom I thank also for supporting, together with Fiona Adamson, a manuscript workshop, which has been essential in the final revisions of this text. This department, in its unique approach to the discipline, its critical thinking, its commitment to politics, and its amazing students and wonderful colleagues, has been more than I could have imagined as an academic home.

There are so many others, in so many corners of the world, friends and colleagues and those who make this distinction impossible, who have been a part of this journey and contributed to it: Andrew Dilts, Ariel Handel, George Shulman, Hellen Kinsella, Uday Mehta, Yair Wallach, Gil Hochberg, Rafi Grosglik, Jeanne Morefield (again), Rob Nichols, Nancy Luxon, Yves Winter, Anne McNevin, Ann Stoler, Onur Ulas Ince, Chris Brown, Michal Givoni, and Yuval Evri. I feel blessed by the long or short conversations we have had, their knowledgeable references or suggestions, the work they have been kind enough to share, and their ongoing support.

Parts of this book have been published in other academic journals, and although I cannot personally thank the anonymous reviewers of these essays, if they happen to read this book, I hope they can identify their contributions. A version of the theoretical overview was published in *Political Theory*; I would like to express my deepest gratitude to Lawrie Balfour, for the engaged and dedicated work she has done as part of this publication. Thinking on this book started many years ago with another publication, the entry "Home" in *Mafte'akh: Lexical Review of Political Thought*. Much like my previous book, which took form after writing the entry "Movement," the roots of this book can be traced back to this intellectual project, which has been one of the most productive scholarly endeavors in which I have taken part. I am indebted to all those who were part of this project, and above all to Adi Ophir, who initiated it and assembled all of us around it.

Mori Ram has worked with me on this research and has helped with so much more than I originally expected or planned for. Phoebe O'Hara and Jordi Lpez Bo have also been incredibly helpful in the research process. Marieke Krijnen and Emma Jacobs provided attentive and careful editing, and the team at Duke University Press has done fantastic work throughout the production process. I am particularly appreciative of Sandra Korn, Susan Albury, and, of course, Courtney Berger, who was involved in this book even before it hatched, who has believed in it, pushed for it to be published with Duke, provided advice, and was patient and accommodating of so many requests. The two anonymous reviewers provided feedback that was simultaneously so uplifting and so perceptive. Their meticulous and careful reading and the productiveness with which they expressed their critique is deeply appreciated.

Finally, there are few people who have not contributed to this book directly, but without whom I would have probably not become the person writing it. Anat Biletzki introduced me to philosophy and to its intimate links to politics. She was my ultimate source of inspiration, and my decision to pursue an academic career was very much a function of my desire to stand, one day, like her, in 144 Gilman (the room where she taught her Introduction to Logic) and open the eyes of others as she did for me. Adi Ophir has taught me what radical, critical thinking looks like, and has provided the philosophical path I have since sought to follow. Judith Butler has shaped my ways of seeing the world and understanding it, first in her writings and then in person; she also opened the world for me, and provided me the opportunity—often rare if not impossible—to escape. Last, Eileen Gillooly created a space—for me and so many others—in which more than I have ever believed to be possible became a reality. So many of the encounters, conversations, and friendships mentioned throughout these acknowledgments are her making, in one way or another.

The Leverhulme Trust generously provided the material conditions for the work of writing, as it gave me the precious gift of time. I am grateful for the opportunity they have given me to complete this book.

Introduction
Home

This is a story of ruination at the foundation of a new political system.
—YAEL NAVARO-YASHIN

Indeed, the house is often made to stand for "the conflict" insofar as it represents the tangible losses and gains that resulted. —REBECCA BRYANT

I suppose part of my critique of Zionism is that it attaches too much importance to home. Saying, we need a home. And we will do anything to get a home, even if it means making others homeless. —EDWARD W. SAID

This is a book about homes that were formed in and through violence; about homes that themselves become tools of destruction and expulsion; and about lives and selves whose very being is a form of injury. "A space of belonging and alienation, intimacy and violence, desire and fear," as Alison Blunt and Ann Varley put it,[1] which is "fundamental to being,"[2] home functions for me here as

Epigraphs: Yael Navaro-Yashin, "Affective Spaces, Melancholic Objects: Ruination and the Production of Anthropological Knowledge," *Journal of the Royal Anthropological Institute* 15, no. 1 (2009): 5; Rebecca Bryant, "History's Remainders: On Time and Objects after Conflict in Cyprus," *American Ethnologist* 41, no. 4 (2014): 690; Edward W. Said, "Interview with Ari Shavit," *Ha'aretz*, August 18, 2000, republished in *Power, Politics, and Culture: Interviews with Edward W. Said*, by Edward W. Said, ed. Gauri Viswanathan (New York: Vintage Books, 2001), 458.

1 Alison Blunt and Ann Varley, "Introduction: Geographies of Home," *Cultural Geographies* 11, no. 1 (2004): 3.

2 T. Peil, "Home," in *International Encyclopedia of Human Geography*, ed. Rob Kitchin and Nigel Thrift (Amsterdam: Elsevier, 2009). For a phenomenological analysis of home as fundamental to being, see Dylan Trigg, *The Memory of Place: A Phenomenology of the Uncanny* (Athens: Ohio University Press, 2012).

a concrete site, but also a placeholder, a metaphor, for thinking identities (collective and individual) that emerge through violence. Most explicitly, home is a site that ties the self to the nation, for which it often serves as "an uneasy metaphor."[3]

This book, then, looks at the systems of injury that have founded the system of property (from which enclosure, imperialism, slavery, or gentrification cannot be cleansed away) and are thus embedded into the concept of home if we think of any industrial, capitalist society.[4] It looks at the violence intertwined with the intimacies of love and sexual desire, which is thus embedded into the concept of home if we think of kinship. But above all, it looks at settler colonies, wherein the construction of one's home, and ultimately one's (national) identity, is the destruction of another's. In this context, this book's main test case is Israel/Palestine, where, indeed, the territorial struggle involved in the formation of homeland often took—still takes—place through various struggles around houses.[5]

My linguistic points of departure are Hebrew and Arabic, in which home and house (affect and architecture, belonging and territory) are merged. This linguistic point of departure, as well as the location from which I write, allow a linguistic slide between several words: *home, household, house, domestic, domos,* and *oikos.* If Hannah Arendt is correct, these words do not merely have different meanings and do not merely represent different political systems; they actually organize and shape different political orders.[6] And yet, the Hebrew word *ba'it* encapsulates this array of meanings. It is

---

3 Amahl Bishara, "House and Homeland: Examining Sentiments about and Claims to Jerusalem and Its Houses," *Social Text* 21, no. 2 (summer 2003): 143. On home as a metaphor for the nation or state, see also, among many others, Alon Confino, *The Nation as a Local Metaphor: Wurttemberg, Imperial Germany, and National Memory, 1871–1918* (Chapel Hill: University of North Carolina Press, 1997); Michael Feige, "Soft Power: The Meaning of Home for Gush Emunim Settlers," *Journal of Israeli History* 32, no. 1 (2013): 109–26; or Erin Manning, *Ephemeral Territories: Representing Nation, Home, and Identity in Canada* (Minneapolis: University of Minnesota Press, 2003).

4 For an excellent analysis tying together capitalism (postindustrialization, globalized markets), ethnic violence, and homes—their shortage, the fantasies constructing and undoing them, their geographies, and the various forms through which they are (re)created at a time of crisis—see Arjun Appadurai, "Spectral Housing and Urban Cleansing: Notes on Millennial Mumbai," *Public Culture* 12, no. 3 (fall 2000): 627–51.

5 Bishara, "House and Homeland," 144.

6 Hannah Arendt, *The Human Condition,* 2nd ed. (Chicago: University of Chicago Press, 1998).

the domos of the domestic sphere and it entails (or is contained within) the *oikonomia* of the oikos; it is a home, a house, and at times a household. In other words, it is the physical site, the social order that is organized within it, and the affectual dimensions that eventually territorialize identity as well as attachment.[7] The Arabic *beit* likewise entails an array of functions that are scattered over several English concepts. But as we shall see, whereas language unites these functions, political history dissociates them in the case of many Palestinians.

"Home" thus represents here the spatial facets of attachment, belonging, community, kinship, identity, and thus subjectivity. These spatial facets render "home" an apt site (or, as stated above, an analogy, an allegory) for understanding settler colonialism: the political system defined by an attachment to space that rests on dispossession, on a primordial act of ethnic cleansing and the many forms of violence that follow.[8]

Accordingly, the task ahead is to understand the cultural, political, and theoretical apparatuses that enable people and nations to construct a home on the ruins of other people's homes, to feel that they belong to spaces of expulsion, or to develop an attachment to sites which subsequently—or even consequently—are transformed into sites of violence. Belonging is thus conceptualized here as and through settlement (homemaking, a mode of taking place) in order to produce an account of the relationship between collective identities and institutional, mass, or state violence.[9] In a way, then, I ask about the affectual conditions of possibility of settler colonialism,[10] which is

7 For a further analysis of this concept, see Hagar Kotef, "Ba'it (Home/Household)," *Mafte'akh: Lexical Review of Political Thought* 1E (2010), http://mafteakh.tau.ac.il/en/2010-01/01/.
8 Achille Mbembe provides a concise yet comprehensive map of these forms of violence in the context of colonization—from the founding violence that creates the space for its own appearance to a violence that "give[s] this order meaning," and to a violence that "recur[s] again and again in the most banal and ordinary situations," which falls "well short of what is properly called 'war,'" yet cannot be reduced to the notion of structural violence. Achille Mbembe, *On the Postcolony* (Oakland: University of California Press, 2001), 25.
9 I am thinking here about belonging primarily in its political form, that is, as a mode of maintaining, demarcating, reproducing, or imagining "the boundaries of the political community." See Nira Yuval-Davis, *The Politics of Belonging: Intersectional Contestations* (London: SAGE, 2011), 204. But as Yuval-Davis proposed, this mode of belonging is tangled up with other forms of belonging—with social categories (of race, class, gender, etc.) or value systems.
10 In Sara Ahmed's words: "The issue is that home is not simply about fantasies of belonging—where do I originate from—but that it is sentimentalized as a space of belonging ('home is where the heart is'). The question of home and being at home can only be addressed by considering the

simultaneously a sociopolitical and a psychic question.[11] After all, without such mechanisms of attachment to violence, "settling" would have been impossible amid the conditions of colonization. In so doing, I follow a rich body of literature that argues that colonization cannot be understood without what Ann Stoler terms the "'emotional economies' of empire," and I try to understand those in their most spatially articulated manifestation.[12] The house, its structure, its ideology, the sentiments invested in it, the social textures within it and those of which it forms a part, are inseparable from the financial systems, policies, and moral economies of empire.[13] I therefore move between "home" as a metaphor for a state or an attachment to wider political constellations (community, territory, nation) and home as a component of the state (which is composed, as Aristotle stated, of many households), that is, the homes of individuals and small kinship units. This movement is a way of weaving together these affective economies, or untangling them to see how they are produced, managed, and regulated.

This means that settler colonialism also serves here as an example (if not an allegory in and of itself) of other political formations in which the existence of some—their lives, their bodies, their security, and their prosperity—is conditioned on inflicting violence on others. This violence can be direct or structural, deliberated or unintentional, celebrated or denied by the injuring persons, or can even hurt their sense of self (as is, for example, the case with progressive, leftist Israelis)—but it is nonetheless part of who they are. Who

---

question of affect: being at home is here a matter of how one feels or how one might fail to feel." "Home and Away: Narratives of Migration and Estrangement," *International Journal of Cultural Studies* 2, no. 3 (December 1999): 341.

11 Indeed, as Butler notes, the ethical and political reflection of the question of violence "must take place precisely at the threshold of the psychic and social worlds" (Judith Butler, *The Force of Non-violence* [New York: Verso Books, 2020], 172).

12 Ann Laura Stoler, *Along the Archival Grain: Epistemic Anxieties and Colonial Common Sense* (Princeton, NJ: Princeton University Press, 2009), 68. See also Stoler's *Carnal Knowledge and Imperial Power: Race and the Intimate in Colonial Rule* (Oakland: University of California Press, 2002); Antoinette Burton, *Dwelling in the Archive: Women Writing House, Home, and History in Late Colonial India* (Oxford: Oxford University Press, 2003); Philippa Levine, *Prostitution, Race, and Politics: Policing Venereal Disease in the British Empire* (New York: Routledge, 2003); and Anne McClintock, *Imperial Leather: Race, Gender, and Sexuality in the Colonial Contest* (New York: Routledge, 1995), among many others.

13 See, for example, Ian Baucom, "Mournful Histories: Narratives of Postimperial Melancholy," MFS: *Modern Fiction Studies* 42, no. 2 (summer 1996): 259–88; Edward W. Said, *Culture and Imperialism* (London: Vintage Books, 1994).

we are. As Jennifer Terry recently showed in regard to war, Bruce Robbins in regard to various modes of privilege, or Michael Rothberg in regard to various orders of systematic violence, systems of injury are woven into social positions in ways that make it impossible to simply renounce them, to simply take a stance against them, to simply say, in Jeanne Morefield's reconstruction, this is not "who we are."[14] Which is not to say that we should accept these systems of injury. "Who we are" always takes form within broken, contradictory schemes that can never be determined once and for all.[15]

THIS BOOK WAS WRITTEN over a period of more than seven years, during which many dominant assumptions concerning political lives have shifted. When I started writing it, around 2012, there was a need, I thought, to question the assumption that those living in liberal democracies disavow violence, if only as a rhetorical maneuver. There was an urgency, I thought, to point to the undercurrents tethered to the political fabric (in Israel, but also in the United States or Europe) that render legitimate the explicit embrace of, and political will to, violence. But as the book was written, with the rise of Trump and the Far Right across the world, the explicit racism that came to light with Brexit, and the slow legalization of apartheid in Israel, these undercurrents rose to the surface. In this sense, the book is both more and less timely than originally planned. The theoretical effort to expose these desires or attachments may be less needed as they are now barer, but understanding them is more urgent than ever.

What I seek to offer here is a theory of the dispossessor. At least in the context of Israel/Palestine, much has been written on the dispossessed subject, and theories of subjectivity that work through the figure of the refugee or through the space of diaspora are quite prevalent. There has also been a proliferation of literature about the state as an actor or state actors, or mechanisms of power

---

14 Jennifer Terry, *Attachments to War: Biomedical Logics and Violence in Twenty-First-Century America* (Durham, NC: Duke University Press, 2017); Bruce Robbins, *The Beneficiary* (Durham, NC: Duke University Press, 2017); Michael Rothberg, *The Implicated Subject: Beyond Victims and Perpetrators* (Stanford, CA: Stanford University Press, 2019); Jeanne Morefield, *Empires without Imperialism: Anglo-American Decline and the Politics of Deflection* (Oxford: Oxford University Press, 2014), 2.

15 See, for example, James Martel, *The Misinterpellated Subject* (Durham, NC: Duke University Press, 2017); or Judith Butler's work, in particular, *Gender Trouble: Feminism and the Subversion of Identity* (New York: Routledge, 1990), and *Bodies That Matter: On the Discursive Limits of "Sex"* (New York: Routledge, 1993).

that explain dispossession. But a theory of the dispossessing subject is largely missing. *The Colonizing Self* thus works at two levels: first, it provides a contextualized analysis of spaces of belonging in Israel/Palestine, and second, it provides a theoretical analysis of the forms of subjectivity at the foundation of both liberalism and settler colonialism (which are, historically at least, inextricable). In this regard the status of Israel as a liberal democracy (albeit an eroding one) merits some explication. "Liberal" and "democratic" are in Israel parameters limited to a dual matrix, combining citizenship status and location: All Jewish citizens (within the 1948 borders and in the settlements) enjoy liberal democracy, and, to a lesser degree, all citizens (Jewish and Palestinian) within the 1948 borders. Thus, even though also within these parameters, both the liberal and the democratic facets of the regime are limited, stratified, and eroding, and even though the "one state" is already the political condition of Israel/Palestine—and within these boundaries it is clearly a nondemocratic state—its matrix of control allows for clearly defined zones of democratic rule.[16] When I refer here to "liberal" or "democratic" I refer to these enclaves, within which most Jewish Israelis reside.

To unfold this dual analysis, the book focuses on three main homes or, better yet, three main figures of home, archetypes of sorts that come to represent different modes of inhabiting violent geographies. The first is the home of one of the most violent settlers in the West Bank, a home that effectively led to the eviction of an entire Palestinian village. It is also the largest organic farm in Israel, and the relation between the ethics of organic agriculture and this form of dispossession is crucial to me, as part of an effort to understand the ethical schemes that are employed to support homes under such conditions of violence (part III). The second home is in fact a plurality of homes: the depopulated Palestinian homes that are inhabited by Israeli Jews, often progressive and left leaning (part II). These Palestinian homes—in Jaffa, Jerusalem, Ein Hod—and this mode of homemaking in the depopulated home/ space serve as an allegory for Zionism at large (if not settlement as such). At the focus of this allegory is liberal Zionism, and, in this sense, there is a wider lesson concerning liberal sentiments here. The duo formed by parts II and III moves between the 1967 and the 1948 borders and endeavors to think together (even if apart) the establishment of Israel and the occupation of the West Bank and Gaza. In very different ways, these two modes of homemaking open questions concerning the various narratives, ideologies, and ethics

16 For an analysis, see Ariella Azoulay and Adi Ophir, *The One-State Condition: Occupation and Democracy in Israel/Palestine* (Stanford, CA: Stanford University Press, 2012), 203–24.

that allow one to live amid the destruction for which they are responsible. Accordingly, this analysis allows us to see the forms of social and political positions—the selves—that emerge through the attachment to these sites of violence. The analysis of these two parts is based on a spatial typology of contested homes, an ethnographic examination of these homes as sites wherein both formal citizenship and claims for place are negotiated, and a cultural analysis of identity production via a study of the representations of homes, national or private. Finally, the third home, which opens this book, is the figure of home as it circulates in political theory (part I). At its core, it is the home I reread into the Lockean concept of property, but in its wider sense, it is the home that I seek to situate as the core unit of political analysis. Via this reading, I show how the structure of dispossession is embedded into different modes of subjectivity, thereby providing a conceptual foundation for the analysis that follows.

Home and Violence: The Wider Scope of the Argument

Home is "the primary site around which identities are produced and performed," a site of intimacy and love, a site defined by attachments.[17] At the same time, home is always also a site of injury: injuries caused by and to the territories we inhabit or the people with whom we share our lives or with whom we refuse to coinhabit; injuries caused by our disposed piles of rubbish or our sewage flows, or by police or military violence that penetrates home or refuses to do so. Furthermore, home is also an exclusionary space: it creates distinctions between those who can come in and those who must stay out; between those who stay overnight and those who must leave; those who have keys and those who must knock on the door—between the members of the household (and, within them, between family and domestic workers or slaves, for example) and guests or unwanted strangers. Or, to apply these distinctions to another context, between the members of the nation-state and its outsiders: guest workers, undocumented migrants, and those who cannot even cross the border. Home is thus a site of differentiations.

Therefore, in its articulation as both a political technology and a political concept, we can think of the home as a place of governing differences—governing by creating differences (by hiding them, containing them) or governing those who have been differentiated: the governance of wives, slaves, servants, and other domestic workers, as well as children or those presumed

17 Peil, "Home," 181.

to be like children (and thus we can think of home as a meeting point for questions of race, class, legal residency, age, and disability). Home is that which can be—indeed is—differentiated (above all from the political),[18] and is that within which difference resides: It is the place of Woman (she who is different from Man); the signifier of private property (which produces class differences); and it is the function through which forms of government are differentiated: differences between those who are thoroughly and fully governed and those who can, in some fields, transcend being governed and are therefore "free" and "equal."[19] If one of the main problems of early modern and modern political theory is the tension between theoretical equality (universalism) and a reality of domination, discrimination, and exploitation, then "home" may provide a theoretical solution. Prefiguring and conditioning the political sphere as a sphere of (presumed) equality, the home (or private sphere, or domestic sphere) allows differences and differentiations to be governed outside of politics and as if they were nonpolitical, making way for "universalism" at the state's level.[20]

At stake, then, is the array of connections between exclusion, often violent, and intimacy—an intimacy that always requires exclusion to maintain its parameters (intimacy, after all, cannot be stretched too far), yet tends to hide this aspect from the stories it tells about itself. This combination means that also at stake is a tension between fantasy and real life, or a tension between the promises of political concepts and the political orders they actually depict. In this sense, too, this book can be read as a parable. The

18 We see this in the Aristotelian demarcation of the oikos as the other of the polis and in a long tradition of both philosophy and historical accounts ever since. It underlies the dichotomy identified by Max Weber between the pure form of rational authority in the modern bureaucratic state, on the one hand, and the traditional state, drawing its form from the household, on the other. Mediated by civil society, this opposition also appears in Hegel; it is central to the rigid distinction between the private and the political that liberalism both assumes and demands—a distinction that preconditions the notion of private property; and it is shared by institutional-historical analyses that depict the emergence of the modern state from the royal court. According to the latter analyses, even though the state in its embryonic form was inseparable from the king's household, the modern state is defined as such *because* of the disentanglement of the sovereign from the persona of the king and of the state's bureaucracy from the management of the king's household.

19 I am thinking here along the lines of Arendt's reading of Aristoteles (see *Human Condition*).

20 As Carole Pateman has observed, or as Marx has made clear. Carole Pateman, *The Sexual Contract* (Stanford, CA: Stanford University Press, 1988); Karl Marx, "On the Jewish Question," in *The Marx-Engels Reader*, ed. Robert Tucker (New York: W. W. Norton, 1978), 26–52.

fantasy (or concept) it captures is a certain fantasy of home, as a sheltering, stable, and peaceful space. The reality is that of violence—the violence of forced mobility, demolition, and dispossession on which this book's argument focuses, but also of rape, incest, beating, imprisonment, confinement, isolation. This is not to say that all these violences are the same, and indeed, I will not consider all of them here.

Many have pointed to this tension before me, and their work can mark the larger scope of the argument, the wider field to which it applies.

Feminists across disciplines, historical moments, and geographical contexts have exposed the frequency of domestic violence, marital rape, or incest; they have shown how domestic work and care are outsourced to those working under conditions of exploitation, often paying with their own homes' collapse. Drawing on their important insights, my book nevertheless centers not on violence in the home, but on homes as a technology of violence that operates outward. Accordingly, working on home here is not a way of foregrounding intimate modes of injustice that often take place in the private sphere. Rather, my focus is *the intimacies of public wrongs.*

The history of public wrongs that is woven into the theory and practice of homemaking is quite diverse. Another one of its main fields is capitalism, and alongside gender and sexuality it, too, provides some of the larger parameters within which my argument can echo. Much like in settler colonialism, which is the focus of this inquiry, in capitalism we find mechanisms of attachment to objects of violence—objects whose production necessitates violence—and a continuous attachment to these objects even after this violence becomes apparent. Most relevant to the subject of this book would be cases of gentrification, or instances in which eminent domain is declared to evict some (most often the less well-off), transferring places of residence to private real-estate enterprises in a process through which new homes are constructed on the ruins of others. But in different forms and under different structures, we are attached to objects in which violence is implicated in even the most mundane practices of domesticity: from our contribution to degrading working conditions when ordering home supplies from Amazon, to the toxicity of mineral dust in the cobalt mines in the Democratic Republic of Congo that goes into the production of almost every battery we use (from laptops to electric cars), to the child and forced labor in those and other mines; the list goes on and on.

Lauren Berlant further shows that desire under capitalism attaches itself not just to objects implicated in violence (through their production, or through the social organizations that coalesce around either production or consumption), but to the very order of violence. I will return to this analogy in detail in the theoretical overview and chapter 2. Whereas it is Berlant's model of attachment that will stand at the basis of one of the main arguments of this book, the analogy between capitalist systems and settler colonialism has other facets which will be considered here only partially. A key analogy here is the capitalist mode of production through destruction that David Harvey identifies, following Marx.[21] For Harvey, it is capitalist production that is at stake here; but creative destruction is also the mode through which settlers' homemaking takes place.

Finally, much like the case of both settler colonialism and intimacy or kinship, part of what shapes capitalist form of destruction is the question of substitution. Presumably, whereas both capitalist consumption and sexual desire are organized according to the logic of substitution, at stake in settler colonialism is precisely the lack of the possibility of substituting the object of attachment: territory. That is, if in capitalism the logic of value or exchange, and certainly practices of surplus consumption, are anchored in the possibility—and the desire—to substitute one object (concrete or abstracted) for another, and if sexual desire is organized around the substitution of one object of desire with another (this is precisely the foundation of the Oedipal complex, the structure of Lacan's *objet petit a*, but also the nature of any new relationship or most fantasies), then in settler colonialism the singularity of the territory, its irreplaceability, is the political principle that drives and justifies settlement. Yet the difference does not hold, and the mechanism of substitution often remains an unrealized potential, even in the former two orders. In this sense, to borrow Berlant's words (themselves borrowed), this book "politicizes Freud's observation that 'people never willingly abandon a libidinal position, not even, indeed, when a substitute is already beckoning to them.'"[22]

---

21 David Harvey, *The Enigma of Capital and the Crises of Capitalism* (Oxford: Oxford University Press, 2010). Gastón Gordillo inverts the famous "creative destruction" into "destructive production" to think of the capitalist production of space. Gastón R. Gordillo, *Rubble: The Afterlife of Destruction* (Durham, NC: Duke University Press, 2014). See also Marshall Berman, *All That Is Solid Melts into Air: The Experience of Modernity* (New York: Penguin Books, 1982), 100.

22 Lauren Berlant, *Cruel Optimism* (Durham, NC: Duke University Press, 2011), 27. Quote from Sigmund Freud, "Mourning and Melancholia [1915]," in *The Standard Edition of the Complete Psychological Works of Sigmund Freud*, vol. 14, ed. James Strachey (London: Hogarth, 1957), 244.

Israeli Homes

"The ongoing requirement to eliminate the Native alternative continues to shape the colonial society that settlers construct on their expropriated land base," argues Patrick Wolfe.[23] The main argument of this book is that not just societies, but also modes of selfhood are shaped by this ongoing requirement. In other words, there is a settler self and it is constituted as part of a project of ethnic cleansing. As Ruba Salih and Sophie Richter-Devroe put it in the Israeli context, "land confiscation, annexation, and fragmentation are foundational not only to the formation of Israeli settler nationalism but also to the definition of its citizens *as political and human subjects*."[24] The story of the "political and human subject" that is formed via "land confiscation, annexation, and fragmentation" (in Salih and Richter-Devroe's words) is the story of the homemaking of the Israeli Jew in Israel/Palestine.[25] And this story must be examined also through all those Palestinian homes whose destruction constitutes this home: homes that are bulldozed or bombarded, at times killing their inhabitants in their collapse; homes that are still standing but have become inaccessible; homes whose keys are kept in the hope of return and that are often inhabited by others; temporary homes in refugee camps that have become permanent; homes that are rendered illegal by discriminatory land regimes; homes that are being demolished cyclically as part of Israel's effort to make more land available for Jewish settlement; but also homes that are being rebuilt, again and again, as a form of resistance—staying put, *sumud*, as a political struggle reasserting identity and belonging.[26]

Zionism is often described as (indeed is) "a massive housing project."[27] Yet as Idan Landau observed,

23 Patrick Wolfe, *Traces of History: Elementary Structures of Race* (New York: Verso Books, 2016), 33.

24 Ruba Salih and Sophie Richter-Devroe, "Palestine beyond National Frames: Emerging Politics, Cultures, and Claims," *South Atlantic Quarterly* 117, no. 1 (2018): 7; my italics.

25 I add here the qualifier "Jew" to "Israeli" in order not to erase the roughly 20 percent of the Israeli population who are not Jews, particularly Palestinians who are citizens of the Israeli state. This qualifier may produce some discomfort, as it may sound essentializing and as such racist (anti-Semitic). This is not my intention here.

26 *Sumud* literally means "persistence," but also refers to the act of Palestinians staying closely, tightly, stubbornly to the land, and building a home and a homeland, despite the effort to dispossess them. See Alexandra Rijke and Toine van Teeffelen, "To Exist Is to Resist: Sumud, Heroism, and the Everyday," *Jerusalem Quarterly* 59 (2014): 86–99; Raja Shehadeh, *The Third Way: A Journal of Life in the West Bank* (New York: Quartet Books, 1982).

27 Yael Allweil, *Homeland: Zionism as Housing Regime, 1860–2011* (London: Routledge, 2017), 5. Allweil analyzes the Zionist project through what she refers to as "Israel's housing regime," which was

if someone were to summarize the Zionist project one day, [they] would have to face one baffling fact: how is it that so many people tie Zionism to construction and production, rather than to destruction and eviction? After all, alongside the obsession with nonstop construction, mostly beyond the Green Line, the roars of bulldozers have always been present: ascending, striking, breaking, and shattering. Migrants' housing projects were built instantly, build-your-own-home neighborhoods, neighborhoods for military personnel, suburbs, and luxurious highrises sprung up like mushrooms after the rain; and at the very same time, the angel of Zionist history amassed a pile of debris which "grows skyward."[28]

Stories of destruction also feature in Israeli identity via the destruction of Jewish homes: above all, the hounding image of the destruction of the temple, which is referred to in Hebrew as the destruction of home, the prolonged exile that followed, and the Holocaust. This duality of constitutive destruction can be a version of Said's claim that both nations share a history of dispossession, but this is not the claim I want to make here. I will not offer a detailed mapping of these various destroyed homes and the diverse courses of their destruction. I rather seek to isolate a segment from this complex map in order to integrate destruction and construction into one history, one identity, of a community, a nation, for which destruction is constitutive.

FOR NOW, AMID all this destruction, I want to focus on the constitutive destruction that took place in 1948 and its long aftermath in order to introduce a wider question regarding knowledge and violence.

In the aftermath of the two grand territorial wars of Israel—in 1948 and 1967—massive projects of demolition have changed the Israeli landscape.

"intended to provide housing for each citizen as a fulfilment of the right of each Jew to the ancestral homeland in which he or she was being rooted" (12). Note the conflation here between "citizen" and "Jew," which has served to deny many Palestinian citizens the right to a proper home.

28 Idan Landau, "House Demolitions: The Enduring Background Noise of Zionism," *Lo lamut tipesh* [Don't die dumb] (blog), June 10, 2013, https://idanlandau.com/2013/06/10/house-demolishions -zionism-background-noise/; my translation. The quoted segment is from Walter Benjamin's "On the Concept of History," in *Selected Writings*, vol. 4: *1938–1940*, ed. Michael W. Jennings and Howard Eiland, 389–400 (Cambridge, MA: Harvard University Press, 2003), ix.

Pictures and maps showing "before" and "after" strikingly present the construction of the Jewish homeland as heavily dependent on destruction (see figures I.1–I.3). Ever since this period, house demolition in its various forms has been a dominant political technology in Israel, and an essential element in its construction.[29]

My argument in regard to this political technology is dual. First, as aforementioned, I argue that this destruction is constitutive. That is, this destruction is not a mere historical contingency. It is rather woven into Israeli subjectivity, as far as such exists (and national selves never fully exist as such). To put it differently, this book sets out to show that Israelis are intimately invested in destruction in various ways. Second and relatedly, I argue that in some cases, this destruction is affirmed rather than denied. This second argument intervenes in a larger debate in the literature concerning the work of collective memory in Israel/Palestine, as well as colonial memory more broadly. I touch on it extensively in the theoretical overview. Within this debate, some emphasize the erasure of Palestinian history and landscape, intended to deny their very existence in the land and, derivatively, the violence entailed in removing them;[30] some focus on

29 There are many dimensions to the transformation of Arab land into Jewish land. On the legal status of territory, see Geremy Forman and Alexandre Kedar, "From Arab Land to 'Israel Lands': The Legal Dispossession of the Palestinians Displaced by Israel in the Wake of 1948," *Environment and Planning D: Society and Space* 22, no. 6 (December 2004): 809–30; Alexandre Kedar, "The Legal Transformation of Ethnic Geography: Israeli Law and the Palestinian Landholder 1948–1967," *New York University Journal of International Law and Politics* 33, no. 4 (2001): 923–1000; Issachar Rosen-Zvi, *Taking Space Seriously: Law, Space and Society in Contemporary Israel* (Abingdon, VA: Routledge, 2017). In regard to the Bedouin minority, see Alexandre Kedar, Ahmad Amara, and Oren Yiftachel, *Emptied Lands: A Legal Geography of Bedouin Rights in the Negev* (Stanford, CA: Stanford University Press, 2018). Noam Leshem emphasizes that the state is not a unified entity in this regard, and many who settled in depopulated Arab houses or areas cannot simply be seen as its agents. They had conflicting relations with the state, which often treated them as illegal trespassers. Noam Leshem, *Life after Ruin: The Struggles over Israel's Depopulated Arab Spaces* (Cambridge: Cambridge University Press, 2016).

30 A very partial list includes Nadia Abu El-Haj, *Facts on the Ground: Archaeological Practice and Territorial Self-Fashioning in Israeli Society* (Chicago: University of Chicago Press, 2001); Salman H. Abu Sitta, *The Palestinian Nakba 1948: The Register of Depopulated Localities in Palestine* (London: Palestinian Return Centre, 1998); Meron Benvenisti, *Sacred Landscape: The Buried History of the Holy Land since 1948* (Berkeley: University of California Press, 2000); Noga Kadman, *Erased from Space and Consciousness: Israel and the Depopulated Palestinian Villages of 1948* (Bloomington: Indiana University Press, 2015); Walid Khalidi, ed., *All That Remains: The Palestinian Villages Occupied and Depopulated by Israel in 1948* (Washington, DC: Institute for Palestine Studies, 1992). I review others throughout this book.

FIGURE I.1. Manshiyya. January 1949 (source: Zalmanya).

the various rationales deployed to justify Palestinians' dispossession when their existence becomes undeniable;[31] some argue that there are large holes in these networks of blindness and denial through which that past constantly emerges;[32] some call for a complete change of metaphors.[33] Rather than working to provide

---

31 The myth of nomadism alongside apparatuses producing nomadism, and with them the notion of terra nullius, is probably the most dominant here, in the context of Israel/Palestine and others. See, for example, Kedar, Amara, and Yiftachel, *Emptied Lands*; Hagar Kotef, *Movement and the Ordering of Freedom: On Liberal Governances of Mobility* (Durham, NC: Duke University Press, 2015); Carole Pateman and Charles W. Mills, *Contract and Domination* (Malden, MA: Polity, 2007).

FIGURE I.2. Shows Tel Aviv in the early 2000s. The minaret of the Hassan Bek Mosque serves here as a visual anchor.

further "proof" of or "support" for this side or the other, I am more interested in the very existence of this debate. The debate itself reflects an unstable dyad of collective memory that can then be translated into an argument regarding the content of what is remembered (did we know? did we see? have we forgotten? erased? denied? could we have been aware?—or unaware?). I contend that this dyad, and the difficulty of accounting for it, is at least partly generated

32 Gil Z. Hochberg, *Visual Occupation: Violence and Visibility in a Conflict Zone* (Durham, NC: Duke University Press, 2015); Leshem, *Life after Ruin*. For other contexts, see Stoler, *Along the Archival Grain*, chapter 7, "Imperial Dispositions of Disregard."

33 Ann Laura Stoler, "Colonial Aphasia: Race and Disabled Histories in France," *Public Culture* 23, no. 1 (winter 2011): 121–56.

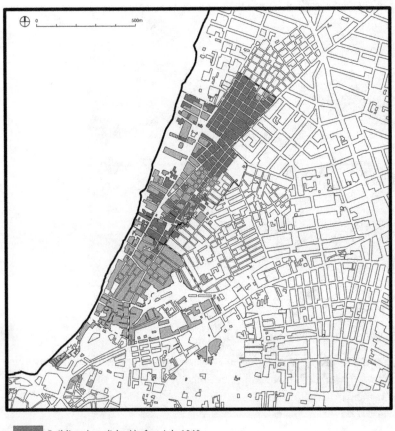

Building demolished before July 1949

Building demolished before July 1980

—·—·— Boundaries of the 1948 demolition operation, 28 hectares version

- - - - - Boundaries of the 1948 demolition operation, 41.5 hectares version

FIGURE I.3. Manshiyya's destruction plan. In dark gray houses that were destroyed by October 1949; in light gray, houses that were destroyed by 1980. Courtesy of Or Aleksandrowicz. Aleksandrowicz's work details these acts of destruction, questions the security claims behind them, and unfolds the long history of destruction behind several of Tel Aviv's neighborhoods. Image from "The Camouflage of War: Planned Destruction in Jaffa and Tel Aviv, 1948," *Planning Perspective* 32, no. 2 (2017): 188.

by the difficulty of settling modes of being-with-violence. Put differently, the inability to settle down colonial memory, as well as the inability to settle the different theoretical frameworks accounting for this memory, is a function of the difficulty of acknowledging that selves can live with their own violence in nonconflictual ways. This difficulty may be of the settler's own memory or the theorist's frame—and I will keep moving here between these levels of analysis. It is this assumption, that people cannot reconcile their self-image with the violence they inflict on others, that I want to question.

A Methodological Note: Settler Colonialism

"Home" can be seen as one of the main criteria differentiating colonialism from settler colonialism. Wolfe famously distinguished between the imperative to work imposed on the colonized in colonialism (part of a racial system that exploits bodies and resources) and the imperative to move imposed on the colonized in settler colonialism (part of a racial system that takes over land for the purpose of settlement). Thus, in the first system, various modes of colonial governance endeavored to maintain the metropole as a home and keep the attachments of Europeans to the colony limited and transient.[34] In the case of settler colonialism, however, at stake is the production and preservation of home in the colony. What will be outlined in this book is therefore a history of sentiments that allow one to stay put, to form an identity unaffected, or less affected, or at least not completely undone by its contradictions and violence.

The facts that "settlers come to stay," that settler colonialism is "first and foremost a project of replacement," and that in the act of settlement settlers "destroy to replace"[35] render the paradigm of settler colonialism an apt lens through which to examine my question concerning home as a tool of destruction (or perhaps render "home" an apt lens through which to examine settler

---

34 This was done via the regulation of sex and kinship, the school system, and the emphasis on constant mobility of bureaucrats across the empire. Such managed circulations—within the empire and between colonies and metropoles—aimed at creating proper attachments and ways of being "moved" that separated "home" (in the metropole) from "away" (in the empire). It generated bonds to people as well as territories, but also cultivated aversions to people and territories in the colony, from whom one had to remain detached. See Stoler, *Along the Archival Grain*, 68 (although the project of narrating these movements reaches beyond this page and book, and can be traced through most of Stoler's writings). Sara Ahmed shows how the result is entire groups, mostly of postcolonized subjects, for whom this distinction between "home" and "away" becomes impossible (Ahmed, "Home and Away").

35 Wolfe, *Traces of History*, 33.

colonialism). This does not mean that settlers necessarily bring about destruction maliciously, but if in settler colonialism the primary identity is the relation to place,[36] and if this belonging is an act of elimination and dispossession,[37] then by being who one is, one is already implicated in violence.[38] Violence, then, emerges as a precondition for the integrity of one's subjectivity. This is the main claim of this book.

Nevertheless, two primary reservations can be made in regard to the framing of Israel as a settler-colonial state and this argument's framing. First, many of the events, modes of attachment, and practices of homemaking that will occupy these pages resonate and have parallels with other historical and geopolitical contexts: Poles, Germans, or Hungarians who moved into the homes of Jews after the Second World War; postpartition "house swaps" in India/Pakistan; or Turkish Cypriots who came to inhabit the homes of Greek Cypriots after partition. I therefore refer here to "settler colonialism" not as an exclusive and excluding framework. Unlike some tendencies in the recent field of comparative settler-colonial studies, I prefer to follow Stoler's insight that there is no one imperial (or colonial, or settler-colonial) case that is identical to the other, which also means that sometimes cases that can be categorized as settler colonialism in some respects resemble civil wars, postcolonial partitions, or national revivals in other facets.[39]

The second reservation has to do with the particular status of Israel within this framework. With the emergence of "settler-colonial studies," there has been much debate concerning the relevance of this framework to the Israeli/Palestinian context. Some have treated it as a clear case of

36 This is the case even if settlement takes the form of a national identity, mostly since such societies are often migrant societies, united primarily by the territory.

37 Patrick Wolfe's famous formulation of settler colonialism as a "logic of elimination" is not an argument that all settler colonies are necessarily genocidal. The imperative posed by such societies is not always about death, but always about *movement*: the imperative on indigenous populations to move. Patrick Wolfe, *Settler Colonialism and the Transformation of Anthropology: The Politics and Poetics of an Ethnographic Event* (London: Cassell, 1999). For the colonial histories and the limits of the concept of dispossession, as well as for the possibility of reclaiming it in radical struggles for decolonization, see Robert Nichols, *Theft Is Property! Dispossession and Critical Theory* (Durham, NC: Duke University Press, forthcoming).

38 With Ariella Azoulay, we can think of this claim somewhat differently but with the same conclusion: by being *governed* as a citizen alongside noncitizens, one is "in effect exerting violence." Ariella Azoulay, "Civil Alliances—Palestine, 1947–1948," *Settler Colonial Studies* 4, no. 4 (2014): 416.

39 Ann Laura Stoler, "On Degrees of Imperial Sovereignty," *Public Culture* 18, no. 1 (2006): 125–46.

settler colonialism, if not one of the primary players in the comparative playing field of the discipline.[40] Others pointed to the limitations of this paradigm—for Israel as well as for other geopolitical contexts.[41] Given the

40 A special issue of the journal *Settler Colonial Studies* (as well as many other essays in it throughout the years) was dedicated to examining this paradigm in relation to Israel/Palestine. For the analytical and political benefits of applying the category "settler colonialism" to the Israeli case, see Omar Salamanca, Mezna Qato, Kareem Rabie, and Sobhi Samour, "Past Is Present: Settler Colonialism in Palestine," *Settler Colonial Studies* 2, no. 1 (2012): 1–8. See also other papers in that volume. One of the first accounts of Israel as a settler-colonial state is Maxime Rodinson's *Israel: A Colonial-Settler State?* (New York: Monad Press, 1973). However, as Patrick Wolfe notes, despite its title, this book does not think about settler colonialism in particular, but about colonialism as such. For Wolfe's account of how this book has shaped his understanding of settler colonialism, see Patrick Wolfe, "New Jews for Old: Settler State Formation and the Impossibility of Zionism: In Memory of Edward W. Said," *Arena Journal* 37/38 (2012): 285–321. Wolfe dedicated a significant segment of his comparative account of settler colonialism to the Israeli case, marking it as a settler-colonialism case par excellence (see *Traces of History*). Just as important, the paradigm has given language to resistance and the imagination of new horizons, particularly among Palestinians who are citizens of Israel, since it allowed for a shift from the discourse of "peace process," "conflict management," or even "occupation" to a language of decolonization that assumes the need to account for the mode of governance also within the 1948 borders.

41 For the limits of this paradigm in this context, see Rachel Busbridge, "Israel-Palestine and the Settler Colonial 'Turn': From Interpretation to Decolonization," *Theory, Culture and Society* 35, no. 1 (January 2018): 91–115, which also provides a comprehensive review of the settler-colonialism literature in relation to the Israeli/Palestinian context. Some have called for thinking within other frameworks, such as apartheid (e.g., Abigail B. Bakan and Yasmeen Abu-Laban, "Israel/Palestine, South Africa and the 'One-State Solution': The Case for an Apartheid Analysis," *Politikon* 37, nos. 2–3 [2010]: 331–51; Hilla Dayan, "Regimes of Separation: Israel/Palestine and the Shadow of Apartheid," in *The Power of Inclusive Exclusion: Anatomy of Israeli Rule in the Occupied Palestinian Territories*, ed. Adi Ophir, Michal Givoni, and Sari Hanafi [New York: Zone, 2009], 281–322); ethnocracy (Oren Yiftachel, *Ethnocracy: Land and Identity Politics in Israel/Palestine* [Philadelphia: University of Pennsylvania Press, 2006]); or simply colonialism (Derek Gregory, *The Colonial Present: Afghanistan, Palestine, Iraq* [Malden, MA: Blackwell, 2005]). Lorenzo Veracini argued that while the occupation of the West Bank and Gaza is a *colonial project*, within the 1948 borders it is a settler-colonial one ("The Other Shift: Settler Colonialism, Israel, and the Occupation," *Journal of Palestine Studies* 42, no. 2 [winter 2013]: 26–42). Others have rejected these critiques altogether, insisting that Zionism is a national project. Between these approaches, Amnon Raz-Krakotzkin argued that "we must rid ourselves of the tendency to think in terms of the dichotomy colonialism/nationalism, which often dominates the discussion of the Zionist consciousness," not just because the term *colonial* seems to entail "a total delegitimating" and "the term 'national' [presumably] justifie[s] anything," but also because, as Raef Zreik notes, both historically and conceptually, Zionism has always entailed both dimensions—the national and the settler colonial. Amnon Raz-Krakotzkin, "Exile, History, and the Nationalization of

first reservation, I have no stakes in arguing that Israel falls or does not fall within the parameters of this paradigm. I nevertheless use it, despite these limits, since—to follow Raef Zreik's useful formulation—in its "praxis and tools," Zionism follows the structure of settler colonialism: "Its takeover of the land, its dream of the disappearance of the native, the importance it allocates to the frontier, its expanding nature and the stories that it tells itself about the land as being terra nullius all match the settler-colonial paradigm."[42] This is even though, as Zreik himself contends, Zionism was at the same time a national movement, a revival of a nation in what was—and still is—seen as its own homeland.

Finally, a conceptual clarification is required. In the Israeli context, the term *settler* is most often used to designate someone living beyond the Green Line, primarily in the West Bank. However, if we think within the framework of settler colonialism, then at least schematically, all Jews in Israel fall under this category. There are several ways in which this categorization can—and should—be problematized. Elsewhere, with Yuval Evri, I do some of this work of problematization in regard to Palestinian Jews (who were natives of the land)[43] and others have done so as well, particularly in regard to Mizrahi Jews.[44] But the work of this book progresses primarily through figures, and the detailed historical work that such problematization necessitates will not be done here.

Jewish Memory: Some Reflections on the Zionist Notion of History and Return," *Journal of Levantine Studies* 3, no. 2 (winter 2013): note 43; Raef Zreik, "Leumit ve colonialit" [National and colonial], *Ha'aretz*, July 21, 2015, https://www.haaretz.co.il/opinions/.premium-1.2688934.

42 Raef Zreik, "When Does a Settler Become a Native? (With Apologies to Mamdani)," *Constellations* 23, no. 3 (2016): 359.

43 Yuval Evri and Hagar Kotef, "When Does a Native Become a Settler?," *Constellations* (forthcoming).

44 Unlike Palestinian Jews—who have been living in Palestine during, and sometimes before, the Ottoman Empire, and were considered as natives by themselves as well as by their fellow Muslim and Christian Palestinians and the authorities, Mizrahi Jews is a term usually serving to mark those who immigrated to Israel, often after 1948. However, because they came from Arab-speaking countries and had been an integral part of the Middle East and the Ottoman Empire, Jews from North Africa and the Middle East ("Mizrahi") are often seen as part of a different logic and structure of immigration and placement, if not the victims of Zionism as a European/settler project. See, for example, Amnon Raz-Krakotzkin, "Zionist Return to the West and the Mizrachi Jewish Perspective," in *Orientalism and the Jews*, ed. Ivan Kalmar and Derek Penslar (Waltham, MA: Brandeis University Press, 2005), 162–81; Ella Shohat, "Sephardim in Israel: Zionism from the Standpoint of Its Jewish Victims," *Social Text* 19/20 (autumn 1988): 1–35.

A Note on Exile (and Politics)

If Zionism can be defined as a negation of exile[45] and a construction of an exclusively Jewish homeland, and if the outcome of this return from exile is destruction, would the key to justice be exile, a refusal of a home that has become a tool of dispossession?[46] Within a state of left-wing despair, some have advocated this as the political solution. But within a global regime in which modes of both mobility and stability are radically differentiated,[47] there are political and ethical risks involved in romanticizing exile. Sara Ahmed questions, as a mode of warning, whether exile and other modes of nomadic and diasporic existence are the coherent choices of the "one that can do so, because the world is already constituted as their home." "Is this," she further asks, "an example of movement as a form of privilege rather than transgression, a movement that is itself predicated on the translation of the collective and forced movements of others into an act of individual and free choice?"[48]

Alternatively, one could advocate exile not as a concrete call, say, for the Jews to leave Israel/Palestine (a call, we must note, that takes the form of ethnic cleansing), but as a conceptual tool that allows a reorganization of political life. Amnon Raz-Krakotzkin proposes to think of exile not as "the opposition to homeland, but [as] a sensitivity that leads towards a process of decolonization that includes Jews and Arabs alike, in which Jews limit their rights in order to create the space for a Palestinian existence, while Palestinians recognize Jewish existence." Such a concept "may become the starting point for thinking about alternatives to partitions, as well as the idea of the nation state, without ignoring national differences."[49] This imagining of political exile will not be a romanticization of what Said saw as "the unhealable rift forced between a human being and a native place, between the self and its true home," but rather, and still after Said, a way of thinking of a

---

45 For a complex analysis of this rejection, see Raz-Krakotzkin, "Exile, History."

46 For such a call, see Daniel Boyarin, *A Traveling Homeland: The Babylonian Talmud as Diaspora* (Philadelphia: University of Pennsylvania Press, 2015); Judith Butler, *Parting Ways: Jewishness and the Critique of Zionism* (New York: Columbia University Press, 2013); and Arendt, to whom we shall return. For a contemporary call for Jewish/Israeli diasporic existence as part of a growing despair in the Israeli left, as well as its critique, see Michal Givoni, "Indifference and Repetition: Occupation Testimonies and Left-Wing Despair," *Cultural Studies* 33, no. 4 (2019): 595–631.

47 See, for example, Tim Cresswell, *On the Move: Mobility in the Modern Western World* (New York: Routledge, 2006); Kotef, *Movement*.

48 Ahmed, "Home and Away," 335.

49 Amnon Raz-Krakotzkin, "Exile and Binationalism: From Gershom Scholem and Hannah Arendt to Edward Said and Mahmoud Darwish" (Carl Heinrich Becker Lecture, Fritz Thyssen Stiftung, Wissenschaftskolleg zu Berlin, Berlin, 2012), 129.

shared condition of displacement from which another politics can emerge.[50] Not a negation of home, but a way of envisioning "political principles that are derived from the diasporic conditions that must also, as it were, be brought home."[51] Such a concept of exile could become, in Butler's words, "an internal criticism of the national, if not a set of qualifications and safeguards that inhere in any possible nation."[52] In times in which, as Adorno famously put it, "it is part of morality not to be at home in one's home" (and were there ever any other times?), would this advocation of exile not be a preferred political solution?[53]

Perhaps. But, again following Ahmed, it may be that by thinking of exile conceptually we are, once more, engaging in a romanticizing move in which the nomads, the exiled, "come to perform a particular kind of theoretical work, to represent something other than themselves."[54] Can one think concretely about exile as a condition that can be employed to organize the political communities at home, as it were? Can one do so in ways that fracture the modes of entrenched, exclusive nationalism but do not further fracture the subject, already in "a discontinuous state of being" generated by displacement?[55]

Perhaps. But in this book, rather than focusing on shared models of diasporic homemaking or the Jewish sense of rebuilding a home postdiaspora, I ask about the meeting point of these two homes—the Palestinian and the Jewish Israeli—as part of an effort to understand how the destruction of homes (of Palestinians) becomes constitutive of the construction of homes: of the construction of Israel as a national home, of the establishment of houses for Israelis to reside in, and of the sense of attachment to territory that is formative of identities. Thinking about this connection urges us to think of the home's absence not as another possible definition of homes (as in the case of diasporic models of homemaking) but as a condition that subtends the being—the presence—of some homes. This again places the conceptualization of home within an analytic of violence, or makes home the embodiment of such an analytic.

---

50 Edward W. Said, *Reflections on Exile and Other Essays* (Cambridge, MA: Harvard University Press, 2000), 171.

51 J. Butler, *Parting Ways*, 208.

52 J. Butler, *Parting Ways*, 209.

53 Theodor W. Adorno, *Minima Moralia: Reflections on a Damaged Life* (London: Verso Books, 2005), 39.

54 Ahmed, "Home and Away," 334.

55 Said, *Reflections on Exile*, 177.

Structure and Main Arguments

The Colonizing Self is composed of three main chapters and six shorter "satellites" organized in three parts. Before each of the main chapters, a brief interlude opens the particular question of the chapter to a different context—sometimes, the interlude examines a different case of settler colonialism; at other times, it serves to offer a different departing point for the main chapter. The goal of these interludes is to gesture toward other domains to which the argument is relevant, even though I cannot fully develop these other directions here. After each chapter, an epilogue offers an analysis of one of the core problems that surfaced in the main chapter. These are more structural interventions, focusing on specific questions the main chapters opened up but did not fully address.

AFTER THIS INTRODUCTION, a theoretical overview sets the ground for my main question concerning the relations between violence and identity. It attempts to map the primary models within which these relations are conceptualized in existing literature, and marks the main theoretical lacuna this book seeks to address. These models are going to be unpacked throughout the book and guide its inquiry.

PART I: HOMES

A home—and identity—that is built on the dispossession (the destruction) of others encapsulates a structure of belonging that is not limited to Israel. Rather than a comparative analysis of settler colonies and their construction of home (which is undoubtedly of value), part I, "Homes," returns to some key moments in political theory to show the conceptual foundations for this book's inquiry. Specifically, I argue that the kind of political self that is formed within a specific theory in which home is the basic unit of analysis is ontologically dependent on violence.

The interlude, "Home/Homelessness," works primarily with Arendt to foreground two claims: (i) Despite an effort to allocate "home" to a separate, nonpolitical sphere, homemaking appears to be foundational in a significant part of the history of political thought, and "Man" emerges as a domestic animal. The ability to sustain a political community is thus seen as a function of sedentary qualities. (ii) Within these texts, the concept of home is narrowed down to particular (European) models. Given (i), this narrowing means that this tradition can see only some subjects as fully human. This global distribution of homelessness and entitlement to homes will be mapped onto the

Israeli/Palestinian context in the following chapters. The main chapter of part I, "The Consuming Self: On Locke, Aristotle, Feminist Theory, and Domestic Violences," looks at the concept of home as it materializes in three moments in political theory: Aristotle's theory of politics, feminist theory's critique of domesticity, and Locke's theory of property. The latter is the focus of that chapter, since it works at the essential converging point of liberalism and settler colonialism. Drawing on Carole Pateman's famous reading in *The Sexual Contract*, according to which it is the family, rather than the individual, that "contracts in," I argue that the basic property-making unit shifts throughout chapter 5 of the *Second Treatise* (the chapter on property). Whereas it begins with the individual body, over the course of the chapter Locke carries it to the household. The household thus appears as the basic political unit, rather than the individual or even Pateman's couple.

My reading of Locke does not merely serve to introduce the home to the core of political theory; it also demonstrates that the Lockean individual had strong expansionist tendencies. This understanding of the expansionist drive at the foundation of liberal subjectivity establishes the basis for the analysis of settler colonialism that is to follow. Moreover, since the household can materialize as a property-making unit in Locke only via enclosure, and since its paradigmatic means of expansion is agriculture, the link to the analysis of organic agriculture in the West Bank (part III) is fully made.

Part I ends with an epilogue titled "Unsettlement," which situates the analysis in the particular space of Israel/Palestine. The epilogue problematizes some of the framings of this book in order to show the multiple positions and possible trajectories that will be sidelined by the focus of my argument. Marking those is necessary not only as part of demarcating the wider picture, but also since this plurality entails alternative political possibilities to the trajectory this book tracks. It thereby also lays bare some of the methodological frames employed in my analysis of homemaking in Israel/Palestine, and as such serves as an introduction of sorts to parts II and III. Thus, even readers less interested in the more theoretical discussion, who may prefer to skip Part I and focus their reading on the more concrete discussion of Israel/Palestine, should probably begin with this brief chapter.

PART II: RELICS

Part II, "Relics," opens with a reading of Lorraine Hansberry's *Les Blancs*. This interlude, "A Brief Reflection on Death and Decolonization," focuses on notions of home among the settler figures in the play and asks about the prospects of decolonization given their modes of attachment to territory. Since the play is situated in an imaginary African country, this reading also opens a path to a comparative analysis vis-à-vis chapter 2. Chapter 2, "Home (and the Ruins That Remain)," looks into identities that are shaped when one's own sense of belonging is saturated with the violence of the past. Focusing on Jewish Israelis who made homes in depopulated Palestinian homes, the chapter develops a model of wounded attachments (following Wendy Brown) to the violence undergirding political belonging. It may be questioned to what degree this attachment is indeed an attachment to violence: Those who live in the ruins of others often do not experience their lives as violent, and those who look at the landscape dotted with half-standing houses may not see it as a remnant of violence. There is here an attachment to a home, a land, but not, one may argue, to the violence that made the former possible, even if such violence was a necessary element of colonization. To address this potential reservation, the epilogue, "A Phenomenology of Violence: Ruins," provides a typology of the violence that is nonetheless there. It is there as a residue that cannot be erased; it is there as a trace that still carries elements of the violent past; it is there in the clash between temporalities of those for whom violence is indeed in the past and those who still experience it as their everyday. The chapter provides a phenomenological map of these modes of violence in order to peel apart—but also weave together—the different forms of violence with which this book engages.

PART III: SETTLEMENT

Part III, "Settlement," moves to the West Bank. Thus, whereas part II focuses on those who inherited the colonized space they came to inhabit, part III looks at the act of colonization as it takes place. Nevertheless, the divisions between the arguments developed in part II and those developed in part III are not necessarily superimposed on the 1948/1967 division. These lines of division are questioned at the end of chapter 3, and feature here only for the sake of clarity and simplification.

Part III presents two stories of two homes in the West Bank, both revolving around the production of food, as an element of domesticity. It begins with an interlude, "A Moment of Popular Culture: The Home of *MasterChef*," that introduces the concept of home in the West Bank through a brief engagement with the Israeli franchise of the popular reality show *MasterChef*. The show's seventh season included a settler from the evicted outpost Amona among its contestants. I follow the way this contender won over the hearts of the Israeli mainstream through this show. His story of loss and homelessness joins the politics of food to provide an account of the normalization of settlements in Israel today. This politics of food remains central to the main chapter of this part, chapter 3: "On Eggs and Dispossession: Organic Agriculture and the New Settlement Movement." Focusing on one extreme outpost in the West Bank called Giv'ot Olam, it analyzes a process of homemaking in which violence and dispossession are ongoing practices. Giv'ot Olam was the forerunner of the new settlement movement that is often referred to as "hilltop youth": a movement aimed at grabbing more land by building illegal outposts outside established settlements. Giv'ot Olam is also, as aforementioned, the largest organic farm in Israel and the largest supplier of organic, free-range eggs in the country. Examining both the ethics of organic food and the material conditions of organic agriculture (land resources, waste, and water), I show how a home is created as a dispositional tool within an ethical scheme. This chapter also tracks the story of the Palestinian village Yanun, which has been almost completely abandoned following constant harassment and severe attacks from Giv'ot Olam's settlers. The epilogue, "An Ethic of Violence: Organic Washing," returns to the question of violence's visibility that is key to the theoretical overview and part II. It asks whether the scheme of organic agriculture sustains settlements' violence by enveloping it with a language of justice and care (toward animals or the earth) that hides violence from sight ("washes" it in green politics). Based on the ethnographic work of chapter 3, the epilogue concludes the book by arguing that we need to find an alternative account, one that shows not how people deny their violence to sustain it, but how life with violence is embraced.

THE THREE MAIN CHAPTERS at the heart of each part thus offer a certain historical journey. I begin with the imaginary past of settler colonialism (chapter 1), move to a more recent history of Israel/Palestine (chapter 2), and end by looking at the present-day West Bank (chapter 3).[56] Yet this chronology is not strictly kept. It presents a present that can be dated to the past, and a past that still lingers in the present, in order to show the ontologies and fractured histories of the settler-colonial project.

Chapter 2 is "historical" not just because it focuses on the homes depopulated in 1948, but also because it represents a position that is becoming less dominant in Israel. In the last decade or so, Israel's attitude toward its own violence has dramatically changed. Though such changes are always fractured, never linear, and appear gradually and unevenly across society—and hence dating them is a somewhat problematic exercise—this change occurred sometime after the 2006 Lebanon War. It was first clearly manifested in Gaza in

56 I thank reviewer number 2 for this observation.

2009. Chapter 2 marks this trajectory from selves who are truly undone by their own violence, who cannot inhabit life once they realize the destruction that this inhabitation generates, to selves who "shoot and cry"—the famous formulation that comes to mark "crying" as both a token paid so that violence can continue and a way of indulging one's own pain when confronted with the suffering one causes to others—and, finally, to selves who do not even cry after shooting, who "shoot and do not apologize,"[57] who fully own their violence and no longer come undone by it. Nevertheless, the subjects featured in chapter 2 are not perpetrators in the classic formulations, but rather those defined by Robbins as *structural beneficiaries* or by Rothberg as *implicated subjects*:[58] They are those who "occupy positions aligned with power and privilege without being themselves direct agents of harm," who "contribute to, inhabit, inherit, or benefit from regimes of domination but do not originate or control such regimes."[59] Their relations to violence accordingly remain more ambivalent than what we see in chapter 3.

In a similar yet mirrored vein, chapter 3 is "contemporary," not just because it depicts the current settlement movement in the West Bank but also because it depicts most clearly the aforementioned nonconflictual approach to violence that is becoming more dominant in Israeli public discourse. It represents, in this sense, a wider tendency in Israel to steer away from the liberal-democratic facets of the state project and more openly embrace its nationalist-settler facets. And yet this chapter, too, is "historical," in the sense that the positions and patterns of settlement it describes have been typical to the project of settling Israel from the very outset. The juxtaposition of chapters 2 and 3 is, accordingly, not a claim that West Bank settlers (the protagonists of part III) inhabit this violent position whereas liberal Zionists within the 1948 borders (the protagonists of part II) do not. My point is precisely that in the historical trajectories this book marks, both positions come to inhabit violence in non- (or less) conflictual ways, albeit differently.

57 To paraphrase the election slogan of the Jewish Home Party from the 2014 campaign. I elaborate on this formulation at the end of chapter 2.

58 Robbins, *Beneficiary*; Rothberg, *Implicated Subject*.

59 Rothberg, *Implicated Subject*, 2.

Theoretical Overview
Violent Attachments

A standard critique of empire holds that imperial rule nourishes and feeds off the cultivation of ignorance, that empire is in the business of limiting, distorting, and obscuring knowledge and that with more of it, empires would be more vulnerable to critique; . . . that knowledge pierces what obscures the workings of power, weakens its hold, and, with sustained exposure, could be made to crash. . . . I argue that these accounts . . . may be for us to question, if not refute. —ANN LAURA STOLER

One way to read this book is as a work concerning the shape a critique of violence should take—its scope and conditions of possibility—when violence is embraced rather than denied by those enacting it. It seeks to unpack a "structure of feeling," in Raymond Williams's words, in which violence becomes an explicit part of collective identities.[1] Of the plural forms violence takes, I think here primarily about mass violence, although to understand it, this overview also passes through individualized forms of violence. The arguments here are therefore not—cannot be—universal; they cannot be applied to all forms of violence in a flat, coherent way. Nevertheless, thinking of them together can shed new light on the mechanisms that allow violence to be sustained across different fields. Indeed, there is a single theoretical-political question driving

Epigraph: Ann Laura Stoler, *Along the Archival Grain: Epistemic Anxieties and Colonial Common Sense* (Princeton, NJ: Princeton University Press, 2009), 248.

1 The expression was coined in Raymond Williams and Michael Orrom, *Preface to Film* (London: Film Drama, 1954), but is usually used in reference to Williams's more extended conceptual work in *Marxism and Literature* (Oxford: Oxford University Press, 1977).

all these different inquiries: how should we theorize the violence that is woven into what gives meaning to our lives?

More specifically, this book seeks to propose a way for theorizing how groups legitimate their political violence that refuses the assumption that violence is sustainable only as long as it remains hidden or somehow unacknowledged. It refuses the assumption, to repeat Stoler's words from the epigraph, that "knowledge pierces what obscures the workings of power, [and thereby] weakens its hold." Accordingly, it refuses the assumption that the role of critique is to render violence visible—an assumption, I propose, that is part of a premise that violence is often denied by democratic, liberal crowds, and therefore that revealing it is a significant political act that can end it. Still with Stoler, I argue that these assumptions "may be for us to question, if not refute." These assumptions, I argue, fail to perceive that people can desire the violent arrangements supporting their communities (not merely deny and suppress them, or see them as a "necessary evil"). They therefore fail to address political settings in which violence becomes an affirmative element of political identities and is embraced rather than denied. In such contexts, a critique rendering violence more visible may lose its critical edge, and participate, despite itself, in a celebration of violence.

What follows interweaves a variety of threads and fields to construct an alternative model for a critique of the relations between violence and identity. Some may seem (indeed are) unrelated, but the eclectic nature of these threads is meant to echo this model's various fields of applicability. As part of this, I move between different kinds of "selves" (individuals, groups, states) and between different modes of violence, or what I will often refer to here as generating injury. "Injury" itself shifts here, and its meaning ranges from a physical wound—a breaking of the skin, corporeal damage—to an extinction of entire nations. These shifts by no means seek to propose that these are one and the same; further, when I argue here that violence is constitutive of selves, this claim will have radically different political implications if we think of one mode of injury or of the other. For now, I leave these distinctions intentionally vague in order to include various forms of harm, keeping the full scope of the argument open. As the argument unfolds, these distinctions will take a more explicit form, and the focus of my particular inquiry will become clearer.

In the first section ("Three Models: Compliance, Cruelty, Dissociation"), I begin by analyzing how mass or state violence is conceived—and, as part of this, often justified—by those engaging in it. I review three primary models of theorizing violence and its modes of justification; all, I propose, rest on questionable assumptions regarding the work of knowledge. I point to the short-comings of these theories not to invalidate them, but to demonstrate the need to supplement them. Indeed, all models of violence reviewed here will be featured throughout this book, as valuable explanatory frameworks.

The next section ("Desire: Theories of Intimate Violence") offers a fourth model to supplement the above three. For this purpose I draw on feminist, queer, and poststructuralist understandings of desire to think of a violence that is woven into the fabric of social relations—not necessarily so and not in ways that require us to simply accept it, but structurally so, in a way that necessitates different modes of struggle. I reconstruct this structure of subjectivity through both a literary illustration and a theoretical analysis/review. This combination is meant to render the claim tangible without fully developing its theoretical infrastructure, whose full unfolding, in its various nuances and challenges, lies beyond the scope of this overview.

As noted above, I do not seek to offer here an analogy between settlers' mass violence and the modes of injury, primarily sexual, that are at the core of queer/feminist analyses of violence (I do not claim, for example, that we should *compare* settlers to men in a heteronormative society, or settlement to rape).[2] I certainly do not claim that these can all be conflated into one phenomenology of violence. Rather, what I seek to illustrate here is a model, which, like any model, is limited in its applicability to different cases and yet is useful for explaining the object at hand. In this sense, the feminist/queer/poststructuralist understandings will be incorporated into my argument primarily through the claim that to understand the dynamics and endurability of settler colonialism we need to understand the networks of sentiments invested in it and the social textures it both works on and fabricates. I further draw on queer/feminist theories of subjectivity to highlight desire as socially constructed. With this framework I argue that the social settings of settlement are likely to facilitate a desire for these very settings and, with them, to violence itself. Significant to this argument is also the understanding introduced by the above body of thought, that we develop attachments to structures of injury. I thus show the affectual mechanisms

2 For a discussion of this analogy in the Palestinian conceptualization of settlers, see Honaida Ghanim, "From Kubaniya to Outpost: A Genealogy of the Palestinian Conceptualization of Jewish Settlement in a Shifting National Context," in *Normalizing Occupation: The Politics of Everyday Life in the West Bank Settlements*, ed. Ariel Handel, Marco Allegra, and Erez Maggor (Bloomington: Indiana University Press, 2017), 244–68.

that sustain social and political identities that are violent due to their mere positionality.

In the final section ("Reversal"), I return to Israel/Palestine to unpack this model more concretely. I propose thinking of mass violence, at least in the context of settler colonialism, as a certain version of Judith Butler's understanding of subjectivity as emerging through injury. While for Butler, injury is primarily conceptualized as an injury caused to the self,[3] I seek to look at forms of subjectivity constituted by social conditions in which the self is a *source* of injury.

Three Models: Compliance, Cruelty, Dissociation

The vast majority of the literature asking how political communities see and understand their own mass violence can be divided, albeit schematically, into three main groups. They offer three rough models that I label as "compliance," "cruelty," and "dissociation." Because the last model will be the most central to my analysis, I focus on it here and merely mark the other two. As stated above, in the next section I will propose a fourth model (we can term it "desire") to add to the first three.

From the outset, it is important to say that even though these models are in tension with each other, most cases of violence can be understood by a combination of some of them. People can be cruel *and* lie to themselves—at different moments, in regard to different uses of violence, or sometimes even in regard to one and the same occasion; we can be constituted by violence, yet still refuse to see it, etc. In most societies, we can find all three of the above models: at times they function as competing narratives, sometimes dividing societies across political lines; at times one may gain more dominance; and at times one may be repressed or may (re)surface.

COMPLIANCE

The first model, compliance, emerges from an effort to understand how people can live *under* atrocity-generating regimes: what enables people to accept, not object to, and even collaborate with state violence? The relevant literature is predominantly engaged with fascism and genocide, and has provided different answers to this question: the power of authority,[4] of

---

3 With some important reservations on which I touch later. See note 50.
4 The Milgram experiment is probably the most famous in this regard, but many authors of the Frankfurt School can serve as more theoretical references here, with various understandings of

ideology,[5] of order itself;[6] the bureaucratization of violence;[7] or lack of an ability to think independently, particularly to think from the point of view of the other.[8] What these explanations have in common, excluding the latter, is

---

"authority" and its workings. Some (particularly Erich Fromm) questioned the very divisions between externality and internality in this regard, seeing authority as an attribute that can at times be internalized, as the individual cancels the self by immersing herself in the large body of the many. This adds a layer of complication to my claim concerning externality, yet can still be reconciled with it because it rests on the authority originated from an external body (plural or individual)—even if it is internalized. See, for example, Erich Fromm, *The Sane Society* (Greenwich, CT: Fawcett Premier Books, 1955; *The Crisis of Psychoanalysis: Essays on Marx, Freud and Social Psychology* (Greenwich, CT: Fawcett Premier Books, 1971). See also Theodor W. Adorno, Else Frenkel-Brunswick, and Daniel J. Levinson, *The Authoritarian Personality: Studies in Prejudice* (New York: W. W. Norton, 1982). For Louis Althusser, whose theoretical implications and contexts go far beyond authoritarian regimes, adherence to authority is built into subjectivity under certain sociohistorical conditions. Interpellation works because we (in the particular era which can perhaps be marked by capitalism, but should be defined more precisely both historically and geographically) are constructed as subjects who are almost wired to obey, because in a way and to some degree, we are always already subjected. Althusser's analysis also shows clearly that the more complex accounts of authority cannot be separated from those focusing on ideology (see note 5). Louis Althusser, "Ideology and Ideological State Apparatuses," in *Essays on Ideology* (London: Verso Books, 1984), 86–98. For a critical reading of such concepts of subjectivity, particularly in Althusser, see Martel, *Misinterpellated Subject*.

5 Hannah Arendt, *The Origins of Totalitarianism*, 5th ed. (New York: Harcourt Brace Jovanovich, 1973).

6 Bauman offers one of the most complete versions of this argument. According to him, the Holocaust, far from being a barbaric counterexample to modern morality, can be explained by modern principles of rationality and order that are seen as morally superior in other circumstances, such as instrumental rationality, rule-following, the ordering and categorization of all social life, and a complex division of labor. See Zygmunt Bauman, *Modernity and the Holocaust* (Cambridge: Polity Press, 1991).

7 Kafka's writing is a lucid illustration of this claim. Arendt's idea of the banality of evil also entails the "breaking down" of evil to mundane, bureaucratic activities that are not murderous in themselves. The activities which mounted and coalesced into the Holocaust "were comprised of office work such as organizing transport, deciding how many Jews should be deported and to where and 'negotiating' arrangements with the countless 'partners' involved in the 'final solution.'" Hannah Arendt, *Eichmann in Jerusalem: A Report on the Banality of Evil* (Harmondsworth, UK: Penguin Books, 1992), 287. Bauman's explanation in *Modernity and the Holocaust* can be read along these lines as well. However, for Bauman, the bureaucratic explanation takes a sociological form, hinging on a rationalized division of labor that substitutes "technical responsibility" for "moral responsibility," thereby creating bureaucratic "remoteness" (101–2), while for Arendt, the explanation has more to do with a certain structure of personality (see the next footnote).

8 This is Arendt's main emphasis in *Eichmann in Jerusalem*. She points to a "curious, quite authentic inability to think" that comes to replace, for her, the explanation emphasizing the power of ideology in *The Origins of Totalitarianism*.

the idea that violence is located in some elsewhere. Violence is situated in something external (a leader, government, or social structure) and there is a psychological or sociological power that renders people collaborative, submissive, even cooperative. That is, people may respond to violence, accept it, even participate in it, but it is not part of *who they are*. If something is to be found in themselves instead of in these external sites where violence resides, it is a disposition to adhere to violent powers (which may have to do with psychosocial factors, economic ones, etc.). It is precisely this externality that I want to question.

Indeed, if we take the idea of democracy seriously, there is another question we need to pose, if not instead of, then alongside the above question: how can one play an *active* role in a violent political order?—not as *subjected* to the regime but as a subject in the second meaning of the term as well,[9] as an "author," as Hobbes would have it, of this violence?[10]

CRUELTY

The second model consists of accounts that see violence as emerging from political sadism, cruelty, or institutional hatred, which are not contradictory, but rather integral to the political identity of those engaging in violence. Some of these explanations focus on fascism in its different articulations. Others look at liberal democracies, yet not for the values they declare they stand for but for the racial schemas subtending them. Some point to political articulations of sadistic erotic pleasure in various cases, ranging from lynching[11] to torture[12] to settler colonialism.[13] Others focus not on sadistic *erotic* pleasure but on the cruelty

9 Judith Butler, *The Psychic Life of Power: Theories in Subjection* (Stanford, CA: Stanford University Press, 1997), 84.
10 Thomas Hobbes, *Leviathan*, Cambridge Texts in the History of Political Thought, ed. Richard Tuck (New York: Cambridge University Press, 1996), 142.
11 Harris, for example, describes lynching as an act of releasing sexual tension that provides a "particular kind of satisfaction." Trudier Harris, *Exorcising Blackness: Historical and Literary Lynching and Burning Rituals* (Bloomington: Indiana University Press, 1984), 23. Harris accordingly focused on the ritual of castration, in which the black lynched body was transformed from an object of (sexual) envy and a presumed (sexual) threat to a substitute for the female body (21–24). This simultaneously sexualized the act itself and reshaped political orders: "by feminizing the black male body, the white male could once again claim his power and superiority over that body, effectively categorizing it alongside the female bodies, both black and white, over which he continued to wield political and social control" (21–24).
12 Sherene Razack, "How Is White Supremacy Embodied? Sexualized Racial Violence at Abu Ghraib," *Canadian Journal of Women and the Law* 17, no. 2 (2005): 341–63.
13 Alexander G. Weheliye, *Habeas Viscus: Racializing Assemblages, Biopolitics, and Black Feminist Theories of the Human* (Durham, NC: Duke University Press, 2014), see especially chapter 6. For an

manifested when crowds rejoice as they witness violence, often spectacular, often inflicted on their perceived enemies.[14] Still others expose different affectual dimensions implicated in practices that shape political cohorts (usually defined by race) through anchoring otherness in suffering. According to the latter accounts, senses of belonging often emerge not merely through the exclusion of othered groups, but through further manifesting and experiencing otherness via a public spectacle of violence. Finally, others have appealed to the notion of political cruelty to point not to personality structures of some individuals but to political and ideological structures that shape people's desires or ways of seeing not precisely as sadistic, but as dismissive of violence. Specifically, these modes of organizing society place people in a different relation to the violence they inflict, allowing them to see it yet erasing the victims as suffering subjects. Here we find schemes of racism and dehumanization that render some lives less accounted for,[15] pseudoscientific assumptions about the lack of pain among some people that erase the possibility of victimhood,[16]

---

analysis of this eroticization in relation to Israel/Palestine, see Alex Shams, "Israeli Discourse of Sexualized Violence Rises amid Gaza Assault," *Ma'an News Agency*, August 6, 2014, https://www.maannews.com/Content.aspx?id=717908; Nadera Shalhoub-Kevorkian, Sarah Ihmoud, and Suhad Dahir-Nashif, "Sexual Violence, Women's Bodies, and Israeli Settler Colonialism," *Jadaliyya*, November 17, 2014, http://www.jadaliyya.com/pages/index/19992/sexual-violence -women%E2%80%99s-bodies-and-israeli-settler.

14 Such accounts have become more common in recent years in relation to Israel, as documented episodes of Israelis watching and rejoicing in spectacles of violence became more widespread. Most famous, perhaps, was "Cinema Sderot" during the 2014 war on Gaza. As missiles, phosphorus bombs, and other weapons lit up the sky over Gaza and ultimately killed more than two thousand people, Israelis were documented sitting on a hill above the Gaza Strip, watching the military attacks, and cheering. More recently, Israelis from Kibbutz Nahal Oz have been photographed as they watch with enjoyment how Israeli Defense Forces (IDF) soldiers shoot at demonstrators in Gaza, a photograph that circulated widely in social media.

15 Zygmunt Bauman, *Wasted Lives: Modernity and Its Outcasts* (Oxford: Polity, 2004). See also Arjun Appadurai, *Fear of Small Numbers: An Essay on the Geography of Anger* (Durham, NC: Duke University Press, 2006). Paul Bloom presents a great critique of this framework, seeing dehumanization as a necessary precondition for violence: "The Root of All Cruelty?," *New Yorker*, November 27, 2017, https://www.newyorker.com/magazine/2017/11/27/the-root-of-all-cruelty/. On the fractioning of humanity in the production of ethical schemes and attendance to suffering, see also Thomas L. Haskell, "Capitalism and the Origins of Humanitarian Sensibility, Part I," *American Historical Review* 90, no. 2 (1985): 339–61.

16 Saidiya Hartman shows how "the purported immunity of blacks to pain" was essential to the system of slavery. Saidiya V. Hartman, *Scenes of Subjection: Terror, Slavery, and Self-Making in Nineteenth-Century America* (Oxford: Oxford University Press, 1997), 51. See also Jennifer L. Morgan, *Laboring Women: Reproduction and Gender in New World Slavery* (Philadelphia: University of Pennsylvania Press, 2004).

or a framing of the other as a dangerous enemy whose killing is always justified.[17]

In this context, I want to linger briefly on Shawn Smith's analysis of the representation and perception of lynching in the American South, since it foregrounds the question of attachment to violence that will be central to my own argument. Many have shown how the mass, if not institutionalized, violence of lynching has been essential to the formation of national (white) belonging, especially in a reality of radical political instability (emancipation, suffrage, the infiltration of a modern economy).[18] Important for me here is not just the *structural* role of violence in the formation or preservation of some hierarchical orders and some selves, but also the array of *attachments* that are vested in violence, or at the very least in the order violence serves (white supremacy in this case). Smith's analysis of the book *Without Sanctuary* is a good illustration of such an analysis.

Without Sanctuary is a collection of images of lynching taken in the last decades of the nineteenth century and the first decades of the twentieth. Examining this book, Smith observes: "It is . . . a disturbing book, not only due to the devastating nature of its images but also due to the beauty and richness of its reproduction and design. Lushly printed on glossy paper, some of the images reproduced in soft warm tones, . . . the work becomes a kind of macabre coffee-table book. One wonders at the range of desires the book may play on."[19] Even if not intended to create some sense of pleasure in the reader/observer, the book's beauty "play[s] on" such a "range of desires." It also makes

17 An example is the declaration of Israel's former defense minister Avigdor Liberman that "there are no innocents in Gaza" to justify using live ammunition to shoot at unarmed demonstrators. Tovah Lazaroff, "'There Are No Innocents in Gaza', Says Israeli Defense Minister," *Jerusalem Post*, April 8, 2018, http://www.jpost.com/Arab-Israeli-Conflict/There-are-no-innocents-in-Gaza-says-Israeli-defense-minister-549173. Butler's gesture toward state violence directed toward African American individuals and communities provides an apt formulation: "If the person [who is the target of police violence] was not doing anything demonstrably violent, then perhaps the person is simply figured as violent, as a certain *kind* of person, or as pure violence embodied in and by that person. The latter claim manifests racism more often than not" (Judith Butler, *The Force of Non-violence* [New York: Verso Books, 2020], 4).

18 Shawn M. Smith, *American Archives: Gender, Race, and Class in Visual Culture* (Princeton, NJ: Princeton University Press, 2000); Ida B. Wells, *Southern Horrors: Lynch Law in All Its Phases* (Auckland, New Zealand: Floating Press, 2014); Amy L. Wood, *Lynching and Spectacle: Witnessing Racial Violence in America, 1890–1940* (Chapel Hill: University of North Carolina Press, 2009), among many others.

19 Shawn M. Smith, *Photography on the Color Line: W. E. B. Du Bois, Race, and Visual Culture* (Durham, NC: Duke University Press Books, 2004), 119.

visible the pleasure of the hundreds and thousands of white people who came to take part in those spectacles of racial violence. Examining the technologies of the photographs, their means of production, and their modes of circulation (particularly as postcards), we see more than how these spectators are "dressed for the occasion," how "they meet the camera unabashedly, even cheerfully."[20] We can further see the ties woven between brutal violence, the construction of community, and desire. Postcards are not merely a means for saying "I was there," Smith claims. "They also serve as mementos with which individuals mark sentimental bonds with others—'I was there and I thought of you while I was there.' The postcard presumes . . . a shared sentiment; . . . [they] function as a fantasy site of desire for distant viewers."[21]

My book similarly examines such modes of attachment, desire, and imagining communities that organize themselves around violence. But for the most part, this model of cruelty seems to be less suitable for the analysis of my cases. This is not merely because when I read the different figures that will be featured in these pages I see an embrace of violence, yet no pleasure taken in it (although this may be my own personal inability to see). It is less adequate also because the "cruelty" model rests on an immediate relation to a suffering body, whereas the vast majority of this book engages primarily, though not exclusively, with the violence of those closer to what Robert Meister and later Bruce Robbins have termed "structural beneficiaries": those who are not active perpetrators, but nonetheless receive "material and social advantage" from various orders of violence.[22] Or perhaps more accurately, those who cannot fully be seen as direct perpetrators, but who live within and as the tentacles of perpetration, beyond the direct act of violence, into the ongoing, systematic, enduring nature of violence. I am interested primarily in those who are part of the oppressive side of these orders, and whose well-being (actual or perceived) is often dependent on the continuation of this oppression and its injuries; those who could therefore be seen as exerting violence even if, and when, they do not actively engage in it. In these cases, attachments to violence are not the cruel attachments to a direct pain inflicted on a body. Indeed, this focus changes by the end of the book, where violence becomes more direct; and yet it rarely takes the spectacular form that the model of cruelty seems to presuppose. Here the third model comes into play, the one I termed "dissociation," which is probably the most common model used to explain imperial and colonial violence.

20 S. Smith, *Photography on the Color Line*, 120.
21 S. Smith, *Photography on the Color Line*, 122.
22 Robert Meister, *After Evil: A Politics of Human Rights* (New York: Columbia University Press, 2012), 26; Bruce Robbins, *The Beneficiary* (Durham, NC: Duke University Press, 2017), 7.

DISSOCIATION

The third model, dissociation, often accounts for political violence in democratic, even liberal, settings and is probably the most common model used to explain the sustainability of imperial and colonial violence. This model can be found—I contend—in a diverse and rich literature, including many liberal texts, significant segments of postcolonial literature, and literature inspired by, or taking part in, projects of truth and reconciliation. In my own geopolitical context, it can be found in most of the relevant literature on the Israeli/Palestinian conflict. These bodies of thought can by no means be reduced to a single account. Yet, within this richness, one principle seems to be shared: if violence is to endure (at least in democratic societies), a gap, if not a rift, must be introduced between the self and the violent actions of herself or her group.

Using Stanley Cohen's very wide mapping, alongside the work of many others who have engaged in such research, we can outline the various modes of such dissociation, even if they are not always as neatly separable as in the list below.[23] For the sake of illustration, they will be accompanied by concrete examples from Israel/Palestine.

- A complete rejection of the facts: "there were no Palestinian villages in this place"; or: "the Palestinians who were here left because their leaders persuaded them to do so in order to aid the war effort"—and we already see that both "rejection" and "facts" come in different types and gradients. Salman Abu Sitta speaks in this context of a "collective amnesia," which further complicates the relation between the known and the unknown, since what is forgotten was known.[24] Janet McIntosh refers to "structural oblivion" as the systematic process by which institutions, communities, and individuals become ignorant or maintain ignorance, not only concerning particular events in his-

---

23 Stanley Cohen, *States of Denial: Knowing about Atrocities and Suffering* (Cambridge: Polity Press, 2001), 21ff.

24 Salman H. Abu Sitta, *The Palestinian Nakba 1948: The Register of Depopulated Localities in Palestine* (London: Palestinian Return Centre, 1998). As Cohen says, "at the heart of the concept" of denial there is a "paradox": denial is about allowing "for the strange possibility of simultaneously knowing and not knowing. The existence of what is denied must be 'somehow' known and statements expressing this denial must be 'somehow' believed in" (Cohen, *States of Denial*, 24). Gayatri Spivak refers to "sanctioned ignorance." Gayatri Chakravorty Spivak, "Can the Subaltern Speak?," in *Marxism and the Interpretation of Culture*, ed. Cary Nelson and Lawrence Grossberg (Champaign: University of Illinois Press, 1988), 291.

tory (she talks about the memories of second- and third-generation settlers in Kenya) but also concerning the long-lasting, structural privileges of colonization. The work that forgetting requires is often done at levels beyond the individual and should therefore not be seen, at least not often, as deliberate.[25] If we take McIntosh's point further, however, it is crucial to note the link between an individual's ability to deny and a state or society's projects of renarration. As Cohen puts it, "it is easier for you to 'know nothing' if your society claims that 'things like that could not have happened here.'"[26]

- A reorganization of the facts within a framework that alters their signification. For instance: reframing violence as self-protection and aggression as victimhood. As in: "the Palestinians who indeed were here, and whom we indeed expelled or killed, were about to exterminate us; we had no choice."[27] Or, alternatively: altering signification by using language that diminishes the violent act (such as the prevalent formulation in the passive "these Palestinians have found their death").[28] These can be tied to Charles Mills's notion of "epistemological ignorance": an expression pointing to the fact that, sometimes, people are unable to understand or interpret injustices, even if they are able to see them.[29]

- Psychological, sociopolitical, or structural mechanisms allowing a continuous sidelining of the truth; not a denial as such, but a marginalization of the facts to the periphery of knowing, of seeing, of the

25 Janet McIntosh, *Unsettled: Denial and Belonging among White Kenyans* (Oakland: University of California Press, 2016), 10.

26 Cohen, *States of Denial*, 133.

27 The very widespread nature of this interpretation was clearly articulated during the "knives intifada" in 2015 and the events that followed. Responding to several cases in which individual Palestinians have tried, and in some cases succeeded in, killing Israelis using primitive weapons such as knives, member of parliament Yair Lapid suggested that "there must be clear instructions to shoot and kill whomever takes out a knife, or a screwdriver, or whatever it might be" (Yair Lapid, "The State of Israel Needs a United Front in Its Struggle against Terror," Facebook, October 11, 2015, https://www.facebook.com/pg/YairLapid/posts/?ref=page_internal). Lapid's use of "whatever it might be" reveals the scope of the possibility of framing Palestinians' actions as terror, thus justifying, almost always, killing them.

28 As Jeanne Morefield states, "liberal imperialists" often use the passive voice to divert attention from illiberal actions, as in: "acts of violence were committed and mistakes were made." Jeanne Morefield, *Empires without Imperialism: Anglo-American Decline and the Politics of Deflection* (Oxford: Oxford University Press, 2014), 17.

29 Charles W. Mills, *The Racial Contract* (Ithaca, NY: Cornell University Press, 1997), 18.

political matter, so that life can continue uninterrupted, despite what is known. A good example is Stoler's notion of "colonial aphasia": a mode of simultaneously denying and seeing, even being obsessed with, the colonial past.[30] Lisa Lowe termed this duality "the economy of affirmation and forgetting that structures and formalizes the archive of liberalism."[31] This is often done alongside various methods of turning a blind eye[32] or, more systematically so, of organizing entire political spaces of visibility in ways that render some truths more difficult to discover. The foresting of destroyed Palestinian villages after 1948, or an elevated road system in the West Bank that renders existing Palestinian villages less visible, can serve as examples.[33]

- Psychological, sociopolitical, and structural mechanisms of deferral, disavowal, and repression that secure the self from the potentially shattering implications of that which is known. We are quite familiar with such mechanisms on the psychological level (e.g., in dealing with childhood trauma); on the political level we can think with Morefield's work on deflection: turning the gaze away from violent actions to a liberal identity that is presumably always already there, regardless of these actions. The alleged stability of identity presumably means that the violent actions cannot contaminate it. Accordingly, by pointing to the liberal identity of the empire, its imperial (illiberal) doings can simultaneously be acknowledged and their meanings and implications for one's identity denied.[34] Ariella Azoulay and

30 Ann Laura Stoler, "Colonial Aphasia: Race and Disabled Histories in France," *Public Culture* 23, no. 1 (winter 2011): 121–56.

31 Lisa Lowe, *The Intimacies of Four Continents* (Durham, NC: Duke University Press, 2015), 3.

32 Cohen refers to this as not having an "inquisitive mind." For Cohen, this is an individual but more so a quite astonishing collective ability of entire societies to deny the past (*States of Denial*, 133).

33 Amira Hass, "To Drive and Not to See Arabs," *Ha'aretz*, January 22, 2003; translation in Ariel Handel, "Where, Where to and When in the Occupied Palestinian Territories: An Introduction to Geography of Disaster," in *The Power of Inclusive Exclusion: Anatomy of Israeli Rule in the Occupied Palestinian Territories*, ed. Adi Ophir, Michal Givoni, and Sari Hanafi (New York: Zone Books, 2009), 206; Eyal Weizman, *Hollow Land: Israel's Architecture of Occupation* (London: Verso Books, 2007).

34 Liberal narratives of imperialism are thus "never simply about repression of uncomfortable memories but always, rather, about the production of national identity through the remembering to forget." In this process, "painful memories" can never "be entirely 'removed from plain view'"; they are rather confronted, and immediately deflected, marginalized, in the name of

Adi Ophir point to a different mechanism operating along the same principles: they show how expressing shock and outrage at violent acts that are allegedly "excessive" allows Israelis to reaffirm their own morality as well as the morality of the occupation.[35] The paradigm of "a few rotten apples" is dominant here. It serves to mark "excessive" violence as the doings of the few and reaffirms the enlightenment of those engaged in these acts of marking.

- Finally, ideological apparatuses that allow violence to be reframed as nonviolence. Such mechanisms range from schemes like "progress" or the "white man's burden" as a mode of framing imperial domination to notions such as "bringing democracy to the world" as a scheme justifying warfare, or the Israeli version of "enlightened occupation."[36] All these allow for framing violence as something that is actually beneficial to its victims, and therefore not in conflict with the liberal-democratic identity of the perpetrators/beneficiaries.

This rough map, which can surely be more slowly unpacked, ties together very different accounts that nevertheless share three connected assumptions: first, that in order to realize the formation and sustainment of political identities

---

a "history of 'who we are'" that is, promoting freedom, individual rights, formal equality, and state sovereignty (Morefield, *Empires without Imperialism*, 15, 3). See also Veracini, who states that the settler imagination "has a tendency to operate by way of disavowal and repression." Lorenzo Veracini, "Settler Collective, Founding Violence and Disavowal: The Settler Colonial Situation," *Journal of Intercultural Studies* 29, no. 4 (2008): 365.

35 Ariella Azoulay and Adi Ophir, *The One-State Condition: Occupation and Democracy in Israel/Palestine* (Stanford, CA: Stanford University Press, 2012), 203–24. Or, as Ann Stoler notes: "Shocked moral outrage may suggest the innocence of those who were duped, ignorant, and not to blame. Feature stories on colonial war atrocities may be 'safe' because they have the perverse effect of suggesting that such individuated truths are redemptive" (Stoler, "Colonial Aphasia," 144). On the notion of "excessive violence" in this context, see Hagar Kotef and Merav Amir, "(En)Gendering Checkpoints: Checkpoint Watch and the Repercussions of Intervention," *Signs: Journal of Women in Culture and Society* 2, no. 4 (2007): 973–96.

36 On the use of the trope "bringing democracy to the world," see, for example, Paul Bloom, "Bush Pledges to Spread Democracy," CNN, January 20, 2005, http://edition.cnn.com/2005/ALLPOLITICS/01/20/bush.speech/. For more on the term *enlightened occupation*, see Gershon Shafir and Yoav Peled, *Being Israeli: The Dynamics of Multiple Citizenship* (Cambridge: Cambridge University Press, 2002). And, famously, Rudyard Kipling's "The White Man's Burden," in *Kipling: A Selection of His Stories and Poems*, ed. Rudyard Kipling and John Beecroft (Garden City, NY: Doubleday, 1956). For a wider theoretical analysis, see, among many others, Uday Singh Mehta, *Liberalism and Empire: A Study in Nineteenth-Century British Liberal Thought* (Chicago: University of Chicago Press, 1999).

within ethical schemes, the violence of imperial and colonial endeavors must be dissociated from the large political communities—or political imaginations—involved in them. This, in turn, rests on a second presupposition—one seldom made explicitly, but that seems to be a logical necessity—that there is some tension, if not a contradiction, between violence and the self. Without this presupposition, there would be no need to assume this vast apparatus of dissociation. In fact, the perplexity that drives it would dissolve. Thus, even though many of the abovementioned authors do see violence as constitutive of identities, they nevertheless see these identities as having to constantly negotiate with this violence.

To take one example: Even though Morefield's argument concerning the politics of deferral *refutes* the idea that the violence of Anglo-American imperialism does not represent "who we are" (as she puts it), it nevertheless sees the sustainability of imperial violence as a function of the ability to constantly disconnect this violence from the "we" engaging in it. Imperial violence is indeed narrated and recognized by Anglo-American liberals, she argues, but via "prolonged and creative forms of deflection that constantly ask the reader to avert her eyes, away from colonial violence and economic exploitation, and back towards the liberal nature of the imperial society." In such accounts, actions are dissociated from identity, and the latter can justify the very actions contradicting it because imperial society "was always, even when it was not, just being who it was," that is, liberal.[37] My point is that the complex apparatus that Morefield identifies is necessary only when, and as long as, the identity of the "we" is perceived as being, or indeed *is*, in contradiction to imperial violence. I do not argue that this apparatus is not in operation; merely that, in some cases, it is insufficient to account for the relations of some liberals to their violence—violence that *they* see as part of who they, indeed, are.

The third shared assumption of the above body of literature is that therefore, in order to resist these endeavors of dissociation, a certain politics of exposure, memory, or recognition is called for. Often, this politics aims to render violence more visible, so there is no possibility to claim it is unknown; other times, when violence and its traces can clearly be seen but are still denied or dissociated from identity, the aim of this politics will be to construct new historical narratives or political frames that can work against the possibility of dissociation. For the sake of brevity, I shall name all these endeavors "politics of visibility." This visibility, or these new ways of knowing and understanding political constellations, would presumably undo the possibility of the gap between

37 Morefield, *Empires without Imperialism*, 3.

the individual/group and their violence, and would thus undo the possibility of sustaining violence. If the denial of violence, as any form of denial, is done to protect the self from the implications of that which can threaten identity, and if, at the same time and for the same reason, denial is also what allows atrocities to go on, then the role of critique according to this model is to remove envelopes of justification. The truth, as it were, must be confronted, in a process that—much like psychoanalysis—is simultaneously traumatic and cathartic. My claim here is not that such political projects of knowledge and visibility are null; nor is it that political awareness of one's status is politically meaningless, or that "implicated subjects" are bound to reaffirm the violent orders they are implicated in. Furthermore, political projects of this nature are not always (not even often) part of a naïve endeavor, and most accounts above are critical and astute in their perception of political reality. My goal here is by no means to refute or ridicule these understandings. My point is that I identify in them a glimmer of hope—a hope I share myself—that such an act of dismantling the mechanisms of dissociation (or justification, or invisibility) would contribute to undermining the façade of liberal identity, force it to confront its reality, and thereby push for political change. I see this hope as politically necessary, being a vehicle for transformation, and yet when I look at the political reality I see something different. Indeed, these assumptions fail to acknowledge that violence is not always in conflict with the self or the community, but is something whose very loss may threaten the self. Accordingly, the model of dissociation is insufficient. This brings us to the fourth model, I want to suggest here, theorizing how violence is negotiated with identity.

Desire: Theories of Intimate Violence

The model for the acceptance of mass/state/institutionalized violence I seek to develop below joins the above three models. Unlike the model of compliance, it sees political violence as rooted in people themselves; unlike the model of cruelty, it does not see this violence as necessarily an outcome of sadism or maliciousness, thereby keeping open the possibility of a shared political future;[38] and unlike the model based on dissociation, it accounts for violence that cannot be explained by modes of invisibility or denial: it refuses the claim that people do not see or do not know or that they distort and reframe their knowledge so its meaning or political implication dwindles. In developing it, I will follow a model of subject formation

38 It would be quite impossible, or at least more difficult, to share life and territory with those who take pleasure in your suffering or those you perceive as such.

to ultimately argue that subjects in positions of privilege are likely to be attached to the conditions allowing these privileges to endure, even when these generate, sustain, or are themselves a form of violence. Moreover, these attachments do not—or do not always—become possible *despite* this violence, or because people are able to ignore it, but sometimes are *mediated* by violence itself.

To demarcate this model, I begin with the context of sexual desire. With important inversions and reservations, this model captures something of the model I want to propose for understanding wide-scale violence. Let us begin, then, on an individual level, and from the injured subject who is often theorized using this model, and then move on to the theorization of the injurious or beneficiary subject, and the large-scale injurious groups.

By way of illustration, consider this conversation from the story *Strangers at Home* by Ronit Matalon. Guiding her friend, who is about to have sex for the first time, this teenager's voice encapsulates the intimacies of violence that are at the basis of my proposed model.

> Look, you are getting undressed, right? Lying in bed—you next to the wall and he next to you. You take off your jewelry, your hairpins, everything, everything, and put it all in a small pile on the bedside dresser. Then you stand in front of him. You do nothing . . . Just don't be alarmed if you start shaking. You always shake at first, in an effort to tear away the voice, the memory of the freezing touch; from the fact that when he imprints his marks on your neck, it is not you his touch addresses; from this thought that you cannot control—a thought preparing you to be a woman . . . Then he gets on top of you . . . You need to open your legs, but be careful, not too much, you'll see . . . if you open them too much . . . it hurts. . . . But it's a good pain, you will want it a little bit, this is how you feel the time passing . . . If you bleed just ask for a towel and all that.[39]

The blood that needs to be cleaned; the body trembling from a touch, or just the thought of a touch that seems to hurt more than it causes pleasure (a freezing touch that might bring to mind an act of strangling as it leaves its imprint on the neck); the act of tearing, tearing the self from herself, but also being torn by another; all these are part of the injury—the pain—that is identified in this paragraph as sex, as the meaning of "be[ing] a woman." It is part of what one learns to want and is inseparable from what will become her desire. This is not to say that any sex is injurious, and it is certainly not to argue that any sex

39 Ronit Matalon, *Strangers at Home* [in Hebrew] (Tel Aviv: Ha-Ḳibuts Ha-me'uḥad, 1992), 67–68; my translation.

is a form of rape (in fact, it is precisely the injury that cannot be identified with acts of raping, or cruel desires, that I seek to point out). It is to rehearse, albeit briefly and anecdotally, what several feminist schools have shown at least since the early 1960s if not before, even if in radically different ways: that the most intimate relations can be violent or that violence can be intimate; that its presence is not a destruction of the familiar fabric of life, but part of it.[40]

Significant to my own argument is that there is not an "I" beyond this structure of desire who is being "misled" to want what harms her. The "I" emerges through this desire and cannot be freed by the power of truth about oppression (which is not to say that oppression must be accepted or that a struggle against it is impossible). To jump ahead, this point will be important for the question concerning the role of critique that I pose in what follows: If these relations to injury and through it to violence are constitutive of the self, then a critique rendering violence more visible (a critique along the lines of the "dissociation" model) would not have the same liberating power often ascribed to it. Much like the injury that cannot be disentangled from the "I," so will be the violence in contexts of social identities based on domination (patriarchy, white supremacy, settler colonialism). What has to be contended with, then, are not questions of exposure or knowledge but of the very conditions that render violence constitutive.

Butler has probably phrased it most eloquently: "Called by an injurious name, I come into social being. . . . I am led to embrace the terms that injure me because they constitute me socially. If we then understand certain kinds of

---

40 A very partial list: psychoanalytical feminists claimed that violence is inseparable from the formation of the self and the self's attachments to others (Melanie Klein's object relations theory might be the best example here, although in different ways one may think about Julia Kristeva's "abject" along such lines; see Melanie Klein, *The Psycho-Analysis of Children* [London: Vintage Books, 1997]; Julia Kristeva, *Powers of Horror: An Essay on Abjection* [New York: Columbia University Press, 1982]); postcolonial feminists have shown how desire organizes imperial domination and how imperial structures partake in the organization of desire (e.g., Malek Alloula, *The Colonial Harem: Images of Subconscious Eroticism* [Manchester: Manchester University Press, 1986]; Anne McClintock, *Imperial Leather: Race, Gender, and Sexuality in the Colonial Contest* [New York: Routledge, 1995]; Ann Laura Stoler, *Race and the Education of Desire: Foucault's History of Sexuality and the Colonial Order of Things* [Durham, NC: Duke University Press, 1995]); and radical feminists argued that we have learned to desire subjection—to see pornography and its violence as sex or the systematic institutional exploitation within the heteronormative family as love (e.g., Andrea Dworkin, *Intercourse* [New York: Simon and Schuster, 1997]; Catharine A. MacKinnon, *Toward a Feminist Theory of the State* [Cambridge, MA: Harvard University Press, 1989]; Carole Pateman, "Women and Consent," *Political Theory* 8, no. 2 [1980]: 149–68).

interpellations to confer identity, those injurious interpellations will constitute identity through injury."[41]

For Butler, this claim has both an ontological dimension and a sociohistorical one. Ontologically, it is a function of the fact that, as corporeal creatures,
we are vulnerable,[42] and of the fact that from birth, bodies are both dependent
on others if they are to survive and are shaped by social norms (even if never
deterministically or fully so).[43] But this is, as Butler puts it, a "social ontology."[44] First, it is social because this vulnerability is precisely a function of our
social interdependence and interconnectivity. It is because of our deep social-
ity that we cannot form significant ties to others and to the world without
being undone, Butler teaches us, and this undoing is both a form of injury and
what makes us so vulnerable to being injured by the other's doings (betraying
us, leaving us, leaving the world, but also sometimes merely a look, a touch, or
the lack thereof). Second, it is "social," or rather "political," because it is a function of the particular social webs, kinship formations, works of power, forms
of rule, and social hierarchies within a given society. In this sense, to insist
on inherent vulnerability is not to ignore the historical and social specificities
of different political structures or organizations; it is to point to a condition

41 J. Butler, *Psychic Life of Power*, 104–5.
42 This is not to say that we are mostly vulnerable or mortal, or to refute the claim that, as, Bonnie Honig rightly insists, we are "natals as well" and that "a focus on natality—which is no
less minimal than mortality, ontologically speaking—may generate new commonalities while
orienting humanism differently than mortality does" (Bonnie Honig, "Antigone's Two Laws:
Greek Tragedy and the Politics of Humanism," *New Literary History* 41, no. 1 [winter 2010]: 9).
It is to say that vulnerability is one essential dimension of our existence, certainly if we think
of it as an existence with others. And whereas Butler emphasizes the body's vulnerability to
suffering in some of her post-9/11 books (particularly *Precarious Life* and *Frames of War*), this
vulnerability, which actually means openness or responsiveness, is also what allows pleasure
and desire—being moved, touched, imprinted upon by others. See Moya Lloyd, "The Ethics
and Politics of Vulnerable Bodies," in *Butler and Ethics*, ed. M. S. Lloyd (Edinburgh: Edinburgh
University Press, 2015), 171.
43 In this regard, it is important to note Butler's emphasis that the work of norms is that of power
and not that of violence. Whereas all norms are a form of power, not all norms—perhaps not
even most, and under some readings, none—are a form of exerting violence. They do, however,
render some bodies more vulnerable to violence (and, under some readings, some of them operate violently on some bodies). For an elaborate clarification of these relations, see Judith Butler,
"Reply from Judith Butler to Mills and Jenkins," *differences* 18, no. 2 (September 2007): 180–95.
44 Judith Butler, "Remarks on 'Queer Bonds,'" *GLQ* 17, nos. 2–3 (2011): 382. Butler emphasizes that
the English translation of Freud's "drive" (*Trieb*) as "instinct" is largely responsible for the reading of these psychoanalytical frames as biologically deterministic (*Force of Non-violence*, 157).

that is articulated differently and with different implications within different orders, and that cannot be taken outside of these concrete social articulations. We all share the condition of vulnerability, but some groups are more vulnerable than others; some political formations and some specific governments increase insecurity, while other forms of politics/governments work to minimize it; some acts or social structures kill, disable, or debilitate—to draw on Jasbir Puar's important distinction[45]—some scar, and some cause temporary discomfort; and finally, some political actors work differently with their own or others' conditions of vulnerability (importantly, being vulnerable does not preclude political action or render one a passive victim).[46]

My case of analysis, however, is situated from the outset within a particular political constellation and is about political positionality rather than ontological conditions of subjectivity as such. This distinction is crucial, because it shifts us from the realm of ontology and thus necessity to the realm of politics, with the potentiality of change it carries. Butler herself insists on this distinction when she states, together with Athena Athanasiou, that it is crucial to distinguish between the conditions of subject formation in and through injury, and the injury that is the outcome of particular political constellations or actions. The former are "at the fundamental level of subjection," while the latter are the object of resistance and transformation.[47] What is nonetheless important for me in this ontology of openness is one insight that will be relevant also to the political analysis: An affective attachment opens us to injury in ways that sometimes make it impossible to dissociate injury from attachment.

Lauren Berlant situates this structure of attachment at the core of capitalist society. She shows that the need to protect the "I" makes us hold on to objects of attachment—or perhaps better, to the very permanency of an object,

---

45 Jasbir K. Puar, *The Right to Maim: Debility, Capacity, Disability* (Durham, NC: Duke University Press, 2017).

46 Butler makes this distinction between a shared ontology and its differentiated social/political materialization most explicitly in *Frames of War*, where she distinguishes between precariousness as an ontological ("existential") fact and precarity as a political condition. Judith Butler, *Frames of War: When Is Life Grievable?* (London: Verso Books, 2009); see also Judith Butler and Athena Athanasiou, *Dispossession: The Performative in the Political* (Cambridge: Polity Press, 2013). For important critiques, however, see Alyson Cole, "All of Us Are Vulnerable, but Some Are More Vulnerable Than Others: The Political Ambiguity of Vulnerability Studies, an Ambivalent Critique," *Critical Horizons* 17, no. 2 (2016): 260–77. Cole observes that the emphasis on the shared ontological condition may "dilute" these observations, and thus "the language of vulnerability may not be able to perform the political work the most vulnerable require and deserve" (274).

47 Butler and Athanasiou, *Dispossession*, 3–5.

or to the idea of permanency itself—even when those inflict injuries of various kinds: "The subjects who have x in their lives might not well endure the loss of their object or scene of desire, even though its presence threatens their well-being, because whatever the content of the attachment, the continuity of the form of it provides something of the continuity of the subject's sense of what it means to keep on living and to look forward to being in the world."[48] Thus, we hold on to objects, even when those are "problematic objects" and even when they generate "compromised conditions of possibility," as part of an almost tragic effort to stabilize identity—the meaning of who we are.[49]

In both Butler's and Berlant's accounts, violence emerges not as something that threatens identities, but as what sustains them; in both, violence therefore also becomes an object of desire, or is at least woven into a desire for other objects; in both, this nexus, wherein violence and desire coproduce each other, is a function of the particular social conditions that constitute identity (images of the good life in Berlant, heteronormative forms of socialization in Butler). These last three points will be central to the analysis of violent identities throughout this book, with one significant difference: In the above accounts, injury and identity are considered from the perspective of those injured—by others, by structures, by a particular construction of identity. In my analysis, however, the optics will be reversed to think of those who *generate* injury.[50]

---

48 Lauren Berlant, *Cruel Optimism* (Durham, NC: Duke University Press, 2011), 24.

49 Berlant, *Cruel Optimism*, 24.

50 We should note that Butler does account for this side of the equation as well, most explicitly when she talks about the "frames" that make some life less grievable. J. Butler, *Frames of War*; Judith Butler, *Precarious Life: The Powers of Mourning and Violence* (London: Verso Books, 2004). However, in these accounts of those who cause injury, she is much closer to some of the threads in the "dissociation" model and seems to sideline these insights about the constitutive role of violence. In her reply to some critiques, Butler further emphasizes that her consideration of the work of violence as constitutive should not be taken to indicate the subjects' own actions. In fact, she insists, "it may be that precisely because—or rather, when—someone is formed in violence, the responsibility not to repeat the violence of one's formation is all the more pressing and important" ("Reply from Judith Butler to Mills and Jenkins," 181). This call for nonviolence is further developed in her most recent book, *The Force of Non-violence*. This book was already in production when *The Force of Non-violence* was published, making a more systematic analysis of it here impossible. It is telling, however, that even when Butler works on agents of violence, she is very much concerned also with what violence does *to them*. Violence, she says, breaks "not only the social bonds of the groups targeted by war but those of the groups waging war as well" (*Force of Non-violence*, 155). Ultimately, working with Freud, she shows that in terms of understanding the psychic structures of destruction, the distinction between aggressors who hurt others and those who become the victims (albeit of their own violent drives) is unstable (see esp. 158–59).

Reversal

What I propose is a structural reversal that can be seen as a hypothesis (one I hope to substantiate in the following chapters): If subjects emerge via the social conditions in which they are born and that continue to form them as they continue living, and if, as Butler and Berlant argue, we come to desire these conditions even when they are injurious, then we should at least entertain the possibility that sociopolitical conditions that are founded on ongoing violence—such as settlement or colonization—are likely to give rise to a particular mode of attachment to one's own violence.

The analysis of such desires must move, then, between individual settlers and their modes of attachment, on the one hand, and settler communities, where such "structures of feelings" become more explicitly political, on the other. It also has to move between an analysis of different and shifting political arrangements and what we may call the ontology of settler colonialism, or what Wolfe would call its structure. And finally, within such a story, the structural and the historical must be unfolded in their distinctness but also in their interdependence. The book will be able to do this only partially, and I hope the reader will be able to connect some of the dots.

The claim, then, is that in the settler's ways of being, her very presence, her very political identity, is a form of violence. There is not an "I," in the case of the settler, without dispossession—if not elimination—of natives, and so the effort to stabilize identity, to hold on to the "continuity of the subject's sense of what it means to keep on living and to look forward to being in the world" (to return to Berlant) is inextricable from this violence. Recall the landscape that is saturated with traces of violence I mentioned in the preface (I return to these in chapter 2). When one longs for and belongs to this landscape, one does not take pleasure in seeing or causing pain (the cruelty model); yet this pain cannot be fully separated from the spaces of belonging that construct the sense of self (political, communal, individual). The desire at play here is not for the suffering body, and the suffering of others may be completely incidental to it. But since this desire is for a territory in which violence is deeply entrenched, suffering becomes immanent to it. The "I" who finds a home in these spaces, in those traces, and who is thus also defined by them, is conditioned (also) by the violence they mark, remind her of, and carry with them from the past, even if this violence is mediated by time and by other people. As in the model developed by poststructuralist feminists, there is no "I" beyond this structure of relationality who is being "misled" to want to harm or to not see the harm she generates. That is, within the structure of settlement, the Butlerian scheme should be reversed: the "I," to paraphrase Butler's quote from the previous section, comes to embrace the terms through which she injures others because they constitute her socially.

Importantly, as aforementioned, the constitutive nature of violence changes with this reversal. Unlike the forms of injury that necessarily constitute the self because it is unavoidably a social being, and as such necessarily open to others and vulnerable to their actions (or neglect), the mass violence that becomes constitutive to settler identity is a function of a particular mode of inhabiting a territory and is not necessary. Even if we accept that structurally necessary to this mode of inhabiting a territory is what Wolfe termed "elimination," elimination itself takes a plurality of forms that bear radically different political implications: genocide, transfer, spatial concentration and isolation, assimilation. The concrete materialization of the structure is thus a matter of politics and history, and the idea of structural necessity becomes more fluid. Further, one can inhabit land in altogether nonsettler ways.

To conclude this overview, let us briefly consider one anecdotal illustration of such an alternative mode of inhabitation, to make clear that the discussion herein is political rather than ontological. In a petition against the Balfour Declaration (March 1920), a group of Palestinians from Nazareth declared: "The Jews are people of our country who lived with us before the occupation. They are our brothers, people of our country and all the Jews of the world are our brothers."[51] The Jews—local and potential immigrants—are placed here by the Palestinians on a par with themselves as indigenous groups, confronting together a colonial order (Britain). Alongside other, similar calls, this petition demonstrates the possibility of imagining Jewish-Palestinian modes of sharing the land based on notions of shared indigeneity.[52] Eventually, however, Jewish presence in the land took a more settler-colonial form, which was a function of many structures: a particular dominant Zionist ideology (which came to triumph over other Zionist and non-Zionist options), a particular imperial constellation that formed in the shift from the Ottoman to the British Em-

51 Cited in Ella Shohat, "Sephardim in Israel: Zionism from the Standpoint of Its Jewish Victims," *Social Text* 19/20 (autumn 1988): 11.

52 See Yuval Evri and Hagar Kotef, "When Does a Native Become a Settler?," *Constellations* (forthcoming). For some examples of literature drawing on pre-1948 history to trace such possible alternative modes of inhabitation in Israel/Palestine, see Ariella Azoulay, "Civil Alliances—Palestine, 1947-1948," *Settler Colonial Studies* 4, no. 4 (2014): 413-33; Yehuda Shenhav, *Beyond the Two-State Solution* (Cambridge: Polity Press, 2012); Salim Tamari, *Mountain against Sea: Essays on Palestinian Society and Culture* (Berkeley: University of California Press, 2008).

pire, the global colonial order, the outcomes of the Second World War and the Holocaust—with the existential fears it produced—and other global and local processes.[53] This mode of settler presence has since then been sustained by and continuously feeds on current global orders (such as the rise of the Right across the world), theological frameworks that see the Jewish people as the sole owners of the land, or a national ethos that encourages a particular, exclusive desire for the territory itself among Israelis from a very young age.

And yet this mode of presence can still be transformed by a shared struggle—Palestinian, Israeli, and international. At the end, the choice to organize this book around the concept of home is to insist on asking how one can stay, and yet stay in different ways. Taking "home" as the primary axis of analysis is a way of saying that I believe that the struggles working to shift these modes of settler attachments, and with them settler violence, should begin with the fact that the land is shared and has become the home of both Israeli Jews and Palestinians. The question, then, is not how one side can triumph, but how the space can be shared in just and nonviolent ways. This question is articulated in this book primarily in regard to Israel/Palestine, but the urgency of having to share the world or so many of its corners in more just and less violent ways reaches far beyond this context. The next part opens up some of these contexts, before I move to my primary geopolitical focus.

53 And once this form was established, the idea of shared indigeneity became, at least to some extent, a way of robbing Palestinians of the only status that can protect them, rather than a foundation for equality. See Honaida Ghanim's critique of Meron Benvenisti's *The Dream of the White Sabra* in "On Natives, Specters, and Shades of Ruins" [in Hebrew], in *Indigeneity and Exile in Israel/Palestine*, ed. Shaul Seter (Tel Aviv: Tel Aviv University Press, 2014).

Part I
HOMES

Interlude
Home/Homelessness

A READING IN ARENDT

"To be human is to have and to know your place"—Tim Cresswell cites a widespread assumption.[1] Indeed, so widespread that Robert Park could argue that "the human creature is a good deal of a vegetable," a fact that is made evident by "the invincible attachment of mankind to localities and places."[2] Park is not unique in appealing to such metaphors, even if he uses them somewhat more bluntly than most. What Liisa Malkki identifies as "a powerful sedentarism in our thinking" "is routinely conceived in specifically botanical metaphors." "People," she explains, "are often thought of, and think of themselves, as being rooted in place."[3] Indeed, Simone Weil referred to rootedness as "perhaps the most important and least recognized need of the human soul."[4] And while she

1 Tim Cresswell, *On the Move: Mobility in the Modern Western World* (New York: Routledge, 2006), 31.

2 Robert E. Park, "The Mind of the Hobo: Reflections upon the Relation between Mentality and Locomotion," in *The City: Suggestions for Investigation of Human Behavior in the Urban Environment*, 2nd ed., ed. Robert E. Park and Ernst W. Burgess (Chicago: University of Chicago Press, [1925] 1967), 156–60. And yet we should not mistake this attachment to stationariness for an absence of movement among human values. After all, for Park "it is the fact of locomotion ... that defines the very nature of society": society, according to him, *is* a "moving equilibrium" that is *composed* "of moving, locomoting individuals" (159).

3 Liisa Malkki, "National Geographic: The Rooting of Peoples and the Territorialization of National Identity among Scholars and Refugees," *Cultural Anthropology* 7, no. 1 (1992): 31, 27. See also Gilles Deleuze and Félix Guattari, *A Thousand Plateaus: Capitalism and Schizophrenia*, trans. Brian Massumi (London: Continuum, 1987), 18.

4 Simone Weil, *The Need for Roots: Prelude to a Declaration of Duties towards Mankind*, trans. Arthur Wills (London: Routledge, [1949] 2002), 40.

saw rootedness as something "natural" and "automatic," she did not see it as an individual need but as a need inextricably linked to life in a community.[5] Thus, even though home is a constant absence from political thought; even though it often functions as the Other of the political; even though it entails, and is further *defined by*, all that is presumably not political (women, children, slaves, property, but also stability, confinement, or biology); and, finally, even though the domestic sphere is conceptualized as that which is, or should be, beyond the reach of the political (and in that it is very much like the sphere marked as "nature," and sometimes as a symbol of nature, though sometimes its complete opposite, as in the case of domesticated animals),[6] despite all these attributes or assumptions, "home" nevertheless emerges as a defining element of humanity, and further—of humanity in its political articulation. Ultimately, humans appear as political animals *because* they are domestic creatures.

Arendt, who will be at the center of this chapter, is indicative of these two, somewhat contradictory, trajectories. On the one hand, she saw humans as characterized by their ability to transcend this vegetative sense, to move beyond the sphere of biology, necessity, and nature that she identified with the household. On the other hand, as I show here, Arendt saw the stability of the home as essential to both human and political life. This conflictual approach to home—as that which must be transcended but which remains constitutive despite this externality—makes it possible to pull out some threads that will be at the heart of this book. The first is the centrality of home to both political action and political theory, and the claim that it stands at the core of both. The second is the insight provided here through Arendt into the ways in which sedentarist assumptions function within global imperial formations. There are two elements here: (i) the refusal to see some forms of being-in-the-land as establishing legitimate territorial claims (the refusal to see some homes as homes) and (ii) the refusal to see those who have lost their legible home—i.e., refugees—as political subjects despite the lack of a collective territorial anchor. Both will become clear later in this interlude. The third thread concerns the models available to collective Jewish homemaking, which allow me to demarcate more concretely the type of home around which this book revolves. This interlude, then, places the home at the foundations of political analysis; it then looks at homes in differentiated global contexts and shows how their configuration or negation is mapped onto patterns of colonial rule;

5 Weil, *Need for Roots*, 40.
6 I am alluding here to a set of common assumptions that can be found in political theory, history, and beyond. See Introduction, note 18.

and it ends with home in Israel/Palestine, which is the main focus of this book's analysis.

THE MOST COMMON READING of Arendt emphasizes the contrast she saw between the domestic and the political spheres. The home, much like the body of which it is the paradigmatic place, was to be "left behind" when one enters politics.[7] This is a spatial dichotomy: the body and the household within which corporeal functions are organized are politics' conditions of possibility, and they must remain *external* to it.[8] And yet it is not simply that the home attends

7 As Anne Norton puts it in "Heart of Darkness: Africa and African Americans in the Writings of Hannah Arendt," in *Feminist Interpretations of Hannah Arendt*, ed. Bonnie Honig (University Park: Pennsylvania State University Press, 1995), 257. The body, biology, needs, are beyond the reach of human action; they are "the fact of difference as such," and should therefore remain contained and confined in order to leave a space wherein things can be *made equal* by the virtue of a political decision (Hannah Arendt, *The Origins of Totalitarianism*, 5th ed. [New York: Harcourt Brace Jovanovich, 1973], 301; all references to Arendt's *Origins* will herein appear as *OT*). There is a great body of literature on the concept of the body in Arendt's thought. Between the different analyses within the relevant debate, the Arendtian body appears as given in limbo: as part of the realm of necessity, it is inevitably situated in opposition to freedom and politics. Accordingly, "one enters politics by leaving the body" (Norton, "Heart of Darkness," 257). On the other hand, however, Arendt is looking for a concept of freedom "which is not an attribute of the will but an accessory of doing and acting" and is therefore anchored in the body (Hannah Arendt, "What Is Freedom?," in *Between Past and Future: Eight Exercises in Political Thought* [New York: Penguin, (1961) 2006], 65). In Linda Zerilli's words: "Arendtian action and speech would be empty without the bodily drives that animate them" (Linda M. G. Zerilli, "The Arendtian Body," in *Feminist Interpretations of Hannah Arendt*, ed. Bonnie Honig [University Park: Pennsylvania State University Press, 1995], 180). The body is what drives and animates action and must appear "for politics to take place" (Judith Butler, "Bodies in Alliance and the Politics of the Street," *European Institute for Progressive Cultural Policies* 9 [2011], http://www.eipcp.net/transversal/1011/butler/en). And yet, it can never cross the threshold of politics, almost as if Arendt "cannot admit . . . that the body is the locus or vehicle of action, hence freedom," as Wendy Brown diagnoses (*Manhood and Politics: A Feminist Reading in Political Theory* [Totowa, NJ: Rowman and Littlefield, 1988], 196). This ambivalence, this liminal position of the body vis-à-vis the political, may indicate that for Arendt, the exclusion of body from politics is a function of two separate—perhaps complementary, perhaps conflicting— frameworks. In one respect, Arendt fails to see the body as political or, as Brown proposes, fails to recognize that her own theory calls for an embodied account of politics. Yet for her, this very failure is the failure of politics itself and therefore must be left unspoken.

8 Elsewhere we see that if we replace the spatial language with a temporal one, this dichotomy is inverted, and should be replaced with, or supplemented by, a dichotomy in which the body's *instability* (its fragility, mortality, its linear *movement* in time—from natality to death) is contrasted

to the needs of the animal part—if not the vegetable part—of the political animal that is Man: Arendt not only criticized but also *reproduced* the assumption
that to be fully human, one needs a place, a source of stability, and eventually
even a certain degree of confinement. Accordingly, on the other side of this
need to transcend domesticity, we find in Arendt's writing a strong "sedentary
metaphysics," as Malkki termed it.[9]

The fact that Arendt saw placelessness as a crisis is most evident in her
discussion of statelessness in *The Origins*. What the refugees of her account lost
was not liberty as individual freedom;[10] rather, they lost the right to *stay*, to
take place, to *reside*, and with it the ability to form a community, or what Arendt refers to as a "social texture." The right to have rights, as she famously puts
it, is thus conditioned on the ability to be *placed*, and, moreover, to be placed in
proximity, so that one is able to come together with others.[11] But we find this
metaphysics also in *The Human Condition*, where the boundless movement of
the very principle of politics—action—carries the risk of destroying the very
world it constructs (*HC*, 190). It is therefore not surprising that when Arendt
speaks of "the world"—the space and product of politics—she constantly relies
on domestic metaphors:[12] It is the table around which we sit—which ties us

---

to the *permanence* and *stability* provided by a political world (e.g., Hannah Arendt, *The Human
Condition*, 2nd ed. [Chicago: University of Chicago Press, 1998], 177); all references to Arendt's
The Human Condition will herein appear as *HC*). As Arendt claims in *The Human Condition*, the
political world is the space in which action becomes stories that provide both agents and actions
some durability. Note that even in this version of the dichotomy, the political can accomplish
its own promise—stability across time—because it transcends the material world, transforming
action into a story. Accordingly, even if from two opposite directions, the individual proves
herself to be (also) a subject (that is, an agent) and not (merely) an object by transcending the
body: first by demonstrating the human ability to not be fully affixed by biology and, second, by
the possibility of immortalization which is the perpetuation (fixity) over time.

9 Malkki, "National Geographic," 31. Accordingly, as Malkki observes, the displaced are often
pathologized by the means of situating this crisis within their bodies and minds rather than in
social and political circumstances ("National Geographic," 33).

10 Understood here as freedom of movement: "There is no question that those outside the pale of
the law may have more freedom of movement than a lawfully imprisoned criminal or that they
enjoy more freedom of opinion in the internment camps of democratic countries than they
would in any ordinary despotism, not to mention in a totalitarian country" (*OT*, 296).

11 "The first loss which the rightless suffered was the loss of their homes, and this meant the loss of
the entire social texture into which they were born and in which they established for themselves
a distinct place in the world" (*OT*, 293). See epilogue to part I for critiques.

12 Jeanne Morefield, "World" (lecture, Conceptual Itineraries workshop, SOAS, University of London, June 2017).

yet separates us, preventing "our falling over each other, so to speak" (HC, 52), and which can disappear, and with it "the power to gather [people] together, to relate and to separate them" (HC, 53). It is the banister—which represents the modern tools of thought or morality). But above all, it is the wall. The wall of the oikos, Arendt tells us, was the etymological base of the Greek concept of law (HC, 63–64).[13] Thus, "the lawmaker was like the builder of the city wall, someone who had to do and finish his work before political activity could begin" (HC, 184), the law as a wall that delimits (and thereby constitutes) the polis (HC, 184). Like the oikos, which is an array of borders—the borders demarcated by its physical walls, the limitations on novelty set by the repetition of reproduction, and the very boundaries of life, as it is the site of birth and death—the law is the set of limitations within which (and against which) the political sphere is constituted as a sphere of freedom. Arendt briefly mentions here what Schmitt further developed: that nomos is based on the division of land, on the logic of spatial separation, or, in his words, that nomos "is a fence word" and that "law and peace originally rested on *enclosure in the spatial sense*."[14] Only after "the solid ground of the earth is delineated by fences, enclosures, boundaries, walls, houses, and other constructs" would "the orders and orientations of human social life become apparent."[15] "In the beginning"—Schmitt reminds us of what we have already learned from Rousseau—"was a fence."[16]

Without these fences—without "the wall of the *polis* and the boundaries of the law"—the public space "could not endure, could not survive the moment of action and speech itself" (HC, 198). We therefore need stability, not just as the biological precondition from which one needs to depart to become a political animal, but also as the condition that contains and thus enables politics itself:

> The fences inclosing private property and insuring the limitations of each household, the territorial boundaries which protect and make possible the physical identity of a people, and the laws which protect and make possible its political existence, are of such great importance to the stability of

---

13 See also Carl Schmitt, *The Nomos of the Earth in the International Law of the* Jus Publicum Europaeum, trans. G. L. Ulmen (New York: Telos Press, 2006), 70.

14 Schmitt, *Nomos of the Earth*, 75, 74. Arendt read Schmitt and quoted his work *State, Movement, People* in *OT*; e.g., 251; see also 339.

15 Schmitt, *Nomos of the Earth*, 42.

16 Schmitt, *Nomos of the Earth*, 74. Schmitt cites Trier here. Rousseau wrote: "The first person who, having enclosed a plot of land, took it into his head to say *this is mine* and found people simple enough to believe him, was the true founder of civil society." Jean-Jacques Rousseau, *The Basic Political Writings*, 2nd ed., trans. and ed. Donald A. Cress (Indianapolis, IN: Hackett, 2011).

human affairs precisely because no such limiting and protecting principles rise out of the activities going on in the realm of human affairs itself. (*HC*, 191)

Stability thus emerges, from this perspective too, as a precondition for politics, a claim many have identified in Arendt's account of rightlessness.

ARENDT CLAIMED THAT the tragedy of the First World War's refugees was "unprecedented" (*OT*, 293), and yet this was not because such atrocities had never occurred on the face of the earth before. On the contrary; they were unprecedented because "a growing number of people and peoples suddenly appeared whose elementary rights were *as little safeguarded by the ordinary functioning of the nation-states in the middle of Europe as they would have been in the heart of Africa*" (*OT*, 291, my italics). One way to read this unprecedentedness, then, is that, unlike in the case of massacres "in the heart of Africa," with those other massacres "everyone ought to have known what they were doing."[17] We can understand this claim as resting on a presumed stratification within humanity itself, dividing it into several "kinds" of people: some clearly present themselves as humans and others do not and thus cannot serve as "precedents" to human tragedy. Many indeed have read Arendt as reproducing such racial logic, yet others insist on more generous readings.[18] We can be more generous, then, and read this unprecedentedness as a function of two related factors. First, the case of the First World War's refugees was allegedly "unprecedented" because, by that time, "there was no longer any 'uncivilized' spot on earth" (*OT*, 297)—or, to put it in Lockean terms, because one could no longer simply go and "plant in some inland, vacant places of

---

17 Famously: "the real crime" only began when Indians and Chinese were treated "as though they were not human beings," "because here everyone *ought to have known what they were doing*" (*OT*, 206; my italics).

18 For the former, see note 24 in this interlude. For the latter, see, e.g., Seyla Benhabib, *The Reluctant Modernism of Hannah Arendt* (Lanham, MD: Rowman and Littlefield, 2000); Ayten Gündogdu, *Rightlessness in an Age of Rights* (Oxford: Oxford University Press, 2014); Manu Samnotra, "'Poor in World': Hannah Arendt's Critique of Imperialism," *Contemporary Political Theory* 18, no. 4 (2018): 562–82.

19 John Locke, *The Second Treatise*, in *Two Treatises of Government and a Letter Concerning Toleration*, ed. Ian Shapiro (New Haven, CT: Yale University Press, 2003), §36. Given that Arendt notes that "through centuries the extermination of native peoples went hand in hand with the colonization of the Americas, Australia, and Africa" (*OT*, 440), it is particularly vexing that at times she cannot avoid repeating the myth of a peaceful settlement of "uncivilized" places on earth. See also the famous statement on page 237: "Unlike their happier predecessors in the religious wars," these new immigrants "were welcomed nowhere and could be assimilated nowhere. Once they had

America."[19] Importantly, then, even under a more generous reading that looks at historical conditions rather than racialized differentiations, Arendt's claim hinges on the myth of vacant lands that has lain at the foundations of imperial and colonial enterprises, reimagining the world as entailing vast patches of terra nullius in which settlement would not entail the dispossession of anyone. The second factor is that, supposedly, what the European refugees have *lost*, the sub-Saharan Africans *never had*. These two facts are closely related, because it is this presumed lack of home that makes it possible to see the land as vacant and available. It is the *lack* of home that preconditioned or facilitated the materialization of many of the horrors of both the Second World War and imperial ventures in Africa alike according to Arendt; but it is the *loss* of home rather than its mere lack, and the *craving* for a home (the reaffirmation of some sense of rootedness) that makes these horrors more tragic, more immoral, more horrifying in her eyes. The latter, she states, are the share of the Europeans alone.[20]

People in sub-Saharan Africa do live in homes that Arendt can name—tents and huts—and yet these cannot fulfill the role of home as outlined in the previous section: creating a stable, contained, and long-lasting platform for transcending nature and engaging in political life. Therefore, for Arendt, African "tribes" do not seem to suffer from the same loss as the European refugees.[21] The tent, she argues in a paragraph from "The Crisis in Culture," "can serve as a home," "but this

---

left their homeland they remained homeless, once they had left their state they became stateless; once they had been deprived of their human rights they were rightless, the scum of the earth."

20 Such a hierarchical ontology of home manifested itself across many other layers of imperial governance. Jonathan Schroeder shows how during the eighteenth and nineteenth centuries, bodies subjected to forced mobility were pathologized through the concept of "nostalgia": a pathological longing for home that was "solely used to diagnose sailors, soldiers, convicts, slaves, and other groups whose labor forcibly separated them from home." But whereas the Swiss soldier was seen as slowly dying from nostalgia because he missed his European home (recall, again, Arendt's emphasis on loss in the case of European refugees), enslaved Africans were seen as dying (slowly or quickly) not because they *missed* their home, but because they believed they would return home *in* death. This racialized stratification of pathology altered how the presumed desire for home (a conceptualization that itself, as Schroeder shows, made it possible to decontextualize and depoliticize the suicide of slaves) was managed. Beyond marking enslaved Africans as irrational in their belief in the postdeath mythical world, as suffering from an even more pathologized pathology as it were, this also marked their real home as irrelevant. Once again, the non-European subject appears as lacking a home or a true sense of home, as part of a system that "had made a business of displacement." Jonathan D. S. Schroeder, "What Was Black Nostalgia?," *American Literary History* 30, no. 4 (November 2018): 655, 658.

21 For such an analysis, see Jimmy Casas Klausen, "Hannah Arendt's Antiprimitivism," *Political Theory* 38, no. 3 (June 2010): 393–427.

by no means implies that such arrangements beget a world, let alone a culture." It cannot exceed its status of an "earthly home" and become "a world in the proper sense," because it cannot "resist the consuming life process of the people dwelling in it, and thus outlast them."[22] In a different formulation of the above negation of homes, this time from "Culture and Politics," huts are added to this list: the "tents and huts of primitive peoples" fail to serve as a boundary, a "dam," Arendt contends, "between the perishability of man and the imperishability of nature that serves as the yardstick for mortals to measure their mortality."[23] Tents are clearly transient, less stable, and with their lack of walls and doors cannot embody the materiality of the dam—they cannot both separate, like a wall, and allow a regulated, protected transition between the "in" and the "out" (recall the importance of such regulated movement in Arendt's metaphysics with which we opened this chapter). They also symbolize nomadism and thus are more clearly contrasted with the oikos. But huts are not defined by the ability to dismantle them easily and keep moving on; they do have walls and seem to be closer to the spatiality Arendt imagines or requires. Why, then, are huts included in Arendt's list of homes that are not sufficient to become the foundation for political life?

Much has been written about the racial grammar of Arendt's writings and I shall not repeat those arguments here.[24] As briefly noted above, other readings are possible. Manu Samnotra even proposes to "read Arendt's argument in 'Imperialisms' in a postcolonial key."[25] Rather than engaging in this debate, I will limit my analysis to two quick points regarding the wider lineages of

22 Hannah Arendt, "The Crisis in Culture," in *Between Past and Future: Eight Exercises in Political Thought* (New York: Penguin, [1961] 2006), 209–10.

23 Hannah Arendt, "Culture and Politics," in *Thinking without a Banister: Essays in Understanding, 1953–1975*, ed. Jerome Kohn (New York: Schocken Books, 2018), 170–71. For an analysis, see Klausen, "Hannah Arendt's Antiprimitivism."

24 Anne Norton probably provides the harshest critique in "Heart of Darkness." See also Robert Lambert Bernasconi, "When the Real Crime Began: Hannah Arendt's *The Origins of Totalitarianism* and the Dignity of the Western Philosophical Tradition," in *Hannah Arendt and the Uses of History: Imperialism, Nation, Race, and Genocide*, ed. Richard H. King and Dan Stone (New York: Berghahn, 2008), 54–67; Lisa Jane Disch, *Hannah Arendt and the Limits of Philosophy* (Ithaca, NY: Cornell University Press, 1996), 132–33; Kathryn T. Gines, *Hannah Arendt and the Negro Question* (Bloomington: Indiana University Press, 2014); or Norma Claire Moruzzi, *Speaking through the Mask: Hannah Arendt and the Politics of Social Identity* (Ithaca, NY: Cornell University Press, 2001). But see Benhabib's critique in *The Reluctant Modernism of Hannah Arendt*, esp. 83–86. Benhabib emphasizes that Arendt does not reproduce the colonial/imperial trope of "Africa," and that rather than viewing it as a monolithic entity, Arendt sees the diversity and plurality within African societies in ways the above critiques miss.

25 Samnotra, "Poor in World," 563.

thoughts and praxes within which the above claims concerning homes might be situated. First, in her dismissal of huts, she should be situated within a long colonial history of construction. This dismissal, importantly appearing in two essays focusing on culture, relied on a particular view that saw construction materials as manifesting the contrast between nature and culture. It was indeed this contrast that stood at the heart of Arendt's understanding of "savagery": "what made [the 'savages'] different from other human beings was not at all the color of their skin but the fact that they behaved like a part of nature." Huts were both an example and a symbol of this inability, or lack of desire, to create "a human world, a human reality" (*OT*, 192). They were not constructed from materials that sought to defy nature, but were rather part of it, and indeed this is how they were understood by various colonial administrators. They were seen as too transient, too vulnerable to natural forces, and straw was often declared an illegal construction material as part of colonial administrations' efforts to master both diseases and the spread of fire. Huts were thus declared as nonhouses not just by Arendt but also by colonial governing apparatuses that refused to register huts as domiciles.[26] The Arendtian "hut" should therefore be read in light of this legacy, in which bricks or concrete were identified with "culture" and doors were seen as "formal attributes of Western architecture."[27] This "hut" reflects, accordingly and consequently, histories of dispossession that were made possible by classifying some materials as proper construction materials and others as improper ones. Sometimes, this classification meant that some houses were deemed "illegal" and were thus demolished,[28] and sometimes it meant that locals who worked with local construction materials lost their jobs and live-

26 See Liora Bigon, "A History of Urban Planning and Infectious Diseases: Colonial Senegal in the Early Twentieth Century," *Urban Studies Research* (2012), https://doi.org/10.1155/2012/589758.

27 Bernhard Siegert, *Cultural Techniques: Grids, Filters, Doors, and Other Articulations of the Real*, trans. Geoffrey Winthrop-Young (New York: Fordham University Press, 2015), 193. See also Adrian Forty: "Concrete . . . is one of the agents through which our experience of modernity is mediated" (*Concrete and Culture: A Material History* [London: Reaktion Books, 2012], 14). Perhaps noteworthy is the fact that Forty talks about the perception of concrete as universal and brings examples from Europe, North and South America, and Asia, but Africa is not mentioned even once in his book. Accordingly, in colonial cities, the white quarters were "meant to be built using permanent materials such as stone, and conceptualized as the very embodiment of 'civilization'" (Bigon, "History of Urban Planning," 3).

28 Liora Bigon, *French Colonial Dakar: The Morphogenesis of an African Regional Capital* (Manchester, UK: Manchester University Press, 2016).

lihoods with the preferences of European newcomers for European ways of construction.[29]

This was the material articulation of a wider tendency we see in both political administration and political theory: to see "home" as both a condition for political existence, rights, or freedom, and an entity which only some subjects may enjoy or have access to. Notwithstanding varied models of localization, the homes of Africans, Indigenous Americans, Irish, but also paupers ("vagrants") were not registered as such or were not seen within these imaginaries as a stable enough backdrop against which freedom could be obtained.[30] Other homes—of Asians, but also of women more or less across the board—were seen as too confining and presumably allowed no transcendence.[31] Put differently, in these cases there is an assumed failure, as it were, of locality itself. This failure, this assumption that having a home is a trait of some and not of others, an assumption regarding a global distribution of homeland-ness across the imperial map, has been essential to the projects of colonization, from Locke to Zionism.[32] Crudely put, if the colonized-to-be have no real homes, if they

29 Or Aleksandrowicz shows how cement replaced *kurkar* (the local building stone) in the construction of Tel Aviv as part of a larger replacement of Palestinian with Jewish work. The new material enabled Jewish workers, who were unskilled in working with the local construction materials, to take over the construction of the first Jewish city as part of a campaign to prefer "Hebrew labor" (*avoda ivrit*) and boycott Palestinian workers. Or Aleksandrowicz, "Kurkar, Cement, Arabs, Jews: How to Construct a Hebrew City" [in Hebrew], *Theory and Criticism* 36 (2010): 61–87.

30 The presumed nomadism of Africans is at the center of this chapter and that of Indigenous Americans at the center of the next one. Barbara Arneil demonstrates how these assumptions regarding improper settlement worked in tandem with presuppositions concerning the lack of discipline and were essentially "colonial." That is, they became part of an order of various colonies, from farm colonies to work colonies to nondomestic colonies, which were confined spaces aimed at managing and disciplining these mobilities. Barbara Arneil, "Liberal Colonialism, Domestic Colonies and Citizenship," *History of Political Thought* 33, no. 2 (2012): 491–523.

31 On the correlation between home and confinement in relation to both Asians and women (specifically, the feminization of the presumed immobility of the Chinese as well as the "Chinesation" of women's confinement within domesticity), see Hagar Kotef, "Little Chinese Feet Encased in Iron Shoes: Freedom, Movement, Gender, and Empire in Western Political Thought," *Political Theory* 43, no. 3 (2015): 334–55.

32 Wolfe states that "nomadism naturalized removal" (Patrick Wolfe, *Traces of History: Elementary Structures of Race* [New York: Verso Books, 2016], 167). For Locke, see chapter 1. For the Zionist context, see, among others, Alexandre Kedar, Ahmad Amara, and Oren Yiftachel, *Emptied Lands: A Legal Geography of Bedouin Rights in the Negev* (Stanford, CA: Stanford University Press, 2018); Edward W. Said, *The Question of Palestine* (London: Routledge, 1980). For other contexts,

are but nomad savages or rootless populations, then colonization is but a project of domesticating vacant lands. Understanding this structure of (presumed) homelessness is therefore fundamental when considering postcolonial theory or struggles for decolonization, but also when trying to decipher the internal logic of colonial efforts and edifices. What is quite surprising is that this structure was shared by some of the greatest critics of imperialism as well, including Arendt.

BUT ARENDT'S ARGUMENT goes beyond this racial distribution of homelessness. She describes the white Boers as rootless, very much along the same lines as her description of the black Africans, particularly Hottentots: they had transformed themselves into a tribe, she argues, since they refused any settlement:

> This does not mean that the Boers did not feel at home wherever they happened to be; they felt and still feel much more at home in Africa than any subsequent immigrants, but in Africa and not in any specific limited territory. Their fantastic treks, which threw the British administration into consternation, showed clearly that they had transformed themselves into a tribe and had lost the European's feeling for a territory, a patria of his own. They behaved exactly like the black tribes who had also roamed the Dark Continent for centuries—feeling at home wherever the horde happened to be, and fleeing like death every attempt at definite settlement. (*OT*, 196)[33]

Again, Arendt explicitly recognizes a sense of home among the Boers, and yet this home does not provide the "European" meaning or political structure, because it is boundless. Recall: "the world" requires some degree of confinement. But the Boers refused any enclosure, and therefore, when the British came in in the mid-nineteenth century and attempted to "impose fixed

---

see Clifton C. Crais, "The Vacant Land: The Mythology of British Expansion in the Eastern Cape, South Africa," *Journal of Social History* 25, no. 2 (winter 1991): 255–75; Selim Deringil, "'They Live in a State of Nomadism and Savagery': The Late Ottoman Empire and the Post-Colonial Debate," *Comparative Studies in Society and History* 45, no. 2 (April 2003): 311–42; Ward Stavig, "Ambiguous Visions: Nature, Law, and Culture in Indigenous-Spanish Land Relations in Colonial Peru," *Hispanic American Historical Review* 80, no. 1 (February 2000): 77–111.

33 This parallelism between oppressed and oppressor eventually meant that the Boers "differ only in the color of their skin" from the "black races" (194).

boundaries on landed property," they simply abandoned "without regret their homes and their farms" (*OT*, 196).

This tangent line connecting the Boers with the Hottentots has led Jimmy Casas Klausen to argue that the line to draw here is not racial. He rather proposes seeing Arendt as antiprimitivist.[34] Another option would be to think here of *geography* as the determining factor: something in Africa itself undermines the possibility of homemaking. Accordingly, and quite amazingly, it is only in slavery—after they have been "domesticated" and permanently "placed" on a different continent—that sub-Saharan Africans become somewhat more human in Arendt's eyes.[35] Unlike the stateless people (a claim Arendt makes explicitly) and unlike the "savages" in Africa (a claim that can be inferred from the series of analogies she draws), a slave has "more than the abstract nakedness of being human and nothing but human" (an abstract nakedness whose meaning is, paradoxically, the loss of the "essential quality of being human"). The slave, "after all, has a distinctive character, a *place* in society" (*OT*, 297; see also 192). This placement is seen here as a social factor (a role, a social position), and yet enslavement was more than "domestication"; it was also a change of location: from Africa to Europe and predominantly America. Accordingly, it was only upon leaving Africa that one could find a home in the Arendtian global scheme.

Alongside antiprimitivism and geography-based biases, there are other explanations for this similarity between the Boers and black Africans in Arendt. Often, Arendt ascribes the failure of the Boers to properly localize themselves to what she sees as their main moral fault: the "early emancipation from work and complete lack of a human built world" (*OT*, 197). Thus, it was the lack of a particular industrious relation to work (already found in Locke) that was the main fault of those in the southern parts of Africa.[36] But in the background of this moral failure, a crucial material element is at play. The story of the Boers begins with the *nature of the soil*. After all, they had a community based on agriculture in the Netherlands, and their abandonment of these agricul-

---

34 Klausen, "Hannah Arendt's Antiprimitivism."

35 This may provide the full and final implications of what Mbembe identifies in his critique of the discourse on Africa. Whereas Africa and Africans were almost always framed through the figure of the animal, "to be exact, . . . the *beast*," the discourse on Africa offers a "path" to "humanization" via "domestication." Achille Mbembe, *On the Postcolony* (Oakland: University of California Press, 2001), 1–2.

36 As Klausen observes, both the Hottentots and the Boers gained this status in Arendt's writing due to a dual failure: the failure to work, which was dependent on the failure to settle and, moreover, to recognize the value of territory (Klausen, "Hannah Arendt's Antiprimitivism").

tural ways of life only began upon their arrival in South Africa, where the Boers found "bad soil" that "made close settlement impossible and prevented the Dutch peasant settlers from following the village organization in their homeland" (*OT*, 191). Rather than some innate moral dysfunction, the materiality of the territory prevented agriculture and dictated a particular mode of expansive settlement with no anchor. I stated above that in Arendt, the right to have rights is conditioned on the materiality of a territory; we now see the degree to which society is shaped by the material conditions of the land.[37]

But the question may need to be reversed. Rather than asking whether Arendt failed to see the African homes as home because she was racist (as in the case of the Hottentots), or because she was antiprimitivist, or rather than reading her as arguing that one can have no home in Africa—because of its location or because of the nature of its soil—we can see Arendt as making an almost opposite claim. When she states, in the famous chapter "Race and Bureaucracy," that "rootlessness is characteristic of all race organizations," and when she later narrates the Boers' contempt for stable homemaking or their fear that the new colonial immigrants who came to settle in South Africa would violate its racial organization by introducing sedentarism, she can be read as pointing to an opposite causality: *rootlessness is what produces racial societies*, or at least what stands at their foundation. "Rootlessness," she argued, "was the true source of that 'enlarged tribal consciousness' which actually meant that members of these peoples had no definite home but felt at home wherever other members of their 'tribe' happened to live." These tribes—in both Europe (with the Pan-European movements and particularly Nazism) and Africa (with the Boers)—created devastating destruction wherever they went, banishing whomever was not a member of their perceived race. The result was "homelessness on an unprecedented scale, rootlessness to an unprecedented depth" (*OT*, 232, vii, respectively). Racism, and perhaps even race, in this reading, is thus the *product* of a mode of territorialization that entails an unrelenting, ruthless, infinite desire for expansion.

37 While Arendt classifies the black Africans as simply "'natural' human beings," that is, not political (*OT*, 192), with the Boers she goes to more length in differentiating them from the model of political life that would later occupy the pages of *The Human Condition*, particularly the model of Greek citizenship. It might seem that while the black Africans are "naturally" nomads, the Boers were *transformed* into this position by the nature of the soil ("regressed" from their agricultural ancestry to a disregard for work). But if the soil is what produces a rootless society (and with it also a race-based society), then the Africans are as shaped by it as the Boers. They were merely there before. In this sense, both groups are fashioned by nature (soil), and thus simultaneously "naturally" nomads and "constructed" as such.

WITH THIS LATTER CLAIM, we can move to the third protagonist who joins the Boers and sub-Saharan black Africans in Arendt's description of South Africa: the Jews.

The chapter "Race and Bureaucracy" teaches us that the Jews brought with them to South Africa "a flavour of essential homelessness and rootlessness" and that anti-Semitism there was a result of their choice to settle down "permanently" (OT, 202, 204). Similarly to the chapter on statelessness, here too we see that the Jewish question is tightly connected to the question of home and homelessness. Because of their "essential homelessness," because of the lack of home in any metropole, the Jews who moved to South Africa for gold, diamonds, and finances ended up *settling*, in numbers that did not resemble any other group. In so doing, they disturbed the racial organization that was—always is, Arendt tells us—based on rootlessness. They were hated because they settled and they settled because they were hated elsewhere; and then, via what she termed "the boomerang effect," (e.g., OT, 155, 206) the social organization of this hatred in Africa was brought to Europe and further produced their dispossession and homelessness.

But eventually, many Jews settled elsewhere: in Palestine/Israel. One may wonder whether the "flavour of essential homelessness and rootlessness" they carried with them to that land led to the fact that when their home there was turned into a homeland, it took the structure of a racial society to which Arendt points: one based on a desire for racial purity (or at least national cohesiveness) alongside a never-ending desire to further expand.[38] At any rate, once they move to Israel, the racial relation Arendt sees in Africa is reversed: Arendt's Jews become a tribe like the Boers, and they end up producing dispossession like so many other racial organizations.

As noted in the introduction, however, there were other options to the creation of a Jewish home in Palestine. Arendt, for instance, saw Palestine as a "home,"[39] yet one that was not based on a national homogeneity. The tight relation she saw in Europe (and differently so, in Africa) between the formation of the nation-state and the mass waves of refugees generated by the effort to manufacture national homogeneity "led her to oppose any state formation that sought to reduce or refuse the heterogeneity of its population, including

38 This would be a variation of the argument linking Israel's nationalism to the trauma of the Holocaust. See, for example, Idit Zartal, *Israel's Holocaust and the Politics of Nationhood* (Cambridge: Cambridge University Press, 2005).

39 For example, Hannah Arendt, "Some young people are going home," in *The Jewish Writings*, ed. Jerome Kohn and Ron H. Feldman (New York: Schocken Books, 2007), 34–37.

the founding of Israel on principles of Jewish sovereignty."[40] She thus preferred a Jewish homeland that did not take the form of a sovereign state and a Jewish nation that was not anchored in territory.[41]

Echoing a sentiment we shall encounter later, that a home that is built on violence and destruction cannot be a wholesome home, Arendt further argued that once the Jewish homemaking takes a form of national state, it will no longer function as a Jewish homeland. This claim was based on a (wrong) prediction, namely that the massive Arab resistance to the establishment of a Jewish state would prevail and end the Jewish adventure in the Middle East once and for all. But more relevant to the trajectory that history did take, Arendt predicted that "even if the Jews were to win the war, . . . the land that would come into being would be something quite other than the dream of world Jewry, Zionist and non-Zionist."[42] It would become a militarized society, surrounded by enemies, which would ultimately "degenerate into one of those small warrior tribes about whose possibilities and importance history has amply informed us since the days of Sparta."[43] "Tribe" again. And tribes, as we learned in Arendt's account on Africa, have no homes. They are characterized as being unable to locate themselves, to root themselves properly. Further still, this would ultimately lead to conflicts with other countries and therefore a clash with Jews living in the diaspora, who would no longer be able to be attached to Palestine/Israel as a cultural, spiritual center.[44] Therefore, "it becomes plain that at this moment and under present circumstances a Jewish state can only be erected at the price of the Jewish homeland."[45]

40 Judith Butler, *Parting Ways: Jewishness and the Critique of Zionism* (New York: Columbia University Press, 2013), 121.

41 This led her to promote notions of federalism—either, in earlier stages, in Europe (wherein the Jews would be one nation among many) or later in Palestine (a Jewish Palestinian federation). For an analysis, see J. Butler, *Parting Ways*, chapter 5.

42 In "Zionism Reconsidered," from 1944, Arendt made similar claims, this time situated in an imperial context, arguing that a Jewish national state, if "proclaimed against the will of the Arabs and without the support of the Mediterranean peoples"—that is, alienated from its locality—would necessarily be dependent on the continuous support of imperial superpowers. Hannah Arendt, "Zionism Reconsidered," in *The Jewish Writings*, ed. Jerome Kohn and Ron H. Feldman (New York: Schocken Books, 2007), 373.

43 Hannah Arendt, "To Save the Jewish Homeland: There Is Still Time," in *The Jewish Writings*, ed. Jerome Kohn and Ron H. Feldman (New York: Schocken Books, 2007), 397.

44 Arendt shared here the vision of Ahad Ha'am and Brit Shalom.

45 Hannah Arendt, "To Save the Jewish Homeland," 397.

Arendt, like many critics of Zionism before and after her, offers alternative views that would allow seeing Palestine/Israel as a Jewish home, even a homeland. Elsewhere, Yuval Evri and I have mapped some other modes of home-making in pre-Mandatory Palestine that are established on a shared language, a shared understanding of the rules of the land, a local culture that does not need to be homogenized and in which various immigrants are invited to participate as either guests or permanent inhabitants.[46] But once the trajectory of Zionism materialized as a tribelike presence in the land (a point Arendt makes), the Israeli Jews ended up reproducing in Israel/Palestine the same failure of home we saw cutting across the multiple strata of Africa's imperial map (a claim she does not make but that we can make with her). In sub-Saharan Africa, this dysfunctionality of home was the trait of the Hottentot "tribes," the Boers, and those who came as guests and ended up staying (specifically the Jews)—and as in the case of Europe, was the foundation for war and genocide. In Palestine, Arendt predicts, a Jewish state would destroy the hopes of a homeland for the vast majority of Jews in the diaspora; it would undermine the homeland also of Israelis, who, if not completely defeated, would become a tribe of sorts; and, importantly and accordingly, it would also destroy the homeland of all Palestinians whom it would undoubtedly end up deporting, Arendt predicted at the eve of the 1948 war.[47] We can continue with and beyond Arendt to argue that if the logic of the tribe endures, the dispossession would continue—as it indeed continued far beyond 1948—since the tribal expansionist tendencies Arendt so incisively identifies in the case of the Boers become part of the state's very structure.

PART OF THE STRUCTURAL claim of this book is that most homes are violent in some way and that violence is constitutive of many selves. However, the home that is inscribed in a national homeland takes a particularly violent form. This form of violence differs in both scale and kind from other cases that can compose the wider scope of the argument, and it is this form that I am most interested in here. Arendt vividly reminds us of this when she insists

---

46 Yuval Evri and Hagar Kotef, "When Does a Native Become a Settler?," *Constellations* (forthcoming).

47 Arendt, "Zionism Reconsidered." For more on Arendt and the nonstate option, see Amnon Raz-Krakotzkin, "Exile and Binationalism: From Gershom Scholem and Hannah Arendt to Edward Said and Mahmoud Darwish" (Carl Heinrich Becker Lecture, Fritz Thyssen Stiftung, Berlin Institute for Advanced Study, Berlin, 2012).

on mentioning that the solution to the "Jewish question" "by means of a colo-nized and then conquered territory" did not put an end to statelessness and all the suffering it entails. It "merely produced a new category of refugees, the Arabs, thereby increasing the number of the stateless and rightless by another 700,000 to 800,000 people" (OT, 290). This particular form of violence goes be-yond Israel/Palestine and beyond settler-colonial societies: "what happened in Palestine within the smallest territory and in terms of hundreds of thousands was then repeated in India on a large scale involving many millions of people" (OT, 290). As part of the shift in perspective from violence in the home to homes as a tool of violence that is deployed externally, scale changes; at stake is an entire society that disposes of another.

1. The Consuming Self

ON LOCKE, ARISTOTLE, FEMINIST THEORY,

AND DOMESTIC VIOLENCES

The settler self is an identity category that is first of all a function of territory. I therefore begin the analysis from its spatial sites of formation. Furthermore, since at stake for me are primarily the affectual conditions of settlement, I begin with the site that is key in the formation of attachment to both people and places: home. A discussion of homes thus becomes the point of departure for the discussion of selves. As the foundation for this discussion, this chapter focuses on the concept of "home" (or its neighboring concepts, particularly "house" and "household") as a basic analytical unit in political theory.

The centrality of the household to political lives and political theory means that we can no longer think of subjectivity, including its liberal model, as reducible to autonomous individualism. The home or household as a basic unit reveals the degree at which we arrive to the world and act in and on it as social beings, always given within intersubjective networks. But whereas theories that foreground intersubjectivity tend to emphasize a politics of care and vulnerability, the analysis here emphasizes home as a space of violence and domination. The "individual," precisely because she is interdependent on the social networks in which she (but usually "he") is given, emerges as part of a matrix of control and subjugation. Rational, autonomous individuality that is essentially averse to violence—a construct that stood at the core of the "dissociation" model in the theoretical overview—is thus exposed as imaginary.

I begin this chapter with Aristotle and the notion of "politics" or "political theory" more broadly to show how home functions as such a basic unit of analysis, even when it is explicitly constructed as the opposite of politics. I move to feminist theory to briefly think about and with those who have always insisted on disrupting the division between private and public, home and politics, but also to point to the intimacy of violence that home entails. I end with Locke, who serves as the protagonist of this chapter. With Locke, I rehearse the claim that home is the fundamental unit of politics (this time: property, contract), but I situate this claim within a more specific historical context of settler colonialism. With this focus, "violence" also shifts; it no longer works inward, but rather outward; it is no longer the intimate violence *in* the home, but mass violence that occurs through and by the means of homes—their movements, their logics of expansion, the national forms they come to take as homelands. But intimacy is not lost in this analysis. Akin to domestic violence, whose intimacy is intertwined with its structural and large-scale societal dimensions, settler-colonial mass violence has intimate facets. These facets are the primary interest of this book, and this chapter begins to take us in this direction: With and through Locke, the household itself is being conceived through its own corporeality—and it is this corporeality that will become significant in my exploration of selves' experience of their own complicity in colonization. This corporeality materializes here through the metaphors, if not material processes, of digestion, vomiting, and other forms of metabolism that become intimate, or even affectual, manifestations of and reactions to one's position as a colonizing self.

In Locke, "home" functions as a particular relation between individuals and territory, mediated by the concept of property. Property therefore becomes the main axis of this analysis, and yet from the outset it cannot but be thought of also through the legal histories of occupancy and occupation: property as "the right of the first occupant." This was a right rooted in Roman law that Hugo Grotius saw as the foundation for all property claims.[1] It was the right of the one who takes hold of, occupies. And, as Robert Nichols and Brenna Bhandar show, albeit in radically different ways, it was a concept that was rooted in the practices and worldviews of Europeans and was not easily disentangled from the habits of empire and colonization. It was carried to the new territories they occupied across the earth, where it quickly came to shape landscapes and human networks.[2] At play is, therefore, a legal history of rights in things (property) that has historically developed in tandem with the right to own the

---

1 "All property (*proprietas*) has arisen from occupation." Hugo Grotius, *The Freedom of the Seas, or the Right Which Belongs to the Dutch to Take Part in the East India Trade*, trans. Ralph Van Deman Magoffin (New York: Oxford University Press, [1609] 1916), 27.

2 Robert Nichols, *Theft Is Property! Dispossession and Critical Theory* (Durham, NC: Duke University Press, forthcoming); Brenna Bhandar, *Colonial Lives of Property: Law, Land, and Racial Regimes of Ownership* (Durham, NC: Duke University Press, 2018).

earth, to enjoy the fruits of war and conquest: the access it gave to laboring bodies, material resources, and, above all, land.

I argue here that the Lockean basic contracting unit—we can call it "the individual"—is in fact a home. The self accordingly emerges as a *territorial unit of appropriation,* whose unlimited potentiality of expansion can be seen as mirroring the structure of colonization. With Locke, in other words, I show the structural formation of the colonizing self and explore how it is tethered to the ideology and theory of liberalism. And vice versa: I show how the ideology and theory of liberalism is forged within conditions of settler colonialism. In this aspect, I join a rich literature whose focus is liberalism and empire.[3] Through the course of this book, however, I shall depart from this paradigm: Liberals play a large role in chapter 2, where I show how they negotiate their colonial violence, but by the end of that chapter, some of the liberal facets of their politics are abandoned for more directly militarized frameworks of justification. Part III is engaged from the outset with those who are not liberals and do not see themselves as such, and the justification schemes for colonial violence there will be of a different order.

Notes on Oikos and Politics: Aristotle and Beyond

Locke's insistence in the *First Treatise* that the household provides neither a model for political rule nor a basis of justification for the latter echoes Aristotle's argument that the rule of a household differs in kind, rather than merely in number, from the rule of a statesman.[4] Indeed, Aristotle defined the home (oikos) as the "Other" of politics or vice versa. The oikos is "this association of persons, established according to nature for the satisfaction of daily needs" (*Politics* 1252b9). It is therefore a "natural" thing and a site organized according to

---

3 Including the works of Uday Mehta, Jeanne Morefield, Jennifer Pitts, Duncan Bell, Dipesh Chakrabarty, Lisa Lowe, Barbara Arneil, and many others who will be cited here.

4 Locke: "The power of the magistrate over the subject may be distinguished from that of a father over his children, a master over his servants, a husband over his wife, and a lord over his slave" (*The Second Treatise,* in *Two Treatises of Government and a Letter Concerning Toleration,* ed. Ian Shapiro [New Haven, CT: Yale University Press, 2003], §2). Aristotle: "It is an error to suppose, as some do, that the roles of a statesman, of a king, of a household manager, and of a master of slaves are the same, on the ground that they differ not in kind but only in point of numbers of person" (*The Politics,* trans. T. A. Sinclair [Harmondsworth, UK: Penguin Classics, 1981], 1252a1). Hereinafter, instead of page numbers, all references to the *Second Treatise* will be by section number; and all references to *The Politics* will appear with indication of paragraph number.

natural needs, or, in other words, a site determined by necessity. As such, the oikos is the opposite of the political—the realm of human action—and of the possibility of transcending necessity. The oikos is the other of the polis, not only in these functions, but also in its form: the household is based on unification and unity, while the polis is based on plurality and variation (*Politics*, 1261a10, 1261a22).

Hannah Arendt saw this contrast as one of the main merits of the Greek political structure. Such a separation of oikos and polis, she argued, is necessary if we are to open up a space (the political space) ruled by a logic that is not submerged by necessity and can thus be governed by freedom. It is therefore only by distinguishing an enclosed site (the household) in which biological needs are attended to that the political space as a space of freedom becomes possible (*HC*, esp. 28–37). What emerges from this separation is an opposition whereby reproduction, stability, (over)determination, and need are all contained within the household, while plurality, change, and the possibility of transcending and creating (the possibility of action) are all enabled by the political. The dissolution of the borders between the two spheres is, for Arendt (as well as for Foucault and Agamben after her), a concrete historical problem of what we can vaguely term *modernity*, which is marked by her as the appearance of "the social." In Arendt, the resultant overflow of domestic functions into the public realm means that public space can no longer be seen as a political space (although Foucault and Agamben would make this space the substance of their notion of bio*politics*).[5] However, a careful reading reveals that this separation of oikos and polis could not be sustained even within the Greek framework, which Arendt craved to reconstruct. The Aristotelian identification of telos with nature leads to a mutual infiltration of the political (the *telos* of man) and the domestic (the realm of *nature* within human space): "Therefore every state exists by nature, as the earlier associations too were natural. This association is the end of those others, and nature is itself an end; *for whatever is the*

---

5 A different route for my argument, which nonetheless intersects with the Arendtian path at a number of points, might accordingly be offered here through Foucault's concept of governmentality and his analysis of the notion of economy. By means of these concepts, Foucault describes a double shift: first, from the governance of life, events, and things in the home to their governance by the state; and second, from the household as a model for government to the household as a part of the population (which in turn becomes a central object of management in the paradigm of governmentality). See Michel Foucault, *Security, Territory, Population: Lectures at the Collège de France, 1977–1978*, ed. Michel Senellart and Arnold I. Davidson, trans. Graham Burchell (New York: Palgrave Macmillan, 2007), esp. lecture 4.

end-product of the coming into existence of any object, that is what we call its nature" (*Politics*, 1252b27; my italics).

Being the ultimate end, and hence also the end of the household, the political becomes the nature of the domestic; that is, the nature (read: essence) of the household resides in the polis. In other words, the political organization is not only the *outcome* of what Aristotle terms "natural associations": the households, villages, and prior to them the pairs of man-woman and man-slave to which I shall return momentarily. Since the political organization is these associations' end, and since "end," "essence," and "nature" are conflated in Aristotelian teleology, the political turns out to be the *nature* of the household, while the essence of the household is revealed to be *political*. These are not two sides of a dichotomy; the meaning of the two parts of this conclusion is identical within the Aristotelian framework. Simultaneously, the naturalness of the household becomes an attribute of the political, being the *nature*, i.e., the telos, of the human realm. To put it differently yet again, since for Aristotle parts gain their essence from the whole, and since the polis is composed of households and can be seen as the whole of which they are parts, the essence of the household is political. At the other end of this equation, the polis "exists by nature" precisely because it is composed of households, which in turn imbue it with their attributes, above all with their naturalness—the very attribute that supposedly distinguishes them from the polis.

We find here, then, the same argument we found in the interlude: some forms of domesticity define, paradoxically perhaps, the individual as a political animal. Without an established oikos, politics becomes impossible. This centrality may reflect a wider Aristotelian ontology, wherein things move only to arrive at their *place* (topos). If in the Aristotelian metaphysics, place has an ontological primacy, whereas movement is secondary (a mere means to *arrive*), then in Aristotle's *Politics*, the oikos seems to have the same role. If politics, as I briefly noted but as Arendt makes explicit, is a space of movement in the Aristotelian framework, topos/oikos is its precondition.[6]

My argument here follows in some ways a move made by Jacques Derrida, according to which the political sphere of Western political thought is con-

---

6 As Arendt narrates it, re-moving herself from the sphere of stability, the individual can inhabit a space "whereby freedom is understood negatively as not being ruled or ruling, and positively as a space . . . in which each man moves among his peers." Accordingly, Arendt explicitly refers to freedom of movement as "the substance and meaning of all things political." Hannah Arendt, *The Promise of Politics*, ed. Jerome Kohn (New York: Schocken Books, 2009), 117, 121. See also Arendt, *Human Condition*, 23–24; Hagar Kotef, *Movement and the Ordering of Freedom: On Liberal Governances of Mobility* (Durham, NC: Duke University Press, 2015), 1, 130.

taminated (always already) with the logic of the family/household. According to Derrida, from classical times until today, we share a political space founded on the principle of fraternity, of *brother*hood, wherein the agents of civic lives are the sons of the same mother—the motherland. Thus constituted, the political not only takes place within the borders of the family; it also subjects itself to the necessity embedded in nature: it becomes (or perhaps always was) a sphere of blood, of dynasty. Moreover, the plurality of this sphere is actually a mere duplication; it is the multitude of the identical.[7] Unity, which is a primary attribute of the home (in Aristotle, in Arendt, but also in Rousseau, and, differently so, in Hegel) and which should be contradictory to the plurality of the political sphere, is reincarnated as a political attribute, and its new opposite—now "difference" instead of "plurality"—appears within the home.[8]

The distinctions in whose name the household was banished to beyond the borders of the political sphere in both Aristotle and Arendt thus fail: the distinctions between freedom and necessity, between the political and the natural (or biological), and, as Derrida shows, between plurality and unity, between (free) action and being conditioned, between change and reproduction. Both sides of the desired dichotomy appear as subject to the same logic.

What is disrupted here is not just the dichotomy bisecting nature from politics or necessity from agency, but also the ideal of individual autonomy. That is, with the collapse of the dichotomy, a notion of political agency that is given

7   Jacques Derrida, *The Politics of Friendship*, trans. George Collins (London: Verso Books, 1997). See also Jacques Derrida, *Rogues: Two Essays on Reason* (Stanford, CA: Stanford University Press, 2005). Indeed, substantial differences—the difference between citizens and those who are not, gender- and sex-based differences, class differences, racial differences—were removed from the polis and (presumably) restrained within the household. It was precisely this "privatization" of difference that enabled and characterized the particular political design of the Greek polis.

8   When read in regard to the Arendtian version of the polis, my claim here may seem peculiar. Arendt, after all, criticized modern society precisely for turning difference into a private matter, and claimed that the unity that emerges undermines the possibility of political action. But her plurality is the matter from which heroes are made, rather than structural, systematic differences that set various groups apart. The difference she sought is better thought of as greatness: "the public realm itself, the *polis*, was permeated by a fiercely agonal spirit, where everybody had constantly to distinguish himself from all others, to show through unique deeds or achievements that he was the best of all." Or see: "unlike human behaviour . . . action can be judged only by the creation of greatness because it is in its nature to break through the commonly accepted and reach into the extraordinary, where whatever is true in common and everyday life no longer applies because everything that exists is unique and *sui generis*" (HC, 205).

in the singular (as a singular) is undone. After Aristotle characterizes oikos as the basic unit that makes up the polis, we discover that, in fact, the oikos conceals a more basic unit, namely the couple, "those who are incapable of existing without each other."[9] By himself, the citizen cannot form a (political) unit; he cannot appear in the singular and "must be united," either with a woman or a slave. He (always a "he") depends on the slave for his material existence and on the woman for reproduction, for fulfilling "the natural urge . . . to propagate one's kind" (*Politics* 1252a24). Politics thus always begins with this dual duo.

This intersubjectivity presents us from the outset with a very specific political model: a model not only of territoriality and later of nationality (the nation being the extension of the family in a given territory) but also a hierarchical model in which intimacy and domination cannot be fully separated. This is a presumably natural domination, anchored in the natural need to reproduce and the natural need to survive (and, taken together, the natural need to exist over time).[10] The "individual" at the core of the theory is thus revealed not merely to

9 "Those who are incapable of existing without each other must be united as a pair. For example, (a) the union of male and female is essential for reproduction; and this is not a matter of *choice*. . . . Equally essential is (b) the combination of the natural ruler and ruled, for the purpose of preservation. For the element that can use its intelligence to look ahead is by nature ruler and by nature master, while that which has the bodily strength to do the actual work is by nature a slave, one of those who are ruled" (*Politics* 1252a24).

10 A new criterion distinguishing the household from the polis thus emerges: the nature of *domination* or *rule* and the fundamental difference between ruling those who are "free and equal" (Aristotle, *Politics*, 1255b16) and ruling those who are by their very nature unfree (women and slaves). Accordingly, the household can be defined as that place in which the unfree are ruled. A parallel distinction can be found in Agamben, who turns to Rome rather than Greece. Following Foucault, Agamben characterizes sovereign power as the power over life and death. He sees its first appearance in the power of the paterfamilias over his children—a power that resides within the space of the home and enters the political when the emperor adopts the citizens as his sons. The father's power over the lives of his children is precisely what makes them free citizens—their lives only become political lives through his possibility of killing them. The father's relationship with his children defines the political by means of the distinction between this relationship and its almost permanent antithesis—the home: while the father's power over his sons (the *vitae necisque potestas*) defines and constructs the model of political life, the father's power over his daughters, his wife, and his servants is "only" power. Like Arendt, Agamben also characterizes modernity as the dissolution of these boundaries: "In the camps"—which, according to Agamben, are the paradigm of modernity—"city and house become indistinguishable." See Giorgio Agamben, *Homo Sacer: Sovereign Power and Bare Life*, trans. Daniel Heller-Roazen (Stanford, CA: Stanford University Press, 1998), 105.

exist only in plural, rendering it more fragile as a basic unit of analysis; he is also revealed to be dependent on subjugating others (a slave, as part of the system of property; a woman, as part of the gendered system of procreation).

Feminist Critiques and the Politicalness of the Household

bell hooks once observed that somehow, the most progressive and even radical politics ends where the housing market begins.[11] Conservative politics, attachment to racial segregation, and securitization of civic spaces all become part of the story when it comes to real estate, even among most liberals. Homes, she accordingly argued, are always about "the politics of race and class."[12] She would probably willingly acknowledge that they are also always about the politics of gender. These lines of social positioning shape the (unequal) distribution of access to resources and political statuses (rights, citizenship) in a network of ties wherein "what assures the domestic tranquility of one is the productivity and regulated discipline of the other."[13]

Both as scholars and as activists, feminists were probably the first to challenge the division between the "private sphere" and the public/political one. Some have critiqued the confinement of women to their homes and the identification of femininity with domesticity that rendered women economically dependent (and hence, dependent in general), and that rendered women's political claims meaningless.[14] Others have called for an entire reconfiguration of political life in light of domestic practices of care. Mostly working in the progressive era at the turn of the twentieth century, they claimed what Arendt would later criticize: that the political sphere should be subjected to the logic and technologies of the household, thereby also giving women the right—indeed, the duty—to engage in politics.[15] Others have called for a re-

11 bell hooks, *Belonging: A Culture of Place* (New York: Routledge, 2004).
12 hooks, *Belonging*, 3.
13 Edward W. Said, *Culture and Imperialism* (London: Vintage Books, 1994), 87.
14 Examples here date back to at least first-wave feminism if not earlier. Before Susan B. Anthony or Elizabeth C. Stanton, who made such arguments, Mary Astell and Mary Wollstonecraft made similar claims. Later on, Betty Friedan and Simone de Beauvoir added their versions.
15 These ideas and platforms received names such as "home protection" (Frances Willard), "civic housekeeping" (Charlotte Perkins Gilman or Margaret Fuller), or "enlarged housekeeping" (Jane Addams). In Rheta Childe Dorr's words: "Women's place is in the Home. But home is not contained within the four walls of an individual home. Home is the community. The City full of people is the Family. The public school is the real Nursery. And badly do the Home and

configuration of domestic rather than public lives, in ways that would facilitate political change, primarily women's equality. Charlotte Perkins Gilman,
for example, advocated communal kitchens and common areas for laundry
in order to free up women's time and change the structure of their obliga-
tions by rendering domesticity itself public. Still others offered an almost
opposite critique, condemning the ongoing breaching of home by the state
and its often violent agents. It was primarily feminists of color who sought
to reclaim home as a site of potential liberation. After it was shuttered, undermined, violated, or deemed illegal under slavery, and after decades of
state violence and mass incarceration, home was a place to recuperate and
protect.[16]

Whether it is a site of intimate violence that the state refuses to even recognize or an intimate site that state violence keeps penetrating, in these very
different accounts, feminists have systematically identified the home as a site
of oppression, domination, and violence. These modes of intimate violence
have often been entangled with violent state formations in ways that urge us
to question the radical distinction between mass, systematic state violence and
the so-called domestic violence inflicted primarily on women and children—a
distinction I have repeatedly made here for analytical clarity. The efforts to
put an end to the polygamous practices of the settler state's indigenous populations (native Americans or Bedouins); the systematic rape of female slaves that
produced further property for slaveholders; the forced sterilization of poor or
black women; housing projects (or gated communities) as a tool, manifestation,

---

the Family and the Nursery need their Mother." Cited in William Chafe, *The Paradox of Change:
American Women in the 20th Century* (Oxford: Oxford University Press, 1991), 15.

16 bell hooks sees the home as a place where black men and women can share experiences of marginalization and foster solidarity and intimacy (*Yearning: Race, Gender, and Cultural Politics* [Bos-
ton: South End Press, 1991]). Chandra Mohanty wants to define home "not as a comfortable,
stable, inherited, and familiar space but instead as an imaginative, politically charged space in
which the familiarity and sense of affection and commitment lay in shared collective analysis of social injustice, as well as a vision of radical transformation. Political solidarity and a
sense of family could be melded together imaginatively to create a strategic space I would call
'home'" (Chandra Talpade Mohanty, *Feminism without Borders: Decolonizing Theory, Practicing Solidarity* [Durham, NC: Duke University Press, 2003], 128). See also Barbara Smith's introduction
to *Home Girls: A Black Feminist Anthology*, rev. ed. (New Brunswick, NJ: Rutgers University Press,
[1983] 2000). For a review of the different approaches outlined here, see Jocelyn M. Boryczka,
"Revolutionary Pasts and Transnational Futures: 'Home Lessons' from US Radical and Third
World Feminisms," in *American Political Thought: An Alternative View*, ed. Jonathan Keller and
Alex Zamalin (New York: Routledge, 2017), 72–92.

and form of racial segregation—these cases, alongside many others, begin to illustrate the series of differentiations separating those for whom home provides privacy, stability, and rights (ownership or other forms of legal protection of tenancy) from those for whom home is a prison or whose homes are constantly encroached on—by state authorities, agents of the free market, or kin and relatives.

Locke: Property and Colonial Digestion

Locke's *property* (unlike the boundless concept of capital) is very much a system of borders, which are above all, or at least first of all, the borders of body and estate. Yet despite the importance of such territorial enclosures to one of his primary political concepts,[17] and despite the fact that the family has a crucial role in the definition of rationality, which was as important for him (and tightly related),[18] the combination of the territorial order in the fifth chapter of the *Second Treatise* (the chapter on property) with the institution of family depicted in the subsequent chapter is made only in passing. At the beginning of chapter 7, and somewhat more explicitly later on in that chapter (§ 87), the unification of kinship ("wife, children") and property (slaves, and perhaps also servants, situated somewhere in between the two categories but not quite belonging to either) composes "the domestic rule of a family," which is explicitly defined as a separate sphere, clearly differentiated from that of political rule. More often, however, in the *Two Treatises*, the several terms that could form the conceptual network of "household" (house, home, domain, etc.) appear in negative form, to assert that it is not there, or, as we shall see by the end of this chapter, that

---

17 Kotef, *Movement*, 9, 73–80, 101–6; Wendy Brown, *Walled States, Waning Sovereignty* (New York: Zone Books, 2010), 44.

18 John Locke, *Some Thoughts Concerning Education* (London: A. and J. Churchill, 1693). For analyses, see Nancy J. Hirschmann, *Gender, Class, and Freedom in Modern Political Theory* (Princeton, NJ: Princeton University Press, 2009); Nancy J. Hirschmann, "Intersectionality before Intersectionality Was Cool: The Importance of Class to Feminist Interpretations of Locke," in *Feminist Interpretations of John Locke*, ed. Nancy J. Hirschmann and Kirstie M. McClure (University Park: Pennsylvania State University Press, 2007), 155–86; Hagar Kotef, "Little Chinese Feet Encased in Iron Shoes: Freedom, Movement, Gender, and Empire in Western Political Thought," *Political Theory* 43, no. 3 (2015): 334–55; Uday Singh Mehta, *The Anxiety of Freedom: Imagination and Individuality in Locke's Political Thought* (Ithaca, NY: Cornell University Press, 1992).

it does not function as it should.[19] Nevertheless, reconstructing a Lockean concept of "household" is significant for understanding Locke's concepts of subjectivity and property, as well as their now long-established relation to colonization.

The argument, however, goes further. I argue that it is the household, rather than the individual, that forms the basic unit of political analysis in Locke, and that the individual somehow comes to stand for this plurality of bodies and thus camouflages it. As aforementioned, in this argument, I follow Carole Pateman's analysis in *The Sexual Contract*, yet since I situate my claims in a different domain—property rather than sex—I end with somewhat different conclusions (that do not contradict, but rather complete hers). This argument is then taken to point to the expansionist structure of these basic units (individuals, households), and to tie their "unlimited expansion,"[20] as well the violence it entails, to the most intimate site of self-definition. This is, accordingly, a preliminary step toward unfolding the intimacies of public wrongs that will occupy this book.

PROPERTY

Locke's concept of property is at the very least dual, and here I work with the narrow concept that is found in chapter 5 of the *Second Treatise*. The wider concept refers, alongside objects or estates, to life and liberty as well, yet—as Arneil makes clear—this is *not* the concept used in chapter 5, where property is indeed understood as property in and of objects.[21] This may not be accidental; as Armitage shows, chapter 5 is "an intruder," inserted into the *Treatise* at a

---

19 In the *Treatises*, the term *home/household* is almost absent (whereas *domicile* and *domain* are completely absent); there are some references to the term *private dominion*, but these are made to deny its existence. The claim that there is no private dominion that could become the foundation for absolute power is Locke's main critique of Robert Filmer. This is a denial of the link between home and political right, which is the denial of the classic patriarchal argument for royalty.

20 As Arendt referred to it in *The Origins of Totalitarianism*, 5th ed. (New York: Harcourt Brace Jovanovich, 1973), 137.

21 On property as "life, liberty, and estate," see James Tully, *A Discourse on Property: John Locke and His Adversaries* (Cambridge: Cambridge University Press, 1980); and a clarification in James Tully, *An Approach to Political Philosophy: Locke in Contexts* (Cambridge: Cambridge University Press, 1993), chapter 4. For Barbara Arneil's argument, see *John Locke and America: The Defence of English Colonialism* (Oxford: Clarendon Press, 1996). See also C. B. Macpherson, *The Political Theory of Possessive Individualism: Hobbes to Locke* (Oxford: Oxford University Press, 2011), 198.

later stage of writing—in all likelihood, while Locke was revising the *Fundamental Constitutions of Carolina*.[22] Considering this preoccupation with the question of settlement in America, the use of different language may be indicative: the conceptual narrowness allowed Locke to delineate a concept of property that works well with some of his political projects, even if it betrays some of his universalist ethics.

Locke opens chapter 5 by marking the two main theories that stand in the way of his own theory of property. The first is the common-law understanding of property as the right of use and the related system of commons.[23] The second is the idea of full, undivided, and unlimited dominion, according to which private property is a derivative of an original right given by God to an original sovereign (Adam).[24] The former is an obstacle to the accumulation of private property; the latter not only renders property a function of the sovereign's consent—a hierarchy Locke would reverse as he turns sovereignty into a derivative of property[25]—but is also historically and conceptually entangled with a theory

---

22 David Armitage, "John Locke, Carolina, and the 'Two Treatises of Government,'" *Political Theory* 32, no. 5 (2004): 602–27.

23 Patrick S. Atiyah argues that the idea of absolute property became established only in the first few decades of the seventeenth century, in both legislation and practice (*The Rise and Fall of Freedom of Contract* [Oxford: Oxford University Press, 1985]). Only in 1628 did the House of Commons declare that "every free subject of this realm hath a fundamental property in goods" (86). It is only "from the sixteenth century [that] we encounter the idea that 'every man's house is his castle'" (86), but until the mid-eighteenth century, these rights were still limited by other rights and traditions, above all the rights of use, which lay at the foundation of the system of commons (88). The vast project of enclosure that ensued from this new conception of property radically changed the models of space and dwelling. On the system of commons as nonetheless establishing private property, see David Tabachnick, "Two Models of Ownership: How Commons Has Co-Existed with Private Property," *American Journal of Economics and Sociology* 75, no. 2 (March 2016): 488–563.

24 This was precisely Filmer's model. This link, between household and sovereignty, was also central to Roman law, wherein property, that is, dominion, "is the power over resources which a *dominus*, that is, a head of a household, exercises over his *domos*" (Daniela Gobetti, "Humankind as a System: Private and Public Agency at the Origins of Modern Liberalism," in *Public and Private in Thought and Practice: Perspectives on a Grand Dichotomy*, ed. Jeff Weintraub and Krishan Kumar [Chicago: University of Chicago Press, 1997], 114). In all these versions, dominion marked a "claim to total control against the world" whose roots, if not model, are God's ownership of the world he created (Richard Tuck, *Natural Rights Theories: Their Origin and Development* [Cambridge: Cambridge University Press, 1979], 15).

25 Locke sought to establish property as *preceding* sovereignty. The sovereign (or contract) emerges to protect *already existing* property. Thus, even though in established countries, enclosure (prop-

of absolute power, whose limitation is one of Locke's main objectives.[26] The *First Treatise* is dedicated to refuting the idea of full, inherited dominion; chapter 5 of the *Second Treatise* focuses on showing how private property can be deduced from an originary state in which the world has been given to men in common. To refute the above and to establish a new—revolutionary yet legally grounded—concept of property, Locke drew on many existing traditions, often strategically, at times partially.[27] And yet, as I show, these frameworks were not, in themselves, sufficient for the tasks that Locke's larger projects required. Theories of labor, improvement, the Roman theory of first occupant—all introduced a set of tensions, if not contradictions, into his argument. My proposition is that these contradictions are relieved if we see the household as basic unit of property.

---

erty) is conditioned on consent, "in the beginning and first peopling of the great common of the world it was quite otherwise. The law man was under was rather for appropriating" (*ST*, §35).

26 "Dominion," as well as the absolute power it contains, is both a component and a marker of the political theory Locke rejects. See Andrew Fitzmaurice, *Sovereignty, Property and Empire, 1500–2000* (Cambridge: Cambridge University Press, 2014). Tully proposes that Locke's entire theory of property is but a "necessary precondition" to counter the theory of absolute political power (*Approach to Political Philosophy*, 102).

27 He writes against Filmer's understanding of property as originating from the dominion of an absolute sovereign, but also against Pufendorf's understanding of property as emerging from *agreement* (here he rather *relies* on Filmer; see Peter Garnsey, *Thinking about Property: From Antiquity to the Age of Revolution* [Cambridge: Cambridge University Press, 2007], 142–43) or, indeed, against Pufendorf's understanding that sees common land as establishing rights of use but not appropriation (Arneil, *John Locke and America*, 57). He needs to salvage Grotius's understanding of original common ownership from Filmer's critique, yet without adopting the absolutist paradigm of Grotius (Tully, *Approach to Political Philosophy*, 101–17). He draws on principles from the Levelers to establish a doctrine of natural right (Richard Ashcraft, *Revolutionary Politics and Locke's Two Treatises of Government* [Princeton, NJ: Princeton University Press, 1986]; Richard Tuck shows the medieval sources of these theories, in *Natural Rights Theories*). Yet he radically departs from their doctrine to protect the prevailing unequal distribution of property (David McNally, "Locke, Levellers and Liberty: Property and Democracy in the Thought of the First Whigs," *History of Political Thought* 10, no. 1 [spring 1989]: 17–40). A thorough analysis of these traditions and sources of influence can be found in Onur Ulas Ince, *Colonial Capitalism and the Dilemmas of Liberalism* (Oxford: Oxford University Press, 2018), chapter 2; and Tully, *Discourse on Property*. Neal Wood further places Cicero's views of the original acquisition of property in a tradition leading to John Locke (Neal Wood, *Cicero's Social and Political Thought* [Berkeley: University of California Press, 1988]; see also Benjamin Straumann, *Roman Law in the State of Nature: The Classical Foundations of Hugo Grotius' Natural Law*, trans. Belinda Cooper [Cambridge: Cambridge University Press, 2015], esp. 27). On the inconsistent, or at least nonuniform, use of Roman law among early modern scholars, see Daniel Lee, "Sources of Sovereignty: Roman *Imperium* and *Dominium* in Civilian Theories of Sovereignty," *Politica Antica* 1 (2012): 79–80.

I proceed by examining two frameworks Locke relied on to support his theory of property. The first is a more conventional and straightforward reading of Locke, seeing labor as the primary foundation for property-making. This would allow me to introduce my argument through a set of more familiar critiques. The second is based on an element of Roman law largely neglected in the literature, even by those who insisted that Locke relies on Roman law in his theory of property: the theory of mixing.[28] Through both possible readings, two arguments are made: a rehearsal of a claim, now quite established in the literature, that Locke's theory of property sought to justify colonial expansion in America;[29] and the argument that the basic contracting units in Locke are households. These two arguments are further linked in a section on enclosure that follows, and I conclude with a brief reflection on destruction in the *Second Treatise*.

LABOR

The question of property has always been also an imperial question. It was the question of the commodification of race, of commercial expansion, of securing foreign markets and the global transport of laboring bodies, or of the extraction of wealth by the displacement and dispossession of native groups. This has introduced a set of limits to both the principle of property, and the major frameworks upon which common theories of property rested at the time. For example, Locke's theory of property could not be based on the consent or the agreement of others, as Samuel von Pufendorf and other natural law theories

28 Exceptions to this are Wolfram Schmidgen, "The Politics and Philosophy of Mixture: John Locke Recomposed," *Eighteenth Century* 48, no. 3 (fall 2007): 205–23; and Roger T. Simonds, "John Locke's Use of Classical Legal Theory," *International Journal of the Classical Tradition* 3, no. 4 (spring 1997): 424–32. The former does not engage directly with the particular theory of mixing I outline here, but does recognize the importance of this concept to Locke's philosophy.

29 Chapter 5 of the *Second Treatise* is, accordingly, dedicated (at least also) to the justification of colonization and is primarily engaged not with ownership proper but rather with establishing the superiority of "European technics of land improvement" over "Amerindian culture." Some of the major accounts on this subject include David Armitage, "John Locke, Carolina"; Arneil, *John Locke and America*; Farr, "Locke, Natural Law"; Herman Lebovics, "The Uses of America in Locke's Second Treatise of Government," *Journal of the History of Ideas* 47, no. 4 (October–December 1986): 567–81; Tully, *Approach to Political Philosophy*, 137–76. For more focused accounts of property or capitalism and colonialism, see Barbara Arneil, "Trade, Plantations, and Property: John Locke and the Economic Defense of Colonialism," *Journal of the History of Ideas* 55, no. 4 (October 1994): 591–609; Ince, *Colonial Capitalism*, chapter 2. Alternatively, see Vicki Hsueh, "Unsettling Colonies: Locke, 'Atlantis' and New World Knowledges," *History of Political Thought* 29, no. 2 (2008): 295–319.

contend. This was not merely because such theory presupposed the same pre-cedence of contract over property that threatened Locke's understanding of contract as a function of property rather than the other way around, but also because—as David Armitage shows—a reliance on contract would have under-mined Locke's colonial efforts in Carolina, where he sought to delegitimize any contract-based acquisition of land in order to delegitimize Indigenous territo-rial claims.[30] A similar limitation arises from the right of first possessor/taker/occupant that Roman law sources cite as part of the Laws of Nations (*jus gen-tium*). This was the idea that if something does not belong to anyone or is given in common, it becomes the property of the first person taking hold of it. Thus, the person who picked up an acorn under an oak that is given in common, or an apple in the forest (to refer to Locke's examples in §27) becomes their owner. Yet even though this doctrine was central to Locke's conceptualization of property,[31] and even though it was central to the justification of colonial en-deavors more generally,[32] it, too, fell short of justifying British colonial expan-sion: ultimately, "most of America, and certainly all that the European powers believed worth developing, was *by their own criteria, already occupied.*"[33]

30 Armitage, "John Locke, Carolina." Locke acknowledged the possibility of property exchange via agreement only in those parts of the world where sedentarist agriculture already existed, and where money had replaced barter—two elements he explicitly states Indigenous Americans are lacking (618). With this periodization he thus disqualified the territorial agreements that colonizers did make with First Nations.

31 Fitzmaurice, *Sovereignty, Property and Empire*, esp. 21–24, 114–22, and chapter 4. See also Richard A. Epstein, "Possession as the Root of Title," *Georgia Law Review* 13 (1979): 1221–43. As both Epstein and others have pointed out, the examples that Locke refers to in this context are identical to the Roman examples: "things captured on land, in the sea and in the sky" (Simonds, "John Locke's Use of Classical Legal Theory," 427).

32 For the centrality of the Roman theory of first occupant to the British (as well as French) le-gitimation of colonial expansion, see Anthony Pagden, *Lords of All the World: Ideologies of Empire in Spain, Britain and France c.1500–c. 1800* (New Haven, CT: Yale University Press, 1998), specifically 76–82. See also Christopher Tomlins, *Freedom Bound: Law, Labor, and Civic Identity in Colonizing English America, 1580–1865* (Cambridge: Cambridge University Press, 2010), 133. According to Tully, the justification of colonial expansion was "one of the leading problems of political theory from Hugo Grotius and Thomas Hobbes to Adam Smith and Immanuel Kant": "Almost all the classic theorists advanced a solution to this problem justifying what was seen as one of the most impor-tant and pivotal events of modern history . . . to justify European settlement on the one hand, and to justify the dispossession of the Aboriginal peoples of their property on the other" (James Tully, "Aboriginal Property and Western Theory: Recovering a Middle Ground," *Social Philosophy and Policy* 11, no. 2 (summer 1994): 156).

33 Pagden, *Lords of All the World*, 82. Accordingly, whereas it was "one of the most effective means with which to address" imperial expansion, the theory of first occupant "was used to argue

If the theory of first occupant was to work as a legitimating apparatus for land appropriation in America, a theory of use, or labor, had to be put into effect. As others have shown in detail, the seemingly commonsensical theory of labor—which begins with eating an apple and is carried through the time and effort invested in picking it if not growing it—was actually based on a very specific model of European agriculture that sought to set distinctions between two modes of engagement with space and things: a distinction between Indigenous "presence" or even "use," and settlers' or landowners' "agriculture." Despite being fully aware of agricultural practices among Indigenous populations, Locke portrayed Indigenous Americans as hunter-gatherers, and yet he did not deny their *labor*, a concept that for him included practices such as hunting and gathering.[34] However, this particular mode of labor generated property rights vis-à-vis objects (those they collect or hunt)—a property right that did not "interfere with England's plans for settlement in the same way that claim over land [would] do."[35] At the same time, by defining labor *on the land* "in terms of European agriculture and industry: cultivating, subduing, tilling, and improving," Locke could argue that this right in objects is separated from right in the land, which Indigenous Americans did not have.[36] In other words, even though Indigenous Americans owned the deer they ate or hunted, according to the basic principle of property, they had no right to the territory—which could thus be marked as "waste" and available. Locke's "labor" could thus become the basis for dispossession in both England (via the elimination of the commons) and America.[37]

As we move to other colonial contexts later in this book, one should note that in this dismissal of native agriculture that served to justify colonial land

opposite viewpoints: namely, either it left little or no place for inhabitants of the lands concerned, or it was used by opponents to claim these people did have rights" (Fitzmaurice, *Sovereignty, Property and Empire*, 87).

34 "Thus this Law of reason makes the Deer, that Indian's who hath killed it; 'tis allowed to be his goods who hath *bestowed his labour upon it*" (*ST*, §30). The same equation of gathering and labor can be found in §28. On Locke's awareness of Indigenous agricultural practices, see Arneil, *John Locke and America*, 23–41; Vicki Hsueh, "Cultivating and Challenging the Common: Lockean Property, Indigenous Traditionalisms, and the Problem of Exclusion," *Contemporary Political Theory* 5, no. 2 (May 2006): 193–214, esp. 200–205; Tully, "Rediscovering America," 65–87, 118–32, 140–41.

35 Barbara Arneil, "The Wild Indian's Venison: Locke's Theory of Property and English Colonialism in America," *Political Studies* 44, no. 1 (March 1996): 62.

36 Tully, "Aboriginal Property," 160.

37 See note 29.

theft, and in this understanding of labor (particularly agricultural) as an essential element of occupation, Locke was just one in a long tradition.[38] Further, the type of agriculture that Locke promoted through his emphasis on enclosure was particularly efficient within the project of colonial expansion. As Patrick Wolfe has shown, and as will be further developed in chapter 3, sedentarist agriculture not only addressed some of the most basic needs of settler colonialism and not only provided an alibi, a technology, and the means for further territorial control through its "ceaseless expansion"; it also—"with its life-sustaining connectedness to land"—became "a potent symbol of settler-colonial identity."[39] Andrew Fitzmaurice can thus claim that Locke "insists on a definition of occupation *as* labour."[40] We could add that given the emphasis on land as the "chief matter of property," this also works in the other direction: labor itself was defined *as* occupation.

Locke's theory of labor, combined with the theory of first occupant, hence allowed him to develop a theory of property that worked well in tandem with justifying colonial expansion. Yet labor introduced a crisis to the Lockean scheme. If physical work were a necessary and sufficient condition for the production of property, it would stand in the way of Locke's theory of accumulation, in which some profit from the labor of others. When Locke argues that "the grass my horse has bit; the turfs my servant has cut; and the ore I have digged . . . become my property," he introduces a break or mediation between labor and property (*ST*, §28). It can be argued that the horse—and even the

---

38 Patrick Wolfe, *Settler Colonialism and the Transformation of Anthropology: The Politics and Poetics of an Ethnographic Event* (London: Cassell, 1999), 391, 395–96. In the context of Mandatory Palestine, this approach was shared by administrators and historians of the time, who framed the commonly held land called *mushāʿ* as "an obstacle to investment that blocked any chance of development." See Amos Nadan, "Colonial Misunderstanding of an Efficient Peasant Institution: Land Settlement and Mushāʿ Tenure in Mandate Palestine, 1921–47," *Journal of Economic and Social History of the Orient* 46, no. 3 (2003): 320. Like Locke, who used this dismissive approach to land cultivated in common to justify the colonization of America, in this case, too, dismissal served as the grounds for transferring land from some hands (Indigenous Americans or English land users in Locke, Palestinian *fallāḥīn* in Palestine) to others' (Europeans colonizers or English landowners in Locke, Jews in Palestine).

39 Patrick Wolfe, "Settler Colonialism and the Elimination of the Native," *Journal of Genocide Research* 8, no. 4 (2006): 395, 396.

40 Fitzmaurice, *Sovereignty, Property and Empire*, 120. Accordingly, when he wrote—together with the Earl of Shaftesbury (Anthony Ashley Cooper)—the constitution of Carolina, Locke prioritized the interests of landed proprietors over the interests of mercantile commercial agents. McNally, "Locke, Levellers and Liberty," 22.

slave, who is not mentioned here but is certainly part of this story—do not have the status of an individual. Lacking such a status, they can be seen as an extension of "my" body in some strange ways, and accordingly their labor can generate my property. But this is not the case for the servant, who is an independent person, merely selling his labor power temporarily. So are other wage laborers, who nevertheless produce property for others, as we see in other writings of Locke.[41] If property is generated through labor, then the labor of the servant should generate property for *them*, rather than for "me." Yet Locke does not make this claim. In fact, Locke does not even make this claim in order to refute it. Whereas he explicitly engages in removing the limits set on accumulation, such as spoilage (i.e., one cannot accumulate beyond what can be consumed before it spoils) or abundance (i.e., the idea that there is enough for everyone, which was an important ethical constraint in Locke's account), he does not engage at all with the limitation set by the power of individual labor: the principle according to which one can accumulate only what one has individually labored on/for or mixed with one's own labor.[42] On the contrary, he assumes that the servant or wage laborer chose to alienate their body (their labor power), rendering it yet another thing to be accumulated by the landowner.[43] Accordingly, even though chapter 5 begins with a close link, if not complete equivalence, between body, labor, and property, somewhere along the way the product of labor is severed from the laboring "hands" and "body" and is annexed to another body (*ST*, §27). Labor is therefore not a sufficient principle in which to anchor property claims. With the question of inheritance, we see it is also not a necessary one (as children can inherit property without laboring).

This predicament concerning the relationships between labor and property can be resolved if we take seriously Locke's choice to identify wage labor with servitude in his main political treatise. Servants were legally defined (as servants) when they came under the title of the master, and in this sense *were part of the household*. Alongside the horse, the slave, the wife and children, the servant and other domestic

---

41 In particular, see John Locke, "On the Poor Law and Working Schools," in *Locke: Political Essays*, ed. Mark Goldie (Cambridge: Cambridge University Press, 1997), 182–200. Locke's logic of rationality, political standing, the ownership of labor, and allocation of work (authoritative or not) is clearly different when considering the poor, working or not. The model of accumulation described here is not applicable in their case. For further analysis, see Hirschmann, *Gender, Class, and Freedom*; Kotef, *Movement*, 107–10.

42 See Macpherson, *Political Theory of Possessive Individualism*, 214–20.

43 Macpherson, *Political Theory of Possessive Individualism*, 214–15. Although see Tully, *Discourse on Property*, 136–39.

workers formed what I propose to see as the real property unit in Locke. If Locke's basic property units are not individuals but, indeed, households, the servant is by definition part of this unit, and his labor incorporated into it by virtue of this legal status. To put it differently: if the "I" were to be extended to the household itself, or encapsulated by the individual who came to represent it as a whole (the landlord), then there is no contradiction in this theory of labor. Not the labor of one's individual body, but the labor of everyone included within the (noncorporeal but very concrete) boundaries of the estate, generated property for "me."

This is, in a way, an extended version of Pateman's argument on the sexual contract, placing the latter within an intersectional framework. It links Pateman's critique to critiques made by Charles Mills, C. B. Macpherson, and others, and further unites them within a single structure: before the social contract takes place, before we come to shape the contours of our shared life and legitimate forms of rule, a set of other "contracts" is instituted (sexual, racial, classed).[44] Through these contracts a plurality of people and animals is united under the rule of a single person; it is this plurality, submerged into that person and politically erased thereby, that enters into the social contract as the "individual." And this plurality only becomes part of a singular principle if we think of it within the framework of domesticity. With this unification of bodies within a unit that is simultaneously an economic unit and one of kinship, the theory anchoring property in labor can be carried from the laboring body to the horse, the servant, and beyond.[45] Locke's theory of labor, then, was based on the expansion of the individual body, which was ultimately morphed into the estate. And estates could be expanded into and within the colonies.

Since it is the question of violence that is at stake here, it is important to note that this expansion (from individuals to households) is never peaceful. As Pateman puts it bluntly, "the true origin of political right," in Locke and other social contract theorists, is rape.[46] Barbara Arneil reminds us that servants and slaves

44 At least in the case of the wife, Pateman shows that the idea that we "contract in" (i.e., join the social contract) in such domestic groups is more evident in Locke than in other social contract theorists, because for him, the state of nature is not an individuated form of existence but a social one. The woman ("wife") is therefore much more easily folded into the "individual" in his version of the social contract, subsumed within the family structure when the game of contracting begins (Carole Pateman, *The Sexual Contract* [Stanford, CA: Stanford University Press, 1988], 52).

45 Arneil proposes that at the heart of Locke's theory of property we find the plantation, placing it in a more explicitly colonial setting (Arneil, "Trade, Plantations, and Property.")

46 Pateman, *The Sexual Contract*, 104–5.

suffered from other regimes of violence.[47] Slaves were part of the family, according to Locke, and upon entering the family, they brought death and war with them:[48] their own death, which was merely suspended ("delayed") in slavery, and a state of war between them and the master that justified subjugating them to his absolute power.[49] This intimacy of war, subjugation, rape, and family life should be kept in mind as we think of the question of selves that emerge in and through violence.

MIXING

Section 27 of the *Second Treatise* makes one of the closest links between corporeal labor and property: "Whatever then he removes out of the state that nature hath provided, and left it in, he hath *mixed his labour with, and joined to it something that is his own*, and thereby makes it his property" (*ST*, §27, my italics). Besides labor, many readers of Locke have focused here on the effect of *removal* from nature,[50] and some have linked it to the notion of *improvement*, tying this argument to the great emphasis Locke puts on the *value* added to things through labor.[51] However, not less significantly, the claim made here by Locke is about *mixing*: the mixing of labor (that is, of the body, or at least its doings or powers) with the thing that thereby becomes property. My proposition is that this concept, too, on its legal histories and lineages, should be understood as central to

47 Barbara Arneil, "Women as Wives, Servants and Slaves: Rethinking the Public/Private Divide," *Canadian Journal of Political Science/Revue canadienne de science politique* 34, no. 1 (March 2001): 29–54.

48 *ST*, §86.

49 *ST*, §23. "The perfect condition of slavery . . . is nothing else but 'the state of war continued between a lawful conqueror and a captive'" (*ST*, §24; see also §85). For an analysis, see David Armitage, *Foundations of Modern International Thought* (Cambridge: Cambridge University Press, 2013); Andrew Dilts, "To Kill a Thief: Punishment, Proportionality, and Criminal Subjectivity in Locke's Second Treatise," *Political Theory* 40, no. 1 (February 2012): 58–83; James Farr, "Locke, Natural Law, and New World Slavery," *Political Theory* 36, no. 4 (August 2008): 495–522; James Farr, "'So Vile and Miserable an Estate': The Problem of Slavery in Locke's Political Thought," *Political Theory* 14, no. 2 (May 1986): 263–89.

50 For example, Stanley C. Brubaker, "Coming into One's Own: John Locke's Theory of Property, God, and Politics," *Review of Politics* 74, no. 2 (spring 2012): 207–32; Onur Ulas Ince, "Enclosing in God's Name, Accumulating for Mankind: Money, Morality, and Accumulation in John Locke's Theory of Property," *Review of Politics* 73, no. 1 (2011): 29–54; Henry Moulds, "Private Property in John Locke's State of Nature," *American Journal of Economics and Sociology* 23, no. 2 (1964): 179–88.

51 Most famous is his claim that "an acre of land" in America produces "not one thousandth" of an acre of cultivated, enclosed land "here" (*ST*, §43). A few paragraphs beforehand, Locke provides the more moderate ratio of one to ten, or perhaps to a hundred (§37).

the interpretation of Locke's theory of property. For now, this is presented here as a hypothesis, still not anchored in the archives of letters, comments, and reading notes that a history of ideas often calls for in demonstrating an interpretational move. It is, nonetheless, anchored in the internal logic of the text.

Locke proposes that for an object to become property one needs to *mix* it with or *join* it to something. As Nasser Behnegar puts it: Locke's language implies that when labor alters an object, "something of the cause of this alteration must necessarily be present in the altered object just as something of venison must be present in me if it is to nourish me."[52] Indeed, in sections 27–28, Locke keeps pointing to annexation as essential to property making.[53] Importantly, mixing and joining should be with/to something that "*is his own*," and there are only two related "things" "that [are] his own" at this stage of the text: the body itself (or rather personhood, which cannot be reduced to a legal status because from the outset it is marked by "hands" and "body") and labor, or the doings of this body ("the Labour of his body, and the Work of his hands"), which is "the unequivocal property of the labourer."[54] And since, as others have argued, in this context labor cannot be conceptualized as anything but a corporeal entity, a thing one can *possess*, "a space-occupying material object to be combined with other such objects," the distinction between the two (body and labor) is evasive.[55] What transpires, then, is a model in which property emerges by *becoming one with the body*. Put differently, when a body is mixed with a thing and a thing with a body, property (that is, right in things) is made.

"Mixing" was indeed a central concept in existing theories of property, specifically the Roman theory of mixing, which, to the best of my knowledge, has not been seriously considered thus far in relation to Locke. According to Roman law, if two materials are mixed to form a new material, the new entity belongs to the person who made the mixture, since he is seen as the first occupant of the new entity.[56] This is only the case, however, if the two mixed objects form a new *body* (a defined *thing*), an indissociable

<hr>

52 Nasser Behnegar, "Locke and the Sober Spirit of Capitalism," *Society* 49, no. 2 (2012): 131–38, 136.

53 "It begins by him removed from the common state nature hath placed it in, it hath by this labour *something annexed to it that excludes the common rights of other men*" (*ST*, §27; my italics).

54 *ST*, §27. More accurately, the body itself, or life, is strictly God's property, as he created it; man has a derivative right to it. But labor is strictly his own, as his own mode of creation, and so would be its products. See Tully, *Discourse on Property*, 108–9, 113–14.

55 Simonds, "John Locke's Use of Classical Legal Theory."

56 See *The Digest of Justinian*, vol. 1, ed. Alan Watson (Philadelphia: University of Pennsylvania Press, 1998), 6.1.1.5.

whole. The example from the *Digest of Justinian* is telling: If "A" "fixes an arm or a leg belonging to 'B' to his own statue, . . . 'A' has become the owner of the whole." Whether B can legitimately claim compensation for the leg depends on the nature of fixing (the wholeness of the new body): "If an arm of a statue has been joined to the rest of the statue by welding, it is merged in the unified whole of the larger part, and once it has become another's property cannot, even though later broken off, revert to its former owner. It is not the same with what has been soldered with lead, because welding effects fusion of two things made of the same material, whereas soldering does not have that effect."[57]

In other words, if the arm has been joined to the rest of the statue without being fused into a *unified body*, B maintains some right in the arm (can demand compensation or reclaim it when the statue breaks), but if it has been merged to the statue to be made part of an indissociable whole, it will remain A's, no matter what happens to the statue. It is only once A has created a unified body then, that his property claim is finalized. This finality is going to be important in the argument to follow.

In the *Digest*, "mixing" serves as a complement to the theory of first occupant, which was one of Locke's main points of reference. The latter established the principle that if something does not belong to anyone or is given in common, it becomes the property of the first person taking hold of it; the former (the theory of mixing) came to clarify the status of being "first" vis-à-vis different "objects." "If corn belonging to two parties has been mixed together," the person who did the mixing is not the first occupant of the mixture, since this mixture does not form a new indissociable whole. The mixture will either belong to the parties to whom the corn originally belonged in common or each will get their original share, depending on the terms of the mixing (consensual or not).[58] However, "if mead is made from my honey and your wine," that is, a new whole is produced, "it belongs rather to the maker, since it does not retain its previous character."[59] Mixing thus determines the status of products of labor in relation to the framework of the first occupant theory, and Locke's reliance on the latter suggests that his adaptation of the language of mixing may not have been accidental or metaphorical, but intended, rather, to provide some familiar legal grounding to his ideas. Moreover, Grotius's critique of this theory was familiar to Locke and hence at the very least we have evidence that

57 *Digest*, 6.1.23.2–5.
58 *Digest*, 6.1.3.2.
59 *Digest*, 6.1.5–5.1.

Locke was familiar with the Roman version.[60] This familiarity seems to have shaped at least the language, if not the argument, of chapter 5. We can further see the notion featuring extensively in Locke in other contexts, with quite a few textual resonances to the examples given in the Roman law.[61]

If we think within the Roman tradition, it is not enough that one "mixes" labor (as a power or an investment of time) with an object. To make property, the mixing of labor (self) and thing must create a unified body. When the mixing does not create a new, fused whole (when the limb is joined with nails rather than welded, for example), the parts can be reclaimed by their previous owners. Within such an understanding, mixing and joining are a way of connecting objects to the body, a form of "annexation," to use Locke's term. Indeed, we saw above that labor for Locke was itself a corporeal entity, or a way of conceptualizing the body itself.

This notion of mixing works well at the beginning of the chapter on property, when the paradigmatic, or at least first, form of property making emerges as digestion: "The fruit, or venison, which nourishes the wild Indian, who knows no enclosure, and is still a tenant in common, must be his, and so his, i.e. a part of him, that another can no longer have any right to it" (*ST*, §26). Digestion is therefore the most elementary form of property making: at least in its rudimentary form, in the case of the "Indian," something—significantly, fruit or venison—must become *"part of him,"* a component of his body, a form of nourishment, to become "his" (i.e., property).[62] Elsewhere, I have argued that Locke applies two different logics of property divided along colonial lines: one is based on labor and the other on digestion. In the case of

60 Tully, *A Discourse on Property*, 118.

61 In his *Essay Concerning Human Understanding*, for example, this is most evident in the realm of reproduction, when bodies emerge as generative in the formation of other bodies: "the mixture of a bull and a mare" produces jumarts, and "the mixture of an ass and a mare" produces mules. Locke then goes on to testify that he "once saw a creature that was the issue of a cat and a rat. And had the plain marks of both about it; wherein nature appeared to have followed the pattern of neither sort alone, but to have jumbled them both together" (John Locke, *An Essay Concerning Human Understanding* [Philadelphia: Hayes and Zell, 1854], 3.6.23). Wolfram Schmidgen traces the significance of mixture to the *Essay* and Locke's other theoretical work, and concludes that it therefore it must be taken seriously also in relation to property (Schmidgen, "Politics and Philosophy of Mixture").

62 The *Essay* once again provides the ontological foundation for this digestive incorporation: "that, which was Grass to Day, is tomorrow the Flesh of a Sheep; and within few days after, becomes part of a man" (Locke, *Essay*, 3.19).

the "Indian," Locke requires that "he" digest the object so that "another can no longer have any right to it," whereas in the case of the "civilized parts of mankind," labor would do.[63] But it may be more accurate to argue that this is not a matter of different logics but of different stages of development within a single logic.

Digestion provides Locke with a powerful model; it conveys a strong sense of injury in the case of infringement on property. With digestion, property gains the same status as the body, and violating it is a clear case of causing harm. Accordingly, the need for nourishment "figure[s] prominently in Locke's political theory of appropriation."[64] Digestion, in this sense, is also the ultimate mixture of body and thing that cannot be separated into its original elements; yet rather than a dispute between two people in relation to a third object, as in the examples given in Roman law, it comes to address a potential dispute between "me" and the rest of humankind (to whom the object has been given in common) over an object that has now become part of "me." This full annexation of the object by one party in the potential dispute makes any effort to contest property nonsensical, and this is its power. But this is also where it meets its own crisis.

If we think through the theory of mixture, but also if we think with other tangential interpretational frameworks such as James Tully's claim that property is based on the act of creation,[65] this model of digestion does not easily lend itself to the subsequent development of the argument. Digestion is part of (a metaphor for?) a direct link between property making and the body with

---

63 *ST*, §30; Kotef, *Movement*, 103–4.

64 Chad Luck, *The Body of Property: Antebellum American Fiction and the Phenomenology of Possession* (New York: Fordham University Press, 2014), 91. Luck further notes that digestion is the principle limiting property: "The language of 'spoilage' indicates eating as the limit to what can be appropriated. We can only take possession of those things we can ourselves consume before they spoil" (Luck, *Body of Property*, 92). It is therefore possible to argue that for Locke, "eating is the epitome of human agency both because it requires work and because that work is transformative. Labour turns acorns and apples into food, which digestion then turns into flesh." It is the transformation done via eating that turns "common matter into personal property, giving all men a property in their own person. The possessive individual of Locke's liberalism eats his way to ownership" (Paul Youngquist, "Romantic Dietetics! Or, Eating Your Way to a New You," in *Cultures of Taste/Theories of Appetite: Eating Romanticism*, ed. Timothy Morton [New York: Palgrave Macmillan, 2004], 241).

65 Tully argues that it is the *creation of something new*, the "act of making," that "gives rise to the right in the product" (Tully, *Discourse on Property*, 41; see also 116–21, on the new status of the object obtained via "making").

which chapter 5 opens;[66] but as early as in section 28, annexation or mixing become more distant from the individual body: the section moves us from digestion to eating, boiling (a mediation between nature and consumption), bringing home (a mediation between the common areas and that which marks the extended borders of the self), and picking up. After Locke has established digestion as an incontestable form of property making ("No Body can deny but the nourishment is his"), he asks: "When did they begin to be his? When he digested? Or when he ate? Or when he boiled? Or when he brought them home? Or when he pickt them up? 'Tis plain, if the first gathering made them not his, nothing else could." (*ST*, §28).

Akin to digestion, "picking up" or "bringing home" are supposed to be processes of mixing body (labor) with object (now property); however, this does not really work. Unlike the case of "digesting," and perhaps even "eating" or "boiling," when I "pick" an acorn or "bring it home," I do not *create* anything new in the world, the outcome is far from being a *mixture*, and its counterparts (me and acorn) are certainly *distinguishable* and dissociable.[67] Many have therefore argued that the idea of property as based on mixing labor with things is nonsensical, or at best bad figurative language.[68]

Note that the structure of both the argument and the question of interpretation proceeds here along the lines of the previous section: a distancing of property from the individual body creates a tension in Locke's theory of

66 It is not merely that the idea of bodily borders, and one's "property in his own person," is the principle from which property rights can be derived (*ST*, §27). It is also not merely that the first *right* (the right to self-preservation) emerges from natality itself—from our existence as corporeal creatures ("Men, once born, have a right to their preservation, and consequently to meat and drink and such other things as nature affords for their subsistence," §25). The body, further, is what *makes* private property: "The labour of his body, and the work of his hands, we may say, are properly his" (§27). See further analysis in John Dunn, *The Political Thought of John Locke: An Historical Account of the Argument of the "Two Treatises of Government"* (Cambridge: Cambridge University Press, 1969); Tully, *Discourse on Property*, 45–48.

67 "One clearly transforms an acorn or an apple when one boils, eats, or digests it, but not when one gathers or picks it up" (Behnegar, "Locke and the Sober Spirit," 137).

68 Robert Nozick's famous critique may be the most vivid: "If a private astronaut clears a place on Mars, has he mixed his labor with (so that he comes to own) the whole planet, the whole uninhabited universe, or just a particular plot?"; or, "If I own a can of tomato juice and spill it in the sea . . . do I thereby come to own the sea or have I foolishly dissipated my tomato juice?" Nozick also questions here the notion that labor always adds value such that improvement can serve as a sufficient principle to establish ownership. Even though he provides a different example for this latter critique, it seems that the case of the tomato juice in the sea is a good example here, too. Robert Nozick, *Anarchy, State, and Utopia* (New York: Basic Books, 1974), 174–75. See also A. John Simmons,

property. I propose that the solution, too, is identical: this tension is resolved with a transition—which indeed occurs throughout chapter 5—from the body as the basis of property (a form of property making whose quintessential model is digestion, i.e., *corporeal expansion*) to a new territorial unit, the household, which can make property according to a similar model of expansion. The "self" that "mixes" acorns with itself in the act of picking up is the household or estate, whose enclosure mimics the logic of bodily borders with which we began. Most significantly, the household can mix land with its "body" thereby making it property; the household metabolizes land, as it were, and assimilates it into the property of the Lockean dominus.[69]

This enlarged ability to mix—mixing land with household rather than digestible objects with body—is crucial. Yet, as briefly noted above, it rested on practices of enclosure, and thus did not equally apply to all. What is in some cases a continuum, moving from digesting to "picking up" or "bringing home," was broken in the case of some subjects. Between section 26, which points to the need for the food to become "part of him" to establish a property claim, and section 30, which takes us to the looser forms of annexation, a latent transition in the concept of the individual seems to take place. Whereas section 26 explicitly points to the "Indian" as an exemplary case of "the individual" through which the logic of property can be deduced, by section 28 Locke is speaking about a general "he," and by the end of the paragraph, about "me." Section 29 already introduces servants, to make clear that the setting is different. And in case it has been overlooked, the division is reintroduced in section 30, with a clear distinction between an "Indian," subjected to an "original Law of Nature for the *beginning of Property*," and "the Civiliz'd part of Mankind" that is subjected to a more convoluted system. What we see here is a shift, which is simultaneously temporal, geographical, and a shift in the application of the principle of property, wherein the "Indian" in America represents an original or primitive logic of property that is then developed. Drawing from Uday Mehta's work, Vanita Seth has called us to see how the Lockean individual is in fact a project. Rationality, alongside freedom, is but a potential, Mehta shows; a universal kernel which needs to actualize, but sometimes fails to do so fully or properly.[70] In the

---

The Lockean Theory of Rights (Princeton, NJ: Princeton University Press, 1992), esp. 266–74; Gopal Sreenivasan, *The Limits of Lockean Rights in Property* (New York: Oxford University Press, 1995); Jeremy Waldron, *The Right to Private Property* (Oxford: Clarendon Press, 1990), esp. 184–91.

69 I want to thank one anonymous reviewer for this useful formulation.

70 Uday Singh Mehta, *The Anxiety of Freedom*; Uday Singh Mehta, *Liberalism and Empire: A Study in Nineteenth-Century British Liberal Thought* (Chicago: University of Chicago Press, 1999); Vanita Seth, *Europe's Indians* (Durham, N.C., Duke UP, 2010).

spaces of the colonies, this failure is the normal order of things.[71] The state of nature thus entails *two* models of individuality, separated by the temporal trajectory of actualization encapsulated in the above transition from §26 to §30: one whose ability to accumulate is limited (the "Indian" who "knows no enclosure" and needs an object to become "a part of him" in order to finalize a property claim) and another, for whom picking up can fully take on the logic of digestion since it takes place within an enclosed unit that is the extension of his own corporeality. The latter is the English landowner, who, in the case of the state of nature as it manifests itself in America, is the settler. It is he, as Mills and Pateman have argued, who is eventually the political agent of the social contract that is imagined through the case of America.[72] And while the "Indian" is the figure beginning this process and logic of private property, he somehow remains stuck in its initial stages, failing to actualize its full potential.

CONSIDERING THE TRANSITION from the individual to a household from the perspective of labor provides a social story of accumulation; it shows the formation of social, specifically classed and gendered divisions between those who work or labor,[73] and those who own. Considering this transition from the perspective of the theory of mixing provides an ontological foundation that allows "picking up" to be aligned with the logic of digestion as corporeality itself expands from the individual to the household. Yet as an ontological formation it can function only—or at least best or in a more stable way—when a clear border demarcates the household, rendering it into a corporeal unit. Here enters the theory of enclosure. With it, the corporeality of the body, which clearly produces property when it mixes an object with itself, becomes part of the configuration of the household as an accumulative entity. Picking would thus be quickly transformed in chapter 5 into sedentary agriculture and, with it, into land accumulation.

71 This is indeed a spatial question: "Had you or I been born at the Bay of Soldania," Locke claims in his argument against the notion of innate ideas in the *Essay*, "possibly our thoughts, and notions, had not exceeded those brutish ones of the Hottentots that inhabit there: and had the Virginia king Apochancana been educated in England, he had, perhaps, been as knowing a divine [one of the supposedly innate ideas Locke considers], and as good as a mathematician, as any in it" (Locke, *Essay*, 1.4.12). While the potential is there (most of the Indigenous Americans Locke has "spoken with" "were otherwise of quick and rational parts enough" [2.16.6]), its development appears here as a function of location.

72 Carole Pateman and Charles W. Mills, *Contract and Domination* (Malden, MA: Polity, 2007).

73 In this respect the wife, who labors to reproduce, is but another servant. See Pateman, *Sexual Contract*, 47–48.

It would not be novel in any way or form to argue that enclosure was important for Locke. But with the above arguments, something additional transpires: Enclosure is the foundation that makes the conceptual shift from body to household possible. If the logic of property began with bodily borders, then enclosed lands could become demarcated objects to which things can be annexed, joined, or mixed with to be made into property. Thus, everything occurring within this unit—picking of apples or eating of grass by horses—can be said to constitute a single whole (as the Roman law requires), thus granting property.[74] In the primitive form of property making, "each human being's right to the exclusion of all other persons from his body was *ipso facto* a right to the exclusion of all other persons from the victuals that had become the stuff of his body";[75] in its extended form, the demarcation of the enclosed domain as a private sphere does the same for everything within the household's territory, and in a global setting, it guarantees England's (or other European countries') worldwide access to land. Perhaps this is yet another reason why fences—as Wendy Brown observed—are such an important element in Locke's theory.[76]

This last point becomes clear if we see what happens to property when its "chief matter" shifts from object to land. Locke famously states that "the chief matter of property [is] now not the fruits of the earth, and the beasts that subsist on it, but the earth itself; as that which takes in, and carries with it all the rest," and that "property in that too is acquired as the former."[77] Once land takes the place of objects (deer, acorns) consumed by the body, the body itself must be replaced with a "body" that can consume land: domain. Rather than mixing a digestible object with the body, in this new model (importantly, still a precontract model) I mix household with land through labor to create a new entity that is thus my property: digestion is replaced with territorial expansion. This is precisely the difference between the "Indian's" claim to property in things, and the European claim to property in the land—a difference whose two sides can still rest on a single structure whose image is digestion. The "Indians" failed to assume the ontological foundation that would allow the mixing of land with "body"; that is, they failed to form stable households.

---

74 *Digest*, 6.23.5.

75 Kramer, *John Locke and the Origins of Private Property*, 116.

76 Brown, *Walled States*, 44.

77 That is: "as much land as man tills, plants, improves, cultivates, and can use the products of, so much is his property" (*ST*, §32).

The "failure" of Indigenous Americans to establish stable households was an ongoing concern among Englishmen in America, particularly those engaged in missionary work. Jack Turner notes the links between Locke's endeavors in America and the work of other missionaries, arguing that his writings on tolerance did not contradict—and indeed, should be read in conjunction with—attempts at (mass) conversion.[78] One missionary with a significant influence on Locke was John Eliot, who, as Teresa Bejan shows, was quite obsessed with natives' sedentarization.[79] From 1650 on, Eliot oversaw the establishment of fourteen English-like "praying towns," which were to become the home of converted Indigenous Americans. Settling down, he believed, was the only way to prevent "scandal" among the Indigenous population; otherwise, they "could easily run away" if they "sinned."[80] As long as "they live[d] so unfixed, confused, and ungoverned a life, uncivilized and unsubdued to labor and order," they "could not be trusted with that 'Treasure of Christ.'"[81] The question of securing settled households and family formations was thus at the root of the English civilizing mission in America; the presumed absence of this domestic configuration was key to modes of colonial governance. In Locke, this presumed failure means that Indigenous Americans could never make the conceptual and physical shift from body to household, which would allow for the theory of mixing to work beyond objects—in this case, to the appropriation of land.

ENCLOSURE CONSTRUCTED THE HOUSEHOLD not just as a unit that can digest (land), but also as one that facilitates a form of vomiting: it spewed out all those who had use rights in the commons, creating a mobile body of labor that could serve the newly emerging capitalist system. These were the people, as we saw above, who had to sell their labor, making its commodification not only plausible but necessary. Without this history one may wonder how we move from a system in which the world is given in common to one in which some feel the need to become the servants of others. Indeed, significant segments of this mobile body were transported to the colonies, primarily as domestic

78 Jack Turner, "John Locke, Christian Mission, and Colonial America," *Modern Intellectual History* 8, no. 2 (2011): 267–97.

79 Turner, "John Locke, Christian Mission," 272; Teresa Bejan, "'The Bond of Civility': Roger Williams on Toleration and Its Limits," *History of European Ideas* 37 (2011): 409–20.

80 Eliot, "Tears of Repentance," quoted in Bejan, "'The Bond of Civility,'" 413.

81 Teresa Bejan, *Mere Civility: Disagreement and the Limits of Toleration* (Cambridge, MA: Harvard University Press, 2017), 63.

servants.[82] Thus new households—plantations—could emerge that, too, kept incorporating land, reproducing enclosure on a global scale. Once again, these households created dispossessed masses condemned into forced mobility: Indigenous peoples who lost access to their land and slaves who were transported to serve as further labor power in the growing fields of the Caribbean's and America's plantations.

What becomes clear with Locke is that this apparatus touches upon, or is set into motion by, not just social, economic, or political structures, but also the structure of individuals' desires. Famously, money removes the limit set by the principle of no spoilage (the idea that the natural spoilage of things limits what can technically and morally be accumulated), thereby paving the way for unlimited accumulation in Locke.[83] Money renders accumulation technically possible, morally justified, and a logical order of things. But not less importantly, money is key in this process because it creates an *urge*, a *desire*, for accumulation. This desire was not there before: without money, the Indigenous Americans are "confining their desires" and have "no Temptation to enlarge their Possessions of Land" (*ST*, §107, §108). But even though money serves here as a mere vehicle, as the last quote insinuates, in an agrarian society, the drive for accumulation is a drive to accumulate *land*. It was land, therefore, that was at stake in securing unlimited accumulation. This was the case not only because Locke was thinking in and from a preindustrial mode of accumulation, wherein land is the "chief matter of property";

82 Peter Linebaugh and Marcus Rediker, *The Many Headed Hydra: The Hidden History of the Revolutionary Atlantic* (Boston: Beacon Press, 2000).

83 Many have made this point; particularly important here is Ince's *Colonial Capitalism*, since it places this argument concerning money in a colonial setting. Locke's limit is most clearly stated in section 46: "He who gathered a hundred bushels of acorns or apples thereby owned them; as soon as he had gathered them, they were his. His only obligation was to be sure that he used them before they spoiled, for otherwise he took more than his share, and robbed others" (*ST*, §46). As C. B. Macpherson shows, the entire argument of chapter 5 revolves around the removal of these multiple limitations set on accumulation (*Possessive Individualism*, 199–221). Tully insists that the limitations Locke sets on accumulation via his emphasis on the principle of use places him in line with the radical Levelers' critique of large estates (Tully, *Approach to Political Philosophy*, 82; see also 128–29). Thus, whereas Locke "certainly argued that the government infringement of property constituted a justification for revolt, . . . by 'property' he meant the civil and religious rights of Dissenters and their possessions, which were confiscated during the great persecutions of the Revolution" (84). This is one of Tully's critiques of Macpherson. However, the use of money alters the notion of use as a principle of limitation, and with it, this entire emphasis collapses. Indeed, Ince claims that "money inaugurates a paradigm shift from subsistence to accumulation" (*Colonial Capitalism*, 54).

it was also because land was at the heart of settler colonialism—which was the mode of global expansion Locke was invested in justifying. Thus, if other modes of imperialism and colonialism were about extraction of resources, labor power, and capital from the colonies and colonized, at stake in America was territory itself. Under these conditions, accumulation *was* expansion, and the desire to accumulate was ultimately what Anthony Pagden describes as a "seemingly inescapable desire for territorial expansion through conquest."[84]

The "Indian's" presumed lack of desire for land allowed Locke to extend the idea that no one is injured by this expansion into and in America. Conquest could thus be portrayed as peaceful cultivation of land. Arneil reads Locke's claim that conquest would not, in and of itself, suffice to justify property (chapter 16 of the *Second Treatise*) and proposes that Locke's emphasis on agriculture as the only legitimate foundation for English colonialism bears an ethical dimension. Colonial expansion for him "must be based on industry and rationality rather than violence."[85] Agriculture thus emerges not merely as an effective technique of colonial land grab, as Wolfe proposes, but as expansion's ethical foundation. We will return to this idea in chapter 3.

HOUSEHOLDS ARE THEREFORE the units that lie at the basis of any significant property claim (i.e., a property claim relating to land)[86] and thus any political claim. Moreover, these are essentially *colonial* households, since they have a tendency—an urge, a reason—to expand and a practice of territorial *expansion through global dispossession*. "Dispossession," because in a reality of limited resources, the desire to possess and the resultant incorporation of land through enclosure ultimately produces an imperial need. Locke seems to have

---

84 Pagden, *Lords of All the World*, 63.

85 Arneil, "Wild Indian's Venison," 72–73. Pagden, however, argues that this principle of colonial ethics only emerged *after* a model conquest based on the Spanish example did not work in North America, because of the different organization of indigenous settlement (lack of large cities) and the scarcity of natural resources available for instant exploitation (particularly gold). The plantation model was therefore not the outcome of an original system of ethics for colonization and industriousness, but rather a necessity that became a mode of justification only in retrospect (Pagden, *Lords of All the World*).

86 Famously: "the chief matter of property being now not the fruits of the earth, and the beasts that subsist on it, but the earth itself; as that which takes in and carries with it all the rest" (*ST*, §32).

been aware of the two sides of this equation. His awareness that resources were shrinking is attested to by his use of the past tense when he refers to the assumption of plenitude: there was a time in which there was enough for everyone, but it seems to no longer be the case.[87] Since the right to accumulate is conditioned by abundance in Locke (by the fact that everyone can have a sufficient share and thus no one can claim injury), an assumption of plenty had to be restored. It is made regarding the "uncivilized" spaces of the globe, where land is still "free." This is the second side of the equation. Indeed, Locke limits the present-time relevance of the availability of resources to America: "And the same measure may be allowed *still* . . . for supposing a man, or a family, in the state they were at first peopling the world . . . let him plant in some inland, vacant places of America, we should find that the possession he could make himself, upon the measures we have given, would not be very large, nor, even to this day, prejudice the rest of human kind."[88] The ethics of capitalism is accordingly fully dependent on the colonial project.

DESTRUCTION

This analysis shows the theoretical model through which the individual—or the household—emerges through various forms of violence or destruction. The basic unit at the heart of liberal (Lockean) concepts of right and freedom is dependent on a constant erasure and dispossession of others. First, it depends on the erasure of all those *in* the household, who are folded into the concept of the "individual" that comes to represent them: the servant, the slave, the horse, the wife. Those lose first the grounds on the basis of which they can make property claims (their work generates property for that "individual," i.e., the head of the household) and then also political claims. Second, it depends on the erasure of the dispossession of all those *outside* the home, who stand in the way of its expansion—Indigenous Americans or English land users. They keep losing their

---

87 Locke thus states that "this measure *did* confirm every man's possession to a very moderate portion"; or: "there is land enough in the world to suffice double the inhabitants, *had not* the invention of money, and the tacit agreement of men to put a value on it, introduced . . . larger possessions" (*ST*, §36; my italics; see the use of past tense also in what follows).

88 *ST*, §36; my italics. Locke refers to a term (*plant*) that was used by many English writers of the time as a synonym for *colonize*: "The Latin word *colonia*, Adam Smith explained, 'signifies simply a plantation.' Both terms were closely tied to the kinds of community the colonies in practice were, and to the arguments for the legitimacy of their existence" (Pagden, *Lords of All the World*, 79). Accordingly, as Karl Olivecrona notes, the "age of abundance"—as he refers to it—is placed in Locke in two places: the past or America. Karl Olivecrona, "Locke's Theory of Appropriation," *Philosophical Quarterly* 24, no. 96 (July 1974): 220.

homes, which are not registered as legitimate and legitimating property units, since they lack the ontological base for mixing, that is, enclosure. And yet surprisingly, destruction becomes a feature of the "civilized" household as well.

On the few occasions that they are mentioned in the *Two Treatises*, *home*, *house*, *domain*, or the conceptual network within which they work, are often mentioned in a negative context, pointing to violation or destruction:

- *Private dominion* is deployed as part of proof that it does not exist (usually as part of the refutation of Filmer's argument).
- *Home* is barely mentioned, and if it is, it is usually referred to somewhat metaphorically: *Home* appears four times in the *Two Treatises*—the first is the mention in section 28 outlined earlier in this chapter, where home functions as a mediation between digestion and picking up. In the other three instances, *home* is a placeholder for a state or sovereign territory or marks the so-called primitive state wherein the two cannot be distinguished.
- But, most interestingly, *house*, in its materiality and spatiality, appears almost always as violated or destroyed. Of the ten times the word *house* is mentioned in the *Second Treatise*, one denotes a family or title rather than a concrete building. As such, it is situated in line with the uses of the term in the *First Treatise*, which it indeed summarizes (in §1); one denotes the ruler of the household, but in order to refute the idea that such domestic rule can be a basis for political rulership (in §76); and the eight other instances mention *house* as it is being destroyed or violated:[89] Once (§159) it burns down and, as it is consumed by flames, it becomes necessary to "pull down an innocent man's house to stop the fire"—an example Locke gives to illustrate the need for executive power. Another time, functioning as an analogy for the relations between conquest and government (§175), *house* appears through the act of demolition, and then through the failure to build "a new one in its place." Three other times, still as part of the argument that conquest cannot establish government, it is being broken into by robbers, who then take it for themselves (twice in §176 and once in §181), and again being broken into as part of an argument about tyranny and the limits of the law (§202, §206). Finally, it is destroyed by an earthquake, and its materials are "scat-

---

89 There are five additional mentions in the *First Treatise*; one of them is to mark a family or title.

tered and displaced by a whirlwind, or jumbled into a confused heap" (§211).

How is it that the unit whose integrity is the foundation for property (or, at least, for the logical possibility of land accumulation) keeps being violated in the Lockean imagination? Why can Locke not introduce it into the text as anything but destroyed, demolished, burned, and burglarized?

It is tempting to play here with the idea that this fragility of the home—which was supposed to provide a protected sphere from potential tyranny, to mark the limits of legitimate rule—is a "return" of its own destruction (a "boomerang effect," if we are to think with Arendt). The destruction of the other's home comes back to hound the colonizing self and becomes its own destruction. But I am not sure of the validity of this reading, both as an analysis of the text and as a historical claim. For now, then, it may be sufficient to argue this: From a claim that violence rarely exists in social relations (Locke's famous state of nature), violence permeates the Lockean self. Eventually, from the peacefulness of state, nature, and domain, debris materializes. This may be hints of debris, more than the "pile of debris" that keeps growing "skyward" in front of the feet of Benjamin's angel of history.[90] Nevertheless, given the project of settlement or the intimate war(s) that constitute the self for who "he" is (a husband, a master—recall Aristotle's requirement of coupling), this debris seems constitutive.

Conclusion

Much like the Aristotelian individual, the Lockean subject cannot endure on its own, and his model of accumulation is based on the *lack* of distinctions between self and object (this is precisely what happens in digestion) or between the self and other members of the household with whom he "must be united":[91] The horse and the grass it eats, the servant and the turf he cuts, and the wife, whose laboring is not even mentioned in the text,[92] are thus constantly folded into the individual or incorporated into it (digested by his image?). Examining

---

90 Walter Benjamin's "On the Concept of History," in *Selected Writings*, vol. 4: *1938–1940*, by Michael W. Jennings and Howard Eiland, 389–400 (Cambridge, MA: Harvard University Press, 2003), ix.

91 Aristotle, *Politics*, 1252a24.

92 The wife, according to Pateman, is just one figure of the servant in Locke (*Sexual Contract*, 47–48).

some of these resonances between Aristotle, feminist theory, and Locke, this chapter sought to establish the household as the most basic unit of analysis for political theory and then identify, more specifically, modes of settler home-making amid destruction and the ruins that remain.

Whereas my engagement with Aristotle and feminism was very brief and sought to mark the terrain more than to offer a thorough analysis, the argument has been unfolded more elaborately in regard to Locke. I proposed that if Locke's idea of property as a function of mixing labor with object is to perform all the tasks underlying Locke's theoretical enterprise—limiting that which is to be limited (sovereignty, commons) and legitimating that which is to be legitimated (colonization, enclosure)—it cannot be contained within the boundaries of the individual body. The property-making unit must expand from body to household. Expansion further becomes essential to the household as a property unit and, with it, global expropriation and dispossession. *The Lockean "individual" is therefore a household, and it is colonial in nature.* Locke's chapter 5 thus provides an initial glance at both the logical structure and the structure of desire that lie at the foundation of dispossession. The rest of the book will continue to unpack such desires and the landscapes of destruction they produce and then feed on. Accordingly, even though the legal histories delineated in this chapter did not play a direct role in the colonization of Israel/Palestine (unlike the colonization of North America), as Said—or, differently so, Wolfe—has shown, the structure of justificatory frames is strikingly similar. Beyond the questions of justification, other themes will be carried from Locke to my inquiry into homes as destructive tools or into the selves as colonizing subjects: digestion (and vomiting) as marks of colonization or of its rejection; agriculture and settlement; the animals that occupy the land and whose labor becomes central to its occupation; the desire to expand and the ontological foundations of expansion (enclosure or, as we shall see by this book's end, a fluid movement that refuses fences); and the effort to reconcile liberal values and ideology with a practice of colonization or perhaps the seamless slide between them. In many senses, then, we can identify an imaginary past and an imaginary self in this chapter that still govern practices and theories of colonization.

Epilogue
Unsettlement

I have learned and dismantled all the words to construct a single one: Home.
—MAHMOUD DARWISH

Home: A Reconceptualization

Amal Jamal traces the uses of the word *beit* by Palestinians, both refugees and internally displaced. As noted in the introduction, *beit*, like the Hebrew word *ba'it*, unites in itself several meanings that are separated in English: *home, house*, even *household*. But Jamal points to a set of dissociations, prevalent among many Palestinians, between the affectual level of belonging (*home*) and the material/institutional one (*house, household*). First, the materiality of the house has been disjoined from the sentimental facets that belong to the home: the home is not necessarily the house where one lives, because the attachment is to the house that is gone; moreover, the house that is gone, in its concreteness, is dissociated from Palestine—the land, the landscape—which becomes home, above, beyond, or instead of the concrete house;[1] and finally, homeland is dis-

Epigraph: Mahmoud Darwish, "I Am There," translated by Anton Shammas from *The Bed of the Stranger* (Beirut: Riad El-Rayyes Books), 1999.

1 Amal Jamal, "The Ambiguities of Minority Patriotism: Love for Homeland versus State among Palestinian Citizens of Israel," *Nationalism and Ethnic Politics* 10, no. 3 (2004): 437. See also Danna Piroyansky, "From Island to Archipelago: The Sakakini House in Qatamon and Its Shifting Ownerships throughout the Twentieth Century," *Middle Eastern Studies* 48, no. 6 (2012): 855–77.

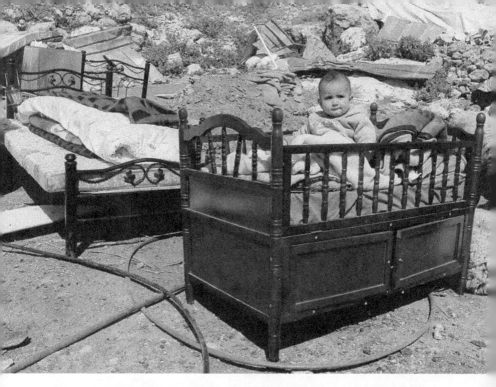

FIGURE I.1. A Palestinian baby inside a crib amid the ruins of what used to be a home in the destroyed village of Khirbet Tana (West Bank), April 2016. Or perhaps: a crib, a baby still inside it, and another bed (the parents'?), empty yet still with bedding, as if ready to be used again, show the home that remains even after the house was demolished by Israel for the fourth time in a period of eleven years (2005–16). Or yet again: a Palestinian house, demolished and shattered, scattered around a hill. Source: Ahmad Al-Bazz/Activestills.org.

sociated from the state (Palestine as a homeland from the state of Israel).[2] If the Hebrew and Arabic words *ba'it/beit* unite the physical construction (*house*), the institutional level (*household*), and the affectual attachment (*home*), the geopolitical context scatters those in the case of the Palestinian home. Therefore, Jamal argues, whereas the etymological roots of *beit* point to the stable, the trivial, the self-evident background of life, the Palestinian *beit* has gained a political meaning that emerges from its absence.[3] It organizes a nationalism that

2 Jamal, "Ambiguities of Minority Patriotism," 442. See also Lila Abu-Lughod, "Return to Half-Ruins: Memory, Postmemory, and Living History in Palestine," in *Nakba: Palestine, 1948, and the Claims of Memory*, ed. Ahmad H. Sa'di and Lila Abu-Lughod (New York: Columbia University Press, 2007), 77.

3 Amal Jamal, "Place, Home and Being: The Dialectics of the Real and the Imagined in the Conception of Palestinian Domesticity," in *Homeless Home*, ed. Ariella Azoulay (Jerusalem: Museum

is based on the experience of diaspora and materializes within practices such as holding onto keys of doors that no longer exist. Therefore, what grants *beit* its meaning as a Palestinian concept is the lack of both the institutional setting and the material conditions that would allow for the anchoring of territorial attachment.[4] Avtar Brah accordingly argues that in the Palestinian "diasporic imagination," home is a "mythic place of desire."[5]

These rifts, however, do not negate or render abstract the Palestinian concept of home. The very concrete home remains a meaningful, essential site and concept, not only for those who stayed—and for whom staying is often a mode of political resistance alongside a mundane mode of managing life and kinship—but also for those who could not stay and are still awaiting return. In other words, pointing to the destroyed Palestinian home does not take here the form of Arendt's understanding of refugeeness (or her view of African tribes for that matter): a way of seeing those who have no home as somehow pushed away from history and politics, if not humanity. Ruba Salih, much like Said before her, urges us to see exile as a "springboard for political subjectivity" rather than as a form of being that undermines it.[6] In this insistence, she reminds us of the dangers of reducing refugees to passive, voiceless victims.

Such an understanding calls on us to further reconceptualize home itself, in ways that also reshape political structures and give way to more flexible— more inclusive—modes of political belonging: rights beyond citizenship; homes beyond land; home that are mobile or shared; communities that can lay claims

---

on the Seam, 2010), 274–301. See also Rosemary Sayigh, "A House Is Not a Home: Permanent Impermanence of Habitat for Palestinian Expellees in Lebanon," *Holy Land Studies* 4, no. 1 (2005): 17–39. Sayigh traces the shift from *beit* as bearing "a connotation of permanence, security and projection into the future" to the scattering of the many elements of *home/house* in the homes of Palestinians refugees in Lebanon (19).

4 Jamal, "Place, Home and Being." See also Helena Lindholm Schulz and Juliane Hammer, *The Palestinian Diaspora: Formation of Identities and Politics of Homeland* (London: Routledge, 2003), 111.

5 Avtar Brah, *Cartographies of Diaspora: Contesting Identities* (London: Routledge, 1996), 192. Or: "The occupation has transformed us from the sons of Palestine into the sons of the *idea* of Palestine" (Mureed al-Barghouti, "Songs for a Country No Longer Known," *Journal of Palestine Studies* 27, no. 2 [winter 1998]: 59–67). For a review of the shifting senses of home across Palestinian generations, see Victoria Mason, "Children of the 'Idea of Palestine': Negotiating Identity, Belonging and Home in the Palestinian Diaspora," *Journal of Intercultural Studies* 28, no. 3 (2007): 271–85.

6 Ruba Salih, "'Intellectuals Know, but People Feel': Palestinian Refugees, Gramsci and Cathartic Politics" (lecture, SOAS University of London, London, October 18, 2017).

to alternative visions of inclusion via the loss of home.[7] Palestinians, alongside other groups of dispossessed, exiled, or migrant peoples, have offered many such conceptualizations. Honaida Ghanim defined home as a border entity, or the border as a home of sorts—a form of inhabiting that which should not be crossed or which is defined as an act of separation. After the border had crossed many Palestinian families and divided them across its line, identity and sense of belonging became anchored in practices of border crossing. "The border came to be a place that the Palestinian ran up against, repeatedly passing and re-passing through it, as when she is expelled or allowed to rejoin her family. It becomes, in the end, a place where she resides, almost a home," in Ghanim's words.[8] These acts of crossing not only change the meaning of home or one's spaces of belonging but also challenge the state's claim to sovereignty. The very attachment to both sides of the border, the reconstruction of home not simply as a border entity but as that which refuses the border altogether or ties both of its sides together, defies the state's project of dividing and defining its own population and territory. It thus runs against the ethnic-based project of the Jewish state, in the most intimate and daily manner. Similarly to the practice of sumud—of staying put and insisting on living in one's own home—which is a key form of Palestinian resistance, in this sense, too, homemaking becomes a form of resistance. Only here, it is the resistance of those who must move (across the border) in order to stay (at home), whose most mundane practices, such as hosting a family member or visiting a relative, become a way of defying the border.

Along similar lines, home can be redefined as a mobile entity whose borders are the borders of the self and can transcend, or work across, national entities, as in Gloria Anzaldúa's famous formulation: "I am a turtle, wherever I go I carry 'home' on my back."[9] Such mobility of home provides grounds for new

7　Sara Ahmed, "Home and Away: Narratives of Migration and Estrangement," *International Journal of Cultural Studies* 2, no. 3 (December 1999): 329–47; Jamal, "Place, Home and Being." Thinking of home from the perspective of absence can take us elsewhere. Alongside the status of refugees, we can think in this context of, for example, the need of individuals to sever ties with their childhood homes, to symbolically kill the head of the household in the process of establishing one's own home and selfhood. This direction will not be pursued in this book, but thinking with it can provide further layers to some of its arguments.

8　Honaida Ghanim, "Being a Border," in *Displaced at Home: Ethnicity and Gender among Palestinians in Israel*, ed. Rhoda Kanaaneh and Isis Nusair (Albany: State University of New York Press, 2010), 3. For other contexts of inhabiting borders as a form of homemaking, see James Clifford, "Diasporas," *Cultural Anthropology* 9, no. 3 (August 1994): 302–38.

9　Gloria Anzaldúa, *Borderlands/La Frontera: The New Mestiza* (San Francisco: Aunt Lute Books, [1987] 1999), 16. A Palestinian female activist likewise declared that "My homeland is my

claims for belonging that are never bound to territoriality and yet, through corporeality (i.e., the body as a form of a home) also do not abandon the link between place and belonging. In a different way, such mobility of homes can work through time rather than space, marking home as something that moves in temporal terms. Adam Ramadan argues that the home in the refugee camp is often imagined through such fleeting temporalities: the space of attachment (the Palestinian homeland, the particular home that was left behind) is often perceived by refugees as a time in the past (before 1948), and their contemporary space of inhabitation often represents to them a transiency that undermines attachment. Contrary to Anzaldúa's home, which seems to be wherever she is, this temporality marks the home as out of sync with the refugees' presence. And yet, as Ramadan goes on to argue, "while this Palestinian time-space emphasizes displacement and transience, the camps have become meaningful places in themselves."[10] Ramadan calls on us to see home in the house of those living in exile, even in the case of refugees still living in camps.

Working with similar assumptions, Sari Hanafi criticizes the argument claiming that development and reconstruction work in refugee camps undermine refugees' claim to return. "There is no opposition," he argues, "between rehabilitation of a place where a refugee lives and the ardent desire of some of them for their return. A refugee is able to place him/herself in a succession or a superposition of many temporalities or spaces of reference." But Hanafi's argument goes further. Beyond the claim that the refusal to rehabilitate destroyed camps will bring suffering to those living there, he argues that (re)building the camps—the houses, streets, and infrastructure—is a material condition for establishing and sustaining a political community.[11] This claim echoes Arendt's

---

mother's womb. I don't want to sound dramatic but that's the only thing I can say that I truly belong to." She was thus claiming "a sense of belonging to a place which she cannot be dispossessed of" at the same time as she "flouts nationalist constructions of the homeland as a fixed territory" (Kim Jezabel Zinngrebe, "Defying 'the Plan': Intimate Politics among Palestinian Women in Israel" [PhD diss., SOAS, University of London, 2017], 11).

10 Adam Ramadan, "In the Ruins of Nahr al-Barid: Understanding the Meaning of the Camp," *Journal of Palestine Studies* 40, no. 1 (2010): 60. "The camps are where Palestinian life has been constructed and maintained for sixty years, where children have grown up and grown old, where parents and grandparents have died and been buried, where memories have been made and accumulated" (53). Significantly, Ramadan shows that the camp becomes a positive place, a home, only after it, too, has been lost (due to other wars, evictions, etc.). It is only then that its residents feel an attachment to it, an attachment they thought they never had.

11 Sari Hanafi, "Palestinian Refugee Camps in Lebanon as a Space of Exception," *REVUE Asylon(s)* 5 (September 2008), http://www.reseau-terra.eu/article798.html.

insistence that having a home is a necessary condition for creating a stable, safe platform from which a political struggle can emerge, and yet Hanafi does something else with this insistence. Rather than dismissing the very political status of the refugees,[12] Hanafi insists on a plural mode of homemaking that allows the refugee to make political claims vis-à-vis several spaces or to develop intimate senses of attachment to those multiple sites. Salih and Sophie Richter-Devroe saw this multifaceted claim as a form of performative politics in the Butlerian sense. By claiming both the right to stay and the right to return, refugees destabilize this binary, thereby destabilizing national boundaries. Salih and Richter-Devroe therefore urge us to find a theoretical place for multiple homes that would also re-demarcate politics.[13] The fact that houses, even the most temporary ones, are made into homes, obtain meaning, and generate attachment, comfort, and life works in tandem with the fact that the house that is lost is still a site of belonging and identity and still generates similar attachments. Moving in between these two houses, Palestinians once again threaten the Israeli logic of homemaking, which rests on a territorial exclusivity.

It is important to remember here, again, that even though such notions of home work against the Israeli logic, they have been central to Jewish diasporic tradition, and in this sense reclaiming them is not necessarily a way of undoing Jewish modes of homemaking, even in Israel. What is being threatened here is a very particular thread in Zionism that Amnon Raz-Krakotzkin has identified as the negation of exile: a complete denial of the home-that-was for the Jew, which is then echoed in the same denial of the home-that-was for the Palestinian.[14] Other visions of home and homelands can construct other geopolitical spaces.

In the current dominant formation of Zionism, however, the very presence of these Palestinian lost homes, the very possibility of repeatedly reclaiming them, even if from afar, is the horizon of the undoing of the Israeli project. Therefore, even their ruins, which will be featured in this book, cannot be conceptualized merely as the relics of disaster. These ruins must be

12 A dismissal of status that most clearly emerges in its tragic form in Arendt's "We Refugees," *Menorah Journal* 31 (January 1943): 69–77.

13 Ruba Salih and Sophie Richter-Devroe, "Palestine beyond National Frames: Emerging Politics, Cultures, and Claims," *South Atlantic Quarterly* 117, no. 1 (2018): 1–20; see also Ruba Salih, "Palestinian Refugees: Homes in Exile," *Open Democracy*, August 18, 2014, https://www.opendemocracy.net/5050/ruba-salih/palestinian-refugees-homes-in-exile.

14 Amnon Raz-Krakotzkin, "Zionist Return to the West and the Mizrachi Jewish Perspective," in *Orientalism and the Jews*, ed. Ivan Kalmar and Derek Penslar (Waltham, MA: Brandeis University Press, 2005), 162–81.

thought of, in and of themselves, as a form of resistance, a material mode of survival rather than mere loss.[15] Beyond being traces of past violence, they are also a mark of a possible future beyond violence. This is precisely why any effort to reclaim these sites of ruin is met with Israel's efforts to further erase any material presence of Palestinian past.[16] But in these sites, too, even the smallest of gestures—picnics held by Palestinian families in their destroyed villages, trips taken to the fields that once were, visits to old neighborhoods and sometimes knocking on the doors of old homes[17]—keep demonstrating that this erasure will necessarily fail in achieving its desired effects and that, despite all, the space remains a site of negotiation. I will return to these in part II.

Israeli Homes: Revisited

The story I will tell in this book is a story of entrenchment—entrenchment in one's home, which is actually the home of another; in one's political position, which is a position that refuses to see the other; in one's own sense of justice, which is so enmeshed with violence that the two can no longer be set apart.

15 Derek Walcott, "The Antilles: Fragments of Epic Memory" (Nobel lecture, December 7, 1992, http://nobelprize.org/nobel_prizes/literature/laureates/1992/walcott-lecture.htm).

16 Norma Mossi describes what happened to depopulated, often destroyed Palestinian villages or neighborhoods after the organization Zochrot conducted visits to these sites in the 1990s and 2000s. Zochrot seeks to bring the Nakba to the Israeli collective memory and public debate, but once villages or neighborhoods became an explicit site of memory, these places were further demolished by the Israeli army so that the little that had remained was erased as well. Memory itself became a threat and its material conditions had to be undermined. Norma Mossi, "To View the Landscape, to See a Place and to Name It: On the Tours of *Zochrot*" [in Hebrew], in *Place Names and Spatial Identity in Israel-Palestine: Majority-Minority Relations, Obliviating and Memory*, ed. Amer Dahamshe and Yosef Schwartz (Tel Aviv: Tel Aviv University Press, 2018), 167–90.

17 Such visits to pre-1948 sites are most often conducted by internally displaced Palestinians, some of whom live very close to the villages depopulated in 1948. After 1967—and before the permit regime that has isolated the West Bank and Gaza from the 1948 territory—many refugees who lived in Gaza and the West Bank were suddenly able to visit their old homes as well. Some, such as the fictive Soraya whom we shall meet in chapter 2, come from abroad as citizens of Western countries. For some descriptions of such visits, see Bashir el-Hairi, *Letters to a Lemon Tree*, trans. D. Brafman (Jerusalem: Alternative Information Center, 1997); Ruba Salih and Olaf Corry, "Settler Colonialism, Displacement and the Reordering of Human and Non-Human Life in Palestine" (unpublished paper); Salim Tamari and Rema Hammami, "Virtual Returns to Jaffa," *Journal of Palestine Studies* 27, no. 4 (summer 1998): 65–79.

To tell it, I work primarily through archetypes that serve me as anecdotes in a Foucauldian sense: emblems of sorts, that crystallize into a wider whole.[18] But being such concentrated emblems, these archetypes also miss and exclude many other positions and modes of relation. Entrenchment, for example, takes different forms across social and ethnic strata in Israel, with radically uneven outcomes.

The Palestinian homes that will be the protagonists of my analysis are mainly the urban houses, often villas, which have been successfully inhabited by primarily Ashkenazi Jews (those of European descent). But the vast majority of Palestinian houses—cities, towns, villages—that have become homes for Israeli Jews were inhabited by Mizrahi Jews (those of Middle Eastern and North African descent), often against the state's desire and under constant threat of eviction. Their attachments to these sites were frequently seen as criminal and were at times broken, or efforts were made to break them, by state authorities or real-estate developers.[19]

These houses or neighborhoods were (re)settled by Jews from North Africa and the Middle East during or in the aftermath of the 1948 war, typically as a "temporary" measure that then became permanent. In some cases, such as in the case of Giv'at Amal in the eastern part of Tel Aviv, the new Jewish residents were brought over by state authorities because their previous residence was under attack or because these depopulated houses were seen as apt temporary residences for new immigrants. But their temporary status became quite permanent—a permanency that does not erase the hardships of the transient. In Giv'at Amal, parts of the neighborhood are still inhabited by some of the original Jewish tenants, and the inhabitants of other parts have only recently been evicted for grand development projects for the city's most affluent population. Those who stayed—but also most of those who were

18 The Foucauldian anecdote entails, and thereby demonstrates, the logic and grammar of a whole domain for which it functions as a sign. Adi Ophir sees it as a "case in which the 'logic of the situation' is consistently brought to the extreme." It is "a crystallization, so to speak, of every significant element present at large in a certain conjunction of power and knowledge" (Adi Ophir, "The Semiotics of Power: Reading Michel Foucault's Discipline and Punish," *Manuscrito: Revista Internacional de Filosofia* 12, no. 2 [1989]: 13). Foucault emphasizes that this is not a form of universalization but a hypothesis, an invitation, for "those who may be interested . . . to join in" (Michel Foucault, "Questions of Method," in *The Foucault Effect: Studies in Governmentality*, ed. Graham Burchell, Colin Gordon, and Peter Miller [Chicago: University of Chicago Press, 1991], 73–74).

19 Noam Leshem, *Life after Ruin: The Struggles over Israel's Depopulated Arab Spaces* (Cambridge: Cambridge University Press, 2016).

evicted—have been struggling for years to get state or municipal recognition and/or compensation. In other cases, such as in the case of Wadi Salib, Jews (mostly from Morocco) moved to the Palestinian houses independently, despite the state's explicit objection. Some moved from the immigrant camps (again, a temporary measure to address the housing crisis created by mass immigration in the immediate aftermath of 1948, which became more permanent than expected).[20] Others moved there after the state tried to settle them elsewhere, often in the periphery and often in nonurban settlements. They preferred the depopulated Arab urban residences over what they perceived as dead-end housing solutions. This preference countered the role central planning assigned to them: they were needed closer to the border, as part of the state's effort to assert territorial control in a disputed territory via settlement; or they were needed in agricultural settlements, as part of the Zionist effort to transform Jewish forms of productivity (the "new" Jew was to be a tiller of the soil). Therefore, when they abandoned their assigned settlement and moved to depopulated Palestinian neighborhoods, they were penalized by the relevant authorities, who refused to transfer this property to them in an orderly manner, as was done in other cases.[21]

In both cases—whether as authorized or nonauthorized occupation of depopulated property by Mizrahi Jews—and unlike the many cases that will be discussed later, these projects of "resettlement" were not regularized and legalized in the years following the war, and thus the inhabitants never obtained rights in their homes. The neighborhoods have suffered from municipal neglect for decades, which was employed as a strategy to ensure the temporariness of these homes, marking and re-marking them as illegal. They became—or were made into, or were left as—slums. Such "slums" could then be evacuated—in some cases after prolonged processes, some of which are still taking place today, more than seventy years after the houses were first repopulated. In their place, massive projects of gentrification emerged. Thus, "areas from which Palestinian population

20 Danna Piroyansky, *Ramle Remade: The Israelization of an Arab Town 1948-1967* (Haifa: Pardes, 2014), 174-75. See also Beni Nuriely, "Strangers in a National Space: Arab-Jews in the Palestinian Ghetto in Lod, 1950-1959" [in Hebrew], *Theory and Criticism* 26 (spring 2005): 13-42.

21 The Absentees' Law from 1950 aimed at securing precisely such a transfer. The law transferred the property not to private hands but, first of all, to the Development Authority. This allowed state planning in regard to the further transference of property to individuals. Such transfers were implemented unevenly along ethnic, economic, and spatial divides. For a detailed historical analysis, see Yfaat Weiss, *A Confiscated Memory: Wadi Salib and Haifa's Lost Heritage*, trans. Avner Greenberg (New York: Columbia University Press, 2011).

was expelled were settled by Mizrahim who later were also forced to leave these places," rendering them available precisely to the socioeconomic group at the focus of chapter 2.[22]

These social rifts between available modes of homemaking and attachment cut across the settler/native divide and somewhat disrupt the settler-colonial paradigm. They fracture lines of alliance but potentially also create alternative lines. The "scars" that run through these urban spaces, the "scene[s] of desolation between mounds of rubble and bulldozers," as Yfaat Weiss puts it, connect the different residents who have lost, or are under permanent threat of losing, their home. Weiss uses the term *diachronic neighbors* to point to the close relations between those who have resided in the same neighborhood, at times in the same house. Despite the fact that one dispossessed the other or has benefited from this dispossession, both groups suffered from loss of "property and compensation" as well as "memory and identity": Palestinian refugees, internally displaced Palestinians, and Jews who came from Muslim and Arab countries.[23] As Ella Shohat shows, the latter were subjected to the same colonial discourse, the same historical process, and the same apparatuses of domination and subjugation that were at work in other contexts of colonial rule. Accordingly, "although Zionism claims to provide a homeland for all Jews, that homeland was not offered to all with the same largess."[24]

The homes made into rubble, confiscated, redistributed, invaded, create broken yet persistent attachments in the case of both Palestinians and Mizrahi Jews, and may be a path for forging new political coalitions that overcome the primary categories of settler colonialism. Nevertheless, most social struggles in Israel revolve around the question of how the material and social benefits of the massive dispossession of 1948 (the real-estate loot) should be distributed among Jews. Most of these struggles do not touch at all on the injustice built into acquiring these possessions to begin with.

THE MAPS OF BOTH destruction and reconstruction or inhabitation are thus more complex and uneven than what this book can offer. Both the

---

22 Haim Yacobi, "Architecture, Orientalism, Identity: The Politics of the Israeli-Built Environment," *Israel Studies* 13, no. 1 (2008): 112.

23 Y. Weiss, *Confiscated Memory*, xii.

24 Ella Shohat, "Sephardim in Israel: Zionism from the Standpoint of Its Jewish Victims," *Social Text* 19/20 (autumn 1988): 1.

agents of violence and its targets, both its tools and its aims are at times fractured and are more dynamic and multilayered than what can be contained within these pages. The histories of dispossessions are also much longer, and their terrains often cut across various divisions within what cannot be neatly mapped onto the settler/colonized divide. They are still carried into the present, not just by the cyclical bombardment of houses of refugees in Gaza or the quiet transfer in the Jordan Valley but also by massive real-estate projects that lead to ongoing evictions of poorer, often ethnically marginalized Jews. Bearing these larger maps in mind, Ghanim reminds us that all these layers of oppression rest on one fundamental duality of erasure and reconstruction: "each and every step of construction and building is a negative of another step: the destruction and erasure of the indigenous society. The erasure of the names and memory of the natives, . . . both physically and symbolically, is not," she argues, "a secondary derivative of the process of Jewish settlement in the land. Nor is it a derivative of a conflict or confrontation, following Palestinian resistance or the invasion of Arab armies in 1948. It is rather the organizing principle and an inherent component of the Zionist colonial project." In this process, a Jewish homeland and Jewish homes are constructed, while Palestinians transition "from nativity to refugeeness, from the home [or house] to the tent, from locality to estrangement."[25]

In a wider reading, the relation between home and homelessness is one articulation of the universal promise of freedom (of politics, of rights), which rests on material divisions and racial hierarchies that condition it, rather than undermine it. This structure—a liberal structure but also a Greek one—means that all those forms of exclusion, those divisions of labor that keep pushing some groups to the margins and beyond, are not the *exception* to this principle of universality but its *precondition*. Some have looked at the very concept of the universal,[26] and others have examined concepts such as contract,[27] time,[28]

---

25 Honaida Ghanim, "'Where Is Everyone!' A Dialectics of Erasure and Construction in the Zionist Colonial Project" [in Hebrew], *Zmanim* 138 (2018): 104; my translation.

26 For example: Étienne Balibar, "Racism as Universalism," *New Political Science* 8, nos. 1–2 (1989): 9–22; Judith Butler, Ernesto Laclau, and Slavoj Žižek, *Contingency, Hegemony, Universality: Contemporary Dialogues on the Left* (London: Verso Books, 2000).

27 Pateman, *The Sexual Contract*.

28 Rahul Rao, *Out of Time* (Oxford: Oxford University Press, 2020).

history,[29] the liberal notion of rationality,[30] the rule of law,[31] or freedom.[32] This book's claim, accordingly, is that destruction is a constitutive element of Jewish homemaking. And it, too, has its history.

A Very Brief History of Destruction

In 1948 and its aftermath, roughly 450 Palestinian villages were destroyed. The exact numbers are under dispute, mostly because of a disagreement concerning what counts as a separate village. The most conservative estimation refers to 360 destroyed villages (official Israeli data from the 1950s) and the largest estimation refers to 472 destroyed villages (research conducted by Palestinians in the 1980s).[33] In these villages and in towns and mixed cities, tens of thousands of Palestinian houses were demolished. This destruction was "meant mainly to create a new geographical landscape from which all traces of Arab presence had been erased."[34] It aimed, in other words, at changing the landscape so that it appeared more "empty" and thus "Jewish" (or available to be made Jewish). This destruction also had the immediate political goal of preventing the return of refugees.[35] Nur Masalha observes that the fact that a "Committee for Abandoned Arab Property" was established in March 1948, before the bulk of the Palestinian exodus had taken place, "raises the issue of 'prior intent.'"[36]

All these houses were in depopulated villages and neighborhoods and were destroyed after they were emptied. Significantly, Aron Shai demon-

29 Dipesh Chakrabarty, *Provincializing Europe.*

30 Mehta, *Liberalism and Empire.*

31 Walter Benjamin, "Critique of Violence," in *Reflections: Essays, Aphorisms, Autobiographical Writings,* ed. Peter Demetz (New York: Schocken Books, 1986), 277–300.

32 Lowe, *Intimacies*; Elisabeth Anker, *Ugly Freedoms* (Durham, NC: Duke University Press, forthcoming).

33 Arnon Golan, "The Transformation of Abandoned Arab Rural Areas," *Israel Studies* 2, no. 1 (spring 1997): 94–110.

34 Ariella Azoulay and Adi Ophir, *The One-State Condition: Occupation and Democracy in Israel/Palestine* (Stanford, CA: Stanford University Press, 2012), 217; see also note 13 there.

35 Farid Abdel-Nour, "Responsibility and National Memory: Israel and the Palestinian Refugee Problem," *International Journal of Politics, Culture, and Society* 17, no. 3 (March 2004): 339–63; Benny Morris, *The Birth of the Palestinian Refugee Problem Revisited* (Cambridge: Cambridge University Press, 2004), 309ff.

36 Nur Masalha, *Expulsion of the Palestinians: The Concept of "Transfer" in Zionist Political Thought, 1882–1948* (Washington, DC: Institute for Palestine Studies, 1992), 185.

strated that this destruction was not primarily a function of war itself. Destruction was rather an orchestrated and planned state project, in the main implemented between 1965 and 1969.[37] This also means that the remnants of past Palestinian lives—the homes and villages—were there for at least two decades after the 1948 war, and *were visible to all*. The last claim is key to one of my main questions here, concerning modes of denial, collective blindness, and dissociation.

Since 1967, however, "destruction" has changed its modes of operation. It is "no longer directed at 'empty' villages and 'abandoned' houses but rather at inhabited ones." House demolition has become an "ongoing project"[38]—directed at houses of Palestinians in the West Bank, Gaza (with more than fifty thousand Palestinian homes and structures destroyed in the West Bank and Gaza between 1967 and 2017), East Jerusalem, and in the towns and villages of Palestinians who are citizens of the state.[39] With this change from

37 During the war itself, destruction of houses was minimal since both sides lacked heavy weaponry. In the immediate aftermath of the war (after local populations escaped) demolition enterprises were limited, as they were considered unnecessary and required manpower and machinery that were in short supply (Shai, "The Fate of Abandoned Arab Villages," *History and Memory* 18, no. 2 [fall/winter 2006]: 97–98). The enterprise was officially meant to "clear" and "level" more than a hundred abandoned villages—some of which had already become the homes of Jewish immigrants via governmental "allocation" (87). This need to "clear" was primarily meant to hide the traces of the Nakba from tourists and Palestinian citizens of Israel, and presumably, in its later stages, also from Palestinians occupied by Israel in 1967, who could at that point travel to see their lost homes. In the archives that Shai uncovered, the depopulated village seems to pose no threat to the Jewish Israeli self-perception.

38 Azoulay and Ophir, *One-State Condition*, 217–18. See also Avi Raz, *The Bride and the Dowry: Israel, Jordan, and the Palestinians in the Aftermath of the June 1967 War* (New Haven, CT: Yale University Press, 2012), 103–36.

39 Data by the Israeli Committee against House Demolitions (ICAHD). Looking more closely at the project of house demolition in more recent years (since 2006, after the second Lebanon War), we can see some of its details. Between 2006 and 2017, Israel demolished 2,173 housing units in the West Bank and East Jerusalem, because they were presumably illegally constructed (a forced illegality, ensuing from Israel's rejection of almost all requests Palestinians submit for building permits), leaving 8,952 Palestinians homeless. Israel also annually demolishes approximately one thousand homes of Bedouins (who are state citizens), who live in the Negev/Naqab region within Israel's recognized international borders. In addition, Israel demolished more than twenty-two thousand houses between 2006 and 2017 as part of military efforts and operations or for allegedly military purposes. Houses are therefore demolished as a mode of "enforcement," as a punitive measure (often houses of the families of those engaged in terrorist or military activity against Israel), or as part of wars or military operations. For data, see B'tselem, "Statistics on Demolition of Houses Built without Permits in the West Bank and East Jerusalem," *B'tselem,*

destroying depopulated homes to destroying inhabited ones, homes become something other than ruins; they become a place and a technology of death. In the last wars that Israel waged on Gaza, the majority of civilian casualties occurred because their bombarded houses collapsed on them. Eyal Weizman has noted that the main targets of military attacks in the 2008–9 campaign on Gaza were houses rather than people. Weizman estimates that fifteen thousand buildings were either destroyed or severely damaged, whereas about fourteen hundred people were killed. But importantly, the two were connected. "Many individuals and families were killed by flying debris— the shuttered concrete and glass of what used to be the walls, ceilings, and windows of their own homes. . . . The built environment became more than just a target or battleground; it was turned into the very things that killed."[40]

In East Jerusalem, in the Negev/Naqab, in the Jordan Valley and other Area C territories in the West Bank, but especially in Gaza, the scale of this destruction keeps mounting. If in the 2008–9 war on Gaza, 4,247 Palestinian homes were completely demolished[41] and roughly fifteen thousand severely damaged, in the 2014 war, seven thousand homes were completely destroyed, roughly eighteen thousand houses were either destroyed or severely damaged to the degree that they became uninhabitable, and almost ninety thousand were damaged.[42]

What is destroyed with this destruction—or what is targeted as an object of destruction—is not just houses, but the territorialization of Palestinians'

last modified August 8, 2019, https://www.btselem.org/planning_and_building/east_jerusalem _statistics; and "Statistics on Demolition for Alleged Military Purposes," *B'tselem*, last updated August 7, 2019, https://www.btselem.org/razing/statistics; Ben Fargeon and Michal Rotem, *Enforcing Distress: House Demolition Policy in the Bedouin Community in the Negev* (Negev Coexistence Forum for Civil Equality, June 2016), https://www.dukium.org/wp-content/uploads/2016/06 /HDR_2016_ENG-1.pdf; ICAHD, "Comprehensive Briefing on Home Demolitions," ICHAD, December 3, 2017, https://icahd.org/2017/12/03/comprehensive-briefing-home-demolitions/.

40 Eyal Weizman, *The Least of All Possible Evils: Humanitarian Violence from Arendt to Gaza* (London: Verso Books, 2011), 100. This data is based on B'tselem's estimations.

41 Data by the Israeli Committee against House Demolition (ICAHD).

42 B'tselem, "Statistics on Demolition for Alleged Military Purposes," *B'tselem*, last updated August 7, 2019, https://www.btselem.org/razing/statistics. An estimation of the United Nations Relief and Works Agency for Palestine Refugees in the Near East (UNRWA) can be found here: "Warning on Funds, UN Doubles Estimate of Destroyed Gaza Homes," *Ma'an News Agency*, December 28, 2014, http://www.maannews.net/eng/ViewDetails.aspx?ID=748278.

attachment to the land, the anchoring of attachment in concrete units.[43] Hence, this destruction works in tandem with the Israeli claim to an exclusive relation to territory. Perhaps, therefore, the products of this destruction (ruins) have a dominant presence in Israeli space (discursive or geographical), as if to prove the success of this project. This is one of the main points that will return throughout this book: since the destruction was/is necessary (constitutive), its traces must be preserved. This is despite and alongside the fact that since this destruction stood/stands in contradiction of some main themes in liberal Zionism (the idea of Israel as a liberal democracy, or the narrative of "a land without a people for a people without a land"), the traces of destruction had to be covered or at least pushed to the edge of the visual field. Political structures, much like psychic ones, are never coherent and consistent, and the residues of their conflicting tendencies make up the Israeli discourse and landscape throughout. Tracking them is one of my main goals here.

---

43 Or, as Weizman puts it, "the war on refugees is an ongoing form of violence that seeks not only to destroy refugee life and property but also to restructure refugeeness—that feature of Palestinian political identity" (*Least of All Possible Evils*, 144).

Part II

RELICS

Interlude
A Brief Reflection on Death and Decolonization

Rice: (. . . *a man perplexed and embarrassed, who desires, like all of us, sympathy*) . . . It may surprise you, sir, but I do not enjoy my present role. I am not by temperament an adventurous sort. Or a harsh one. I have become a military man only because the times demand it. (*A curious, urgent and almost sad defensiveness*) This is my country, you see. I came here when I was a boy. I worked hard. I married here. I have two lovely daughters and, if I may presume an immodesty, a most charming and devoted wife. At some other time I should have liked to have had you out to our farm. This is our *home*, Mr. Morris. Men like myself had the ambition, the energy and the ability to come here and make this country into something . . . *They* had it for centuries and did nothing with it. It isn't a question of empire, you see. It is our home: the right to bring up our children with culture and grace, a bit of music after dinner and a glass of decent wine; the right to watch the sun go down over our beautiful hills . . . And they are beautiful, aren't they? We wish the blacks no ill. But—(*simply, matter-of-factly, a man confirmed*)—it is our home, Mr. Morris.—LORRAINE HANSBERRY

"Major Rice of the Colonial Reserve," as he is first introduced in Lorraine Hansberry's *Les Blancs*, insists he is not a "harsh" man and is attributed by Hansberry a certain "sadness," an embarrassment, that comes to accompany his violent identity at this moment in the play.[1] He does not rejoice in violence (so he declares here), and yet he represents most concretely the violence of settlement, which, we must note, comes in many forms in *Les Blancs*, and as the play

Epigraph: Lorraine Hansberry, *Les Blancs: The Collected Last Plays: The Drinking Gourd/What Use Are Flowers?*, ed. Robert Nemiroff (New York: Random House, 1994), 70–71; italics in original.
1 Hansberry, *Les Blancs*, 72.

unfolds, we see that very few of the white figures, if any, do not themselves become, in one way or another, agents of violence.

Les Blancs depicts an imaginary African state amid decolonization. On one level, it is a story of a mission, established by Rev. Nielsen to bring medical support and education to the local population. Its story is revealed through the eyes of Charlie Morris, an American journalist who comes to cover the goodness of the place but slowly discovers its ugly sides. What is first being understood by him as a "sacrifice" for the benefit of African natives is slowly revealed in its full colonial meanings.[2] Through his eyes, we find out that rather than a site for progress (if we assume we can adopt this term uncritically), the mission is a site that constantly reproduces oppression and violence.[3] But let us return to Rice's words in the epigraph.

At least according to his own account of himself, he is not a violent man. It is rather the structure ("the times" that "demand it" but also the fact that "this is my country"—an insistence on belonging amid a process of decolonization— which *is* what "times" means in this context) that summons violence or positions Rice as an essentially violent power.

Despite insisting that "it isn't a question of empire," Rice's entire scheme of belonging is depicted by Hansberry as imperial: it depends on a strict, color-based division between "us" and "them," on an assumption that the former's right to the land is derived from the inability of the latter to cultivate and improve it ("men like myself had [. . . made] this country into something . . . *They* had it for centuries and did nothing with it"), and it is rooted in arriving from an elsewhere and in an effort to import that elsewhere ("culture") into the occupied space (home as "the right to bring up our children with culture and grace, a bit of music after dinner and a glass of decent wine").[4] Rice's effort to

2 Hansberry, *Les Blancs*, 78.
3 Much has been written, in the context of the critique of humanitarian intervention, about such symbiosis. See Ariella Azoulay and Adi Ophir, *The One-State Condition: Occupation and Democracy in Israel/Palestine* (Stanford, CA: Stanford University Press, 2012), 163ff; Adi Ophir, "The Two-State Solution: Providence and Catastrophe," *Theoretical Inquiries in Law* 8, no. 1 (2007): 117–60; John Prendergast, *Frontline Diplomacy: Humanitarian Aid and Conflict in Africa* (Boulder, CO: Lynne Rienner, 1996); Alex de Waal, *Famine Crimes: Politics and the Disaster Relief Industry in Africa* (Bloomington: Indiana University Press, [1996] 2009); Eyal Weizman, *The Least of All Possible Evils: Humanitarian Violence from Arendt to Gaza* (London: Verso Books, 2011).
4 According to Veracini, settler colonialism is defined by this form of coming from elsewhere: "Colonialism is primarily defined by exogenous domination. It thus has two fundamental and necessary components: an original displacement and unequal relations. Colonisers move to a new setting and establish their ascendancy." But settler colonialism has its unique mode of coming to dominate: "If I come and say: 'you, work for me' [colonialism], it's not the same as saying

dissociate imperial formations from "home" is an effort to separate what may be called the "private" from the "political," and then reinsert the private into the political domain in order to alter the latter's meanings: presumably *because* it is his home, it is *not* a question of empire (a political question); but at the same time, precisely because an assertion of home has been made, the imperial presence can be justified. This is why a "but" must arrive between the claim "we wish the blacks no ill" and the statement "it is our home." The two parts of the sentence cannot really coexist, and a long dash after the "but" asks us to pause and ponder the necessary connection between this form of homemaking and causing—even if not wishing to—harm.

Nevertheless, despite any critique that can be made, this *is* his home, and there is something in his words, almost a plea for recognition supported by the stage directions, that foregrounds the tragedy of Rice himself: the tragedy that is settlement, which is the rendering of one's home into an apparatus of systematically hurting others. This tragedy may become more digestible (as a tragedy) in the case of other white figures in the play, who are less appalling in their worldviews and life practices. DeKoven, one of the doctors working at the African mission, is one such figure, whose ability to clearly see the genocidal nature of the mission's work is quite rare. He tells Charlie, the reporter, that he came to Africa to save lives (and indeed, "I have saved hundreds of lives; all of us have. I have arrested gangrene, removed tumors, pulled forth babies"), but only two pages later, he admits he "helped provid[e] the rationale for genocide."[5] He thus explicitly accepts what Rice seems to acknowledge only in modes that cleanse him from responsibility: that his very presence in the colony is a form of violence and/or necessarily brings about violence. Perhaps, therefore, unlike Rice, when violence is directed against him, he accepts it: "They will murder us here one day, . . . all of us," he states, but refuses to see this murder as anything but just. Reflecting on how this death—his own death—will be remembered, he says it will be portrayed as an attack of savages, who irrationally killed those who came to bring them progress. But this is not

'you, go away' [settler colonialism]" (Lorenzo Veracini, "Introducing: Settler Colonial Studies," *Settler Colonial Studies* 1, no. 1 [2011]: 1). Most importantly, Veracini relies here on a distinction made by Mahmood Mamdani between immigrants, who come from elsewhere wishing to inhabit the law of the land, and settlers, who come in order to become this law. Mahmood Mamdani, "Beyond Settler and Native as Political Identities: Overcoming the Political Legacy of Colonialism," *Comparative Studies in Society and History* 43, no. 4 (October 2001): 651–64; Lorenzo Veracini, *Settler Colonialism: A Theoretical Overview* (London: Palgrave Macmillan, 2010).

5 Hansberry, *Les Blancs*, 112, 114.

the real story, he insists. "The sun really *is* starting to rise in the world, so we might just as well stop pretending it is the middle of the night. *They* are quite prepared to die to be allowed to bring it to Africa. It is *we* who are not prepared. To allow it *or* to die."[6] I will return to the meaning of this "or" at the end of this brief chapter.

The play, however, is woven from other stories as well. One of them is that of Tshembe, an African friend of the mission who returns to Africa after a long stay in Europe, having married a white European woman and had a baby with her. His struggle concerning what "home" may mean—the place in Britain where his wife and baby are waiting for him, or Africa that calls him to join the fight for decolonization—is an important thread of the play, which also problematizes the one-dimensional trajectory of "settlement" (usually, from Europe to Africa). Joining the fight means, he knows, drifting away from his family, potentially dying, but also killing the people he loves. It means participating in a discourse of hate, which he tries so hard to refuse. Between him and DeKoven, the tragedy of the violence of both colonization and decolonization emerges in its full brutality and inevitability. To play on Albert Memmi's formulation of the impossibility of the colonizer who refuses, we can see here the impossibility to transcend the order of violence once the structure of colonization is put in place.[7] Both DeKoven and Tshembe would like to refuse racial hatred and violence but are pushed—or pulled—into this violence by the reality of colonization.

The impossibility of this refusal is perhaps best captured in the figure of Madame Nielsen, the wife of Rev. Nielsen, who established the mission. Madame Nielsen came to the mission not only to "teach" the locals but also to learn from them; she came to share the land and become part of its habitus (opposite to Rice's, but also Rev. Nielsen's effort to change it and bring it the European way of life); she forms deep friendships with local women; and she truly supports the struggle for decolonization. (One can hear in this description Lorenzo Veracini's or Mahmood Mamdani's distinctions between an immigrant and a settler.[8]) At the end of the play, when the struggle for decolonization escalates

---

6 Hansberry, *Les Blancs*, 106.

7 Memmi argues that there are two positions that can be adopted by a colonizer: accepting his role in the order of colonial violence or refusing it. But in a chapter titled "The Colonizer Who Refuses," he displays the impossibility of this refusal: to refuse his role as colonizer would be to refuse everything he is, a death of sorts. I will return to this point as well. See Albert Memmi, *The Colonizer and the Colonized* (London: Souvenir Press, [1974] 2016).

8 See note 4 in this interlude.

and the drums of war are clearly heard approaching, she sits outside the mission with Tshembe. "You will stay on, then?" he asks her, and she replies: "At my age, one goes home only to die. I am already home."[9] Much like Rice's, Madame Nielsen's home is a space that is defined partly by violence. But if his home is defined by the violent aggression it necessitates, hers is a site of her own death. "Our country needs warriors," she urges Tshembe to join the fight, knowing very well that her home is the target of the next attack. Her refusal of the colonial structure (a refusal embedded here in the words *our country*—so different from Rice's "my country" or "our home") demands she renounces *herself*, does away with *herself*.[10]

In the play, this means Madame Nielsen has to die.[11] She does so not as a martyr (a death that would have made her the center of the political situation, rather than the moment of vacating the stage for the struggle of liberation). Instead, she dies—to echo Hansberry's stage directions from the paragraph featuring Rice with which I opened—"simply, matter-of-factly." What would it mean to think of such a death as a political act, even a political call? (And I should preface this question by stating that I do not call here for killing all settlers or so many others whose social positions, security, and prosperity generate a world of insecurity for others.) There is at least one easy answer to this question, which I shall outline here only to question it. My own response, which is less of an answer and more of an impasse, will follow.

Veracini recently offered such an easy answer. In a talk with a similar title, he argued that decolonization amounts to killing the settler in the man but letting the man live.[12] Following Patrick Wolfe's claim that settler colonialism

---

9 Hansberry, *Les Blancs*, 124.

10 As Memmi would put it, this refusal demands that she renounce "part of [herself], and what [she] slowly becomes as soon as [she] accepts a life in a colony." Ultimately, Memmi claims, to truly become part of the process of decolonization requires a form of self-renunciation that would mean she "no longer recognizes [her]self." This is why, he tells us, this position is, in fact, impossible (*Colonizer and the Colonized*, 64, 76).

11 Hansberry converses here, as in the entire play, with Jean Genet's *Les Negres* (The Blacks). Beyond the title, and her own account of how Genet's play affected her and how she wanted to write a "response," *Les Blancs* carries many parallels in the plot: the missionary and the military man as main figures, and the fact that the murder of a white woman is at stake. I thank Kristina Hagström-Ståhl for her thoughts on these parallel lines and for much more. For Hansberry's quote, see Robert Nemiroff, "A Critical Background," in *Les Blancs: The Collected Last Plays: The Drinking Gourd/What Use Are Flowers?*, by Lorraine Hansberry, ed. Robert Nemiroff (New York: Random House, 1994), 32–33.

12 Lorenzo Veracini, "Decolonising Settler Colonialism: Kill the Settler in Him and Save the Man" (lecture, SOAS, University of London, June 5, 2017).

is a structure, Veracini's claim is that killing the settler would mean chang-ing the structure. Knowingly or not, Veracini follows arguments made by both Mamdani and Raef Zreik in a correspondence of sorts under the title "When Does a Settler Become a Native?" Both propose, even if in different ways, that with a radical change in the structure of the settler state, the categories set-tler/native can be dissolved; not, as the title of their dialogue might propose, in ways that turn the settler into a native, but in ways that make this distinc-tion less meaningful, at least in its political bearings.[13] Decolonization is thus the process through which the settler ceases to be a settler.[14] This provides an institutional/structural path for decolonization without violence and, as such, seems quite tempting.

But if the "I" of the settler, her very being, is shaped by, and immersed in, this structure, as I argued in the theoretical overview and will continue to argue throughout this part of the book, then this change must go deeper than a change in legal categories and access to rights, as Zreik claims when he pro-motes the idea of equal juridical citizenship, or deeper even than equal access to material resources, as a more Marxist account would insist. To kill the settler in the man is to kill so much of the man himself that the distinction becomes questionable. This is not just because it is analytically messy, but also because, politically, I cannot imagine it taking place: it is to demand that he give up his property (or at least some of it), his language, his cultural references; but also, if I am correct, that he change his "structures of feeling,"[15] modes of desire, and attachments—to places, to people. I do not say that these are not just demands; but these changes are not easily manufactured. And would encounter fierce resistance.

13 See Mahmood Mamdani, "When Does a Settler Become a Native? Reflections of [sic] the Colo-nial Roots of Citizenship in Equatorial and South Africa" (inaugural lecture as A. C. Jordan Pro-fessor of African Studies, Centre for African Studies, University of Cape Town, May 13, 1998); Raef Zreik, "When Does a Settler Become a Native? (With Apologies to Mamdani)," Constella-tions 23, no. 3 (2016): 351–64; see also Patrick Wolfe, "New Jews for Old: Settler State Formation and the Impossibility of Zionism: In Memory of Edward W. Said," Arena Journal 37/38 (2012): 285–321.

14 These categories are flattened here and in reality they do not always work in unified "blocks." Settlers can belong to different groups, some more easily "nativized" than others; some were actually natives before becoming settlers. For such a critique, see Yuval Evri and Hagar Kotef, "When Does a Native Become a Settler?" Constellations (forthcoming).

15 Raymond Williams, "Structures of Feeling," in Marxism and Literature (Oxford: Oxford Univer-sity Press, 1977), 128–35.

Although undoubtedly necessary, institutional change consisting of the democratization of the settler state is not sufficient, because it leaves intact the deep structures of racialized hierarchies, violent desires, and attachments to dispossession. These are not *psychological* structures, but *sociopolitical* ones, since they have to do with our modes of living together. As Marx argued in "On the Jewish Question," liberation that occurs on the (ideological, institutional) level of the state leaves unregulated, even protected, an entire domain of human existence that is still governed by oppression. But whereas a Marxist solution involving a redistribution of material resources is also necessary, it, too, leaves intact a domain of human existence where oppression can reside: structures of feelings, sentiments, attachments, or what Ann Stoler refers to as "'emotional economies' of empire."[16] Thus (still following Marx's argument), if Bruno Bauer proposes to free humankind from religion by making it a nonstate matter (by freeing the state from religion, by privatizing religion), and if Marx's response to this proposition points to America as a secular state where religion nonetheless thrives (that is, proof that freedom at the institutional level is insufficient, if not destructive), my response to Zreik or Veracini is to point to America as a democratized settler state where racism and white supremacy nevertheless thrive.[17] Further, it is to argue, together with Marx, that material reality changes consciousness, but, beyond him, to suggest that when we think of material reality, we must think beyond domains of economy and take into account affectual politics as well. All this is to say that I am not persuaded that the settler will no longer be a settler if state institutions become democratic and even egalitarian, or even if the land and its resources are redistributed.

"It is too much to ask one's imagination to visualize one's end," argues Memmi after insisting that this form of annihilation—by self or other; ideological, national, or corporeal—is the only goal of decolonization.[18] "There would be no place," he states, for the colonizer in the new social order, no matter how close he is to the colonized in his practices and political alliances, how much he struggles with them and for them. "Even if he is in no way guilty as an individual, . . . he shares a collective responsibility by the fact of membership in a

16 Ann Laura Stoler, *Along the Archival Grain: Epistemic Anxieties and Colonial Common Sense* (Princeton, NJ: Princeton University Press, 2009), 68.
17 Karl Marx "On the Jewish Question," in *The Marx-Engels Reader*, ed. Robert Tucker (New York: W. W. Norton, 1978).
18 Memmi, *Colonizer and the Colonized*, 84.

national oppressor group. Being oppressed as a group, the colonized must necessarily adopt a national and ethnic form of liberation from which he cannot but be excluded."[19] To resolve this ambivalence, one must therefore leave or die. Which brings us back to the "or" in DeKoven's words above: "It is *we* who are not prepared. To allow it *or* to die." This "or" between allowing (decolonization) and dying can be an exclusive "or," marking the two options given to the settler: to allow it *or* to die. But it may be that DeKoven says something different here: one must be prepared *both* to allow decolonization to take place *and* to die, to allow it *by* dying (such as in the death of Madame Nielsen) and one is prepared to do neither.

Madame Nielsen prefers dying over leaving—one form of negating the self over the other. Her death, and with it the sounds that may symbolize decolonization, conclude the play. But I am not sure where it leaves us in terms of an answer to the question of this ending's political lesson.

The question of this political lesson and its addressees is itself quite ambivalent. It foregrounds the colonizer's role in the process of decolonization and yet immediately negates this role; it manifests the claim that it is not the role of the colonizer to set the terms of decolonial justice (one can leave or die, but not take part, it seems), and yet it shows the existential stakes of the colonizer in this conversation. In this sense, it is a paradoxical question to begin with and the difficulty is not just to answer it but also to pose it. And still, I do not—cannot—call here for either individual, collective, or political suicide. I also do not think that "leaving" is a valid solution. At least if we think of the Israeli/Palestinian context, but probably of most other settler contexts as well, leaving is the privilege of a few and is conditioned on both economic and ethnic advantages. I also do not—cannot—refuse the possibility of alliances, of a shared future, of a horizon where people can live, together or separately, but *live*, protected from the violence of the other or the state. I want to be able to imagine a future, say, with Said, in which the just solution for one is not the destruction of the other. But all I have to work with is Madame Nielsen's death. Analogies come to an end somewhere, one may contend, in order to move us forward. But I am not quite sure that we have reached this end.

Here I stop writing. I do not know how one writes dead ends or how one writes themselves out of history.

---

19 Memmi, *Colonizer and the Colonized*, 83.

AND YET RELINQUISHING hope is itself a privileged position.[20] And if the settler has any role in this hope for a decolonial future, if, that is, this hope takes the form of shared life rather than replacement (after Fanon), if it goes beyond the choice to leave or die, then change must occur at the level of desires as well. The following chapter engages with some failures to being moved in particular ways—to feel but also to act, to form, perhaps, a movement (a political one) based on the impasses we met in this chapter and will continue meeting in the next one. But, Michal Givoni reminds us, "what people cannot (yet?) feel is also the ground for the glimmer of hope,"[21] a glimmer of hope that she finds in the continuous effort to narrate wrongdoings, even in the very insistence on dead ends.

20 Above all, I want to thank Omar Tesdell for insisting on this and on hope. For analyses of hope amid conditions of despair, see Michal Givoni, "Indifference and Repetition: Occupation Testimonies and Left-Wing Despair," *Cultural Studies* 33, no. 4 (2019): 595–631. See also Robyn Marasco's claim, according to which despair is a vitalizing political power, in her *The Highway of Despair: Critical Theory after Hegel* (New York: Columbia University Press, 2015).
21 Givoni, "Indifference and Repetition," 2.

2. Home (and the Ruins That Remain)

EMAD: Do you know whose house this is?

IRIT: Yes; it is mine.

EMAD: But before . . . ?

[Irit shrugs her shoulders, signaling "no"]

EMAD: It's hers. [Points to Soraya, who stands behind him]

IRIT: Really? Do you want to come in? Please, come in. . . . You can stay here for as long as you want.

[Soraya, Emad, and Marwan, who accompanies them, enter the house. We hear background conversations between Irit, a young Jewish Israeli woman, and the two Palestinian men. Soraya walks around the house quietly, as if trying to anchor memories (stories) in the concreteness of the space]

SORAYA: What happened to all the furniture?

IRIT: I don't know. I guess my parents got rid of it at some point.

Epigraph: Annemarie Jacir, dir., *Salt of This Sea,* Augustus Film, Clarity Productions, JBA Production, Louverture Films, Mediapro Philistine Films, Tarantula Thelma Film, 2008; all descriptions in brackets are mine. This experience of trying to attach memories, or, in the case of younger generations, stories, to a space that has changed over the years is repeated in many descriptions of return, primarily of those belonging to the third generation of the Nakba, who "experienced the Nakba through the imaginary of parents and grandparents" and returned to visit their family homes after Oslo. (Salim Tamari, "Bourgeois Nostalgia and the Abandoned City," in *Mixed Towns, Trapped Communities: Historical Narratives, Spatial Dynamics, Gender Relations and Cultural Encounters in Palestinian-Israeli Towns,* ed. Daniel Monterescu and Dan Rabinowitz

This dialogue, from the movie *Salt of This Sea* (2008) by Palestinian film-maker Annemarie Jacir, describes the first encounter between Soraya and Irit. Soraya is a Palestinian woman from Brooklyn, and Irit is a Jewish Israeli who lives in the Jaffa home that used to belong to Soraya's family until they lost it in 1948. Now, sixty years later, Soraya returns to Palestine in search of what her family left behind. After this scene of encounter, the camera cuts to the seaside, where Soraya vomits.[1] It is clear why Soraya cannot bear the situation, seeing her home—a home in which she never lived and probably never will, but that still is hers—both there and gone; for the first time so close and so unachievable, even partly disposed of; an entire world thrown into the garbage ("got rid of at some point"). Irit, on the other hand,

---

[Aldershot, UK: Ashgate, 2007], 38). For some narration of such visits, see Ghassan Kanafani, "Returning to Haifa," in *Palestine's Children: Returning to Haifa and Other Stories* (Boulder, CO: Lynne Rienner Publishers, 2000), 149–96; Ghada Karmi, *Return: A Palestinian Memoir* (London: Verso Books, 2015); and Salim Tamari and Rema Hammami, "Virtual Returns to Jaffa," *Journal of Palestine Studies* 27, no. 4 (summer 1998): 65–79. These stories and many others can be compared to similar stories from other contexts, such as stories of Cypriots returning to their homes postpartition and finding them occupied by others. See, for example, Rebecca Bryant, *The Past in Pieces: Belonging in the New Cyprus* (Philadelphia: University of Pennsylvania Press, 2012); Yiannis Papadakis, *Echoes from the Dead Zone: Across the Cyprus Divide* (New York: Palgrave Macmillan, 2005). They can also be compared to the stories of Jews returning to their homes in Eastern Europe after the Holocaust (for example, in Claude Lanzmann's *Shoah* [France, 1985]; I will return to the meaning of this analogy soon). Rosemary Sayigh notes that these narratives of return, in which the "emotional climax of the narrative is the finding of the original family house," is typical of refugees from urban areas. Those returning to their lost villages tend to emphasize family and social ties or their tour in Palestine, which is, in its entirety, their lost homeland (Rosemary Sayigh, "A House Is Not a Home: Permanent Impermanence of Habitat for Palestinian Expellees in Lebanon," *Holy Land Studies* 4, no. 1 [2005]: 33).

1 Vomiting here follows the comment about the loss of furniture—significantly, the loss of the very materiality of the world, through the loss of *belongings*. Belongings, Rebecca Bryant emphasizes, are a way of upholding a connection not just to a home that has been looted but also to history. They "bring other possible futures into our present," and thus open the possibility to imagine other outcomes in a reality of conflict (Rebecca Bryant, "History's Remainders: On Time and Objects after Conflict in Cyprus," *American Ethnologist* 41, no. 4 [2014]: 684). Their loss might be therefore the loss of this horizon of alternative solutions or futures—a world closing. With Sartre, we can add that nausea arises from this closing of the world (Jean-Paul Sartre, *Being and Nothingness: A Phenomenological Essay on Ontology* [New York: Open Road Media, (1943) 2012]; Jean-Paul Sartre, *Nausea*, trans. Lloyd Alexander [New York: New Directions, 1964]).

seems almost unaffected by the encounter. The scene begins as she opens the door, saying "hello" in Hebrew to the unknown persons knocking. Once she learns who they are, there is no moment of hesitation, of doubt; she immediately invites the visitors in and is very hospitable and friendly. As the camera focuses on Soraya while she walks around the house, we hear a background conversation between Irit and the two Palestinian men. In this dialogue, Irit expresses her aversion to violence (although somewhat simplistically: "I think everyone wants peace, except for the leaders"); she shows sympathy for the situation of Soraya and the plight of Palestinians in general (although without assuming any responsibility: "it is terrible the situation, all this violence . . . Your grandfather left in '48? It's so sad, I wish they stayed"). Irit even entertains the thought of a love affair with Marwan, one of the Palestinian men—a violation of any regime of separation. But this relaxed dialogue does not erase the violent infrastructure of the encounter, the primordial act of expulsion.

What makes this scene so disturbing is precisely the hospitality and kindness with which Irit accepts her Palestinian guests. The moment Soraya knocks on the door is the moment at which Irit cannot but face the act of expropriation in its most concrete form. Soraya's knock forces Irit to confront the history—and present—of violence by her state, her family, and in a way herself. And yet somehow, all this does not undo her own sense of belonging and entitlement. Amahl Bishara observes that "even in the least controversial contexts, we might feel a shred of displacement or disbelief if a former resident of a house we have long inhabited knocks on our door to remember past lives." This is since, she says, "the house is 'our corner of the world,' and it is difficult to imagine sharing it."[2] Irit's peacefulness when faced with a much more politically charged knock on the door therefore seems like an act of indifference, an acceptance that is in fact a refusal to see the past lives that inhabited her current home and a refusal to imagine a demand to share. She is willing to be *hospitable* (a very charged political concept) but does not stop to wonder whether she is the host or the guest in this situation. Watching this scene, I always want her to vomit at its end, too.

Vomiting—this visceral, nonrational reaction of a body that cannot contain the current moment—guides my query here. In a way, this chapter is an effort to decipher this lack of existential nausea. If with Locke we met digestion as a metaphor or structure for colonization, vomiting can be seen as its antidote—a

2 Amahl Bishara, "House and Homeland: Examining Sentiments about and Claims to Jerusalem and Its Houses," *Social Text* 21, no. 2 (summer 2003): 143–44.

refusal of the habit of digestion. Fanon's critique of Sartre places existential nausea in colonial settings.[3] It shows how the radical inequality of the colonial world produces the nausea of some (the colonized) and not others (the colonizers). Nausea is, for Fanon, the outcome of a racial world pressing against the self, producing a corporeal scheme the body comes to inhabit yet cannot fully inhabit; it is a racial mode of alienation in which the self and the black body are dissociated via the racist gaze:

> "Look, a Negro!" It was an external stimulus that flicked over me as I passed by. I made a tight smile. "Look, a Negro!" It was true. It amused me. "Look, a Negro!" The circle was drawing a bit tighter. I made no secret of my amusement. "Mama, see the Negro! I'm frightened!" Frightened! Now they were beginning to be afraid of me. I made up my mind to laugh myself to tears, but laughter had become impossible. . . . In the train I was given not one but two, three places. I had already stopped being amused. It was not that I was finding febrile coordinates in the world. I existed triply: I occupied space. I moved toward the other . . . and the evanescent other, hostile but not opaque, transparent, not there, disappeared. Nausea.[4]

But if nausea is the outcome of meeting a world whose reality we cannot bear, as both Sartre and Fanon argue, then would the colonial encounter not also produce nausea in those among the settlers who, much like Irit, do not see themselves as such?[5] Would this moment, in which one realizes their own role on the colonial playing field, not fracture the very being of those who see the "political situation," in Irit's terminology, as the product of the unwillingness

---

3 For Sartre, nausea was the product of a direct encounter with the absurdity of existence (its contingency). It was the product of, a symptom of, or the meaning of alienation that for him began as a psychological phenomenon, but became a sociopolitical question (Sartre, *Being and Nothingness*; Sartre, *Nausea*). Even without working in detail with the ontological dimensions of existential phenomenology in which nausea is a mode through which Being is disclosed or an outcome of this disclosure, the main insight remains worthy of investigation: nausea is the outcome of meeting a world whose reality we cannot bear.

4 Frantz Fanon, *Black Skin, White Masks* (New York: Pluto Press, [1967] 1986), 112. See analysis in David Trotter, "Fanon's Nausea," *Parallax* 5, no. 2 (1999): 40.

5 As stated in the introduction, here I am using the concept of the "settler" broadly to refer to the primary division assumed by the paradigm of settler colonialism. In the Israeli context, it is common to contrast "settlers" with those living within Israel "proper," using the former to refer to those living beyond the 1967 borders. Analytically, however, if one works with the paradigm of settler colonialism, at least most Israeli Jews belong to this category as well.

of "leaders"?[6] Would it not disturb the identity of those who are sure that they belong to a peace-seeking, liberal, democratic majority—like so many Israelis and so many others who are implicated, in Michael Rothberg's terminology, in systematic violence, and often systematically benefit from it[7]—and who, therefore, see themselves as neither responsible for the violence of the past nor as current usurpers (to refer to Memmi's definition of settlers)?[8] If one perceives oneself as such—if one indeed *is* a nonviolent, liberal, progressive person—would the contradiction of the colonial situation not become too difficult to bear with this encounter? And if one can remain indifferent, what are the "habits of the heart and the redirections of sentiments fostered by colonial regimes"[9] that give rise to such peacefulness, such confidence, even when one can no longer deny their own role in history?

THIS CHAPTER IS A STORY of various encounters with colonial reality in an effort to offer some reflections on how and when identity overcomes, or bypasses, the potential crisis produced by the Palestinian knock on the door. This knock can be metaphorical or concrete; it can be sudden (as in the case of Irit) or much subtler and more enduring, since the traces of the act of dispossession were there all along, visible to all. Israelis live amid a multiplicity of Palestinian homes in many physical states: some are but rubble and some, like Irit's, are still whole. Ultimately, my argument is that the possibility to live amid the destruction one generates is key to understanding projects of settler colonialism wherein attachment to places of settlement always generates violence, if not constitutes a form of violence in and of itself. I shall argue that this is not merely the possibility to turn one's gaze and consciousness away from violence but also the possibility to develop an attachment to violence itself. Indeed,

---

6 I allude here to one mechanism of dissociation examined in the theoretical overview.

7 Michael Rothberg, *The Implicated Subject: Beyond Victims and Perpetrators* (Stanford, CA: Stanford University Press, 2019); Bruce Robbins, *The Beneficiary* (Durham, NC: Duke University Press, 2017).

8 "Accepting the reality of being a colonizer means agreeing to be a non-legitimate privileged person, that is, a usurper. . . . This amounts to saying that at the very time of his triumph, he admits that what triumphs in him is an image which he condemns. . . . This self-defeating process pushes the usurper to go one step further; to wish the disappearance of the usurped, whose very existence causes him to take the role of usurper, and whose heavier and heavier oppression makes him more and more an oppressor himself." Albert Memmi, *The Colonizer and the Colonized* (London: Souvenir Press, [1974] 2016), 96.

9 Ann Laura Stoler, *Along the Archival Grain: Epistemic Anxieties and Colonial Common Sense* (Princeton, NJ: Princeton University Press, 2009), 3.

sometimes, the very normalization of living amid the remnants of violence allows one not to see, to deny. And yet the decision to place this chapter's main parable in the depopulated Palestinian house that has been repopulated by an Israeli Jew is meant to highlight, rather, the degree to which people *must* know. Irit—as a placeholder or a symbol—clearly exhibits some of the mechanisms of denial mapped in the theoretical overview. Yet working through the figure of her home, and particularly through the moment Soraya enters it, I want to emphasize here the extent to which Irit also occupies the position of those who see and ultimately embrace violence, those who become attached to it, or perhaps have always been, in this way or another.

In a sense, my argument follows Wendy Brown's understanding of liberal identity as constituted by wounded attachments, by "logics of pain" that work in tandem with, or against, the "emancipatory democratic project[s] within which they are constituted."[10] The wounds and pain that transpire through these pages are very different from the ones Brown exposes, but something of the structure is nonetheless identical. In both Brown's and my analysis, various political projects and genealogies of selves (or communities) carry certain attachments to identity itself. The need to hold on to this identity thus remains, even if it eventually does not abide by the democratic ideals that shaped it to begin with. Liberal Zionism can be seen as one such attachment, since it contains an image of the self (as liberal, progressive, democratic, leftist) that is carried through a project (the state of Israel in its current formation) that eventually subverts the "emancipatory aims" of this "politicized identity."[11] Liberal Zionism, in other words, is sustained through a political project that undoes the very liberalism on which it is based. There is, therefore, a "wound" at its foundation. To be clear, the "wound" at the basis of this attachment is a function of this identity being an *injurious* one—an identity causing the very concrete wounds of others. But the self cannot really renounce the injurious facets of her being, despite refusing to see herself in them, because she is attached to the very structures that necessarily produce them (the Jewish state in our case, at least in its current formation).[12]

Differently put, the Israeli attachment to territory is at least derivatively also an attachment to the act of colonization, since the latter is the condition

---

10 Wendy Brown, "Wounded Attachments," *Political Theory* 21, no. 3 (August 1993): 390–91.

11 Brown, "Wounded Attachments," 391.

12 On the historicity and contingency of this formation and the fact that it was not a necessary form of the state-to-be, see Ariella Azoulay, "Civil Alliances—Palestine, 1947–1948," *Settler Colonial Studies* 4, no. 4 (2014): 413–33; Yuval Evri and Hagar Kotef, "When Does a Native Become a Settler?," *Constellations* (forthcoming).

for the self's placement in the land. But this is a wounded attachment, because the attachment to colonization is imposed on the self: it is the inevitable outcome of the attachment to the land (which is also an attachment to a national identity), and it materializes despite an attachment to the emancipatory political aims of the democratic state/society, with which it is in tension. The story of this chapter is a story of the surfacing of these attachments as an outcome of the colonial encounter—of the moment when one has to confront the injurious elements of her identity.

To tell the story of Israel's politics or culture through these attachments is to refuse, on the one hand, simple tropes that are often used to describe the nondemocratic elements of the Israeli state and society (e.g., "fascism"); it is to show the conflicting elements within Jewish Israeli identity that call us to move beyond such simplifications. On the other hand, such a mode of storytelling also refuses the refusal to recognize how deep and structural these antidemocratic elements are within Israeli identity. To tell this story is to insist on talking about the impossibility of the democratic project in Israel (in its current formation) while also refusing to dismiss the democratic desires of many of its architects and citizens, as well as its concrete democratic facets.[13] It is to work with the assumption that identities, as well as political constellations, are ambiguous and self-contradicting in ways that allow both these sides to coexist—the democratic and the colonial, the emancipatory and the oppressive—and to consider the deep, structural attachments to both these sides.[14] However, this is just one political story to tell. This chapter focuses on liberal Zionism and Zionists who see themselves as part of the liberal Left but still live inside, and are conditioned by, the ruination of the Palestinian home and homeland. As will become clear by its end, and as the epilogue for part I insisted, these are usually Ashkenazi Jews (of European descent), whose appropriation of Palestinian space is different from parallel appropriations in the case of other ethnic groups among the Jewish citizenry. It is a story of people of means, or people who came to acquire means also through this appropriation of Palestinian land, which is different from stories of those whose settlement in Palestinian neighborhoods was rather a step in their economic deprivation. The story here, then, does not pretend to tell a unified story of "Israelis." An altogether different story will be at the focus of the next part of this book. There are many more stories to tell.

13 On the democratic facets of Israel, see note 16 in the introduction.
14 Here, I follow Raef Zreik's insistence that Zionism has always been both a settler-colonial project and a national movement, albeit from a different perspective and through a different lens. Raef Zreik, "Leumit ve colonialit [National and colonial]" [in Hebrew], *Ha'aretz*, July 21, 2015.

THIS CHAPTER IS COMPOSED of two ways of telling the stories of these wounded attachments. One focuses on Israeli Jews, much like Irit, who live in Palestinian houses—concretely, or more metaphorically, as a form of inhabiting the land. I begin with some stories of encounter similar to the story presented in *Salt of This Sea*. I do so both to substantiate the scene's status of example and to continue tracing the sentiments and narratives that entrench the Israeli presence in these homes. At the same time, these stories are brought here from the perspective of Palestinians as a way of insisting on their presence in these chronicles, not merely as "absent," expelled, or disposed of, but as narrators and agents. I continue in the second section with a historical sketch of the physical reaction to the colonial encounter (nausea, pain). While it does not fully unpack a history of Jewish immigration to Palestine, this section nevertheless marks some important moments in what can be thought of as the encounter with an inhabited land and the inability to contain the implication of "settling" this land on one's identity and sense of home. More crudely put, this section points to moments of nausea of the type Irit failed to inhabit, moments that emerge from the friction between the promise of Zionism—the self-image and the fantasy of home in the land of Israel (*Eretz Israel*)—and the material reality of dispossession and violence. The third section offers some observations about the attachment to violence and destruction that may explain why in some cases this friction does not lead to a form of existential nausea. I show how ruination was integrated into the Israeli identity in a way that resolves the conflict that would otherwise emerge from the colonial encounter. The act of inhabiting the depopulated house thus becomes an *example* for a wider process, but also a metaphor for a mode of inhabiting the land.

The next section, "Home and Away," moves to a different mode of storytelling. Rather than the depopulated home/land that has been repopulated, it focuses on landscapes of ruins. This section also begins from a very different theoretical framework: it begins by looking at the mechanism of denial and invisibility that allows the bypassing of the above crisis of identity. It looks at people's ability to not see—an explanation for violence's endurance that I will seek to question. Indeed, Irit's lack of nausea is a way of marking that perhaps the fantasy of home and homeland itself has changed, so that violence no longer contradicts it or that one found other ways to negotiate her being with violence. In other words, ultimately, I argue not merely that the efforts to erase, deny, or turn a blind eye to

---

15 Arguments that were made most efficiently by Gil Z. Hochberg's *Visual Occupation: Violence and Visibility in a Conflict Zone* (Durham, NC: Duke University Press, 2015); and Noam Leshem's *Life after Ruin: The Struggles over Israel's Depopulated Arab Spaces* (Cambridge: Cambridge University Press, 2016).

violence fail,[15] but also that we must recognize and explore the ways in which violence is affirmed, embraced, and becomes constitutive of selves and communities. Accordingly, the following two sections shift analytical frames and point to the integration of violence into Israeli identity: The fifth section, "Home in the Ruins," shows the ruin's integration into the landscape as an object of desire. The sixth section, "The Self and Its Violence," moves to the appropriation of other elements of Palestinians' lives into Jewish Israeli locality and identity and shows to what extent this appropriation is an appropriation of violence. This latter argument is more fully developed in the epilogue to this part. The sixth section also provides a brief sketch of the ethnic as well as temporal boundaries of this chapter's argument. In the concluding note, I offer a brief and anecdotal history of the outcome of this appropriation: the full embrace of current Israeli violence.

In some sense, then, this chapter offers a historical narration, tracing a shift from modes of dissociation wherein the colonial encounter (the knock on the door, the confrontation with one's position as a settler) still generates crisis to the adoption of a nonconflictual approach to violence. To some extent, if one traces general shifts in public opinion, this is a historical story about Israeli society from pre-1948 until today. But, as we shall see with Irit, this "process" often occurs almost instantly and can also be seen as the coexistence of conflictual positions within a single individual.

Other Stories

Even though the possibility of Palestinians' return often produces profound anxieties in the Israeli public and brings about aggression, active rejection, or persistent entrenchment in hegemonic Israeli narratives, Irit's peacefulness is nonetheless representative of something I wish to capture here. It is the calmness of someone who can no longer be undone by the presence of the other; a settled way of inhabitation; an established mode of living-in (in violence, in another's home). This calmness is the triumph of the project of settlement. To substantiate this claim beyond the cinematic moment, I bring here two stories (two out of many that could have replaced *Salt of This Sea* as a gateway for this chapter), some data, and supporting literature.

The number of Jews who live or have lived in abandoned Palestinian homes is far from clear. In regard to the formative years of the state, this ambiguity arises because of the dynamic nature of housing at the time and the obscurity of the object measured. There were Palestinian homes that served as temporary houses for Jews who were later evicted; there were Jewish immigrants who infiltrated Palestinians' abandoned homes despite policies that required their eviction and demolition; there were contradictory policies, wherein some ministries ordered new immigrants or soldiers (or both groups, or one over the other) to take over depopulated apartments while others ordered them to wait; there were those who were officially sent to settle in Palestinian houses but soon left—either because they did not find the accommodations fitting or because they were forced out by other families.[16] There was therefore a wide range of categories created between official policies and individual, sometimes illegal actions; between temporary residences and permanent homes; and between different moments on the timeline. But no matter how one counts, the numbers are significant.[17]

Story I

The documentary *Stranger in My Home* (2007) by Sahera Dirbas follows eight Palestinians who return to Jerusalem to visit the homes they lost in 1948. The film chronicles them as they tell stories about their home and its loss, accompanies them as they wander anxiously around the staircases and the yards, too nervous to bring themselves to knock on the door. These nervous moments prepare us for the encounter between past and present homeowners, but the encounters themselves are brought into the frame only in the last few minutes of the film, if at

16 For a detailed narration of many of these processes, see Benny Morris, *The Birth of the Palestinian Refugee Problem Revisited* (Cambridge: Cambridge University Press, 2004), 282–95. On the role of state as well as private "initiatives" in this effort of settlement, see Arnon Golan, "The 1948 Wartime Resettlement of Former Arab Areas in West Jerusalem," *Middle Eastern Studies* 51, no. 5 (2015): 804–20; see also Leshem, *Life after Ruin*, esp. 83–97.

17 According to Arnon Golan, "most of the 72,000 Jewish 1948 refugees found shelter in former Arab urban areas, and among them almost 30,000 remained permanently." Those remaining thus amounted to 4 percent of the population at the time, yet this data does not include nonrefugees who moved to Arab houses, and Morris claims that several thousand nonimmigrants found at least temporary residence in houses in Palestinian neighborhoods. The phenomenon expanded during the next wave of immigration, between 1949 and 1951: "Of the 690,000 Jewish immigrants who streamed into Israel [during these years], about 125,000 were housed in former Arab areas." Most of those were settled in Arab houses immediately after the war: 110,000 out of the 190,000 who arrived between June 1948 and April 1949. Roughly 22 percent of the total population at the time, then, lived in depopulated Arab houses. Arnon Golan, "Jewish Settlement of Former Arab Towns and Their Incorporation into the Israeli Urban System (1948–50)," *Israel Affairs* 9, nos. 1–2 (2002): 149; Morris, *Birth of the Palestinian Refugee Problem Revisited*, 395. See also Yael Allweil, *Homeland: Zionism as Housing Regime, 1860–2011* (London: Routledge, 2017), 173, for slightly different data that nevertheless reflects a similar scale.

all. In most cases, the Jewish homeowners are almost as welcoming as Irit; most express sympathy for the pain of the Palestinian who was the previous owner, and most—who are much older than Irit—claim they can understand this loss since they went through the same experience in Europe. Some also share stories about their recent visits to their old homes in Poland or East Germany, as if to echo the current situation. They mention how they felt when seeing their prewar home inhabited by others and the awful sense that ensued after seeing that so much was still there, or the awful feeling that came from witnessing that everything had changed. Evoking this sense of familiarity places them on a presumably equal grounding with their "guests," thereby cleansing them of their responsibility. In all cases, the Palestinians insist (usually in Arabic, speaking to the director rather than the homeowner) that the ground is not equal, and that the experience is not a shared one. Whereas the movie provides but a glimpse into the state of mind of the Jewish occupants, this narrative of equality begins to show how one negotiates their status as dispossessor within an ethical frame. Pointing to the suffering of the self—the self who causes the suffering—mitigates the recognition that one has caused another to suffer. Danna Piroyansky sees this claim as a means to "settl[e] the score" and to assert that the act of resettlement of the house is a "fait accompli."[*] Tom Segev's critical analysis of 1948 replicates something of this pattern when he frames the Nakba as a replacement: "Free people—Arabs—had gone into exile and become destitute refugees; destitute refugees—Jews—took the exiles' places as a first step in their new lives as free people. One group lost all they had, while the other found everything they needed—tables, chairs, closets, pots, pans, plates, sometimes clothes, family albums, books, radios, and pets."[**] My claim here is not that this

---

[*] Danna Piroyansky, "From Island to Archipelago: The Sakakini House in Qatamon and Its Shifting Ownerships throughout the Twentieth Century," *Middle Eastern Studies* 48, no. 6 (2012): 869.

[**] Tom Segev, *The Seventh Million: The Israelis and the Holocaust* (New York: Hill and Wang, 1993), 161. See also Walid Khalidi, ed., *All That Remains: The Palestinian Villages Occupied and Depopulated by Israel in 1948* (Washington, DC: Institute for Palestine Studies, 1992), xxxii, for a description of all the belongings that were left behind—the "furniture, silver, pictures, carpets, libraries and heirlooms." There are countless stories of such items left, and then found.

symmetry is either faulted or accurate; I am interested only in how it is deployed and how, in these cases of encounter, it helps dismantle a potential sense of guilt. At any rate, keep in mind those tables, chairs, pots, and pans—that furniture that Irit's parents "got rid of." They keep returning in these stories as a way of bringing homes to life and making present those who lived between the walls now occupied by others.

But perhaps more interestingly, the film shows where a complete deadlock emerges—when the very effort of justification halts and gives way to full negation. A woman arrives at her beautiful, large home. The man currently living there is the most welcoming Israeli in the film. He says he has been looking for the Palestinian family and wants to hear about their fate. He writes down their names and stories as the woman tells them and invites the woman to stay longer. As she turns to leave, she asks about the market value of the house. He replies: "about a million and a half." Not a pause to wonder who is entitled to this significant real-estate yield. The material demand (even if latent) generates a silence. Not even a refusal.

In 1950, right after the war, the Development Authority (Transfer of Property) Law had regularized the transference of sixty-nine thousand apartments, houses, and buildings of Palestinians to centralized Israeli hands (that is, to the Development Authority), yet some of the process continued in later years and some was less centralized.[18] Benny Morris provides some of the most systematic data regarding the years preceding this law. Morris shows the gradual shifts in policy in regard to emptied Palestinian houses: in the early stages of the war, houses were to be kept intact for the return of refugees and houses deemed unfit for reinhabitation were demolished. But as the war continued, the idea of a Palestinian return was gradually pushed aside, and in opposition to it we see explicit efforts to make Arab houses (sometimes still populated, sometimes already emptied) available for

18 Yfaat Weiss, *A Confiscated Memory: Wadi Salib and Haifa's Lost Heritage*, trans. Avner Greenberg (New York: Columbia University Press, 2011), 82. For a detailed account of the transference of property, see Geremy Forman and Alexandre Kedar, "From Arab Land to 'Israel Lands': The Legal Dispossession of the Palestinians Displaced by Israel in the Wake of 1948," *Environment and Planning D: Society and Space* 22, no. 6 (December 2004): 809–30.

new immigrants or soldiers and their families.[19] First were the mixed cities of Jaffa, Haifa, and Jerusalem, where immigrants and internally displaced Jewish families were accommodated in abandoned houses immediately after the flight of Palestinian families and sometimes, at least in Jaffa, following an active removal of Palestinian families for the explicit purpose of providing such accommodations. Later, Jews were settled in Palestinian cities such as Lydda or Ramle. Very few of the depopulated villages were resettled using existing houses; even when new Jewish settlements were established to replace the Palestinian ones, "it proved easier to simply level the villages and build completely new settlements on the site or nearby."[20] Ghazi Falah conducted an extensive survey of depopulated villages during the late 1980s to early 1990s. By this time, roughly forty years after the war, he managed to access 407 out of the 418 villages that were depopulated during the war.[21] Of these, 81 villages were completely obliterated, so that no trace remained to attest that they had once existed; 140 villages were completely destroyed, but rubble was still identified; and 134 villages were mostly destroyed, with some walls or even houses left, but no houses reoccupied by Jewish families. In 50 villages some houses were left intact and were repopulated by Jewish families while all other houses were destroyed, of which 15 villages were repopulated by one or two Jewish families, while in 35 villages more than two families moved to the Palestinian depopulated village.[22] Sharif Kanaana offers a slightly different categorization that makes it possible to discern villages that became part of the urban landscape in Israel, with half-destroyed villages turned into parks, intact buildings used by Israeli institutions, or partly destroyed villages surrounded or partly covered by Jewish neighborhoods.[23]

19 Morris, *Birth of the Palestinian Refugee Problem Revisited*, 369–95.
20 Morris, *Birth of the Palestinian Refugee Problem Revisited*, 382–83, 386, 390.
21 According to Falah's count. I elaborate on this number in the epilogue to part I.
22 Ghazi Falah, "The 1948 Israeli-Palestinian War and Its Aftermath: The Transformation and De-Signification of Palestine's Cultural Landscape," *Annals of the Association of American Geographers* 86 (June 1996): 264.
23 Sharif Kanaana, *Still on Vacation! The Eviction of the Palestinians in 1948* (Jerusalem: Jerusalem International Center for Palestinian Studies, 1992). Kanaana's categories are: (i) villages completely obliterated and replaced by reforestation; (ii) villages destroyed, with some structures remaining on the landscape; (iii) villages destroyed and land cultivated by Israelis; (iv) villages destroyed and replaced by Israeli settlements; (v) villages partly destroyed with some buildings in use by Israelis (e.g., for ranches); (vi) villages partly destroyed but with many buildings

Several recent ethnographic works have engaged with the meaning of living in someone else's home, appropriating the intimate spaces of the enemy, and populating "the emptiness left by recurring demolitions and destruction"—in Israel and elsewhere.[24] In a different geopolitical context, Yael Navaro-Yashin's ethnographic work shows how life in the depopulated home of one's enemy produces a fragmented, if not failed, sense of belonging. When "one's very dinner table, lounge or bedroom" and "the night gown she wears or the cookery she uses" are items belonging to others, collected or found in the aftermath of war, one is unable to be fully at home, she argues.[25] But it seems that over time, this conflictual attachment ("melancholic," in her terms) is negotiated and sublimated. Tovi Fenster's work on home and belonging in Israel/Palestine includes several interviews with women who used to live in depopulated Palestinian homes. Her mother, one of these interviewees, claimed: "We didn't steal it" (referring to her home as well as the furniture she collected from other Palestinian houses in Jaffa). "We got it, that's why I felt at home. The table where we used to eat every Friday night even after I got married, the bed I slept in, we were having guests and we were laughing and talking and this was a family."[26] Note again the role of the table and the bed, which emphasize the

still standing, usually surrounded or partly covered by Jewish neighborhoods; (vii) villages only partly destroyed or intact, which have been taken over by Jewish residents; (viii) preserved villages that have been transformed into museums or artist colonies; (ix) intact buildings used by Israeli institutions; (x) destroyed villages turned into parks; and (xi) Arab villages preserved and repopulated by Palestinian refugees.

24 Leshem, *Life after Ruin*, 17. See also Tovi Fenster, "Do Palestinians Live across the Road? Address and the Micropolitics of Home in Israeli Contested Urban Spaces." *Environment and Planning A: Economy and Space* 46, no. 10 (2014): 2435–51; Susan Slyomovics, *The Object of Memory: Arab and Jew Narrate the Palestinian Village* (Philadelphia: University of Pennsylvania Press, 1998).

25 Yael Navaro-Yashin, "Affective Spaces, Melancholic Objects: Ruination and the Production of Anthropological Knowledge," *Journal of the Royal Anthropological Institute* 15, no. 1 (2009): 6. Navaro-Yashin's work focuses on Turkish Cypriots who have come to inhabit the homes of Greek Cypriots after the partition and mass expulsions. She shows how such practices of appropriation produce political and personal melancholia. They shape a sociopolitical system that is based on the integration of that which it wants to reject (the enemy). Ruins are conceptualized by her as abject, yet unlike the models of Kristeva and Mary Douglas, in her case study "the abject, or 'the ruin', is not that against which the social order or political system was defined. Rather, the abject has become central to the social order or the political system itself" (6). Bryant, however, questions this conclusion, based on ethnographic work in similar sites during the same time (Bryant, "History's Remainders").

26 Tovi Fenster, "Moving between Addresses: Home and Belonging for Jewish Migrant and Indigenous Palestinian Women over Seventy in Israel," *Home Cultures* 10, no. 2 (2013): 172. There are many autobiographical or ethnographic accounts of Jews who became owners of Palestinian homes that

material life that ended and the lives that came to replace them. In the syntax of this sentence, the bed connects the intimacy of the couple (the marriage that precedes it in the sentence) with the wider community of friends and family. Indeed, Rebecca Bryant observes that it is often belongings—which are objects she defines via "possession, desire, and mutual interdependence"—that maintain or interrupt the attachment to homes, communities, and even historical narratives and political horizons.[27] Furniture therefore returns in many of the accounts in this chapter, as in the trigger for Soraya's vomiting, Segev's analysis, or the conversation between Said and Ibrahim Abu-Lughod below.

The fact that the history, told by Fenster's mother, of both house and belonging remained a secret for years attests to the threat that this history en-

Story II

Edward Said never knocked on the door when he visited his home in Jerusalem. "More than anything else, it was the house I did not, could not, enter that symbolized the eerie finality of a history that looked at me from behind the shaded windows, across an immense gulf I found myself unable to cross."* Therefore, the current story of encounter takes a slightly different form. Rather than a story of Said's encounter with the persons inhabiting his home, it is a story of Said's encounter with the Israeli news reporter Ari Shavit, who interviewed him for the Israeli daily *Ha'aretz*. Nonetheless, the first lines of the interview in the Hebrew edition frame it as a story of encounter between present and former homeowners: "Fifty-three years ago, Edward Said's family lived in the Jerusalem neigh-

* Edward W. Said, *The Politics of Dispossession: The Struggle for Palestinian Self-Determination 1969-1994* (New York: Knopf Doubleday, [1995] 2012), 181. Said visited his home several times—the first was in June 1992, and several others followed. He accounts for these visits in many interviews, essays, and books. As we shall see in the notes below, different sentiments are reported in some of them. But he could never bring himself to go in.

just "stood there." See, e.g., Nimrod Eshel, *The Seamen's Strike* [in Hebrew] (Tel Aviv: Am Oved, 1994); Einat Fishbein, "Eviction-Construction: The Story of the Argazim Neighborhood" [in Hebrew], Adva Center, April 2003, http://www.adva.org/UserFiles/File/pinui%20binui%20shhunat%20argazim.pdf.

27 Bryant, "History's Remainders," 684.

borhood of Talbieh. Ari Shavit lives in it now."** Indeed, Shavit keeps referring to Talbieh as *his* neighborhood, and significant segments of the conversation revolve around the question of Said's entitlement to it. Long descriptions of Said's family home in Jerusalem open the interview and later become a platform for Shavit's fear of Palestinian return. "Do you personally have a right to return, a right to return to Talbieh in Jerusalem?" Shavit asks, and Said replies: "For me, Talbieh is a house. The family house, located on Brenner Street, by what is today a small park. When I went there for the first time in 1992, I had with me a deed to my family's house, given to me by my uncle. He wanted me to see what could be done." Shavit finds such a demand difficult to digest. He re-asks the question regarding this return several times, at some point realizing (though he still must ask, as if finding it impossible to conceive): "So the demand to return is not abstract. It's not only a metaphor. Do you really mean it?"*** Said insists that he does. In the most concrete way. Probably unable to endure the implications of Said's response, Shavit completely reframes it at the end of the interview, in a paragraph that merits quoting in full. This paragraph is brought only to the Hebrew-speaking reader (this paragraph, too, was not translated in the English version of the article) after the interview has ended, in Shavit's voice rather than Said's—above the latter's words, despite them, against them:

** Ari Shavit, "My Right of Return," *Ha'aretz*, September 25, 2003, https://www.haaretz .co.il/misc/1.912891; my translation. The English translation begins differently. English version at Edward W. Said, *Power, Politics, and Culture: Interviews with Edward W. Said*, ed. Gauri Viswanathan (New York: Vintage Books, 2001).

*** It might be important to note, however, that in a visit to his home documented in *In Search of Palestine* (1998), Said himself insists that his attachment to the place is not physical, as he has "resigned [himself] to the loss." It is rather "intellectual and cultural, and in some sense spiritual" (he would later add: moral). Whereas Said comes to insist on the materiality of return in the interview with Shavit, in the documentary it is Ibrahim Abu-Lughod, who accompanies him, who refuses to relinquish the materiality of loss—of home and attachment. Abu-Lughod asks, if only as a joke, whether Said thinks the bed in which he was born is still there, embodying, once again, through the reference to furniture (and moreover, a bed) the most intimate, physical, direct sense of attachment to the place. (See also the analysis in Amahl Bishara, "House and Homeland," 150–51.)

What characterizes the New York scholar is a combination of several fascinating paradoxes: on the one hand, Said is probably the most famous Palestinian refugee in the West, but on the other, he is not entirely a refugee, at least not according to his own definition. . . . On the one hand, Said is considered to be a resolute critic of imperialism, particularly British imperialism, but on the other, he is not a victim of this imperialism but rather a typical and successful product of it: he was educated in the schools of the British Empire in Egypt, to which he was sent owing to the capital his father made as a merchant under the patronage of the Empire and thanks to his close ties with it. So perhaps the real personal drama of Said has to do with the fact that his *real lost homeland was not Palestine*. Said's lost homeland is *not geographical at all, but rather cultural.* It was a Mediterranean bourgeois culture, Christian-Arab, open, pluralistic, that evolved in the eastern *Mediterranean* in the second half of the twentieth century. But this culture was dependent on the patronage of the large European powers, and when they retreated from the Middle East, it dissolved. Thus, the *real disaster* that defined the life of the individual person Edward Said *was not the 1948* Nakba but the collapse of the class and culture to which he belonged. *This collapse turned Said, his family members and his fellow Christian-Arab bourgeoisie into placeless, stateless people, without any cultural home.*[****]

Not the Nakba but the collapse of empires; not an imperial domination but its very decline; the loss not of place but of cultural affiliations; not land but culture; not concrete homes but metaphorical, abstract ones. Thus, Shavit, representing the voice of Israelis, does not carry any responsibility for this loss, which is an outcome of imperial realignments, and his own home in Talbieh no longer represents any form of dispossession. But this paragraph is so foreign to the words preceding it that one must wonder how the two can inhabit the same article. Ann Stoler reminds us that "people know and do not know, not sequentially but at the very same time." This paragraph illustrates how "knowing is disabled, attention is redirected, things are renamed, and disregard is

[****] Shavit, "My Right of Return"; my translation, my italics.

revived and sustained."****** It is not that Shavit is blind; he goes to *see* Said's house and describes it elaborately at the beginning of the piece. It is not that he refuses to *listen*; he conducts a lengthy interview and brings Said's words to print. But *at the same time*, he does something to these words; he "renames," "disables," and "disregards" them, to use Stoler's terms.

****** Ann Laura Stoler, "Colonial Aphasia: Race and Disabled Histories in France," *Public Culture* 23, no. 1 (winter 2011): 141, 153.

tails. Thus, even though she declares she did not steal anything and felt at home, she also tells Fenster in another interview: "I'm uncomfortable with it, because it shows that the Arabs were right."[28] Yet ultimately, this threat has been negotiated so that it would not disturb the sense of belonging and home. The mother does not exhibit the same conflictual attitude to place and belonging found in Navaro-Yashin's accounts. The threat is still present and still calls for a variety of strategies to defuse it (such as the claim of symmetry in *Stranger in My Home*, the reframing of words in Shavit's account of Said, and the secrets kept by Fenster's mother) but has been almost dissolved. In such cases, knowledge of past injustices and the realization that one's home is indeed an act of theft might lead not to a rejection of this violence and a search for more justice but, rather, to further entrenching oneself in one's position, one's home. In a way at least, this process of confrontation and entrenchment is the story of this chapter.

A Home That Is Another's

According to a famous tale that has been cited (in slightly different versions) by several scholars, a fact-finding delegation sent to Palestine in the 1890s by the Jewish Congress reported back that "the bride is beautiful but is married to another man."[29] Several decades and a few wars later, Levi Eshkol, then prime minister, expressed a similar sentiment when, three months after the 1967 war, he told Golda Meir, then the Labor Party's general secretary: "I

28 Fenster, "Do Palestinians Live across the Road?," 2437.
29 E.g., Benjamin Beit-Hallahmi, *Original Sins: Reflections on the History of Zionism and Israel* (London: Palgrave Macmillan, 1992), 74; Ghada Karmi, *Married to Another Man: Israel's Dilemma in Palestine* (Ann Arbor: Pluto Press, 2007); Avi Raz, *The Bride and the Dowry: Israel, Jordan, and the Palestinians*

understand . . . you covet the dowry, but not the bride."[30] As Neve Gordon argues, this articulates the "first separation principle" of colonization (which he ascribes to the 1967 occupation but, as we see with the case of the first delegation, is embedded into Zionism from its outset): the separation of land (the bride in the first story or dowry in the second) and people (the other man in the first and the bride in the second).[31] In these domestic, if not sexual analogies, the object of desire—be it a married woman or money—is the land. Other people (the bride herself or her husband) interrupt the possibility of peacefully consummating it. Those others, however, are an obstacle not only to settlement (the realization of the love of territory) but also to desire as such: in the first story, a married woman may be an object of desire, but this desire is likely to be more ambivalent, and the object of desire may be abandoned eventually; this was indeed the proposal made by the Zionist delegation. In the second case, we may wonder about the failures in the order of desire when desire is not attached to its intended object—bride—but to a materiality that comes to replace it—dowry. The pattern follows those of familiar thrillers: the obstacle for desire must be removed. If the settlers' "libidinal economy," as Veracini has called it, is invested in the idea of the virginity of the land (its "emptiness"), then the most proximate alternative to virginity is to turn the married wife or, in the second version, the newly wedded husband, into a widow(er).[32] What is revealed in this analogy goes beyond the need to separate land and people by various means, on which many have elaborated.[33] What is important for the

in the Aftermath of the June 1967 War (New Haven, CT: Yale University Press, 2012). Shai Afsai, however, claims this myth was never established in any primary resource. Shai Afsai, "'The Bride Is Beautiful, but She Is Married to Another Man': Historical Fabrication and an Anti-Zionist Myth," *Shofar: An Interdisciplinary Journal of Jewish Studies* 30, no. 3 (spring 2012): 35–61.

30 Cited in Neve Gordon, "From Colonization to Separation: Exploring the Structure of Israel's Occupation," *Third World Quarterly* 29, no. 1 (2005): 29.

31 Gordon, "From Colonization to Separation," 29. See also his *Israel's Occupation* (Berkeley: University of California Press, 2008).

32 Lorenzo Veracini, "Settler Collective, Founding Violence and Disavowal: The Settler Colonial Situation," *Journal of Intercultural Studies* 29, no. 4 (2008): 370. Or, in Francis Jennings's words in regard to a different context: "The American land was more like a widow than a virgin. Europeans did not find a wilderness here; rather, however involuntarily, they made one." Francis Jennings, *The Invasion of America: Indians, Colonialism, and the Cant of Conquest* (Chapel Hill: University of North Carolina Press, [1975] 2010), 30.

33 E.g., Falah, "1948 Israeli-Palestinian War"; Forman and Kedar, "From Arab Land"; Gordon, *Israel's Occupation*; Nur Masalha, *Expulsion of the Palestinians: The Concept of "Transfer" in Zionist Political Thought, 1882–1948* (Washington, DC: Institute for Palestine Studies, 1992); Ilan Pappé, *The Ethnic Cleansing of Palestine* (London: One World, 2006).

sake of my argument here is that the domestic/sexual analogy shows the collapse—or at least destabilization—of the attachment to the object of desire. It renders vivid the "painful conflict between fantasy and reality" that, according to Veracini, is "bound to produce a traumatic outcome."[34]

SHORTLY AFTER HE IMMIGRATED to Palestine in 1909, Yosef Haim Brenner, one of the pioneers of Hebrew literature and an important Zionist figure, expressed the radical impossibility embedded in the Zionist desire for Palestine and the ethos of a Jewish homeland: "Who can imagine the pain of the unfortunate intelligent Jew who comes here, desirous of a different life, more wholesome, filled with physical labor, the fragrance of the fields—and who, after a few days, realizes that the dream was false, that the land already belongs to Arab Christians, that our farmers are but farmers in the abstract, and that there is no hope here for our people?"[35]

As Anita Shapira notes, this "traumatic realization that haunted him all the years of his life in Palestine" created a dubious sense of belonging, manifested by the fact that "Brenner referred to Palestine as 'my land' in quotation marks."[36] The erasure of Arab Muslims in the above quote notwithstanding, I am interested here in the pain—the physical reaction to what Shapira refers to as a "traumatic realization" that others inhabit the land. It is a pain that comes from the sense of a fraudulent desire, a fantasy falling apart; the pain of loss of what was never there: a home that cannot be realized. Brenner acknowledges here that a home that can be inhabited only via an act—acts—of violence, a home that already belongs to someone else, does not provide a "wholesome" sense of belonging.[37]

This collapsing fantasy of both Brenner and the Zionist delegation has to do with the nature of the land, its being inhabited by someone else. But as the process of settlement evolves, the content and form of both fantasy and its col-

---

34 Veracini, "Settler Collective," 365, 368.

35 Yosef Haim Brenner, *The Writings of Yosef Haim Brenner* [in Hebrew], vol. 4 (Tel Aviv: Shtibel, 1937), 153; translated in Anita Shapira, *Land and Power: The Zionist Resort to Force, 1881–1948* (Stanford, CA: Stanford University Press, 1999), 54–55. The farmers are abstract because, in fact, it was Palestinian workers who cultivated the land.

36 Shapira, *Land and Power*, 54.

37 There are many other such stories from the time. Ahad Ha'am, who visited Palestine in 1891, wrote a description of the journey organized around a fantasy breaking apart. It opens with the "meditations and fantasies" (in Hebrew: *dimionot*, also translatable as "illusions") he had

lapse change. Above all, the fantasy itself must reckon with one's active role in the dispossession of these others.

In 1949, S. Yizhar wrote *Khirbet Khizeh*, a novella describing the destruction of a Palestinian village in 1948. In the novella, years after the destruction of the village, its ruins continued to hound those passing through them, those who, we presume, took part in its demolition but perhaps also those who followed: "These bare villages, the day was coming when they would begin to cry out. As you went through them, all of a sudden, without knowing where from, you found yourself silently followed by invisible eyes of walls, courtyards, and alleyways. Desolate abandoned silence. Your guts clenched."[38] A gut clenching; nausea. These desolated houses should not, will not, give rest to those who destroyed them. Several years later, reflecting on the process of writing this text, Yizhar commented: "When I wrote the story . . . I wrote it as someone who'd been hurt. Hurt because something happened there that I was completely unable to reconcile myself with. . . . [T]he act of expelling the residents and blowing up the houses of the village shook me to the very core. There was something here that went against my whole outlook on life."[39] Again: unbearable pain that undoes the sense of who one is. A wound in the attachment. Have the walls stopped crying out by Irit's time?

IN HER ANALYSIS of "cruel optimism," Lauren Berlant identifies "a binding to fantasies that block the satisfactions they offer, and a binding to the promise of optimism as such that the fantasies have come to represent."[40] Bringing Berlant's framework into this context is an effort to identify fantasies of home that block the very promise of settlement, alongside a binding to the promise of

---

about Eretz Israel and moves quickly to the reality on the ground—a reality of "ruins" and "wretched conditions." The essay is accordingly titled "Truth from Eretz Yisrael" ["Emet M'eretz Yisrael"], published originally as a series of essays in the *Ha'aretz* newspaper. After his fantasies of a "virgin land" crumble, Ahad Ha'am leaves "the land which [he] craved" "with a broken heart and spirit" (see also Shapira, *Land and Power*, 42–43). For similar such reports of fragile belonging, see Baruch Kimmerling, "Sovereignty, Ownership, and 'Presence' in the Jewish-Arab Territorial Conflict: The Case of Bir'im and Ikrit," *Comparative Political Studies* 10, no. 2 (July 1977): 168.

38 S. Yizhar, *Khirbet Khizeh*, trans. Nicholas de Lange and Yaacob Dweck (London: Granta Books, [1949] 2011), 26.

39 Quoted in Anita Shapira, "Hirbet Hizah: Between Remembrance and Forgetting," in *Making Israel*, ed. Benny Morris (Ann Arbor: University of Michigan Press, 2007), 86–87.

40 Lauren Berlant, *Cruel Optimism* (Durham, NC: Duke University Press, 2011), 51.

these fantasies that makes them linger. This lingering means that even though these fantasies of home hinder settlement, they are not replaced by others, and hence people tend to put down roots in the land nonetheless. As noted, these are fantasies of home that create pain and injury—of others, but therefore also of the self, as in the case of Brenner and Yizhar. And it is not sufficient to dismiss this pain to self as a mode of "shoot first, cry later,"[41] because the self is genuinely coming undone here and is no longer capable of fully inhabiting a stance or a place. What we see with Irit, with Shavit, with the homeowners in *Stranger in My Home*, what I want to understand here, is the very disappearance of this mode of being undone.

Temporality plays a crucial role in this disappearance. As generations progress, the Nakba disappears from Jewish consciousness and the ability to deny Israeli violence is perfected.[42] This is a claim I shall problematize in this chapter but that has truth to it; as we are bordering questions of the collective psyche, explanations can—must—remain inconsistent. Irit, unlike her grandmother (or we can say: unlike Fenster's mother, or Yizhar), did not have an active part in dispossession, did not see it in its eventual form. She may not even have seen the more intimate reminders of Palestinian lives—the bed, the table, the picture frames—as her parents disposed of them at some point. She could therefore sideline it, dissociate it from herself. And, moreover, it was never "hers" in the same way (Said would say the same thing about how he relates to this violence from the point of view of its victims).[43] But when Soraya knocks on her door, Irit's own reality as a settler becomes inescapable, and she has to

41 "Shoot first, cry later" is a cynical phrase often used to refer to Israelis who articulate a left critique based on their own participation in war, occupation, or human rights violations. Rather than refusing to "shoot" at all (that is, to participate in the forces that generate political oppression and death), these people, so the phrase claims, participate and then criticize. Furthermore, in their critique, they tend to center on their pain ("cry"), a pain that has been caused by committing injustice and thus rests on a recognition that injustice has indeed been done, but a pain that comes to take center stage, rather than injustice itself. "Shoot first, cry later" is accordingly often seen as a token paid for justice rather than an actual fight for justice.

42 However, the passing of a generation may not be necessary for such a shift. Dan Rabinowitz provides an analysis of memory—collective and personal—that shows the disappearance from memory of the 1948 Palestinian exodus among those who experienced it directly. He shows how quickly Haifa's Jewish residents forgot (or sidelined from their memory) the city being emptied of Arab presence ("'The Arabs Just Left': Othering and the Construction of Self amongst Jews in Haifa before and after 1948," in *Mixed Towns, Trapped Communities: Historical Narratives, Spatial Dynamics, Gender Relations and Cultural Encounters in Palestinian-Israeli Towns*, ed. Daniel Monterescu and Dan Rabinowitz [Aldershot, UK: Ashgate, 2007], 51–64).

43 Edward W. Said, "Zionism from the Standpoint of Its Victims," *Social Text* 1 (1979): 7–58.

come to terms with the violence that is nonetheless at the foundations of her political existence. If settler colonialism is a political project whose logic is its own elimination[44]—a project whose success is dependent on its ability to hide its own structure, bury its traces, and reemerge as a national project[45]—then at this moment the project should have failed.

My desire to see Irit vomiting in response to this moment is a desire to see her simultaneously recognizing and refusing her role as a settler. It is a desire to see a bodily reaction (much like Brenner's or Yizhar's pain) to the loss of the fantasy of home—that is, of identity, a place, a world. The failure to vomit is a failure to both recognize and refuse, or (which might be just another way of saying the same thing) proof that the fantasy is in fact a different one and that the self has already accepted its role as a settler. Rather than a failure in the order of desire, as we see in the analogy of the bride, it attests to a desire that is already embedded into and cannot be undone by this violence's resurfacing. This is where I end this chapter. What follows is a fragmented account of the process through which this attachment that is intertwined with violence is produced.

Appropriating the Colonized Home

"Home" means more than just the narrow confines of one's apartment; it also implies a sense of belonging to the immediate surroundings, to the neighborhood in which we were born, to the people who live next door, to the places where we grew up, went to school and played. "Home" is the sum total of all the physical and social components that form the flesh and bones of the built-up area; and the relation between those components provides the background that permits the satisfaction of our desires and contributes to the residents' pride in the place where they live—or leaves them empty, lonely, frustrated, and uninvolved.

—RAM KARMI

In this piece,[46] Ram Karmi, a famous Israeli architect of the "second generation" who at the time also served as chief architect in the Israeli Housing and

---

44 This is a paraphrase of Wolfe's claim that the logic of elimination (of the native) is the principle of settler colonialism, but Wolfe's claim is also the logical outcome of this point: if settler colonialism must eliminate its own traces as a colonial project in order to succeed (see next note), then the native cannot be seen, i.e., must be eliminated.

45 Patrick Wolfe, *Traces of History: Elementary Structures of Race* (New York: Verso Books, 2016); Raef Zreik, "When Does a Settler Become a Native? (With Apologies to Mamdani)," *Constellations* 23, no. 3 (2016): 351-64.

46 Ram Karmi, "Human Values in Urban Architecture," in *New Trends in Urban Planning: Studies in Housing, Urban Design and Planning*, ed. Dan Soen (Oxford: Pergamon Press), 159.

Construction Ministry, tries to decipher the key to transforming houses into homes, to design a city, a neighborhood, a building that generates a sense of belonging. For Karmi, this is a way of addressing what he identifies as a crisis of blending in migrant societies. The problem to be addressed, then, is the creation of *roots* and what Karmi refers to as the "imprint of the locality" where those roots are missing. As Eyal Weizman remarked in this context, architecture here seeks to carry an "emotional message" rather than mere functionality, to construct "homes" rather than "housing."[47] And since roots are at stake, Karmi argues, cities cannot be planned "on, as it were, a blank sheet of paper."[48] To become a "home," the house must be constructed in a dialogue with the history of the place. Karmi immediately generalizes this history as "Mediterranean," thereby detaching it from its immediate Palestinian context (a familiar technique),[49] and yet, as several theories of architecture have shown, the "Mediterranean" architecture he takes as his model is very clearly Palestinian, inspired primarily by the vernacular architecture of East Jerusalem.[50]

A number of scholars have now written about this process through which Israeli architecture shifted in its attitude to "locality." The effort to protect, preserve, and even mimic Palestinian vernacular architecture as a mode of establishing an Israeli locality followed an almost opposite tendency that endeav-

47 Eyal Weizman, *Hollow Land: Israel's Architecture of Occupation* (London: Verso Books, 2007), 32, 36.
48 R. Karmi, "Human Values in Urban Architecture," 163.
49 According to Alona Nitzan-Shiftan, this shift "from the Arab village to Mediterranean architectural," which was "engrained in a larger architectural culture, . . . relieved the Israeli architect of the disturbing conflict between admiration of native architecture and disregard for the larger Palestinian culture that produced it." Alona Nitzan-Shiftan, "The Israeli 'Place' in East Jerusalem: How Israeli Architects Appropriated the Palestinian Aesthetic after the '67 War," *Jerusalem Quarterly* 27 (2006): 24. Although see Alexandra Nocke, *The Place of the Mediterranean in Modern Israeli Identity* (Leiden: Brill, 2009), for a more complicated analysis of Mediterranean identity in Israel. See also Allweil, *Homeland*, 5ff.
50 Weizman, *Hollow Land*, chapter 1; Nitzan-Shiftan, "Israeli 'Place' in East Jerusalem"; Haim Yacobi and Hadas Shadar, "The Arab Village: A Genealogy of (Post)colonial Imagination," *Journal of Architecture* 19, no. 6 (2014): 975–97. Haim Yacobi, however, shows that the "importance of the house as a source of a collective sense of identity and belonging, as a means of transforming immigrants into 'natives,'" was addressed rather by a tendency of *modernization* in architecture when it came to Mizrahi Jews (migrating from Arab countries). This allowed distancing the house/home from the local architectonic style and its inhabitants from their Arab tradition (Haim Yacobi, "Architecture, Orientalism, Identity: The Politics of the Israeli-Built Environment," *Israel Studies* 13, no. 1 [2008]: 105). The Arab house as an "imprint of the locality" is an ethno-economic privilege. I will return to this point later.

ored to move the landscape westbound and to import European architectonic trends as part of developing a "European taste."[51] According to Haim Yacobi and Hadas Shadar, this incorporation of the Palestinian landscape into Jewish Israeli identity only began after 1948, culminating in the late 1960s and early 1970s (after the 1967 war). Accordingly, if in 1938 the dominant Israeli approach was that "the Arab village is not a model for replication by us,"[52] by 1977, the Arab village or city became (for Karmi and others) the primary route allowing Jews to develop "connections, roots, identity, and the imprint of the locality" in Israel/Palestine.[53] Indeed, Karmi explicitly claimed that being "a harmonious part of its surroundings," the Arab village, unlike many tendencies in Israeli architecture, "feels 'at home.'"[54] As Jewish Israelis, we learned to feel at home in Palestinian ruins.

WHEN EXPLAINING THIS tendency to adapt Palestinian vernacular architecture, Haim Yacobi speculates that the fascination with "the Arab house" was dependent on the expulsion of the inhabitants of these houses, which rendered them "available" for Jewish cultural appropriation. This created a gap between the physical construction (the ruin) and its past residents. A ruin rather than a Palestinian village, its houses can reemerge on the cultural surface not as homes of those who were expelled (and are sometimes merely miles away) but as homes belonging to Jews who presumably inhabited them (or the space) in some ancient past. Paradoxically, then, *it is the destruction that clears Israelis from moral responsibility*. In Sharon Rotbard's words, "the ruin had always been

---

51 Yacobi and Shadar, "Arab Village," 977. The quote is from an article from an urban construction magazine called *Habinyan* (the building). The article then observed that "people are no longer captivated by the Oriental appearance. Anyway, we have relinquished the Oriental character created by the construction of domes and arcades. This reaction is necessary as well as suitable to the real demands of Jewish taste" (977–78).

52 Quote from the first issue of the architectural magazine *Habinyan*; quoted by Yacobi and Shadar, "Arab Village," 978. For an analysis of this process, its paradoxes, and its rationales as they pertain to Jerusalem, see also Nitzan-Shiftan, "Israeli 'Place' in East Jerusalem"; Danna Piroyansky, *Ramle Remade: The Israelization of an Arab Town 1948-1967* (Haifa: Pardes, 2014); Weizman, *Hollow Land*, chapter 1; Yacobi, "Architecture, Orientalism, Identity." All these sources also place this shift in a wider tendency in architecture worldwide.

53 R. Karmi, "Human Values in Urban Architecture," 164.

54 Ram Karmi, "Merkaz HaNegev: Architecture of Shade" [in Hebrew], *Kav* 3 (1965); quoted in Yacobi and Shadar, "Arab Village," 984.

but a ruin—that way one could forget that it had actually been a house once inhabited."[55] Violence and morality thus become inseparable.[56]

But while the availability of houses was surely important, something else is at play with the fact that the appropriation of "Arab" architecture followed the Nakba. This temporal proximity also means that the attachment to the Palestinian landscape and space was an attachment to largely *destroyed* houses, if not to destruction itself or the conditions of violence that brought it about. Whereas this obviously reflects Orientalist desire, and whereas it is true that destruction was aestheticized to decontextualize its violent context,[57] something additional occurs here. What we see in this attachment is the possibility that political identity is constructed, not despite destruction, beside it, through overcoming it, or ignoring it, but through and by means of destruction itself.

"Once, when I climbed Mount Carmel in search of a suitable area for a park, I suddenly heard loud explosions," famous architect and Dada painter Marcel Janco has recounted. Janco was in charge of conducting a landscape inventory survey for the state and of planning national parks during the 1950s. In this role, he was able to see the destruction of the Palestinian village Ayn Hawd—to become the Jewish village Ein Hod—but also to stop it in its midst:

> A multitude of houses were being destroyed in front of my very eyes. I asked for an explanation and was told that the army had gradually demolished an abandoned village for the past five or six years. For security reasons, it was decided that the houses should be razed. . . . I decided to get a closer look, and since I was a senior official of the Ministry of the Interior, my request to halt the explosions was granted. Thus, I was able to recognise, being an architect and an artist, that it was no ordinary Arab village, but rather an historical site . . . And indeed, Roman ruins were discovered there. . . . Undoubtedly, other archaeological remains are yet to be discovered. However, it is reasonable to think that in ancient times it was inhabited by Jews.[58]

---

55 Sharon Rotbard, *White City, Black City: Architecture and War in Tel Aviv and Jaffa*, trans. Orit Gat (London: Pluto Press, 2015), 133.

56 For a more systematic analysis, see James Eastwood, *Ethics as a Weapon of War: Militarism and Morality in Israel* (Cambridge: Cambridge University Press, 2017); Anat Matar, "What Enables Asa Kasher" [in Hebrew], *Mita'am* 6 (2006): 121–42. I return to this point in part III.

57 See discussion in the epilogue of this part: "A Phenomenology of Violence."

58 Quoted in Yacobi and Shadar, "Arab Village," 987. Yacobi further notes that "Janco's initiative has inspired many architects and urbanists who started to appreciate the 'authentic' value of the

Several things should be noted regarding these words. First, we see here, once again, a Jewish past that transpires through destruction: the Arab house, having been destroyed, can be replaced with a Roman ruin and then with biblical Jewish inhabitants. Second, destruction here is not a matter of the past but an ongoing state: As the case of Ayn Hawd/Ein Hod makes exceptionally clear, the materiality of the Arab ruin had to be preserved to withstand this aesthetic quality of ruination.[59] Furthermore, it had to be preserved as *destroyed*: Only a destroyed Palestinian house can be categorized as "antique" and come to represent a Jewish biblical ruin. Only then can it become a relic that is attached in some collective unconsciousness to a certain Jewish continuum in which "antiques" are always reminiscent of Jewish presence.[60] But since it is not really possible "to separate older ruins from new ones,"[61] the Palestinians' ruination becomes constitutive of Israeli identity. Indeed, those who came to populate these houses—in Ein Hod, Jerusalem, Jaffa, Safad, or Acre—did not come to inhabit "biblical houses"; explicitly, these houses are referred to as *Arab houses*. With this term, something in the *active destruction* enacted by Israel remains present in these traces. Finally—and this may be the most important point for me here—in these words of Janco we see quite bluntly that the attractiveness of the Palestinian ("Arab") house emerges *during the acts of demolition itself* and is sustained through keeping it at least partly destroyed.

'abandoned' villages and neighborhoods" ("Architecture, Orientalism, Identity," III). In other sources, Janco refers to this moment as a "discovery." Janco used this expression even though the villages' original inhabitants resided merely 1.2 miles away, in an unrecognized village they established after they were denied the possibility of return (it is probably these inhabitants whom the quote refers to as "infiltrators"). The discursive mechanism of "discovery" is a well-known justificatory tool in imperial formations. However, here it has a unique variant: the village has been serving various purposes for Israel itself—from temporary housing for Jews who had to abandon their homes during the war to a site for military drills in "constructed zones"—and yet it is only at the moment of destruction, as demolition takes place and as loud explosions can be heard, that its beauty can be "discovered."

59 As Susan Slyomovics shows, the ruins in these artists' colonies have been "reinforced by inserting hidden iron bars to maintain the sentimental look and mood of vernacular architecture frozen in time at the last stages of decay." The ruin had to be preserved as such, and even created if needed, for the sake of "sentiments" and "mood" (Slyomovics, *Object of Memory*, 51).

60 Nadia Abu El-Haj, *Facts on the Ground: Archaeological Practice and Territorial Self-Fashioning in Israeli Society* (Chicago: University of Chicago Press, 2001).

61 Gastón R. Gordillo, *Rubble: The Afterlife of Destruction* (Durham, NC: Duke University Press, 2014), 1.

Home and Away

We can point to two main mechanisms often seen as necessary for the endurability of violence, as they create a distance between violence and the self (see theoretical overview). The first is dissociation (refusing to see this violence as having anything to do with myself or my identity), and the second invisibility (refusing to see this violence at all). By anchoring this chapter thus far in the Jewish Israeli making-of-home within the depopulated Palestinian home, I have questioned the possibility of *dissociating* the self from violence. Since home is the place where the self is formed and a part of who one is, if this home carries violence within its walls, this violence somehow becomes part of what defines the self. In the following sections, by scaling up the lens from the concrete home to the homeland and, specifically, to the Israeli landscape, I turn to questioning the related mechanism of *invisibility*.

Much along the lines of my critique concerning dissociation, Yves Winter offers a critique of the claim that violence can endure only as long as it remains hidden or denied. Rather than a framework in which "invisibility . . . allows violence to be repeated and reproduced," he proposes we see "repetition and reproduction [of violence]" as the source of its endurance.[62] Winter refers to the repetition and reproduction of violence as that which then produces its invisibility: because it is there constantly, it becomes transparent. We are familiar with similar claims from critical discussions concerning humanitarian work: overexposure to representations of human suffering can lead to apathy, overload, and, with them, forms of not seeing.[63] And yet instead of "invisibility" we might want to talk here about "normalization"—a significant distinction, as the visual field is not re-called upon in order to mark a presumed absence of that which is there. Either way, Winter's proposition rests on the same skepticism: it questions the assumption that people do not resist orders of violence because they do not *see* them or *know* about them and proposes that this assumption "rests on a mistaken view of the public sphere, a view that assumes that making evil visible will necessarily lead to its eventual eradication."[64] Therefore, I now move to the Israeli landscape to argue that violence is both there and seen. In this argument, the ruin will replace the standing, repopulated house in order to make the same argument concerning the appropriation or even embrace of violence from a different perspective. Let us begin, however, with the more com-

---

62 Yves Winter, "Violence and Visibility," *New Political Science* 34, no. 2 (2012): 198.
63 I want to thank Michal Givoni for this analogy.
64 Winter, "Violence and Visibility," 202.

mon understanding of violence's endurance as rooted in some form of invisibility or willful blindness.

WHEN THEODOR HERZL ARRIVED in Palestine in 1898, he neither became nauseated nor was he in pain, but he instead contracted an eye infection (an outcome, perhaps, of the "dirt [that] resides in [Jerusalem's] stinky streets").[65] This intriguing combination, in which one craves a place they find so disgusting, may reflect the ambivalent structures of desire identified by Berlant or Brown, but for now I want to focus on the bodily response to the existential contradiction. The eye infection, rather than some more internal pain, is almost too perfect as a metaphor here. It embodies, first, a superficial crisis (limited to the retina) and, second, a crisis that can be solved by modes of *invisibility*: a refusal to see the violence that takes place allows this violence to endure without troubling the self-image of the liberal individual.

Even though for Herzl, too, the "moment of encounter between dream and land" was "a moment of crisis,"[66] this moment did not easily shatter his Zionist fantasy, perhaps because his fantasy was itself somewhat colonial.[67] Whereas it was clear to him that others inhabited the land—a land that could accordingly no longer be seen as "empty" or "virgin"—those others could be easily transformed into European-like people in his imagination. Those would join a diverse, yet Western-oriented society that could work as part of the imperial landscape. Haifa could thus become, in his phantasmatic descriptions of Palestine, a place easily mistaken for "some Italian port" or the French Riviera. In the city, "brilliant Oriental robes mingled with the sober costumes of the Occident, but the latter predominated." Therefore, even though there

---

65 Quoted in Rotbard, *White City, Black City*, 71. In *Altneuland*, Herzl described Jerusalem as "yet a miserable provincial town." In its streets, "shouting, odors, a flurry of dirty colors, crowds of ragged people in narrow, musty lanes, beggars, sick people, hungry children, screeching women, shouting tradesmen. The once royal city of Jerusalem could have sunk no lower." The travelers "were revolted." A "miserable railway" led to the city, and "the landscape through which they passed was a picture of desolation." Theodor Herzl, *Altneuland* (1902), trans. D. S. Blondheim, Jewish Virtual Library, [accessed August 2019], https://www.jewishvirtuallibrary.org/quot-altneuland-quot-theodor-herzl, book I, chapter 6.

66 Leshem, *Life after Ruin*, 50

67 Herzl used classical colonial tropes, such as describing the future Jewish state as "a portion of a rampart of Europe against Asia, an outpost of civilization as opposed to barbarism" (Theodor Herzl, *The Jewish State* [New York: Dover Publications, 1989], 96).

were "many Chinese, Persians and Arabs in the streets," "the city itself seemed thoroughly European."[68]

The novel *Altneuland*, from which the above descriptions are taken, shows how this apparatus of homemaking takes shape through violence, blindness, and conflicted desires. The story is of two imagined journeys to Palestine separated by twenty years, during which the protagonists travel in both the Mediterranean and the Indian Ocean, while the land changes its face, if not its geographical orientation. From "a most disagreeable" place, characterized by dirt and neglect, bad smells, and loud shouts, it is transformed by Zionist presence into Europe in the Mediterranean. Much like Herzl, whose vision may have been blurred by the eye infection, Herzl's protagonists do not see this transformation in the making, as they travel away, to reside in an island in the Indian Ocean. They return to Palestine only after the transformation— the movement of the land itself westbound, as it were—has taken place. This gap, Raef Zreik contends, "is the condition of possibility for the Jewish state to emerge." In this gap resided "the dirty demographic job that still allows Herzl to maintain his surface liberalism."[69] *But the need to not see shapes what one can want and how one can want it; it makes some modes of being and staying structurally impossible.* Dimitry Shumsky observes that "home" in *Altneuland* is made through constant movement, if not *as* mobility, "established on the journey, or more precisely—as the journey"—to the extent that "there is no [more] clear distinc-

---

68 Herzl, *Altneuland*, book II, chapters 1, 2. Importantly, it was Haifa that could appear as modern and normal. The first visit described in the book focuses on another city: Jerusalem. But Jerusalem was too tangled up in what Ernst Simon would later refer to as "the immense weight of the historic Jewish landscape and tradition." Upon seeing it, Friedrich, the protagonist of *Altneuland*, felt compelled to cry "Jerusalem!" but he could not quite understand "why the sight of this strange city affected him so powerfully." Jerusalem brought the memories of religious ceremonies from his childhood, which created a mixture of personal (familial) and collective past ("suddenly he saw himself a little boy going to synagogue with his father"). This past is contrasted with the individualized, secularized present, wherein "faith was dead . . . , youth was dead, his father was dead." And thus, while he could not but burst into tears as he saw the city's walls, he could find "nothing in common with these traffickers in the national misfortune." Jerusalem was both too religious and too rooted in the East to fit into Herzl's utopia. It could never be normalized. Ernst Simon, "What Price Israel's 'Normalcy'? A Young Nation and Its Ideals," *Commentary* 7 (1949): 47; Herzl, *Altneuland*, book I, chapter 5.

69 Raef Zreik, "Theodor Herzl (1860–1904): Sovereignty and the Two Palestines," in *Makers of Jewish Modernity: Thinkers, Artists, Leaders, and the World They Made*, ed. Jacques Picard, Jacques Revel, Michael P. Steinberg, and Idith Zertal (Princeton, NJ: Princeton University Press, 2016), 46–60.

tion between 'home' and 'away.'"[70] Thus, even as part of his colonizing fantasy, Herzl was unable to settle down in Palestine. Indeed, after his eye was infected, Herzl tried to expedite his return to Europe. Unable to find a ship leaving Palestine early enough, he embarked on a ship docking in Jaffa's port and waited on board for several days until it was ready to leave for Alexandria.[71]

ZREIK'S CLAIM THAT "the condition of possibility" of the Jewish state is the ability to not see the "dirty work" of cleansing the land (an ability that bridges violence and liberalism) echoes a large body of literature that I assembled in the theoretical overview under the title "dissociation." This body of literature explains the endurance of political violence of perpetrators or beneficiaries by pointing to various manners in which violence is distanced from the self (political or individual). The very basic claim is that violence can endure as long as it remains denied, unseen, or detached from the self. Accordingly, Zionism is often described as a vast political project of erasing the Palestinian landscape, history, and presence. This project of erasure included a destruction of Palestinians' homes during and in the aftermath of 1948–49 to prevent the return of refugees;[72] foresting the ruins of Palestinian villages to obliterate them from the visual field;[73] erasing those villages from the map by changing the names of Palestinian sites to Hebrew (often biblical) names;[74] recasting relics as belonging to a Jewish past; and erasing the more proximate Muslim and Christian past

70 Dimitry Shumsky, "'This Ship Is Zion!': Travel, Tourism, and Cultural Zionism in Theodor Herzl's 'Altneuland,'" *Jewish Quarterly Review* 104, no. 3 (summer 2014): 478, 492–93.

71 Rotbard, *White City, Black City*, 70–72.

72 Farid Abdel-Nour, "Responsibility and National Memory: Israel and the Palestinian Refugee Problem," *International Journal of Politics, Culture, and Society* 17, no. 3 (March 2004): 339–63; Arnon Golan, "The Transformation of Abandoned Arab Rural Areas," *Israel Studies* 2, no. 1 (spring 1997): 94–110; Morris, *Birth of the Palestinian Refugee Problem*, 309ff.

73 Ghazi Falah, "The 1948 Israeli-Palestinian War and Its Aftermath," 256–85; Tovi Fenster, "Zikaron, shayachut ve-tichnun merhavi be-yisrael" [Memory, belonging, and spatial planning in Israel], *Theory and Criticism* 30 (2007): 189–212.

74 Meron Benvenisti, "The Hebrew Map," in *Sacred Landscape: The Buried History of the Holy Land Since 1948* (Berkeley: University of California Press, 2000), 11–54; Liora Bigon and Amer Dahamshe, "An Anatomy of Symbolic Power: Israeli Road-Sign Policy and the Palestinian Minority," *Environment and Planning D: Society and Space* 32, no. 4 (January 2014): 606–21; Joyce Dalsheim, "Settler Nationalism, Collective Memories of Violence and the 'Uncanny Other,'" *Social Identities* 10, no. 2 (2004): 151–70; Nur Masalha, *A Land without a People: Israel, Transfer, and the Palestinians 1949–96* (London: Faber, 1997).

FIGURES 2.1–2.3. The Hermon River at the edge of the Golan Heights (2.1); Hulata (2.2); and Katzrin (2.3). What is seen in these scenes of war's integration into daily life in Israel? Are those tanks and airplanes still remnants of violence? And if so, which violence? Is it the violence of Israel during the war or the violence from which it suffered? Is it victory that is commemorated here or victimhood? Might or survival? And is there any commemoration taking place? Are we reminded of lost lives—and whose lives?—or of vanquishing an enemy? These are the traces of that which has been destroyed, but also the tools of destruction. Photographs by Oded Balilty. © Oded Balilty/AP/Shutterstock.

of archaeological sites.[75] All this has been done alongside reviving the past Jewish presence: biblical myths have been attached to concrete loci; archaeological sites have been constructed to produce a continuum of a Jewish presence in the land; history has been condensed to and within spatial gravitation points that are taken to prove and produce Jewish ownership.[76]

But the tale about Herzl may be a way of arguing that efforts to erase, deny and dissociate, to not see violence, to outsource it to others while one takes a

75 Abu El-Haj, *Facts on the Ground*; Nur Masalha, *The Bible and Zionism: Invented Traditions, Archaeology and Post-Colonialism in Israel-Palestine* (London: Zed Books, 2007).
76 A slightly more ambivalent version of this story of denial and resurrection can be found in Anita Shapira's account of the debates around the book *The Story of Hirbet Hizah*. Anita Shapira, "Hirbet Hizah," 81–123.

trip to the Indian Ocean, are eventually doomed to fail; and when one is forced to see, one's eyes become sick, nauseated perhaps, like an effort of the body to vomit the vision itself by secreting mucus. As noted, however, the larger part of this chapter seeks to move beyond these mechanisms as a sufficient frame for explaining living with one's own violence—not to say that denial, invisibility, or deferral do not take place, and also not to say that often, these mechanisms necessarily *fail*, even though they do; but beyond both these arguments, to suggest that we should see that they are *insufficient, even misleading at times, as frameworks through which to understand the durability of violence.*

Home in the Ruins

Unlike Herzl, who visited Palestine and immediately left (or had to come and go so as not to see too much, as in *Altneuland*), those who stay cannot but see. Their vision becomes accustomed to violence and their eyes remain clear and free of infection. A complete denial or erasure of violence is never possible in contexts of settler colonialism; the violence of the past (if not the present) confronts us too often, too intimately.

The Israeli visual field is inlaid with remnants of past violence that, in being part of the daily view, are simultaneously denied and asserted. Israeli tanks or old military airplanes can be found in parks or playgrounds, and ruins of Palestinian homes often "decorate" serene scenery for hikes or family picnics. The violence that these remnants constantly remind us of, but with this constant reminder also make banal, has become an essential part of the personal history of many who grew up in this place. "When one travels in Israel," Noga Kadman writes, "it is almost impossible to avoid seeing piles of stones, ruins, collapsing walls and structures overgrown with uncultivated almond and fig trees, rolling terraces crumbling with disuse, and long hedges of prickly cactuses."[77] These scenes of what appears to the willingly blind eye as "uncultivated" beauty (or, as a more critical account would suggest, as that which has been carefully "preserved and presented as an organic part of the landscape")[78] are woven into the memories of family leisure time, after-school activities, youth mischiefs, or simply being at home. The point, then, is not that we could not see the remnants of violence, but that we saw them all the time and almost everywhere.

77 Noga Kadman, *Erased from Space and Consciousness: Israel and the Depopulated Palestinian Villages of 1948* (Bloomington: Indiana University Press, 2015), 1.
78 Hochberg, *Visual Occupation*, 39.

Many Israelis with whom I spoke about this project insisted that, even though the destroyed Palestinian houses were there, even though the traces of the Nakba were there, even though some of us inhabited those houses, even though some of our parents or grandparents collected "memorabilia" that were left behind by escaping Palestinians (recall the pots and pans, beds and tables), we could not *really* see them or, at least, could not understand what they represented. But of course we could, and we often did. "The parameters by which we determine what is or isn't included within the realm of the visual is itself a matter open to dispute," Gil Hochberg reminds us.[79] And even though it is true that we might have narrated those objects or landscapes in ways that have distanced the violence they make visible, blindness is not a sufficient concept here. Stoler's observation that colonial memory is unruly and that what is remembered and acknowledged is also denied and forgotten, only to be "rediscovered," might be more appropriate in this context, or Cohen's insistence on denial as a mechanism that already assumes preexisting knowledge.[80] Such alternative frameworks call us to see the dialectic of visual memory, the conflicted and complex relations to facts that cannot be reduced to a refusal to see or know.

Noam Leshem's critique of Meron Benvenisti is a telling example in the current context. Benvenisti coined the term *white patches* to explain how the Arab landscape was erased as part of the Zionist project: whereas the Jews were, "of course, aware of the Arab communities," he argues, the Arab "towns, villages and neighborhoods had no place in the Jews' perception of the homeland's landscape."[81] "But," writes Leshem,

> at the end of that same paragraph, Benvenisti goes on to claim that, "The attitude of the Jewish population toward the Arab landscape— physical and human alike—was a strange mixture of disregard, anxiety, affection, superiority, humanitarianism, anthropological curiosity, romanticism and above all, European ethnocentricity." The reduction of such a plenitude of interests and diversity of motivations to all-encompassing notions of "white patches" or to the common trope of "empty land" is illustrative of the broader analytical need for a more

---

79 Hochberg, *Visual Occupation*, 37.

80 Stanley Cohen, States of Denial: Knowing about Atrocities and Suffering (Cambridge: Polity Press, 2001); Stoler, "Colonial Aphasia"; see also Shapira, "Hirbet Hizah." For further analysis, see theoretical overview.

81 Meron Benvenisti, *Sacred Landscape*, 56.

FIGURES 2.4–2.5. Destruction as beauty: Soreq stream, Jerusalem. Source (top): Israel Antiquities Authorities. Another image on this website notes: "retaining wall of farming terrace, built on ancient wall." Source (bottom): Yehuda Dagan and Leticia Barda, "Jerusalem, Upper Nahal Soreq, Survey," *Hadashot Arkheologiyot*, October 4, 2009, http://www.hadashot -esi.org.il/report_detail_eng.aspx?id=1222&mag_id=115.

nuanced approach to the contradictory actualities of colonized space in Israel/Palestine.[82]

What Leshem identifies here goes far beyond Benvenisti's own blind spot—an inability to see not so much the Palestinian communities themselves but the fact that they were, indeed, seen. Benvenisti's need to replace the plurality of relations to the Palestinian presence with an account of a complete "erasure" might be a function of his own inability to deal with the implications of seeing and knowing. After all, it is easier to explain one's ability to destroy in light of one's blindness to destruction and its effects. Perhaps this is why, as we saw, so much of the critical literature on the Israeli landscape emphasizes erasure and so much of the literature on Israeli discourse and memory in this context emphasizes blindness. Without these paradigms, an affirmative relation to destruction must be contended with. It is this affirmative relation that I seek to explain through the work of memory or visibility. What is of interest to me here, then, is how a collective can take a form that integrates these remnants of violence into its identity and how this collective identity then feeds into present, and ongoing, violence.

My argument in regard to this visual saturation of traces of violence in the Israeli landscape is similar to, yet crucially different from, Gil Hochberg's claim concerning the (necessary) failure to erase the violence of the past: "these repeated attempts to erase, resignify, and evacuate the historical meaning of the Palestinian ruins . . . nevertheless fail (they are *bound to fail*) to successfully repress the haunting impact that these ruins continue to have over Israelis and Israeli culture," Hochberg argues.[83] This impossibility to erase and deny the past (as well as the present, we must add) is, according to her, what animates resistance and what disrupts Zionist narratives.[84] At this point, our arguments depart: The last claim concerning animated resistance as a function of the inevitable visibility of the past must rest on the idea that the resurfacing of violence *interrupts* identity,

---

82 Leshem, *Life after Ruin*, 52. Leshem quotes Benvenisti from *Sacred Landscape*, 56.

83 Hochberg, *Visual Occupation*, 41.

84 Hochberg, *Visual Occupation*, 41. See also Noam Leshem, "Anti-Erasure: The Survival of Space between Salameh and Kfar Shalom" [in Hebrew], in *Place Names and Spatial Identity in Israel-Palestine: Majority-Minority Relations, Obliviating and Memory*, ed. Amer Dahamshe and Yosef Schwartz (Tel Aviv: Tel Aviv University Press, 2018), 164–65. Leshem argues that focusing on the violence of erasure and neglecting to account for all that has remained takes for granted the success of the endeavor to create a hegemonic space and thus undermines, or refuses to recognize, possibilities of resistance.

and this is indeed Hochberg's claim. Yet her words also open the possibility of making an altogether different argument (again, not to contradict, but to add to this cyclical destruction): Since, as she says, the "visible invisibility" of such traces is "a central feature in Israeli cultural and political imagination,"[85] one cannot simply talk in this context about an *interruption* of identity; one must seriously consider the possibility that Israeli identity *cannot be separated* from these landscapes of violence. Thus, while some sites of destruction were erased, forested, or flattened, others became sites of attachment: the "rolling terraces" and fig trees serving as a picnic site, the pools or semi-destroyed *khans* in which children play.

The Self and Its Violence (Appropriation) and the Parameters of the Argument

What we have seen thus far are modes of appropriating houses that are both symbolic (the adoption of an architectonic style or the attachment to a landscape) and material (the occupation of depopulated houses). In both, the home of the Palestinian—most often a *destroyed* home—becomes a mark and an anchor of Israeli identity. "What is more Israeli than an abandoned Palestinian area?" asks Alona Nitzan-Shiftan. "What conveys local Israeli ambience more than Ein-Hod, old Jaffa, or Ein Kerem—all populated by artists who incorporated the abandoned villages into their existence and their lifestyles? These villages of exile, the heart of Palestinian pain, were transformed by their hands into artists' colonies, or, more significantly, into inspirational models for 'local' Israeli building." Hebrew nativity is thus "constructed on the ruins of the localness of the other."[86]

It is as if this attachment to a landscape of ruination comes to resolve the dual crisis of belonging that this chapter has thus far hinged on: the crisis, identified by Karmi, of a migrant society without roots and the crisis of belonging, depicted in the second section of this chapter, in which one's place is revealed to be another's. If the land is both not-yet-mine (a lack of roots) and someone else's, identity can be formed in a less conflictual way by entangling my identity with the Palestinian's, thereby rendering myself indigenous or indigenous-like.[87] Indeed, alongside architectonic style or concrete homes,

85 Hochberg, *Visual Occupation*, 42.
86 Alona Nitzan-Shiftan, "Seizing Locality in Jerusalem," in *The End of Tradition?*, ed. Nezar Al-Sayyad (London: Routledge, 2004), 236–37.
87 See, for example, Baruch Kimmerling, *Clash of Identities: Explorations in Israeli and Palestinian Societies* (New York: Columbia University Press, 2010).

food,[88] dress or body language,[89] vocabulary,[90] names of places,[91] symbols,[92] and even local people[93] have been incorporated into the Israeli Jewish identity in an

88 What is celebrated as authentic Israeli food is often taken from local Arab cuisine: hummus, labane, falafel. The lineages of culinary heritage and ownership of food have been a matter of many heated debates, including an escalation into a "hummus war" in 2008. For more, see Nir Avieli, "The Hummus Wars Revisited: Israeli-Arab Food Politics and Gastromediation," *Gastronomica: The Journal of Critical Food Studies* 16, no. 3 (fall 2016): 19–30; Rafi Grosglik, "Organic Hummus in Israel: Global and Local Ingredients and Images," *Sociological Research Online* 16, no. 2 (June 2011): 1–11; Yonatan Mendel and Ronald Ranta, *From the Arab Other to the Israeli Self: Palestinian Culture in the Making of Israeli National Identity* (London: Ashgate, 2016), chapter 3; see also the interlude to part III of this book.

89 Gil Eyal shows how in the prestate years, *hashomer* members and other paramilitary organizations used to dress up as Bedouins and adopt their appearance. Gil Eyal, *The Disenchantment of the Orient: Expertise in Arab Affairs and the Israeli State* (Stanford, CA: Stanford University Press, 2006), chapter 2. See below for further analysis.

90 Arabic has been marginalized and derogated in Israeli culture and is taught and perceived mostly as the language of the enemy. In a survey quoted by Mendel and Ranta, 50 percent of the participating Jewish citizens reported that hearing Arabic "made them fearful" (*From Arab Other to Israeli Self*, 46). However, many Arabic words did find their way into common Israeli vocabulary, mostly as curses. See Yonatan Mendel, *The Creation of Israeli Arabic: Political and Security Considerations in the Making of Arabic Language Studies in Israel* (London: Palgrave Macmillan, 2014).

91 In the course of crafting what Meron Benvenisti refers to as "the Hebrew map," two processes took place. The first was an erasure of Arab names, to eradicate any memory of the destroyed places. The map was meant to erase "in print what had been already eradicated in actuality—or what 'should have been.'" But often, a second process took place: the Arab names were not erased but incorporated and appropriated. Presumably, this process of Hebrewizing names was a "restoration" of the biblical origin from what was claimed to be the Arabic distortion of the ancient Hebrew name. Yet actually, in a manner that at times "bordered on outright falsification," it was *Arab* names that were borrowed, distorted, and adapted to a Hebrew ear without any proven anchor in some ancient "origin." Benvenisti, *Sacred Landscape*, 41, 35.

92 From Jaffa oranges to the very ideal of the *sabra*, symbols that marked the Arab communities in Palestine were taken to represent the new Jews in Eretz Israel. In this process, many of these symbols "were validated through a process of reconstructive historical writing." They were "either given a Jewish and Zionist identity or were related to biblical and Jewish historical precedents" (Mendel and Ranta, *From Arab Other to Israeli Self*, 52). Honaida Ghanim observes that at the edge of this process, there is an effort to appropriate indigeneity itself ("On Natives, Specters, and Shades of Ruins" [in Hebrew], in *Indigeneity and Exile in Israel/Palestine*, ed. Shaul Seter [Tel Aviv: Tel Aviv University Press, 2014]).

93 Bedouins and Palestinian peasants were seen as embodying modes of living of the ancient Hebrews. "The noble savage meets the biblical Israelite," Raz-Krakotzkin puts this tendency in a wider, orientalist perspective (Amnon Raz-Krakotzkin, "Zionist Return to the West and the Mizrachi Jewish Perspective," in *Orientalism and the Jews*, ed. Ivan Kalmar and Derek Penslar

effort to craft a "Jewish-Israeli 'localness' and 'indigenousness.'"[94] Almost para-doxically, then, Palestinian *presence* was taken to produce the same continuum that was produced by the myth of "empty land" and by the concrete removal of a long history of Arab presence in Palestine.

The incorporation of local/Palestinian elements into Jewish Israeli identity is often analyzed alongside Homi Bhabha's account of colonial mimicking.[95] Yet it may also be seen as a colonial reversal of Fanon's fantasy of decoloniza-tion. The latter is not simply a fantasy of demolition or destruction but of "possession": "to sit at the settler's table, to sleep in the settler's bed, with his wife if possible."[96] Again: the table, the bed—the furniture through which the attachment to the home/space becomes tangible. It is a fantasy of—a process of—*replacement*; re-place-ment; taking place; taking *the* place of the settler. (De)colonization here is not strictly a mode of *becoming* the other (though see the analysis of Gil Eyal below) but of appropriating place, belongings, furniture, wives, as if to ground the act of taking place in the most concrete and intimate materiality; new political orders as established, or at least symbolized, by mov-ing into someone else's home, the home of the defeated.

Central to my argument is that the appropriated trace is a trace of *violence* and that, through it, violence itself is being appropriated. Thus far, I have fo-cused on destruction as that which is appropriated; Gil Eyal's account provides a different vantage point from which to support this claim. Eyal shows that in the prestate years, Jewish militant groups tended to corporeally mimic Bed-

[Waltham, MA: Brandeis University Press, 2005], 169). For other contexts, see Rahul Rao, *Out of Time* (Oxford: Oxford University Press, 2020).

94 Mendel and Ranta, *From Arab Other to Israeli Self*, x. At stake was the possibility to "become 'na-tives' in their new homeland," which passed through the Palestinian as "a son of the land, rooted in its landscape" (Benvenisti, *Sacred Landscape*, 61).

95 Homi Bhabha, "Of Mimicry and Man: The Ambivalence of Colonial Discourse," *October* 28 (spring 1984): 125–33. Some such accounts include: Ariel Handel, Galit Rand, and Marco Al-legra, "Wine-Washing: Colonization, Normalization, and the Geopolitics of *Terroir* in the West Bank's Settlements," *Environment and Planning A: Economy and Space* 47, no. 6 (June 2015): 1351–67; Mori Ram, "White but Not Quite: Normalizing Colonial Conquests through Spatial Mimicry," *Antipode* 46, no. 3 (2014): 736–53. For other contexts, see James G. Ferguson, "Of Mimicry and Membership: Africans and the 'New World Society,'" *Cultural Anthropology* 17, no. 4 (Novem-ber 2002): 551–69; Sara Ahmed, "'She'll Wake Up One of These Days and Find She's Turned into a Nigger': Passing through Hybridity," *Theory, Culture and Society* 16, no. 2 (April 1999): 87–106.

96 Frantz Fanon, *The Wretched of the Earth*, trans. Richard Philcox (New York: Grove Press, [1963] 2004), 39. Although it is certainly also about "demolishing the colonist's sector, burying it deep within the earth or banishing it from the territory" (6).

ouin fighters. In their effort to shed diasporic passivity and transform them-selves into active national figures, they began to embody the militarized form of those who were often considered enemies.[97] As Anita Shapira puts it: what was adopted and imitated as part of the constitution of a new corporeality were "the symbols of power . . . : horseback riding, carrying weapons, and wearing a *kaffia* headdress."[98]

Eyal argues that this form of bodily mimicking disappears after 1948 because, among several other reasons he lays out, the might of military power could at that point be attached to the new Jewish nation without passing through Arab identity. To substantiate this claim, he moves from bodies to homes: in contrast to the *corporeal* mimicking through which the Jew sought to *resemble* an Arab warrior during the prestate years, in the first years of the state the Arab *village* emerged as that which must be maintained *separated* and controlled. This com-parison between Arab bodies to be mimicked and, in the later period, Arab houses to be enclosed, controlled, and surveilled represents, according to Eyal, a shift from hybrid identities to rigid boundaries.[99] But if we consider this shift from body to home alongside the architectonic shift delineated earlier, which had an opposite trajectory—from mimicking Western architectonic style to mimicking Palestinian vernacular architecture—we see that roughly when the Arab village becomes an inappropriable, enclosed "discursive object," whose entire logic is that of securing separations, as Eyal claims, the "Arab house" becomes, as Yacobi and Shadar claim, an object of aesthetic desire and real-estate value.[100]

I propose that this shift from corporeal to architectonic mimicking is a re-placement of one mode of violence (my own, *via* the other's) with another (my own, *against* the other). The mimicking of Arab militarism is replaced with an attachment to the spaces of their defeat—the destroyed house or the evicted one.

EYAL'S HISTORICAL FRAMING, and particularly his focus on the fate of hy-brid identities, calls us to draw another important distinction that demarcates the contours of my argument. In almost all the examples of Arab houses as ob-jects of desire—or, to return to Karmi's words, as "imprint[s] of the locality"—

97 Eyal, *Disenchantment of the Orient*, chapter 2.
98 Shapira, *Land and Power*, 61.
99 Eyal, *Disenchantment of the Orient*, 178–79.
100 On the real-estate allure of Arab houses, see Daniel Monterescu, "The Bridled Bride of Pales-tine: Orientalism, Zionism, and the Troubled Urban Imagination," *Identities: Global Studies in Culture and Power* 16, no. 6 (2009): 643–77.

these houses were either destroyed enough to become part of the "landscape" or repopulated by Ashkenazi Jews. In the many examples in which Mizrahi Jews were settled (as a state project) or chose to settle (often as infiltrators) in Arab houses, neighborhoods, and villages, these sites were soon marked as areas of criminality and disorder to be "modernized" (see epilogue for part I).[101] Unlike refugees from Eastern and Western Europe, the Mizrahi Jews carried the "risk" of (re)immersing themselves in their Arab identity, which threatened their incorporation into the Zionist project. Therefore, they were often evicted—quickly or slowly—from the Arab houses, which either remained in their state of ruin, were erased to become large-scale real-estate projects, or were repopulated by Ashkenazi Jews who could presumably "'understand' and 'appreciate' the 'local' landscape."[102] Ongoing projects of ruination must therefore be understood not just alongside national grids but also within ethnic and class ones, subjected to identity-based differentiations alongside economic interests (gentrification and development). They should also be mapped across the long duress in which they take place, when different points in history tell a different story. This means that the position of the settler cannot be thought of in the singular. The analysis here focuses on one position within a larger mosaic (others will be considered in other parts of this book, but even in its totality, this book provides only a partial image). But what this particularity makes clear, and this is what is significant for me here, is that appropriation was dependent on a presupposed notion of *separation* and was therefore a privilege of particular ethnic (and classed) groups in Israel. Hybridity was never the goal but was rather that which must be overcome. In this sense, too, appropriation was fully dependent on destruction: the destruction of social identities, particularly of Mizrahi Jews, and of life and property, particularly of Palestinians, although the two sides of this equation often flow into each other.

From Karmi to Janco to Eyal, we therefore see different fragments illustrating the processes through which a particular Israeli identity was forged of which violence is a constitutive element. Accordingly, when violence presents

101 Although in the case of Ramle, Piroyansky's analysis shows how, despite the desire to "purify" the "Oriental Jews" from "Arab elements in their existence," this was not translated to moving them out of the depopulated Palestinian houses to modern ("European") housing complexes. It was rather the more well-off Ashkenazi immigrants who managed to move to the new neighborhoods. The immigrants from North Africa and Iraq stayed in the Old City, on Arab property (Piroyansky, *Ramle Remade*, 177–83). The Old City, however, has remained a site of neglect and poverty and was not elevated to the real-estate or cultural status of the previously Arab neighborhoods of Jaffa or Jerusalem.

102 Yacobi, "Architecture, Orientalism, Identity," 112.

itself, when it becomes undeniable, such as when a Palestinian knocks at the door, it no longer destabilizes, undoes, or fractures the sense of self—one's image of oneself or even one's sense of justice.

Conclusion and Beyond

Dafna Levin presents a concise summary of the two roles that the Palestinian ruin—the *hirbe*—plays in Israeli political discourse, both of which were demonstrated throughout this chapter: it is either (i) an object of complete erasure that seeks, first, to hide traces of violence and, second, to dismantle the specter of return it holds or (ii) a romanticized "antique," an oriental, naturalized, historicized, appropriable, cherished "decoration" for a Jewish claim to the land. In its first role, the hirbe makes visible a history of violence and dispossession and must therefore stay out of sight; in its second role, it becomes an object of attachment.[103] This chapter sought to problematize this neat analytic separation. It wondered whether it is possible that as well as (i)—a remnant and trace of violence and destruction—the ruin becomes an object of attachment, part of one's identity and belonging to a place and a community.

My argument here sought to point to both a historical and a structural mode of being attached to these traces of violence. The claim that the object of attachment (the house, the home, the landscape) indeed carries violence within it still requires justification. Except for the case of Janco's words, violence does not appear here at the moment of its arrival, as an event, but is rather embedded in traces, as a residue or excess that cannot fully be done with. Moreover, the attachment I seek to identify is (probably) most often not *experienced* as an attachment to violence. In *Salt of This Sea*, Irit, like so many others who came to occupy the homes (the land) of others, does not feel the violence embedded in her position and does not see herself as committing acts of violence (though see DeKoven's, Madame Nielsen's, or Rice's understandings of their colonial presence in the interlude to this chapter). Indeed, the violence of Irit's mode of belonging probably cannot be seen as an "act." Nevertheless, the experience of violence or lack thereof is to be differentiated from a phenomenology of violence; the latter can point to violence that is there despite being absent from experience. The epilogue that follows will engage with such a phenomenology to better articulate the violence that the

---

103 Daphna Levin, "Our H'irbe: The Representation of Arab Ruins in Israeli Culture" [in Hebrew], *Yisraelim* 6 (2014): 53–67.

current chapter sought to identify. For now, it is important to note that the gap between the experience and the phenomenology of violence means that finding a home in a ruin is not a cruel rejoicing in the face of suffering or a sadistic pleasure in inflicting pain on others (compare with the cruelty model in the theoretical overview). It means that Irit can be genuine when she asserts that "it is so sad" that Palestinians "left" in 1948, that her attachment to a site that represents such a great loss to others is *not* necessarily a celebration of their loss and her triumph. Still, an "I" emerges in this process that can only see herself via destruction.

Irit (to stay with the allegory) grew up in a home that *is* a trace of violence—a constant reminder of past violence that in its saturated presence constantly reminds, but in so doing also banalizes, the Nakba. The point goes beyond the claim that this banalization, this normalization, depoliticizes and dehistoricizes violence.[104] The point is that this violence has been integrated into Irit's identity—it is part of her sense of selfhood, part of her childhood memories, part of how she defines herself. Perhaps this is why she fails to feel an existential nausea when the knock on the door comes: this knock does not undo who she is but ultimately, even if despite herself, confirms it. Accordingly, when (if) a moment of confrontation presents itself, this violence is likely to be embraced rather than renounced, and with it, one's identity as a settler.

It may be the case that Irit ends up having an affair with Marwan; it may be that this affair shifts altogether how she sees the possibility of sharing her home and homeland. It may be that they just become friends; that she travels to Ramallah, that she meets his family, that through these encounters she slowly changes her mode of attachment. But this is not how Irit of *Salt of This Sea* concludes her relations with her Palestinian "guests" on screen. At some point, Soraya demands that Irit confront the past violence. "Admit this is mine, that you took it away from me," she says. But Irit does not admit. She also does not become nauseated. Rather than vomiting, Irit threatens to call the police. Her choice, facing the Palestinian call, is to summon more violence.

Farid Abdel-Nour argues that, confronted with the reality of their past (and present, I keep having to add), Israelis face two options: "either a wholesale rejection of their national identity or a rejection of their very humanity." The first would push to "conversion and rehabilitation, so that they can wash off every trace in themselves of the kinds of persons who could have committed the criminal deeds." The second is to "embrace their own criminality wholeheartedly

---

104 Merav Amir and Hagar Kotef, "Normal" [in Hebrew], *Mafte'akh* 9 (2015): 111–31.

without any tension or difficulty."[105] Whereas the terminology here seems to me somewhat flattened, the idea stands: coming to terms with the violence embedded into the very logic of one's national existence requires either a complete undoing of identity or a nonconflictual embrace of violence. The latter may be "a more logical attitude, materially more coherent than the tormented dance of the colonizer who refuses and continues to live in the colony."[106]

ARI SHAVIT INTERVIEWED Edward Said for *Ha'aretz* in 2003. Above, we saw his efforts to negotiate Said's call for recognizing past injustice, a call that he posits, much like Soraya, as the grounds from which any process of reconciliation and/ or decolonization can begin. We saw Shavit's refusal, somewhat similar to Irit's, to acknowledge his role in dispossession by "distorting" or "disabling" Said's words. By 2013, in his book *My Promised Land: The Triumph and Tragedy of Israel*, Shavit no longer remodels knowledge so as not to confront his responsibility as we saw in story II above. He faces Israeli violence directly. Writing about the massacre that took place in 1948 in the then-Palestinian city of Lydda, he does not try to explain it away as an isolated incident or an accidental event. This was, he says with somewhat surprising honesty, "an inevitable phase of the Zionist revolution that laid the foundation for the Zionist state. Lydda was an integral part of our story."[107] When he looks at it candidly, Shavit confesses, "I see that the choice is stark: either reject Zionism because of Lydda, or accept Zionism with Lydda"— crucially, not *despite* Lydda, but *with* Lydda.[108] This is "a reality [he] cannot contain": "I am not only sad, I am horrified," he states. And yet only half a paragraph later, Shavit's horror is replaced by acceptance. Those who committed the massacre should not be condemned by "Israeli liberals" with "bleeding hearts" who "enjoy the fruits of [these commanders'] deeds." "If need be," he therefore concludes, "I'll stand by the damned." Shavit, then, begins with marking his sadness and even horror, but these seem to be tokens that can very easily be dismissed. If we thought that his heart bled as he faced an uncontainable reality that made him "not only sad" but "horrified," this is not the case. What could have been a mark of a conflicted self—a heart that is torn or injured—is actually not his, and it is those

105 Farid Abdel-Nour, "Responsibility and National Memory: Israel and the Palestinian Refugee Problem," 355.

106 Memmi, *Colonizer and the Colonized*, 87.

107 Ari Shavit, *My Promised Land: The Triumph and Tragedy of Israel* (Melbourne: Scribe Publications, 2014), 131.

108 Shavit, *My Promised Land*, 131.

with the bleeding hearts who should be condemned, rather than the massacre it-self or those who committed it. "Because I know that if it wasn't for them, I would not have been born. They did the dirty, filthy work that enabled my people, my-self, my daughter, and my son to live."[109] What seemed to be an existential crisis (sadness, horror, inability to contain one's world) is instantly resolved.[110] What is significant here is not merely the swift switch of positions—from sadness/horror to the very condemnation of those—but also the explicit recognition that Shavit's very identity and his ability to "enjoy the fruits" of prosperity are conditioned on ethnic cleansing.[111]

I MOVED BACK to Israel in 2012 after living in the United States for almost eight years, just in time for "Operation Pillar of Defense," the Israeli Defense Forces' (IDF) name for that particular round of military strikes on Gaza. I left Israel in 2015, after the 2014 war they called "Protective Edge." I remem-ber sitting in a café in a northern neighborhood of Tel Aviv, just a few days after returning. The neighborhood is typified by its bourgeois, generally left-leaning demographic. At the two tables next to me there were two people, a man and a woman, who seemed to be unfamiliar with each other. One was reading the newspaper, the other asked for the sports section, and a conver-sation developed. They quickly arrived at the conclusion that (I am quoting from memory) "if the world blames us for committing crimes against human-ity in Gaza we might as well commit genocide and get it all over with." During the Nakba memorial ceremony of that year at Tel Aviv University, activists of the then-new right-wing organization Im Tirtzu (in Hebrew: "if you will it,"

---

109 Shavit, *My Promised Land*, 131.
110 Bruce Robbins compares this paragraph to Jack Nicholson's famous speech in *A Few Good Men* ("you cannot handle the truth . . .") to argue that, in both cases, what transpires is a realization that the immoral, violent, unacceptable deeds that were done were done to protect and sustain the self. Therefore, the self cannot renounce what has been done, or at least so he comes to grasp, "because to do so . . . would be to will his own undoing" (Robbins, *Beneficiary*, 143).
111 We can find in Shavit's words elements from the model of dissociation outlined in the theoretical overview, such as the notion of a lack of choice as part of a struggle for survival. And yet, unlike the typical dissociation strategy, this does not become a discourse of reversed victimhood. Lydda is depicted explicitly in terms of a massacre. Moreover, unlike the strategy of pointing to one's own shock and outrage facing "excessive" violence as a way of reaffirming one's morality through expressing horror (akin to what we saw in the dissociation model), Shavit points to the "exces-sive" violence itself as part of the story of the self. Shavit, even if horrified, does not seek to fix, condemn, or isolate the massacre. It is the very massacre, he claims, that is part of who he is.

after the famous words of Herzl) surrounded the demonstrators and, mimicking a famous Israeli song, chanted: "we brought Nakba upon you," ironically paraphrasing the original words: "we brought peace upon you" (*hevenu shalom alechem*). Rather than attacking the demonstrators by denying that the Nakba ever took place (the common attitude at the time), the right-wing activists celebrated the fact that it did and perhaps also called for a new one. By 2014, the right-wing party the Jewish Home (Haba'it Haiehudi) launched a campaign under the title "no longer apologizing" (*mafsikim lehitnatzel*).[112] This was four months after Israel had killed more than twenty-two hundred Palestinians and destroyed more than eighteen thousand houses in Gaza.[113] Although not directly so, given the predominant public debate at the time, one could not but wonder whether the Jewish Home's campaign was a call to stop apologizing for what Israel had just done in Gaza. The campaign was accompanied by a concrete program to annex vast parts of the West Bank (all area C territories), thereby making the state of apartheid explicit.[114] As I write these words, in London in the summer of 2018, this plan is being slowly coded into the Israeli legal system: with the new semi-constitutional law "Israel as the Nation-State of the Jewish People,"[115] the new legislation limiting Palestinians' access to the High Court of Justice and subjecting them to the municipal Israeli court system,[116] the Israeli government's passage of the "Judea

---

112 See video campaign at Naftali Bennett, "No Longer Apologizing" (*mafsikim lehitnatzel*) [in Hebrew], December 6, 2014, YouTube video, 2:46, https://www.youtube.com/watch?v=PBNonq QX5x0.

113 See B'tselem, "50 Days: More Than 50 Children: Facts and Figures on Fatalities in Gaza, Summer 2014," *B'tselem*, last accessed September 13, 2018, https://www.btselem.org/2014_gaza_conflict/en /; B'tselem, "Statistics on Demolition for Alleged Military Purposes," *B'tselem*, last updated August 7, 2019, https://www.btselem.org/razing/statistics. The *Independent* reports higher numbers of house destructions: Lizzie Dearden, "Israel-Gaza Conflict: 50-Day War by Numbers," *Independent*, August 27, 2014, https://www.independent.co.uk/news/world/middle-east/israel-gaza -conflict-50-day-war-by-numbers-9693310.html.

114 Program available at "The Stability Initiative" [*tochnit ha'arga'a*]: A Practical Pathway for the Management of the Israeli/Palestinian Conflict" [in Hebrew], https://www.inss.org.il/he/wp -content/uploads/sites/2/2019/01.

115 In the Israeli political system, "basic laws" function as laws of constitutional-like status in the absence of a fully formed constitution.

116 Justice Minister Shaked has claimed this law "normalizes" the lives of Jewish settlers. Jonathan Lis, "Israel Passes New Law Limiting Palestinians' Access to Court," *Ha'aretz*, July 17, 2018, https://www.haaretz.com/israel-news/.premium-knesset-advances-bill-barring-palestinians -from-petitioning-high-court-1.6271237.

and Samaria Settlement Regulation Law" that retroactively legalized sixteen outposts built on privately owned Palestinian land as part of a larger effort to regularize settlement in the West Bank,[117] and the government's now-official declaration that no territorial compromise will be considered.[118] The nonapologetic approach became an official policy.

117 For a detailed analysis of this process, see part III of this book.
118 This book was completed before the announcement of the Trump Plan in January 2020, which sought to further anchor this process by American support, facilitating its final formalization.

Epilogue
A Phenomenology of Violence

RUINS

In the mid-1960s, amid a vast enterprise to demolish more than one hundred depopulated Arab villages that had remained part of the Israeli landscape since 1948, many Israelis wrote to complain and demand that the demolitions stop. Aron Shai, who researched these letters of complaint, did not find ethical or political arguments pointing to the unjust act of destroying someone else's home, preventing the possibility of return; in fact, the past lives that used to inhabit these houses were not mentioned at all. Rather, what was mourned was the loss of sites with "narrow alleyways bursting with grapevines and figs, and clear spring water rushing between the rocks" or "magnificent stone houses," which were seen as "place[s] for artists" or tourists who "used to come there to admire" these sites.[1] This attachment to sites of destruction was one of the main themes of the previous chapter, and with it emerged the question: can this be seen as an attachment to *violence*?

One may contend that the eviction of ethical and political facets from the above complaints, an eviction we encountered in various forms in the previous chapter, suggests that these cannot be seen as sites, or even traces, of violence. These sites are indeed depicted as sites of almost-natural beauty rather than sites of destruction (although "magnificent houses" cannot really be seen as natural). As Hochberg puts it, Palestinian ruins (or other traces of past violence such as the weapons of war in figures 2.1–2.3 of chapter 2) "are included in the [Israeli visual] frame but only through the selective gaze of the new colonial settlers who overlook the immediate historical context of violence

---

1 Aron Shai, "The Fate of Abandoned Arab Villages in Israel, 1965–1969," *History and Memory* 18, no. 2 (fall/winter 2006): 97.

and destruction and instead incorporate the ruins as elements of lyrical and abstract composition." This abstractness joins mechanisms of resignification, dehistoricization, and naturalization, rendering them "an integral part of the landscape: part of a beautiful, romantic, and pastoral unity."[2] The common claim, then, is that the remnants of the war(s) are integrated into identity, but only after violence has somehow been cleansed away.

Indeed, when I played in the ruins of depopulated Syrian spaces as a child (see preface), when I walked with friends to pick the fruits from the trees that were presumably naturally there, or when those Israelis from the mid-1960s mourned the loss of sites they had come to "admire," I/we/they did not form an attachment to these sites *as* sites of defeat. Mine/ours/theirs was not a triumphant attachment. It was not violence that I/we/they craved or longed for. And yet, in this chapter, I want to insist that violence cannot be cleansed away from these sites, and is thus also tethered to the attachment to them.

Insisting on the violence in the ruin is first and above all a political claim. It is to insist that a past injustice cannot simply be erased; that when an atrocity takes place, its meaning cannot be completely altered by those who generated it or those who come to benefit from it; that the significance of all that remains cannot be canceled. As a theoretical insistence, this follows Azoulay and Ophir's claim that violence must be judged through its effects, and, furthermore, through how these effects impact its victim: violence appears only when there is a victim and in relation to this victim.[3] The insistence here, then, is that especially if we adopt the point of view of the target of violence (the house, the people who used to live in it), violence still resides in the site of destruction long after the bulldozers are gone.

There are ideological apparatuses that prevent people from seeing violence as violence: the naturalization or dehistoricization that Hochberg points to and that was further reviewed in the previous chapter, or ideologies that turn victims into enemies or bearers of their own disaster. But it seems to me that, while these ideological apparatuses do play a role in the construction and justification of political projects, the tendency of theorists of violence to emphasize them is itself a form of ideology. As I proposed in the theoretical overview, it is

2 Gil Z. Hochberg, *Visual Occupation: Violence and Visibility in a Conflict Zone* (Durham, NC: Duke University Press, 2015), 39, 52—the latter quote is from the Israeli artist Larry Abramson.

3 Ariella Azoulay and Adi Ophir, *The One-State Condition: Occupation and Democracy in Israel/Palestine* (Stanford, CA: Stanford University Press, 2012), 134. See also Ariel Handel, "Violence" [in Hebrew], *Mafte'akh: Lexical Review of Political Thought* 3 (2011): 53–80.

an ideology that is rooted in some form of unfounded belief in human nature that makes them/us unable to fully grasp the idea that people can willingly and consciously embrace such forms of disaster making. But there is something too easy about explaining the Israeli gaze, the attachment to these sites of ruin, to the ruined (or standing) houses, via ideological mechanisms that explain violence away (from denial and blindness to naturalization or resignification, or to the claim that most has been erased). The explanation that so many scholars use and that I used to employ myself, namely that we could not see or that we were not seeing things for what they were, seems insufficient to me—not utterly wrong, but conveniently partial. The aim of this brief chapter is to provide an alternative—or, better, supplementary—framework for answering the question of how violence is present in those traces. I cannot offer a complete phenomenology of this violence here. What follows, then, are fragments through which such a phenomenology can begin to be reconstructed.

A Ruin (or, a Brief Phenomenology of Violence)

Before I begin this typology of violence, but also as part of this typology, it is important to better define the ruin itself. Stoler distinguishes between (i) "ruins of empire," which make present the "wider structures of vulnerability" that imperial formations constantly produce and reproduce, and (ii) a melancholic gaze on ruins that re-presents an "image of what has vanished from the past and has long decayed" (such as the Acropolis, the Roman Colosseum, Chichén Itzá).[4] Two distinctions are made within this distinction, only one of which I want to keep for my current purpose.

The first is a *temporal* distinction: between a ruin that re-presents a past whose bearing on the present is a reminder of that which is *gone*, on the one hand, and an "imperial ruin" that carries with it, into the *present*, the violence of the past that never passed, since it is part of a structure of ongoing ruination. The Palestinian ruin is an example of the latter temporality: the Nakba is not a closed event to be relegated to the past, and the ongoing destruction of Palestinian lives and community, polity, and indeed homes is not merely *marked by* but is also *present in* the ruin. This chapter explores several modes of such presence. For now, we can say that the Palestinian ruin makes present the "wider structures of vulnerability," to return to Stoler's words, because, at the very least, it is situated within wider structures of violence that are very much in

---

4 Ann Laura Stoler, *Imperial Debris: On Ruins and Ruination* (Durham, NC: Duke University Press, 2013), 194.

the present. Israeli violence is present in its cyclical eruptions, as wars, military operations, and spectacles of physical oppression; it is there in its structural form, in the organization of the political community in the territory through radical exclusions, in the construction of space so as to disable Palestinian freedom;[5] and it is there via its constant traces that saturate the visual field, which, despite all efforts, cannot be erased. The first two forms, the eruptive and the structural violence, render the violence embedded in the third, that is, in the trace, a matter of the present. These different forms of violence are in close spatial proximity: the bombing of Gaza, the eruptive violence of settlers and soldiers in Hebron, the constant house demolitions in the Jordan Valley, the indefinite detentions and torture in military prisons, the arbitrary arrests (including of children), the tear gas, the exploding ammunition that cuts through the bones of demonstrators, are in close proximity to the prickly groves, the olive and fig trees alongside the half-preserved terraces, the artists' houses in Jaffa or Ein Hod, the sea reflected in their windows. This proximity renders the museumization or the longing and belonging that occur on one end of this duality a museumization *of*, longing *for*, or belonging *to* the violence that occurs on its other side.[6] And this would be the case even if a Jewish Israeli eye may not *see* the bombarding, expulsion, or demolition when it looks at the beautiful arches of an Arab house in Jaffa. I will return to this point later. In addition to this proximity, another proximity is in place that renders these sites (ruins, houses) places of present violence: the proximity of those who were displaced but remained nearby, who can still see their homes—ruined or reinhabited—sometimes on a daily basis. But let us return to Stoler's typology.

Alongside this temporal differentiation, the second distinction at play in Stoler's distinction is based on the question of affect: the ruins that re-present the past are objects of melancholic attachment, a medium through which loss is mourned and the past is glorified. This is not the case with imperial ruins, however, according to her. In shifting the emphasis from ruin (as a given, finalized object) to ruination (as an active process), this melancholic attachment

---

5 On the legal and institutional facets, see Azoulay and Ophir, *One-State Condition*, esp. chapter 7; Amal Jamal, "Beyond 'Ethnic Democracy': State Structure, Multicultural Conflict and Differentiated Citizenship in Israel," *New Political Science* 24, no. 3 (2002): 411–31; Oren Yiftachel, *Ethnocracy: Land and Identity Politics in Israel/Palestine* (Philadelphia: University of Pennsylvania Press, 2006). On the spatial disablement of Palestinian freedom, see Azmi Bishara, *Yearning in the Land of Checkpoints* [in Hebrew] (Tel Aviv: Babel Press, 2006); Sari Hanafi, "Spacio-cide and Bio-Politics: The Israeli Colonial Conflict from 1947 to the Wall," in *Against the Wall: Israel's Barrier to Peace*, ed. Michael Sorkin (New York: New Press, 2005), 251–61; and chapter 3 of this book.
6 I thank Laleh Khalili for this thought.

dissipates. With this shift, what transpires is an enduring violent quality, an ongoing form of disaster production that almost necessarily replaces the melancholic gaze with "a critical vantage point."[7] And yet, in my inquiry (though not *as such*), the Palestinian ruin does not contain this difference in affect between the objects of melancholic attachment and those objects that still produce violence; it seems to be viewed by the Israelis inhabiting the pages of this book with similar melancholic attachment, *at the same time* as it is—and perhaps is even viewed as—a player in an ongoing form of disaster making. To explain this claim, we need to unpack the subject position in relation to which attachment is considered.

Stoler thinks primarily about the subjects of empire, for whom imperial processes of ruination mean that life is structured by the enduring remains of imperial destruction: a material and bureaucratic infrastructure that keeps failing; a landscape that has been scarred, if not maimed, by colonial mining; bulldozed homes that were demolished for the passage of colonial forces; scattered family formations as the outcome of slave trade, a system of concubinage, or a broken economic infrastructure that pushes people abroad in search of survival. These are certainly not traces to be glorified or longed for. But what happens to the affectual dimension when, as in the case of this book, the objects of inquiry are those who generated this destruction and do not suffer its consequences? When the ruin that always carries with it the traces of the disaster does not represent, or affect, their own ruination? Ian Baucom's work on the English country house—an imperial formation that is slowly decomposing—begins to provide an answer to this question.

As a mark of a decaying empire, as well as the very concrete outcome of the slowing circulation of wealth as the empire declines, the English decomposing country house is not itself an agent of destruction, akin to the imperial debris of Stoler, but is rather the trace, emblem, effect of, or participant in a destruction that is taking place further away—in the Atlantic routes of the slave trade, the sugar fields of the Caribbean, the impoverishment of India. Unlike Stoler's case of gutted infrastructure, the crumbling of Baucom's English country house does not continue to ruin, that is, to exert imperial violence. And yet, this ruin becomes "not a simple allusion to the nation's imperial past. It accommodates that past, but accommodates it by signaling that past's terminus, by marking, in fallen stones, its boundary."[8] The ruin therefore both *still entails*

---

7 Stoler, *Imperial Debris*, 12.
8 Ian Baucom, "Mournful Histories: Narratives of Postimperial Melancholy," MFS: *Modern Fiction Studies* 42, no. 2 (summer 1996): 282.

the imperial past (accommodating it, housing it), but only as that which can no longer be present.

If Baucom's ruins contain the imperial past in its *present form*, as its temporal (and perhaps also geographical and political) limit, and if Stoler's ruins represent imperial formation as that which has not passed, the Palestinian ruin's dialogue with continuing Israeli violence bridges past and present differently. I develop this claim in the fourth section of this epilogue ("Trace"), and for now want to mark the fact that in Baucom these forms of ruin, too, can become the object of attachment. For Baucom, this is an attachment to "pure presence," which does not tow along the "past towards which it gestures." And yet, even with such an aestheticized, decontextualized form of attachment, Baucom cannot but argue that decay, collapse, and ruin become something one yearns for. "If there is an order of nostalgia operative, it is a proleptic nostalgia which does not see wholeness in the ruin, but the promise of ruin in the whole."[9] A mode of attachment sneaks into this analysis, or perhaps an element within attachment we cannot quite get rid of: a desire for the ruin as a desire for ruination. In Baucom's reading, the ruination is of empire and its collapsing order, and so attachment to ruination appears to be egalitarian in a way; but the same desire is relevant to my case, when the colonial order is still very much present.

A Mark (or, Signifier and Signified): A Derridean Reading

"To a considerable degree, we have already said what we *meant to say*," that is, that the violence in the ruin cannot be a matter of the past, and thus it is *there*.[10] But in what way is it "there"? And in what way is one attached to "it," as I keep claiming? In "Plato's Pharmacy" (from which the above quote is taken), Derrida works on the relations between writing and speech or logos as an example (*the* paradigmatic example) of the relation of signification. With Stoler, we thought of the violence the ruin still exerts; with Derrida, we can think of the ruin as a *signifier* of violence that is no longer there while questioning the metaphysics in which the signifier is a lesser trace of the thing itself (violence).

Derrida's argument is dual (at the very least dual, or "dual" for the sake of the current purposes). First, he traces a "metaphysics of presence" that prefers the "source" over the substitution, the signified over the signifier; and second,

9 Baucom, "Mournful Histories," 280.
10 Jacques Derrida, "Plato's Pharmacy," in *Dissemination*, trans. Barbara Johnson (Chicago: University of Chicago Press, 1981), 65.

he points to the impossibility of this metaphysics—to the fact that from the outset, we are "trapped" in the realm of signification and can never arrive at a pure, unmediated source. If we look at the paradigmatic example of writing, we see a process in which the source, that is, the author, renders themself absent in the very act of writing, a process in which the source is never there and cannot be there. *To signify is to anchor an absence.* I will return to this point soon when thinking of the Palestinian ruin and the Palestinian absentees.

Derrida moves here between a series of "substitutions": writing substitutes speech, speech substitutes thought or logos, and the logos substitutes the truth (in its strongest version: the Platonic Ideas). But even the Platonic Ideas are given within a series of substitutions, metaphors, allegories, parables, myths, and can only be present through such substitutions: the "sun" as a substitute for the "truth" within a "parable" that itself signifies the need to substitute. We can never look at the sun itself; it would render us blind. We must look at reflections—at least for a while. For Derrida, this process of substituting is a matter of violence: a murder is at stake—the murder of the father in an Egyptian myth of the invention of writing—but also a process of violent replacement: erasure (in which writing "murders" the speaker, or speech, or perhaps the "author" as a "source," who, as Foucault tells us, is "dead").[11] There are more assassinations at play here: what Plato wants to "kill" in *Phaidros*, the dialogue Derrida reads here, is writing itself, in the name of the metaphysics of presence Derrida deconstructs; but also—always with Plato—another murder is looming: that of Socrates.

If Derrida needs to read violence into the game of signifying in the case of writing, the *ruin* as a sign is very clearly a *signifier of violence*. Our task of reading violence into the example is therefore more straightforward. Nevertheless, there are quite a few questions that this claim opens.

First, if we are in the game of signification, we are also playing a game of *interpretation* that, Derrida tells us as he reads Plato, is always a question of faith and can never be fully justified. More concretely, we can claim that in the current context, interpretation tends to be split across national lines: if for Palestinians and those who identify with their call, the ruin *signifies* the violence of the Nakba, for Israelis it may signify something else (we saw some of these options: a Jewish past or natural beauty). With Lyotard's *differend*, we can argue that the violence of the ruin as a signifier is to be found precisely *in the gap between different interpretations*, between the violence Palestinians see and the violence Israelis fail to see or see differently.

11 Michel Foucault, "What Is an Author?" (lecture, Collège de France, February 22, 1969).

But I want to stay here with Derrida and the question of presence. In the ruin, the victim of violence is absent. This is probably best captured by the legal concept "present absentees," which refers to internally displaced Palestinians who were nonetheless declared "absentees" to allow the state to confiscate their property. In the marches of return, in which internally displaced Palestinians walk to their destroyed villages and neighborhoods, the victims re-presence themselves in relation to this signifier, and in so doing, re-signify it as a signifier of (and a site of) violence. But most days, the ruin—much in line with Derrida's claim about the act of signification itself—is the means, the technology, the fact, of producing their absence. And this production *is* the ruin's form of violence. If we think with Derrida about the structure of signification, we see the violence of the ruin itself that, like the writing that murders, is embedded into the act of rendering absent performed by all forms of signification, and that is done here not by making an author, a speaker, or a thought absent—as in Derrida's object of analysis—but by wars, dispossession, occasional massacres, and a population transfer.

This is a way of reading the violence of and in the ruin without attempting to go into the "source," i.e., the original violence that created the ruin and that the ruin *signifies*. Indeed, one of the lessons from reading *Phaidros* with Derrida may be that we need to read the ruin for and from itself; not for what it "marks," which can never be made present, but for what it *does* and what it *entails*, or *is*. To insist that the meaning of the ruin is to be situated in a violence that has passed and cannot be re-presented is to uphold the metaphysics of presence Derrida seeks to undo. To think against such a metaphysics in this case is also to insist on thinking beyond a positivist account of violence, in which violence appears only as an event, in the moment of the physical act. In a way, it is this positivist understanding of violence that renders the ruin but a "signifier," and as such not "really" a site of violence.

IN WHAT MAY BE read as an effort to avoid this question of signification, Gastón Gordillo proposes to abandon the concept and metaphysics of "ruin" and adopt, instead, "rubble." The former, he claims, prioritizes the past of the whole (what has been ruined; what the ruin "points towards," signifies) over the life of its leftovers, thereby abstracting and thus denying "the multiplicity of places, forms, and textures that define actually existing nodes of rubble."[12]

12 Gastón R. Gordillo, *Rubble: The Afterlife of Destruction* (Durham, NC: Duke University Press, 2014), 8.

In this movement from ruin to rubble, we move from signification to the materiality of what is left. Much like Stoler, Gordillo thinks of "ruins" (contra to "rubble") primarily as sites of heritage, to be protected and conserved. Moreover, as he looks at colonial ruins in Chaco, these sites of heritage are often colonial sites. Hence, prioritizing the new life of matter is a form of resisting colonial legacies: rather than a mark of a whole whose meaning is to be found in the colonial past, the sporadic, movable materiality of rubble becomes part of a world that cannot be contained within the parameters of those acts of colonization. It is a way of looking at what indigenous populations do with the ruins they are "left with" (to quote Stoler). My case is almost the opposite in its political trajectory, since *the new life of Palestinian ruins is colonial* in essence (such as when piles of stones are integrated into the landscape, or into new Jewish domiciles, or when various artifacts that were left behind are reappropriated by Israelis). In this case, to work with the texture of rubble and allow the whole it once was to evaporate from the matter that remains would be to erase the indigenous meaning of this matter. Eventually, the metaphysics of the ruin is a political question. Accordingly, rather than an abstraction, what may emerge if we insist on the whole is a reconstruction: a way of summoning—not a moment contained in the past as a whole (the Arab house that once was), nor a materiality of the present (rubble, the piles of stones), but the temporality in which the whole has been ruined to become the trace that it is now: a protracted pain from the past that lingers in the ruin.

A Residue (Material Excess)

At stake in the attachment to the ruin is not violence in its direct, physical appearance; it is also not an individualized violence, targeting a specific body or generated by an individual agent whose intention to cause injury defines this act as violent. But it is also not structural violence, which is built into the inequality of social relations and works by increasing the "distance between the potential and the actual," as Johan Galtung defines it.[13] Neither is it withheld violence, in Azoulay and Ophir's terminology, which unlike eruptive violence is present through the permanent possibility of its unregulated, uncodified eruption, a displayed potentiality, if you will.[14] Nor is it slow violence, which

13 Johan Galtung, "Violence, Peace, and Peace Research," *Journal of Peace Research* 6, no. 3 (1969): 167–91.

14 Withheld violence is not eruptive violence nor the threat of violence (it is therefore not fully captured by the ideas of potentiality and suspension, whose actualization/materialization is subjected to some logic or rule). See Azoulay and Ophir, *One-State Condition*, 137.

is slowly unfolded, usually out of sight, both because destruction is delayed and is proximate in neither time nor space to its cause and because it is often not seen as violence at all.[15] In all these non-positivist accounts of violence, the temporality of violence is key: in all, violence gains its meaning from what might happen in the future. It is a function of what does not but *can* happen at any future moment (Azoulay and Ophir) or *could* happen but probably will not (Galtung); or it results from the process of this future's unfolding (Nixon, and to some degree Azoulay and Ophir as well). The violence I consider here is of a different temporality—not one of unfolding, but one of lurking long after the event; one that, in this lurking, does not allow the present to completely free itself from this past violence.[16]

Yael Navaro-Yashin defines ruination as "the material remains or artefacts of destruction and violation" as well as "the subjective and residual affects that linger like a hangover, in the aftermath of war or violence."[17] *The ruin is a material reminder of destruction.* As a "reminder," it is both what remains (that is, "there") and what "reminds" (that is, carries this affectual "hangover," the sense of loss that remains through it, with it, attached to it). As long as the matter is still there, some violence continues to reside, as a residue, in the materiality of the ruin.

Precisely because the ruin is what Leshem names "a *partial* presence, a remnant of a whole that is no longer there,"[18] the matter that is still there keeps presencing, almost as if insisting on bringing back memories of the act of destruction. Destruction is what is presented in its very partiality. *A ruin is a re-presencing of erasure.* In this sense, the violence of the ruin is not a matter of *interpretation.* Kathleen Stewart's reading of the ruin itself as that which *remembers* rather than *reminds*, and as such *sustains*, is telling:

> The vacancy of a lot in Rhodell *remembers* the fire that burned Johnny
> Millsap to death while he cried out for help and the others could do

15 Rob Nixon, *Slow Violence and the Environmentalism of the Poor* (Cambridge, MA: Harvard University Press, 2011).

16 Significantly, once we abandon the positivist understanding of violence itself, we also change the language of responsibility: this abandonment "indicates the need to reflect on modes of responsibility and justice that exceed the legal frames in which crimes are usually adjudicated" (Michael Rothberg, *The Implicated Subject: Beyond Victims and Perpetrators* [Stanford, CA: Stanford University Press, 2019], 7).

17 Yael Navaro-Yashin, "Affective Spaces, Melancholic Objects: Ruination and the Production of Anthropological Knowledge," *Journal of the Royal Anthropological Institute* 15, no. 1 (2009): 5.

18 Noam Leshem, *Life after Ruin: The Struggles over Israel's Depopulated Arab Spaces* (Cambridge: Cambridge University Press, 2016), 69–70.

nothing but watch; the exposed electrical wire in the hills above Amigo mines #2 *remembers* the image of Buddy Hall, a nine-year-old boy, hanging from it. . . . Here, you could say, history stands before people, as it does for Benjamin's famous Angel of History, as a pile of refuse that is also the site of dreams of redemption. . . . When people go out roaming the hills, whether in mind or in body, it is this "refuse" and its illuminations they encounter. They come up against places and are stopped dead in their tracks by re-membered images they can't help but recall. Every time Tammy goes to the river now, she "cain't he'p but recall that pore man drowned."[19]

At stake, then, is not what the ruin reminds us of (and hence what it can fail to remind some people of) but what it remembers and embodies, always in excess of what others may try to make it be. This is a phenomenological question that can be discussed separately from the epistemological or interpretational ones ("what do people *see*?" or "how do they *understand or narrate* what they see?").

Trace: Time as Violence

Let us return to *Salt of This Sea*. When Soraya insists that the house in Jaffa where Irit now lives is her home, that it is up to *her* to decide whether Irit can stay ("and you can," she promises immediately, perhaps after Said,[20] "but you must admit that all this is stolen"), Irit says that this is a matter of the past: "You want to speak about history and the past; let's forget it." "Your past is my every day," Soraya replies; "my right now." She continues talking in the present tense: "This is not your home," she insists. But Irit takes the present to be less determined by history: "It is [my home] now," she replies. As Lila Abu-Lughod would phrase it, for Soraya "the past has not yet passed."[21] The house does not bring *memories* but carries what Stoler refers to as the long duress of colonialism.[22]

19 Kathleen Stewart, *A Space on the Side of the Road: Cultural Poetics in an "Other" America* (Princeton, NJ: Princeton University Press, 1996), 90–91.

20 Said kept insisting that in claiming the right to return, he does not want to see the current inhabitants of the many Palestinian homes and cities deported. Justice cannot be achieved through producing further injustice, he argued. But a recognition of the act of dispossession is nevertheless a necessary one. See, for example, the epigraph opening this book.

21 Lila Abu-Lughod, "Return to Half-Ruins: Memory, Postmemory, and Living History in Palestine," in *Nakba: Palestine, 1948, and the Claims of Memory*, ed. Ahmad H. Sa'di and Lila Abu-Lughod (New York: Columbia University Press, 2007), 79.

22 Ann Laura Stoler, *Duress: Imperial Durabilities in Our Times* (Durham, NC: Duke University Press, 2016).

Soraya's house is not a ruin, and the fact that it still stands and is now in-habited by a Jewish Israeli carries an altogether different set of meanings and political implications concerning both the past and possible futures. But since my question here concerns the attachment of Israeli Jews to sites of the de-struction of Palestinians, the depopulated and the destroyed house carry many similarities. Here, I am still thinking about time.

"In the ruin, history itself is brought into the present,"[23] but it is brought into the present not merely as a pale leftover from the past, a haunting spec-ter, but as an enduring history of colonization in the present. "When a trau-matic event is allied with a specific architectural space," Susan Slyomovics ar-gues, following Jung, "such traumas of loss are more tenaciously maintained, reproduced, relived, memorialized, and mourned."[24] Again, the materiality of the house, combined with the affectual trauma of the loss of home, re-structures time so that the past lingers; a hangover. *The ruin is dispossession relived.*

WHEN MUREED AL-BARGHOUTI visited his old village in the West Bank, an old man sent him to see the monastery's spring that is "in ruin": "It is over-run with brambles. The jackals come and go as they please; they cavort there. Go and see for yourself. Everything is as it was when we left it. Nothing has made progress here, except the ruins."[25] The ruin, then, freezes time. Indeed, the two—the destroyed space and the temporality embedded in the ruin—can hardly be disentangled. Al-Barghouti observes:

> My relationship to place is, in fact, a relationship to time. I live in islands
> of time, some of which I already have lost; others I possess for a moment,
> then lose them, because I am always placeless. The monastery spring is
> not a place, it is a period of time. Specifically, it is the time when I was a
> child . . . the time of rising with the first morning prayer in order to taste
> figs picked at dawn. . . . It is also the time when jugs of olive oil arrive
> fresh from Abu Yusif's steam press, and the oil is united with the fresh
> tabun bread in my hand before going to school.[26]

23 Stewart, *Space on the Side of the Road*, 95.
24 Susan Slyomovics, *The Object of Memory: Arab and Jew Narrate the Palestinian Village* (Philadelphia: University of Pennsylvania Press, 1998), xix.
25 Mureed Al-Barghouti, "Songs for a Country No Longer Known," *Journal of Palestine Studies* 27, no. 2 (winter 1998): 64.
26 Al-Barghouti, "Songs," 64.

But what is frozen for the Palestinian time may have passed in Israeli temporality.

In the aftermath of 1948—when Irit's grandparents moved into Soraya's family home, when Fenster's mother settled in another depopulated house in Jaffa, when many Jewish migrants or those who had been in Palestine for some time moved into the depopulated Palestinian houses, when they went to the cities' streets and picked up furniture, when they strolled in the ruined villages and found items of clothing, pots, pens, plates, and cutlery, when they saw pictures of families and loved ones thrown on the ground—it was more difficult to see these ruins or homes as disconnected from the ruination that had just taken place, from the lives that had just been destroyed. But over time, these sites, especially those ruined, lost the tangibility that connected them to past lives. The furniture has been got rid of, as Irit mentions.

Time changes forms of seeing. Perhaps, over time, the destroyed Palestinian home beside the crumbling terraces may indeed begin to resemble the type of ruins Stoler has endeavored to dissociate from imperial ruin: the Roman Aqueduct in Caesarea, for example—a trace from a distant past that can be foreclosed by Irit's insistence to talk about the here and now. Time changes meanings; it also changes one's mode of being implicated in the original violence that generated ruination. This is the case also because time changes what is there to be seen: no more items of clothing or pictures or pots, no more belongings that embody the life that was once there. When Soraya leaves her/Irit's house, she goes to the seaside, where a huge garbage dump holds thousands of pieces of unrecognizable debris: pieces of wood and stone, wires, and rubble. She walks through these unnamable fragments of objects—this happens immediately after Irit tells her that her family's furniture has been disposed of. We—and she—may imagine that this is where this furniture ended up. Can one still see the violence in this rubble?

We may argue that there is a difference here, not merely in *interpretation* or what one sees (one sees rubble and the other her family's lost furniture; one sees a site of natural beauty and the other her destroyed home), but in the different *temporalities* of the various actors on this political stage. Irit's past is Soraya's present. But this clash means that the act of erasure is *always taking place*, precisely by the means of turning a present into a past. In other words, given this rift in temporalities, it is the passage of time for one side that makes violence recurring—an ongoing erasure of the other's present.

FIGURE 2.6. Israeli security forces accompany the destruction of thirteen buildings, in which seventy families lived, in Sur Baher, East Jerusalem, July 22, 2019. Source: Mussa Issa Qawasma/סרטיור, in Jecky Huri et al. "The House Demolition in East Jerusalem Is a Ruthless Attack on Simple People," *Ha'aretz*, July 22, 2019, https://www .haaretz.co.il/news/politics/.premium-1.7547975.

WHILE TALKING ABOUT these different meanings or forms of violence, it is important to remember again that violence does not flow evenly. The violence that entails living in a depopulated home is very different from the violence of invading a populated home, which we shall meet in the next chapter, for example. In this book, these are separated by both time and geography: the violence of active expropriation and transfer is situated either in the past of homes such as Irit's (homes situated within the 1948 borders) or in the present of the West Bank (homes to which we shall move now). But this is a simplification made for some analytical clarity. Active, ongoing projects of invasion and house demolition occur in "Israel proper," with families and individuals losing entire lives to bulldozers, often accompanied by police forces (in the case of Mizrahi Jews evicted as part of municipal gentrification projects) or military units (in the case of Palestinians or Bedouins within the Green Line and in East Jerusalem). Feeding on destruction is not a matter of the past.

FIGURE 2.7. A screenshot from Netanyahu's Facebook page (post from January 10, 2017, screen-shot taken July 25, 2019). The text says: "Our forces are now destroying twelve homes of Arabs in Qalansawe [an Israeli Palestinian town in central Israel]. 800 police officers enforce security." The houses in Qalansawe were constructed without permits, much like the more than 100,000 buildings of Palestinians who are Israeli citizens. Israel halts all development enterprises of Palestinian towns and villages, and "illegal" construction is the only solution for the growing population. Since its establishment in 1948, Israel has built more than one thousand settlements (towns, villages, cities) for the Jewish population, and not a single one for the Palestinian popula-tion (except for towns in the Negev/Naqab aimed at concentrating the Bedouin population that was to be evicted from their places of residence). The rejoicing text of the Israeli prime minister facing the destruction came in the context of the eviction of Amona, which the government was forced to conduct shortly beforehand. The destruction of the Qalansawe houses was a formal "price tag" of sorts. Let us shift to Amona, then.

Part III

SETTLEMENT

Interlude
A Moment of Popular Culture

THE HOME OF *MASTERCHEF*

EYAL SHANI [CHEF AND JUDGE]: Perhaps because of [the evacuation of] Amona [an outpost in the West Bank evacuated in 2017] you do not feel like you belong to Israel?

YEHO'IADA NIZRI [CANDIDATE]: Look, I was deported from my home, I mean, when the policemen entered the house, I felt violated. Home is a shelter, a fortress; it is the safest place for me, for my family, for my children. And suddenly, when they came and penetrated this [shelter], it was a tremendous pain. And I still carry this pain with me. I will probably carry it with me forever. —MASTERCHEF

The seventh season of the Israeli franchise of the popular reality show *MasterChef* began airing in October 2017. It was shot, however, a few months earlier, four months after the eviction of Amona: an isolated outpost (basically, an illegal settlement) located east of Ramallah, in the heart of the West Bank.[1] With forty-two families at its heyday, Amona was one of the first outposts, founded in 1995 on land owned by Palestinians from the villages of Silwad, Ein Yabrud, and Taybeh. While the government issued demolition orders against the outpost

Epigraph: MasterChef Israel, season 7, episode 1, October 2017; all translations from the show are mine.

1   It was the last of the six more established outposts and small settlements evacuated in the West Bank since the Oslo Accords: Kadim, Ganim, Sa Nor, and Homesh as part of the disengagement plan in 2005; Migron in 2012; and Amona.

as early as 1997 and several times since, and while the Israeli government itself acknowledged that this outpost (alongside 105 others) was illegal *according to Israeli law*, different Israeli governments throughout the years did everything they could to avoid actual eviction.[2] Perhaps because the original Palestinian owners held documentation proving their ownership, which is often unavailable to many Palestinians, and perhaps because a rare police investigation exposed that the settlers' claims that they had legally purchased the land were based on a vast act of forgery, the long legal struggle ended with a far-from-common High Court of Justice insistence on Amona's eviction.[3] Government efforts to legitimize the land grab via legislation were thus futile in the case of Amona, although they ultimately led to the current "Judea and Samaria Settlement Regulation Law," which retrospectively grants land-use rights to settlements built on Palestinian land. The eviction itself took place in two steps. During the first, in 2006, nine houses were demolished, and during the second, in 2017, the entire settlement was cleared. The effort to demolish the first nine houses ended with dozens of demonstrators and policemen in hospitals, a Parliamentary Inquiry

2 All settlements in the West Bank are illegal according to international law. However, Israel's law recognizes the legitimacy of settlements built on state land—land officially confiscated or legally purchased. Illegal settlements ("outposts") are those built on privately owned Palestinian land, without any central planning or authorization (for more on these distinctions, see chapter 3, note 15). Despite their illegality, the vast majority of these outposts receive de facto support, as the state provides access roads, electricity, water, and—above all—military protection. Above data from (respectively): "The Amona Complex," *Ha'aretz*, October 16, 2013, https://www.haaretz.com/opinion/israel-s-messianic-anti-zionist-dream-1.5274437; Talya Sason, "Summary of the Opinion Concerning Unauthorized Outposts," Israel Ministry of Foreign Affairs, March 10, 2005, https://mfa.gov.il/mfa/aboutisrael/state/law/pages/summary .aspx.

3 See Yesh Din, "Petition to Remove the Unauthorized Outpost of Amona," *Yesh Din Website*, November 25, 2008, https://www.yesh-din.org/en/petition-to-remove-the-unauthorized-outpost -of-amona/. For a copy of the submitted petition to the High Court of Justice [in Hebrew], see www.yesh-din.org/en. On the police investigation, see Chaim Levinson, "Police Discover That Entire Amona Outpost Was Built on Palestinian Land," *Ha'aretz*, May 26, 2014, https://www .haaretz.com/premium-police-amona-built-on-palestinian-land-1.5249597. There are relatively few instances of Israel's High Court of Justice insisting on actually evicting Jewish settlers, with the most famous being Ellon Moreh in 1979. In some cases, the court allows the state to delay the eviction indefinitely. Often, the time that passes makes it possible for the state to declare the contested plot as state land; in other cases, the court accepts the state's position that the land is needed for security reasons. See Idith Zertal and Akiva Eldar, *Lords of the Land: The War over Israel's Settlements in the Occupied Territories, 1967–2007*, trans. Vivian Eden (New York: Nation Books, 2005).

Committee, and a traumatic memory of what looked like—or was constructed as—the launch of a civil war. There were more casualties during the evacuation of these few houses than during the entire 2005 disengagement from Gaza several months earlier.[4] Before the second evacuation, Benjamin Netanyahu's government promised to build a new settlement for Amona's evacuees, deep in the eastern part of the West Bank. The new settlement, Amichai, was populated by the first twenty-five families on March 25, 2018, three weeks after the final episode of *MasterChef* (season 7). The new settlement is not mentioned in the show at all, but the demolished homes of Amona play a significant role in it.

FROM ITS BEGINNING, when pita bread is announced as the dish each candidate must prepare, the opening episode is framed by a national theme: pita is presented as the ultimate Israeli dish and becomes, in the words of the various candidates appearing throughout the episode, a mark of both the national and the personal home (disregarding, first, that at least to some extent, this is originally *Arab* food that was adopted by the Jewish Israeli kitchen later, and second, that pita is often eaten *outside* the home, as street food).[5] Yeho'iada Nizri—one of the candidates, a settler from Amona, and the main figure in this chapter—defines the pita as an allegory of Israeli society: "Pita represents a kind of unity; like the Israeli people [*Am Yisrael*].[6] There are sour people, there are people who are sweet, there are seculars and religious people. Everything goes into a single

4 Efrat Weiss and Anat Bershovsky, "Amona's Takeover Has Been Completed, Hundreds Were Hurt," *Ynet*, February 1, 2006, https://www.ynet.co.il/articles/0,7340, L-3209281,00.html.
5 On such modes of appropriating Middle Eastern food, see David Louis Gold, "Another Look at Israeli Hebrew *Pita* 'Flat Bread': A Borrowing from Judezmo and Yiddish," *Romance Philology* 42, no. 3 (1989): 276–78; Rafi Grosglik, "Global Ethical Culinary Fashion and a Local Dish: Organic Hummus in Israel," *Critical Studies in Fashion and Beauty* 2, nos. 1–2 (2011): 165–84; Liora Gvion, "Cooking, Food, and Masculinity: Palestinian Men in Israeli Society," *Men and Masculinities* 14, no. 4 (October 2011): 408–29; Dafna Hirsch, "'Hummus Is Best When It Is Fresh and Made by Arabs': The Gourmetization of Hummus in Israel and the Return of the Repressed Arab," *American Ethnologist* 38, no. 4 (November 2011): 617–30. The ordinary, daily consumption of food makes claims to the national origins of food always partial. Versions of pita bread exist across cultures, including China, South America, and Turkey. The Israeli version of pita is to some extent a unique adaptation of the Middle Eastern version from which it was born (in terms of size and thickness) and so, in some sense, it has become Israeli. Within its geopolitical context, however, this becoming is tightly linked to Arab roots. I thank Rafi Groslik for some of this information.
6 Am Yisrael is a concept, if not a speech act, which creates a direct and exclusive link between the Jews who are Israeli citizens, non-Israeli Jews in the diaspora, and the idea of the nation. It thereby excludes all other citizens of the state and marks the state's borders as essentially ethnic.

pita, and when you take a bite, it's tasty."[7] Whereas stories of nation and home (often indistinguishable) are present throughout the episode (and the season at large), it is with Nizri that these themes become most explicit.

Nizri's home—his ruined home—is the main theme of the segments focusing on him throughout the season. From the moment he appears on screen, he is presented as a family man, a master of his household, and, as if to draw on the stereotype of domesticity to emphasize this connection to his home, as a "mommy." To those unfamiliar with the format, the opening episode of *MasterChef* is an audition. Several dozen candidates are requested to make a dish as a preliminary test (in this case, their unique version of pita bread), which is then sent, anonymously, to the judges—four of the leading chefs in Israel. The best candidates are called forward to meet the judges and cook a dish of their choice in front of them. The last candidate was Nizri, one of the first settlers in Amona and a leading figure in the struggle against its eviction. As one of the judges, Haim Cohen, tastes his pita, still unaware of who made it, he speculates that it was prepared by a mother who needs to feed many children. Cohen then adds, poetically: "I can imagine here a unity of the family around this pita."[8] Nizri is presented as a domestic figure and, as such, a bearer of unity—of both nation (in a pita, in his own words) and family (through and around a pita, in Cohen's version).

This unity, however, seems to be broken when Nizri steps into the room. Unity becomes otherness and otherness becomes a conflict. The chef and judge Eyal Shani serves as the adversary in this conflict and represents, supposedly, some Israeli Left attitude that is to be remolded throughout the episode and season. As Nizri enters the audition room, Shani immediately asks him about his large yamaka (because "it's beautiful," Shani says, as if to tone down the clear othering effect of his question). In case we have missed Shani's disdain, he also snorts when Nizri says his name (a very unusual Israeli name, clearly marking a particular religious milieu). He asks Nizri where he is from, his tone attacking, as if he already knows the answer. "Until four months ago, I was from Amona," Nizri replies. At this point, Michal Anski, another judge, asks: "Were you among those evicted?," marking Nizri as a victim. But Shani

---

7 *MasterChef Israel*, season 7, episode 1. At the same time, this national symbol is placed as a hallmark of home: "For me," Nizri says, "pita is a way to indulge my children." Other candidates state that "pita is the most Israeli thing in existence" and that "this pita is my home; this is what would make you feel at home at a Shabbat dinner in my home."

8 During the semifinal, Shani would say: "His cooking is round and maternal . . . and it feels 'home' because of this softness and roundness."

refuses her definition and interrupts her: "You are a settler," he says to Nizri, harshly.

The conversation continues, with Anski and Shani being the main judges speaking and Nizri masterfully altering his word choice and attitude as he answers them, addressing their two very different voices. With Shani, he insists (kindly, politely, and with a sense of humor) on his right to settle and, more so, refuses the claims that the West Bank is not "in Israel" and that to be a proper part of the collective, he needs to "return" to the recognized borders of the state. He replies softly to Anski's more personal questions about his household. Anski, the only woman among the four judges, stereotypically keeps urging everyone to "put politics aside" in the name of unity obtained through food. But this effort to steer clear of "politics" is futile (a futility that makes it the most successful strategy of the normalization of settlements). The personal household cannot be extricated from its political settings; its very existence *is* the political action. By merely living in his home, Nizri stole land; much later in the season (in episode 19), Nadia, a Palestinian candidate from Jerusalem, reminds him of this. Cooking a "family dinner" together, she mentions that Nizri had taken her for a "tour" in "greater Palestine" ("greater Israel," he corrects her), to show her "all the settlements, all that they stole from me" ("where our fathers were born and raised," he corrects her again, "our fathers who gave us the right to be here"—"Really? Really?," she responds). But beyond this moment, Nizri will not be held accountable for this robbery, and the only pain we will see is his own pain, the outcome of a traumatic house demolition.

Simply "being there," as a settler in the West Bank, is itself a political act and an effort to re-demarcate national borders (erasing the Green Line), but it is also a constant appeal to the state and its military might. Even if Nizri merely sought to reside there peacefully, *because* he sought to reside "peacefully" *there*, his home constantly summons military violence; his very homemaking *is* occupation. Thus, when he tells the judges about waking up his children every morning as the sun rises above the mountains or about the spices they used to pick outdoors (spices he uses in the show, thereby re-presencing the occupied land when he cooks), the very minute details of his family life are woven into the politics of settlement. Anski's efforts to retrieve the former from the latter are thus futile, and it is precisely through the ongoing failure of this retrieval that the latter (settlement) becomes foldable into the former (home) and becomes normalized and more acceptable (recall Rice's words from part II—"It isn't a question of empire, you see. It is our home"—which seek to perform the same depoliticization).

This is perhaps most evident when Shani's accusation "you are a settler," which is political in its terminology, is transformed into an individualized accusation concerning parental responsibility: "You know," Shani says, "you live on very fragile ground. You are responsible for eight children and you build a home for them that can also be torn down. Do you see yourself as a responsible father?"—"Yes, I am a responsible father," Nizri declares immediately.[9] "Without venturing into politics [and Shani interrupts: 'as a family man'], as a family man [Nizri adopts Shani's words], life in Israel, life in Judea and Samaria [the West Bank] is not a political matter . . . Four hundred thousand people live in Judea and Samaria; no one is going to evict them or expatriate them. This is not an option." The question of settlement has been settled (eviction is "not an option") and can thus be declared as "not political."[10]

Significant parts of the dialogue revolve around the materiality of Nizri's home (house). As part of his effort to evoke otherness at the first stages of the conversation, Shani asks whether Nizri's family used to live in a mobile home in Amona—a stereotypical image of home in the more extremist settlements. Nizri replies: "No. We lived in a house; a big house with a large kitchen." The kitchen opens the possibility of rearticulating the materiality of dispossession (settlements) in colors that appeal to all the judges (and presumably viewers as well). Through it, a transition is made in the discussion, which shifts from denunciation to a discourse of loss and pain. The kitchen is no longer there. After the eviction, Nizri and his family were moved to a youth hostel, where there was no kitchen at all (just one sink in which "one both brushes their teeth and makes sandwiches"). This loss of the possibility to cook seems to bring everyone closer, a process culminating when Nizri responds to the question "why did you come to *MasterChef*?" with the ultimate Israeli cliché of unity: the IDF, the alleged "melting pot" of Israeli society. "I feel that *MasterChef* is like being in the military: you meet everyone, all types of people," Nizri opens his re-

9 On the wider frame of these debates concerning "responsible parenthood" as part of the settlement project and the insistence on constructing family homes as a political project, see Michael Feige, *Settling in the Hearts: Jewish Fundamentalism in the Occupied Territories* (Detroit: Wayne State University Press, 2009), esp. 243ff.

10 As Michael Feige puts it, "the home serves as a statement that the settler project is one of homecoming and is therefore connected to peaceful families wishing to live on their land, whose evacuation would be a moral outrage and a crime against their basic human rights." "Creating homes can therefore be considered to be 'soft power.' It is an invasive strategy, intended to 'Judaize' space at the expense of the Palestinians, but it is meant to be portrayed as friendly, peaceful, and 'homely'" (Michael Feige, "Soft Power: The Meaning of Home for Gush Emunim Settlers," *Journal of Israeli History* 32, no. 1 [2013]: 110; see introduction, note 3).

sponse, marking the Israeli army as a space of encounter rather than an agent of violence. "I finished my reserve service a few years ago and I missed meeting the entire 'tribe,' the people of Israel [Am Yisrael]."

With this unity, Shani can reintroduce the otherness and externality, only to allow it to be resolved. This is where the moment that opened this chapter arrives: "Perhaps because of Amona you do not feel like you belong to Israel?" he asks in response to Nizri's craving for unity. "Look," Nizri replies, "I was deported from my home. . . . It was a tremendous pain. And I still carry this pain with me. I will probably carry it with me forever." This is the final moment of catharsis. At this point, both the audition and the episode are brought to an end, and Nizri's family is invited to enter the room. This is the only family invited to do so. They join the judges in singing traditional Jewish songs, and the final images of the episode are of the judges hugging Nizri's family members. None of the other candidates has received any physical affection. Anski's final words recapitulate the trajectory of the conversation and its message: "I may be far away from you in my political views and geographically," she tells the eight sons and daughters, "but I feel as close to you as someone can feel because I felt a Shabbat dinner at your home." A "Shabbat dinner" was Nizri's dish of choice for the audition. He will continue to cook challah bread and talk about Shabbat family dinners throughout the season. This is the ultimate Israeli symbol of home, and he indeed declares that this is the dinner he used to prepare "at home—the home that was." But reminiscing about the destruction of that home, which is no longer there, is not to abandon the settlement project. The dinner includes herbs from the "Judea Mountains" in the West Bank and his own wine, made in the vineyards that "still stand firm" in the lands of Amona.[11] Amona became present, as a tragedy and as a legitimate home, as the trauma of eviction that is not to be reproduced, in the living rooms of the Israeli households watching the show.

PART OF THE STORY of Nizri and Amona consists of the dialectic of violence and normalization revolving around the threats (decreasing, I should add) to

---

11 Following the order to evict and to demolish all the houses, Amona's settlers petitioned the High Court of Justice to stop the eviction of their agricultural land. Their claim was that the Palestinian landowners who originally appealed to the court explicitly asked for the eviction of the settlement alone, and not its annexed agricultural land. Nizri was one of those petitioners. Fifty-five dunams (5.5 hectares) of agricultural land are still under dispute and are still being cultivated by Amona's settlers. Data courtesy of Kerem Navot, April 22, 2018, https://www.keremnavot.org/feed/Date/2018-04.

evacuate settlements. Nizri's participation in *MasterChef* was one of many acts that were taken as part of an endeavor to prevent future evictions of settlements. The endeavor was framed as an effort to "settle in the hearts" of the Israeli public, to normalize the settlement project, and to halt the prospect of a territorial compromise that entails dismantling settlements.[12] But this is not the story I want to tell here.

To write this chapter, I watched many YouTube videos of Amona's evacuation. I saw homes that were evidently embedded in violence. To see this violence, one does not need to have previous knowledge of the theft of land, the lies involved to justify it, and the acts of violence toward neighboring villages.[13] It is enough to look at the houses' walls, sprayed with slogans such as "death to all Arabs," to see this violence clearly. To see the hate. The racism. And still, the pain of the evicted people is there as well. As they lie on the ground, hug it, holding on to whatever possible, are forcibly carried away by security forces. Or as they turn their bodies into passive heavyweights, letting police officers lift them up and carry them outside of their home—resisting without resistance, refusing to leave yet accepting to be moved. Or as they stand outside their homes, looking at the bulldozers demolishing everything they have built, everything that has been them for so long, crying. Even though these people lost only what they stole, even though much of this act was an orchestrated spectacle whose participants often arrived from elsewhere to enhance the effect of eviction in order to prevent the next one, even though this very loss seems to me necessary if one is to imagine a better future for that land, it is still a loss. And the loss and the sorrow accompanying it are impossible to dismiss; but also impossible to contain alongside all that I know about the history, geography, and politics of that place.

It is impossible to hold on to the pain while simultaneously recognizing that it is necessary, to share the grief of anyone who is uprooted but understand that these people cannot stay where they are—not just because their homes are an act of robbery (an injustice that can be resolved via compensation), but also because they are built to establish a hierarchical domination that prevents all possibility of a just solution: they are built on the top of the hills, establishing

---

12 Feige, *Settling in the Hearts*.

13 On some of these justificatory lies, see Hagit Ofran and Aharon Shem-Tov, "Unraveling the Mechanism behind Illegal Outposts," Settlement Watch, *Peace Now*, 2017, 2018, http://peacenow .org.il/wp-content/uploads/2017/03/unraveling-the-mechanism-behind-illegal-outposts-full -report-1.pdf; see also note 3 in this interlude.

visual control,[14] making sure that water sources are fully in Jewish hands,[15] and their sewage often runs into the Palestinian villages below.[16] As long as these homes are there, there is a structural impossibility of any solution, whether it is based on separation (because the settlements bisect the West Bank into small land cells and create what Meron Benvenisti understood as early as the 1980s as a spatial reality in which a separation into two territorial entities is impossible),[17] or whether it takes the form of reconstructing a just shared space (because of the above architecture of control). Watching from the Left, the images of the eviction are so difficult to process not because they show the injustice done to settlers but because they show how justice itself hurts others so much. This sense of impasse is suffocating.

14 Israeli settlements and their unauthorized outposts have almost always been built on hilltops overlooking Palestinian villages, so that they could serve as mechanisms of civilian surveillance. The desire to maximize the visibility of the indigenous Palestinian population dictated the mode of design of the settlements, "down to the positioning of windows in houses," thus transforming settlements into "optical devices, designed to exercise control through supervision and surveillance." Eyal Weizman, *Hollow Land: Israel's Architecture of Occupation* (London: Verso Books, 2007), 111–39, 131; see also Neve Gordon and Moriel Ram, "Ethnic Cleansing and the Formation of Settler Colonial Geographies," *Political Geography* 53 (July 2016): 20–29.

15 Israel and the Palestinian Authority share two water systems: the Mountain Aquifer and the Jordan Basin. Israel receives 79 percent of the water from the Mountain Aquifer, the Palestinians 21 percent; the Palestinians have no access to the Jordan Basin, and Israel has full control over this resource. Thus, Israel maintains almost complete control over all the water resources in the West Bank. Average water consumption in Israel (per capita) is five times that in Palestine. See Yehezkel Lein, "Thirsty for a Solution: The Water Shortage in the Occupied Territories and Its Solution in the Final Status Agreement," *B'tselem*, July 2000, https://www.btselem.org /publications/summaries/200007_thirsty_for_a_solution.

16 Israel transfers different types of waste to the West Bank: sewage sludge, infectious medical waste, used oils, solvents, metals, electronic waste, and batteries. Israel supported the construction of at least fifteen waste treatment facilities in the West Bank, which manage waste that is produced in Israel. Six facilities handle hazardous waste (which requires special processes and regulatory supervision due to the dangers of toxicity, mutagenicity (carcinogenicity), infectiousness, flammability, and combustibility). It also created a different legal framework from the one used inside Israel to manage waste. Adam Aloni, "Made in Israel: Exploiting Palestinian Land for Treatment of Israeli Waste," *B'tselem*, December 2017, https://www.btselem.org/sites /default/files/publications/201712_made_in_israel_eng.pdf.

17 Meron Benvenisti, *The West Bank Data Project: A Survey of Israel's Policies* (Washington, DC: American Enterprise Institute for Public Policy Research, 1986).

WHILE THIS LOSS must be contended with, while it cannot be dismissed, to point *merely* to this loss, to allow it to guide political decisions and/or political sentiments, is to decontextualize these houses and homes from what they are. And all this contextualization disappears in the reality show. In *MasterChef*, but also in the Israeli media at large, the only painful evictions we see are those of settlers—never of the many Palestinians who have lost their homes, who have been evicted, their homes demolished, their land taken. The Palestinians residing in Silwad, Ein Yabrud, and Taybeh—the other victims of Amona, on whose lands Amona was built—are invisible.[18] The home in Amona can thus become the symbol of such losses, such destruction, despite the fact that the overwhelming majority of houses demolished by the Israeli state are not those of settlers but those of Palestinians.

In this sense, Nizri's appropriation of pita bread or Arab food more widely is a fragment of, or a symbol of, a much deeper appropriation: that of Palestinian pain and loss. The hundreds of thousands of Palestinians who have lost their homes—through eviction or demolition or expulsion—are replaced by the several dozen Jewish families evicted, as homelessness itself is appropriated. The fact that herbs and grapes (wine) are key to the descriptions of his loss also constitutes, moreover, appropriation of the *medium* of grief. Herbs, plants, or fruits often become a tangible metaphor for the Palestinian home that is gone as well as concrete objects to which one can return. Often, these herbs or fruits are the only trace left of the house that is no longer there.[19] Nizri, too, returns to his herbs, to the vineyards that "still stand there," that are, in his case too, the sole remnant of the demolished house. The reversal is thereby completed; the settler becomes a refugee. And yet never fully so: unlike most Palestinians, Nizri enjoys protected, secured access to his herbs and grapes; and while the Amona home emerged as fragile, the territorial rights remain unchallenged. And above all, we must not forget the new settlement that by the time of the show's broadcast was already there. Accordingly, if, in the case of Palestinians, reclaiming the land by

18 Even the accusation "you are a settler" is likely to be read as a violation of some Israeli national integrity and not as a reference to the systematic, structural, and physical violence inflicted by this group, at large, on the Palestinian population in the West Bank.

19 See, for example, Bashir el-Hairi, *Letters to a Lemon Tree*, trans. D. Brafman (Jerusalem: Alternative Information Center, 1997). The lemon, the spices, the herbs are further what Efrat Ben-Ze'ev terms "mnemonic devices and memory containers" for Palestinian refugees. They add the texture of taste and smell to the memories of the pre-1948 life, a visceral object that is more than a memory, as it is the very presence of the thing lost. Efrat Ben-Ze'ev, "The Politics of Taste and Smell: Palestinian Rites of Return," in *The Politics of Food*, ed. Marianne E. Lien and Brigitte Nerlich (London: Bloomsbury Press, 2004), 141–60.

FIGURE 3.1. Land, or Jerusalem: a dessert by Meir Adoni. On the right-hand side is the white chocolate mousse ball representing the Dome of the Rock. Source: Meir Adoni, "Adama Dessert: A Recipe to the Marvelous Dessert by Meir Adoni," *Mako*, February 25, 2018, https://www.mako.co.il/food-recipes/recipes_column-masterchef/Article-7d3840a805cc161006.htm.

claiming the fruit trees and herbs is a "minor act of political opposition,"[20] in the case of Nizri this is the entrenchment of the order of settlement.

BUT PERHAPS APPROPRIATION is too weak of a word to describe what is at stake here. Perhaps more than an act of appropriating homelessness in order to secure the project of Palestinians' dispossession in the West Bank, and perhaps more than cooking Arab food as a way of appropriating indigeneity, there is here a collective effort to consume Palestine itself. To eat it, that is.[21] Whereas this may be a mere metaphor, it almost materializes in episode 31, when the candidates are asked to replicate an intricate dessert by the Israeli chef Meir Adoni that represents, or is inspired by, Jerusalem. The dessert includes mountains made of marzipan, olive trees that are olive oil candies, stones made of chocolate, and a frozen ball made of white chocolate mousse, frozen with liquid nitrogen, which stands for the Dome of the Rock.

20 Ben-Ze'ev, "Politics of Taste and Smell," 144.
21 This thought—among others—was kindly offered to me by Murad Idris.

Nizri feels like this is the dessert made for him, a dessert through which he can experience a sense of place once again. As soon as she tastes his creation, Anski confirms that she can savor the soil, the land, the roots, in Nizri's dessert. Shani, known for his poetic language, reflects on the quiet, solid connection to the land (the territory, the soil, *adama* in Hebrew) that one can taste in Nizri's cooking. "There is a feeling here," he says, "of something that happened on the ground, stood still, and turned silent." At that point, Nizri cannot stop his tears. He tells them about how, when he arranged the plate, he imagined the road leading from Amona to Jerusalem, the mountains seen from his home that is no longer there, "a ruin that still exists—my home that is being destroyed, the temple that is being destroyed, and I wanted to rebuild it." "I miss the land [again: *adama*, also soil, ground, territory]," he later says. "[I miss] my home . . . the feeling of stability . . . Now, everything is destroyed."

His voice cracks. The background music, the sympathetic looks on the judges' faces, make it easy to sense his grief. But Nizri's dessert is missing something: it has no Dome of the Rock. When Nizri tries to make the delicate ice ball, it explodes. Nizri is alarmed for a moment and then shrugs: "I do not really need that Dome of the Rock, anyway; we want to see the [Jewish] temple built there." Nizri expresses here, in and through a dessert that has failed—but thus succeeded beyond expectations—a fantasy of the Jewish extreme Right to detonate the Muslim holy sites located where the temple once stood and rebuild the temple instead. This enterprise (which has become a concrete effort since the 1980s led by a group, "the Jewish Underground," that includes many leaders of settlers' organizations today) is more than likely to initiate an unprecedented regional war. Nevertheless, its small-scale culinary version passes without much attention. It does not seem to remind anyone of all the homes whose destruction the construction of Nizri's old, but also new, home entails. Only one of the judges finds it important to comment on this absence. "I wonder what Freud would have said [about this omission]," he laughs.

3. On Eggs and Dispossession

ORGANIC AGRICULTURE AND
THE NEW SETTLEMENT MOVEMENT

Building a house equals wiping out a hundred Arabs; building a new settlement is like killing a hundred thousand.—MOSHE ZAR, A LAND MERCHANT AND MEMBER OF THE JEWISH UNDERGROUND

The mobile home and later the small red-roofed single family house replaced the tank as a basic battle unit; homes, like armoured divisions, were deployed in formation across a theatre of operations to occupy hills, to encircle an enemy, or to cut its communication lines.—EYAL WEIZMAN

Through its ceaseless expansion, agriculture (including, for this purpose, commercial pastoralism) progressively eats into Indigenous territory, a primitive accumulation that turns native flora and fauna into a dwindling resource and curtails the reproduction of Indigenous modes of production.—PATRICK WOLFE

The story of this chapter provides a small piece of history of the new settlement movement in the West Bank—a movement whose historical and structural parameters will be outlined below and that has been radically reshaping area C after the Oslo Accords.[1] At the same time, this is a structural story,

Epigraphs: Moshe Zar, words said at a formal convention at the Israeli Ministry of Education, Jerusalem, July 2, 2018; see report by Adir Yanko, "On Stage, in a Conference of Ministry of Education," *Ynet* July 3, 2018, https://www.ynet.co.il/articles/0,7340,L-5302979,00.html; Eyal Weizman, *Hollow Land: Israel's Architecture of Occupation* (London: Verso Books, 2007), 83; Patrick Wolfe, "Settler Colonialism and the Elimination of the Native," *Journal of Genocide Research* 8, no. 4 (2006): 395.

1 The Oslo Agreement divided the West Bank into three areas: area A, under Palestinian control; area B, under Palestinian civil administration but with Israel retaining security control; and

encapsulating a larger pattern of settlement: not just of the settlement movement at large or even Zionism to the extent that it was a movement of settlement; it is also a classic story of settler colonialism. Unlike the stories of part II, this is not a story of a home found in the ruins of another but of a home that emerges through ruining other homes. This is a chapter about ruin in-the-making.

Presumably, at stake in the shift from part II to this part is a shift between two primary subject positions of settlers. The one that occupied part II—we can call it liberal—is internally contradictory. Its different pieces simply do not fit together and hence it is bound to self-destruct in different ways (to abandon the liberal project, to subsist with internal wounds, or to self-negate somehow, as in the case of Madame Nielsen in *Les Blancs*). The story here seemingly has no conflicts. It is a story of settlement supported by a theological framework in which the land belongs solely to the Jewish people, of stable racial hierarchies; but also—as this chapter sets out to show—it is a story of settlement supported by a certain vision in which sustainability is essentially and necessarily violent. If this book seeks to understand modes of attachment to violence via an attachment to place, and attachments to place via an attachment to violence, the story of this chapter is one in which violence is woven into the attachment to territory in seemingly coherent ways. And yet there are conflicts and contradictions in this story too, through which, perhaps, political potentialities can be opened. Before we begin, however, it is important to emphasize yet again that even though the two models of settlement are presented here as radically different, and even though they are marked here by separate geographical and temporal lines (the 1967 borders versus the 1948 ones, the history of settlement versus its presents), the distinctions are in fact often blurred and the models often converge. This is where I end.

ON THESE PAGES, the story of one home in the West Bank unfolds—a mini-scale "empire" called Giv'ot Olam (in Hebrew, "hills of the world" as well as "hills for eternity"). This is the largest organic farm in Israel and the largest supplier of organic, free-range eggs in the country.[2] In 2018, eggs were the sec-

---

area C, under Israeli security control and civil administration. The latter area is also where almost all settlements are built (excluding Hebron, which is in area A). Area A comprises approximately 18 percent of the West Bank, and Area B about 22 percent; together, they are home to some 2.8 million Palestinians. Area C amounts to 40 percent of the entire West Bank.

2   It currently employs about seventy people, and all bachelors among the workers live on its grounds (author's fieldnotes, June 25, 2017, Giv'ot Olam). The yearly amount of eggs it produces is incomparable to other suppliers of organic eggs in Israel. See last section of this chapter.

ond thing in the West Bank to be officially annexed by Israel.[3] After the Israeli parliament placed Ariel University under the authority of the Israeli Council of Higher Education in February 2018, thereby effectively asserting Israel's sovereignty over academic education in the West Bank, in June of that year, the parliament approved a single system uniting egg production in Israel with egg production (by settlers) in the West Bank.[4] Giv'ot Olam's eggs are therefore a significant player in the process of annexing land and dispossessing Palestinians, both directly and allegorically.

Much has been written about agriculture as both a technology and a justificatory scheme for colonization: particular modes of agriculture have served to take over land as well as to frame it as "empty" and available for appropriation.[5] Wolfe identified agriculture as "a potent symbol of settler-colonial identity" due to its expansionist qualities.[6] However, *organic* agriculture, alongside slow-food movements, also undercut this justificatory framework—not just because it emphasizes an ethical approach to food but also because it promotes some "return" to localness. "It is difficult to talk about fairness [in food production and consumption] when Jewish Israelis make hummus or call labaneh produced in Hebron a local Israeli product," says Amit Aharonson, one of the leading figures in the Israeli slow-food movement. "Most Israeli cooking arrives from a different *terroir*; it has no real connection to the land here [whereas]

---

3 Settlements and settlers themselves, however, have been subjected to Israeli law from the outset, even though the territory in which they live is subjected to military rule.

4 Ariel University was established by and operated until that time by a different council, the Council for Higher Education in Judea and Samaria. This council was explicitly limited in its authority, and subjected to the military administration of the West Bank. On the unification of egg-production quotas, see Jonathan Lis, "In Israel, Even Eggs Are Cause for Conflict: New Poultry Law Slammed as 'Creeping Annexation,'" *Ha'aretz*, June 12, 2018, https://www.haaretz .com/israel-news/.premium-new-law-passed-for-west-bank-farmers-slammed-as-creeping -annexation-1.6173080.

5 For various contexts, see William W. Bassett, "The Myth of the Nomad in Property Law," *Journal of Law and Religion* 4, no. 1 (1986): 133–52; Naved Hamid, "Dispossession and Differentiation of the Peasantry in the Punjab during Colonial Rule," *Journal of Peasant Studies* 10, no. 1 (1982): 52–72; Gershon Shafir, *Land, Labor and the Origins of the Israeli-Palestinian Conflict, 1882–1914* (Cambridge: Cambridge University Press, 1989); James Tully, *An Approach to Political Philosophy: Locke in Contexts* (Cambridge: Cambridge University Press, 1993); Eyal Weizman and Fazal Sheikh, *The Conflict Shoreline: Colonization as Climate Change in the Negev Desert* (Göttingen: Steidl, 2015); Christopher Zambakari, "Land Grab and Institutional Legacy of Colonialism: The Case of Sudan," *Consilience: The Journal of Sustainable Development* 18, no. 2 (2017): 193–204; and chapter 1 of the present book.

6 Wolfe, "Settler Colonialism and the Elimination of the Native," 396.

slow food is a movement preoccupied with roots." For Israel, Aharonson says, it may be best to establish a movement of rootless food.[7] Accordingly, this chapter looks at how settler locality is produced, how an "organic" relationship between people and land is cultivated, and how this project takes on an ethical form.

Through the analysis of organic agriculture I seek to put forward a few themes concerning the structure and mechanisms of settlement: the relations between settlement and mobility, in particular the identification of a mobile (expansive) mode of settlement that stands at the core of settler colonialism; the relations between aesthetic and settlers' homemaking, which is also a way of questioning the relations between the desire for beauty and the reality of ugly homes; the different modalities of violence that are woven into the daily practices of homemaking; and the relations between violence and ethics that envelop such a mode of homemaking, as well as the role of organic agriculture within the latter. In regard to the question of ethics, what must be made clear—and what I hope is already clear—is that when I refer to the ethics of violence or dispossession, I do not argue that dispossession itself is "ethical." By "ethics," I refer to the stories people tell themselves and others about the rights and wrongs of their actions or ways of being. Specifically, I look at organic agriculture as an ethical scheme for homes that are built very concretely, directly, and explicitly as tools of dispossession.[8] This particular ethical framework was

7 Ronit Vered, "Why the 'Slow Food' Movement Was Never Successful in Israel" [in Hebrew], *Ha'aretz*, November, 2, 2016, https://www.haaretz.co.il/food/dining/.premium-MAGAZINE-1 .3109626. Relatedly, we can state that whereas, on the one hand, organic agriculture is about "locality," on the other hand, the production of organic food in Israel is often based on imported products and consumption is very much about a global politics/identity. See Rafi Grosglik, "Organic Hummus in Israel: Global and Local Ingredients and Images," *Sociological Research Online* 16, no. 2 (June 2011): 1–11.

8 IFOAM, the "international umbrella organization of the organic world," defines organic agriculture as an ethics and outlines the four "inter-connected ethical principles" guiding it: principles of health ("Healthy soil, plants, animals, humans = a healthy planet"), fairness ("Equity, respect and justice for all living things"), ecology ("Emulating and sustaining natural systems"), and care ("for the generations to come") (all quotes from IFOAM, "Principles of Organic Agriculture," IFOAM Organics International (accessed August 2019), https://www.ifoam.bio/en/organic -landmarks/principles-organic-agriculture). Accordingly, Rafi Grosglik argues that "the term 'organic' has become a symbol of the ethically responsible person; responsible for his health, his environment, and his fellow men." *Organic Food in Israel: Resistance, Assimilation, and Global Culture* [in Hebrew] (Tel Aviv: Resling, 2017), 55; my translation. For more on the ethics of organic food production and consumption, see Clive Barnett, Nick Clarke, Paul Cloke, and Alice

chosen not just because of its prevalence in this geopolitical context,[9] but also because it calls for an analysis that connects the ideological level of justification mechanisms to the material level (land resources, waste, and water).

The protagonist of this chapter will be called Dov Golan, a fictive name, whose status as fictive will be discussed later. He is the man who built Giv'ot Olam and has become a guru of sorts. Golan is also notorious for his violence. When his name is mentioned to Palestinians in the villages surrounding the farm, they often freeze; their initial reaction tends to be a complete refusal to talk, out of fear. "He is the master of all this land, all these hills," said one man I met in Yanun, a small village on the outskirts of Nablus whose lands have been gradually confiscated by Golan in the process of expanding his farm. When one reads about Golan—and most articles about him open with descriptions of his strong personality; his fiery, mesmerizing eyes; his strong grip; a corporeal presence that is almost enchanting at the same time as it is chilling—or when one meets him and sees that these descriptions are quite accurate, it is easy to see Golan almost as a fantasy figure of the settler. Indeed, in the interviews I conducted, it sometimes seemed that for Palestinians, his name came to represent the figure of the settler as such, or of a particular type of extremely violent settler. Accordingly, Golan, much like the fictive figure of Irit in chapter 2 or the Lockean "individual" in chapter 1, functions here as an archetype, a parable. These are figures that, whether real (like Golan) or fictive (like Irit), are ideal-types that as such both capture something essential and serve as constitutive models. Thus, for example, even though Irit represents the minority of Jews who settled in Palestinian houses (the majority were marginalized populations, mostly from Arab-speaking countries, who were never offered the legal support that allowed settlement, were often evicted—sooner or later—and whose houses and neighborhoods were subjected to ongoing municipal and state neglect), she also represents the desired model of such settlement, desired also by the many who never enjoyed her privileges. In a different vein, even though Golan represents an extreme model, one often rejected even by fellow settlers, the extreme is what makes him the ideal-type. As a man from Itamar frankly

---

Malpass, "The Political Ethics of Consumerism," *Consumer Policy Review* 15, no. 2 (2005): 45–51; Josée Johnston and Kate Cairns, "Eating for Change," in *Commodity Activism: Cultural Resistance in Neoliberal Times*, ed. Roopali Mukherjee and Sarah Banet-Weiser (New York: New York University Press, 2012), 219–39.

9   According to Shlomo Kaniel, more than 50 percent of hilltop youth are engaged in agriculture. "The Hilltop Settlers: Are They Biblical Sabras?" [in Hebrew], in *Religious Zionism: The Age of Change* (Jerusalem: Bialik, 2004), 533–58.

admitted, immediately after criticizing Golan: "At the end, we need people to be present out there, and to my regret there are no standard people who are able to do so. Only strong personalities with strong ambitions can actualize our vision. . . . My fear is that without people such as [Golan], we shall end up like the people of Gush Katif [who were evicted from the Gaza Strip in 2005]."[10]

The analysis below is based on conversations with Golan himself, one of his daughters (who is also a worker on his farm), Palestinians from Yanun, and human rights activists, as well as news reports and data collected by human rights organizations. Originally, I wanted to weave these stories together to produce a single, if messy, story of a home constructed through ruination. But the more I tried to write such a story, the more impossible it became—Golan's stories about himself, his farm, its beauty, and the care he invests (in animals, nature, or other people) are irreconcilable with the stories of death (of both humans and animals), intimidation, land theft, people hit in the face with a pistol's butt, young children clubbed until their bones crack, a man left to bleed to death in an olive grove, and other stories told by Palestinians and activists.

THE FIRST SECTION of this chapter reconstructs the construction of Golan's farm through these different stories. It also places the story of the farm within the wider context of the outposts, or what has been called "the new settlement movement" or "hilltop youth."

The chronology this section offers is not complete and may not be fully precise. The Palestinians with whom I talked often did not recall dates of events, and it was difficult to obtain all details of particular episodes. Reports collected by human rights organizations are at times somewhat inconsistent, probably because they rely on the testimonies of traumatized witnesses and perhaps because, occasionally, details are lost in translation. Narrating the process of land grab itself also proved incomplete sometimes, since the illegality of Golan's enterprise means that it is not altogether clear which land is cultivated by Giv'ot Olam and which by nearby outposts, themselves illegal. I cross-checked information to provide as precise an account as possible, but it remains a proximate chronology and, later in the chapter, a proximate reconstruction of ideology. Nevertheless, and even though I tried to be as accurate as possible, my aim here is conceptual more than historical or sociological.

10 Quoted in Yehuda Yifrach, "The Meteor of Jewish Settlement in Samaria: 'I Am the Sovereign'" [in Hebrew], NRG, February 2, 2013, http://www.nrg.co.il/online/1/ART2/433/429.html; my translation.

The four sections that follow provide an analysis of the violence entailed in this homemaking from different perspectives. The second section narrates direct, physical violence. The third section explores the mundane violence of daily practices of homemaking in the settlement as well as some of their gendered dimensions. The subsequent section reconstructs Golan's own understanding of violence through his account of organic agriculture as an ethical scheme. It can be read against the concept of "organic washing" depicted in the epilogue. The final section ends this chapter by moving from the narratives that envelop violence to the material resources, particularly land, that tie together organic agriculture and Israeli violence.

A House upon a Hill: Chronology, Background, and Wider Context

Golan moved with his family to the settlement Itamar (located roughly five kilometers from the Palestinian city of Nablus) following the Oslo Agreement. He said he felt an urge to "do something," facing the potentiality of the land being divided into two states.[11] Already back then, he preferred to live in a mobile home at the outer limit of the settlement.[12] The mobility of homes is a key feature of the new settlement movement, a point to which we shall return. Quite quickly, however, in 1995, Golan moved to the other side of the fence, to the first "hill" he occupied without authorization. He made the decision as a response to Yitzhak Rabin's resolution to "freeze" the construction of new settlements as part of the Oslo process.[13] This move amounted to building a wooden chicken coop that joined the first organic chicken coop the family built next to their mobile home in Itamar. The importance of chicken coops to

---

11 These are the words of Golan's wife, quoted in Atya Zar, "Price of Freedom" [in Hebrew], *B'Sheva Online*, September 22, 2005, https://www.inn.co.il/Besheva/Article.aspx/4910.

12 Zar, "Price of Freedom."

13 On November 22, 1992, as part of the Oslo negotiations, the Rabin government decided to stop all public construction in the settlements (Resolution 360). Private construction was still allowed. For an analysis of the resolution, and especially of the extensive construction that took place before and after it, see Idith Zertal and Akiva Eldar, *Lords of the Land: The War over Israel's Settlements in the Occupied Territories, 1967–2007*, trans. Vivian Eden (New York: Nation Books, 2005), 134–35. In response, the settlers began to initiate informal annexations of space beyond the "recognized" settlements. In 2005, the Sason Report provided a provisional estimation, according to which there were 105 unauthorized outposts in the West Bank. See Talya Sason, "Summary of the Opinion Concerning Unauthorized Outposts" [in Hebrew], Israel Ministry of Foreign Affairs, March 10, 2005, https://mfa.gov.il/mfa/aboutisrael/state/law/pages/summary.aspx; Neve Gordon, *Israel's Occupation* (Berkeley: University of California Press, 2008), 197–223.

land theft will return throughout this story: organic, free-range eggs as a tool of dispossession.[14] Later on, some mobile homes were brought over, and other workers joined Golan in populating the hill. Thus was established the first outpost in the West Bank.[15]

In the following two years, Golan moved from one hill to another, establishing outposts that were then occupied by his family members or some of his followers, allowing him to keep moving, until in 1997 he settled in Giv'ot Olam.[16] Driving from Itamar to Giv'ot Olam displays the outcome of this movement: the road winds on hills' ridges, between small outposts very close to each other, often amounting to just a few sheds, a trailer, or a tent, sometimes merely marked by numbers reflecting their topographical latitude: hill 830, hill 777.

But this movement extends well beyond Golan. As a larger movement, it is usually referred to as "hilltop youth." The name may be misleading, Assaf Harel notes, since not all members are young and not all live on hilltops. Yet the term "does capture the romantic and religious desire of these settlers to connect to nature and depart from the organized structures of power of the older and more established settlements."[17] Although, largely speaking, the

14 This formulation, "organic, free-range," is for clarity only. All organic eggs are laid by "free-ranging" chickens (no organic eggs are produced by caged chickens, and the regulations regarding the minimum free space per chicken are usually stricter for organic eggs than for free-range ones). The term *organic*, however, refers also to regulations concerning food and authorized medicine.

15 As stated in the interlude to part III, all settlements in the West Bank are illegal according to international law (for an analysis, see Aeyal Gross, *The Writing on the Wall: Rethinking the International Law of Occupation* [Cambridge: Cambridge University Press, 2017]). However, Israeli law recognizes the legitimacy of settlements that are (i) built on state land—land officially confiscated—or land legally purchased, (ii) constructed according to an approved municipal plan, and (iii) located within the municipal area of the relevant local authority (all three conditions must be fulfilled; see Sason, "Summary"). Illegal settlements ("outposts") are those built without any central planning or authorization, often on privately owned Palestinian land. In actuality, however, the distinction is questionable. Many settlements were built on land not formally confiscated from Palestinians (that is, "illegal" according to [i]), and many were built without any permit (that is, "illegal" according to [ii]). Zertal and Eldar detail this process in *Lords of the Land*. On the other side of this equation, many outposts were authorized and supported by various Israeli government institutions. For some examples, see Zertal and Eldar, *Lords of the Land*, 308–15. See also Weizman, *Hollow Land*, 87–111.

16 Golan's wife, Sarah (fictive name) describes this process in a YouTube video: yersha, "From Messiah to Cheese" [in Hebrew], July 30, 2009, YouTube video, 1:20, https://www.youtube.com/watch?v=WXSjRoApKcQ.

17 Assaf Harel, "'A Blessed Deviation in Jewish History': On Contemporary Forms of Messianism among Religiously Motivated Settlers in the West Bank," in *Normalizing Occupation: The Politics of Everyday Life in the West Bank Settlements*, ed. Ariel Handel, Marco Allegra, and Erez Maggor (Bloomington: Indiana University Press, 2017), 135.

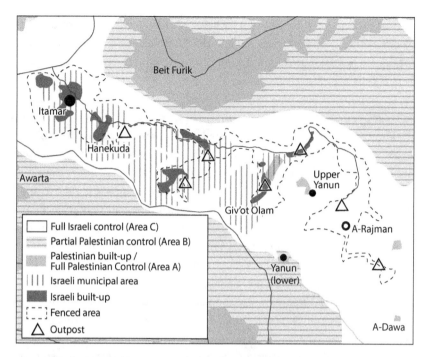

MAP 3.1. Peace Now settlement map (redrawn), August 2018. The map shows that the municipal area of Itamar was enlarged by the movement of outposts expanding eastward and now includes all outposts (triangles) and the roads leading to them that aid in dissecting Palestinian land (the territory demarcated by a dark line). Beyond this territory—already extending far beyond the territory of the original settlement, as well as the built area of both settlement and outposts—lies more agricultural lands. Some of these lands have become part of the "municipal area" of Itamar (marked here in vertical stripes), and some have not and are therefore not marked here (compare with figure 3.3). Adapted from Peace Now, "Settlements Map, 2018," *Peace Now*, August 1, 2018, http://peacenow.org.il/en/settlements -map-2018.

movement strategically serves the state's desire to expand and annex land (albeit at times undercutting other considerations of military rule in the West Bank), and although more often than not the state both materially and legally supports these acts of settlement (although not consistently so and differently in different periods), the movement emerged more or less organically. It began sporadically as a protest movement around the aforementioned injunction to freeze the expansion of settlements; it never had a system of centralized ideological planning; and it frequently takes the shape of spontaneous, individual acts of settlement.[18] Nevertheless, Golan is often seen as its forerunner.[19] Today, with more than 127 outposts in the West Bank joining the 126 formal settlements (true, more or less, to the time of writing these lines, with numbers rapidly increasing), we can say that Giv'ot Olam was one of the first actors in what was to become the most significant political movement in Israel in recent years.[20]

The exact number of outposts is unknown, partly because they play an intricate game of legality with the Israeli government. On the one hand, they are officially illegal, and by disavowing them, Israel can claim it does not establish new settlements; on the other hand, by turning a blind eye and, much further, by supplying them with infrastructure and military defense, the state ensures that its desire for territorial expansion is being pursued.[21] But this duality, in which privately built outposts serve the interests of the state, though not in the state's name—protected and yet denounced, supported militarily and materially yet subjected to a rhetoric of eviction—does not capture the full complexity of this game. As Foucault has taught us, "the state" does not really exist as a unified entity, and decisions are made by various authorities, local and central: attorney generals, commanders on the ground, the civil administration, the prime minister, defense ministers or their deputies in charge of enforcing the law in the occupied territories, the

18 The first outposts were established in 1995, but the name *hilltop youth* itself became common later, just before the 2005 disengagement from Gaza, when the younger generation of settlers participated in large-scale demonstrations against the disengagement. Michael Feige, *Settling in the Hearts: Jewish Fundamentalism in the Occupied Territories* (Detroit: Wayne State University Press, 2009), 229–47; Shimi Friedman, "Hilltop Youth: Political-Anthropological Research in the Hills of Judea and Samaria," *Israel Affairs* 21, no. 3 (2015): 391–407. Shimi Friedman's ethnographic work points to the sporadic, eclectic, and unorganized nature of this group, which he interprets in generational terms through the concept of adolescence. According to Friedman, many of these new settlers arrived at the outposts not driven by ideology but as part of an act of rebellion. Ideology developed later on ("Hilltop Youth," 394–99). Indeed, many of the younger men and women who passed through or settled in Golan's farm fit these descriptions. They were often youth at risk, who found shelter and an outlet in the farm.

19 Feige, *Settling in the Hearts*, 237.

20 Data (unpublished) were kindly provided by Hagit Ofran from Peace Now and Dror Etkes from Kerem Navot, based on ongoing research. For the most up-to-date official publication, see Yotam Berger, "At Least 16 Israeli Unauthorized West Bank Outposts Established since 2017," *Ha'aretz*, July 22, 2019, https://www.haaretz.com/israel-news/.premium.MAGAZINE-at-least-16 -israeli-unauthorized-west-bank-outposts-established-since-2017-1.7546752.

21 The alignment of the state's desires/interests with this enterprise is best demonstrated by a recent retroactive legalization of thirteen outposts as a first step in the legalization of at least

housing or transportation ministries that sometimes do not enforce decisions of the former authorities or embark on their own initiatives, supreme court justices, local council heads or bureaucrats, and many others. The conflicts between them sometimes provide the gaps that allow these outposts to flourish, and other times mean that what has been authorized, actively supported, or simply ignored by one authority is then demolished by another. Moreover, sometimes, the Israeli state follows the outposts to new territorial "edges," even if sometimes reluctantly at first. The relations, in other words, are uneven and unstable, and change from one case to another, one institution to another, and across time.

Schematically, however, we can identify a clear trajectory of the relations between the state and this movement. Until 2012, Israeli governments did work to evacuate some of the smaller, more provisory outposts.[22] This was done because they wanted to maintain a semblance of the rule of law and some commitment to international decisions. It was also done, however, because some of these outposts did operate against these governments' interests, as they increased conflicts with Palestinians. Therefore, some of the outposts remained provisory, hidden; they moved around or masked themselves as neighborhoods of existing settlements in their efforts to hide from state authorities or, sometimes, to hide from international inspection. Others were destroyed and reestablished frequently. Around 2012, this attitude changed, and the state shifted from a rhetoric of evacuation (which was almost never enforced) to a rhetoric of regulation and legalization.[23] Nevertheless, due to

---

thirty-five more. This legalization should be understood as part of a shift from a rhetoric of evacuation (in which the state pretends it has an interest in evacuating outposts) to a rhetoric of "regularizing." The Levy Report, published in 2012, was the legal pinnacle of this change, with a formal claim that the law of occupation, and thus the Geneva Convention (IV), does not apply in the West Bank and that, therefore, Israelis have the right to settle there. Even though it was not formally adopted, the Israeli government followed the report's "spirit" in its new policies regarding outposts. See Gross, *Writing on the Wall*, 158ff. See also note 23.

22 For a review of the changes in this policy, see Peace Now, "The Outposts System (2018)" [in Hebrew], last updated March 2018, http://peacenow.org.il/wp-content/uploads/2018/03/OutpostsUpdateMarch2018.pdf.

23 A brief history of this shift dates back to 1996, when the first Netanyahu government reversed Rabin's decision to freeze construction in the settlements. In the 1993 Oslo Agreement, no formal decision concerning the settlements was made, and alongside refugees and Jerusalem, this was one of the subjects to be discussed as part of the final agreement. There were, however, understandings that there would be no expansion of settlements, which the Netanyahu

legal constraints, much of the state's support still had to remain informal. Therefore, data regarding the outposts is largely speculative. Such was the case with Giv'ot Olam in its first stages. Here we return to Golan's story, and to 1997, when he established Giv'ot Olam.

The territory that was to become Giv'ot Olam was settled by Golan with two young men, who joined him to cultivate the land and guard the area. At first, they had a small tent; later, they brought an old car in which they slept. After some

government then canceled. The new regulations nevertheless subjected the establishment of new settlements to governmental decision, which was immediately violated via the construction of more outposts. The official policy at the time was that outposts were to be evacuated, yet after an attempt at evacuating one outpost next to Yizhar in that same year (1996), which was met with violent resistance, no other evacuation efforts were made.

The 1999 Ehud Barak government declared that it would evacuate fifteen of the dozens of outposts. Barak eventually evacuated only one: Havat Ma'on. During the time of his government, more units were built in the West Bank than during any other government since Oslo. In 2003, Ariel Sharon's government accepted the "Road Map to Peace," which included a commitment to evacuate all outposts. This policy was further supported when the government commissioned Sason's report in 2005 (as a result of pressure by the United States). However, only two outposts were evacuated during these years (alongside two other West Bank settlements, as part of the disengagement). Reelected as prime minister, Netanyahu ratified this commitment in response to UN and US pressure in a formal policy that was valid between November 2009 and September 2010. This included a temporal suspension of construction commencement of new houses in all the settlements throughout the West Bank, excluding East Jerusalem. However, projects already underway could continue. For data and analysis, see Zertal and Eldar, *Lords of the Land*, esp. 160–62, 174–76. In September 2010, Netanyahu terminated the freeze. As we saw (note 21), the effort to formalize construction in the West Bank culminated in 2012 with the Levi Report, and in 2016 become official government policy. The official policy first appeared as part of the government's response to an appeal to the High Court of Justice. See Isabel Kershner, "Israel Quietly Legalizes Pirate Outposts in the West Bank," *New York Times*, August 30, 2016, https://www.nytimes.com/2016/08/31/world/middleeast/israel-west-bank-outposts-mitzpe-danny.html. Soon thereafter, the so-called Regularization Bill (passed in February 2017) decreed that Jewish settlements in the West Bank that were built in "good faith," and without knowledge that the land was privately owned, could be retroactively recognized by the government if settlers show that they received some kind of state support in establishing the site. In August 2018, the Israeli court approved, in a precedent judgment, the retroactive legalization of another outpost built on privately owned Palestinian land. This was the first outcome of the reform initiated by Minister of Justice Ayelet Shaked, which was mentioned in chapter 2—subjecting the West Bank to the municipal court system rather than to the High Court of Justice. See also data concerning the "regularization" of settlements by Peace Now, "The Outposts System (2018)" [in Hebrew], March 2018, http://peacenow.org.il/wp-content/uploads/2018/03/OutpostsUpdateMarch2018.pdf; Yoam Berger, "Israeli Court: A West Bank Outpost Can Be Legalized if Land Was Seized in Good Faith," *Ha'aretz*, August 29, 2018, https://www.haaretz.com/israel-news/.premium-israeli-court-a

FIGURE 3.2. Giv'ot Olam, 2018. A view from the farm's gate. Photo by author.

time, Golan's family moved to reside on the hill. Since, at the time, the Israeli government was still (reluctantly) enforcing limitations on construction in the settlements, they had to camouflage their presence by dismantling the tent every morning and rebuilding it in the evening. But slowly, the tent that was a transient home was replaced by a shed, to which a small paddling pool with nets for shade and even a refrigerator were added. The transient became more permanent. It also became larger. Then, more tents were built, which were no longer dismantled every day.

Today, the nucleus farm is spread out over 220 acres, and Golan cultivates an additional 105 acres beyond this territory (see figure 3.3).[24] Some of it is occupied by his ten large chicken coops (again, the number is under dispute and is an approximation). Other parts are used as grazing areas for goats and as vineyards. About 110 acres of this territory has been declared as state land; the

-west-bank-outpost-can-be-legal-if-built-in-good-faith-1.6429511. All this joins other processes to achieve what can only be understood as a gradual effort to annex the West Bank to Israel.

24 Data kindly provided by Dror Etkes from the NGO Kerem Navot. Etkes emphasizes that, since all of these are illegal outposts and since there are several other outposts in this area, it is not always possible to determine which territory is cultivated by whom, and so these numbers are an estimation. I am grateful for the work he put into collecting the data for this book. Peace

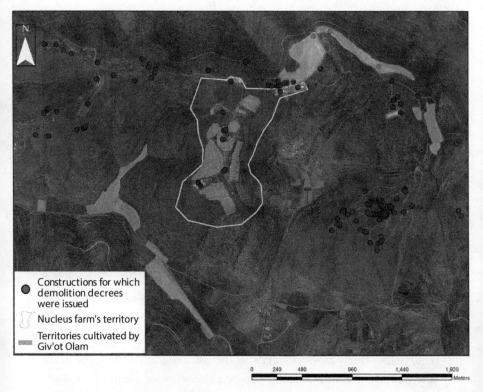

FIGURE 3.3. Land cultivated by Giv'ot Olam and area of the nucleus farm (estimated territory). The cultivated land (in light gray) reaches far beyond the farm. Access roads to these territories take further territory and, more significantly, further dissect Palestinian land. Image and analysis courtesy of Dror Etkes, Kerem Navot.

rest (about 215 acres) is privately owned Palestinian land that was previously cultivated, predominantly by people from Yanun.[25]

Now's estimations are lower, reporting 137 acres as the nucleus farm, with 53.5 acres on privately owned Palestinian land.

25 For the history and context of land grab and agriculture in the West Bank, see Weizman, *Hollow Land*, 117–20. Throughout the story herein, it is important to bear in mind that the vast majority of Yanun's lands (85 percent) were confiscated not by Golan but by the "recognized" settlement Itamar as early as 1983. Between Itamar and its outposts, the original 4,065 acres of Yanun's land parcels have been confiscated almost in their entirety, leaving less than five hundred for the village's inhabitants. See Lena Meari, "Colonial Dispossession, Developmental Discourses, and Humanitarian Solidarity in 'Area C': The Case of the Palestinian Yanun Village," *Community Development Journal* 52, no. 3 (July 2017): 506–23. In this respect, Itamar is an almost entirely illegal

Violence #1 (Beating, Killing)

"In the beginning he was nice," Ahmad from Yanun told me, referring to Golan.[26] "He offered to help watering the sheep, built a water tank we could use, and told us we can ask him for help whenever we need it." This was Golan's way—Ahmad and others in Yanun agree—to slowly establish his dominance. Ahmad and Shukri, his neighbor, describe a reality of good neighborly relations lasting roughly from 1995 until 2000. Golan's account, in contrast, is of constant confrontations; "days of violence," as he refers to them.[27] He likes to talk about being on his own on this hill or another, with nothing but a coffee kit; about those who were always out to get him— the Palestinians ("Arabs" in his terminology), but also state authorities and other settlers; about having to stitch his own wounds after encounters with the local Palestinians (in his descriptions they were always many, and he always confronted them on his own). Ever since those days in the mid-1990s, according to his own account, Golan has not taken his shoes off; always ready for a fight.[28]

The tension between the accounts of Golan and his Palestinian neighbors in regard to their initial neighborliness may be owing to the fact that it seems that Golan—much like many Israelis and, in a way, the state apparatus itself— perceives the very presence of Palestinians on what he sees as his land as a form of attack. As Wolfe puts it, in a colonial/racial framework, "a people in the wrong place is experienced as an assault on the body."[29] Therefore, attacking those who merely came to water their sheep in their own grazing areas, who traveled on a road leading from one village to another, or who picked their own olives, can constitute a form of self-defense for Golan.[30]

construction. See a B'tselem report from 2010: Eyal Hareuveni, "By Hook and by Crook: Israeli Settlement Policy in the West Bank," *B'tselem*, July 2010, https://www.btselem.org/download /201007_by_hook_and_by_crook_eng.pdf.

26 The interviewees asked to remain anonymous. Their full details are with me. Interviews took place in Ahmad's home, December 31, 2017.

27 Roy Sharon, "Avri Ran, 'I Am the Sovereign: Soldiers Will Serve Wherever I Will Tell Them To'" [in Hebrew], *10 News*, February 16, 2013, https://www.10.tv/hamagazim/127132.

28 Sharon, "Avri Ran."

29 Wolfe, *Traces of History*, 17. Wolfe concludes: "the remedy for people being out of place . . . is ethnic cleansing" (17).

30 Golan testified to this explicitly when he defended himself as part of a criminal trial, after being charged with assault occasioning actual bodily harm. In February 2001, Nimer Abu Amar, an

Either way, sometime after 1998—he did not remember the exact dates—Golan approached Shukri. Shukri owned the well uphill, which was the source of water for the aforementioned water tank Golan built. Golan announced that he was taking over the well. The villagers, he noted, could still use the water tank, but they would have no more business next to the well itself.[31] A few weeks later, Golan moved the water tank a few meters down the hill. "You can now water your sheep here," he said, according to Shukri, referring to the water tank and its new location, "and I do not want to see you above this point." The water tank was slowly pushed further down the hill, becoming a moving (fluid?) border, re-marking Golan's new territory, annexing more and more of the agricultural lands of Yanun.[32]

Intimidation soon began. Testimonies are too many to count. Golan or his people would come to the village's homes on Saturdays, "strolling" with their families and dogs, destroying property, throwing stones, and attacking people. Sometimes, at night, they would march on the village's rooftops. Yanun was disconnected from the electricity grid for years after Golan and his men set fire to the UN-funded electric generator (in April 2002). Golan also destroyed the water pump, explaining to the villagers that he had to punish them for not asking his permission to install the generator

---

Palestinian citizen of Israel (a Bedouin from the Negev) drove onto Golan's farm. He was working for the Jewish National Fund (JNF) and accidentally entered the farm in search of one of the JNF's working tools. Golan forced him out of the car, shouting that he was a "stinking Arab," a "dog," and screamed: "This is a Jewish place; your place is not here. Your place is six feet under." He then hit Abu Amar until the latter started bleeding. During the trial, Golan, who did not get a lawyer and chose to defend himself, asked Abu Amar questions such as: "Did you have prayer beads hanging from your front mirror?" and "Did you listen to music in Arabic as you were driving?" Golan's defense rested on the claim that Abu Amar's visibly Arab presence was rightly seen by him as a threat. In this logic, Arab presence is a sufficient justification for violence. For details of the case, see Aviv Lavie, "When Avri Ran Gets Angry" [in Hebrew], *Ha'aretz*, March 15, 2004, https://www.haaretz.co.il/misc/1.953193; my translation. Lawrence Susskind et al. put it in a wider perspective when they argue that "when asked about the conflict between Jews and Arabs, most Hilltop Settlers perceived their reality as a continuous war, which would either be won or lost, with the losers facing expulsion and revenge" ("Religious and Ideological Dimensions of the Israeli Settlements Issue: Reframing the Narrative," *Negotiation Journal* 21, no. 2 [April 2005]: 185).

31 Author's field notes, December 31, 2017.

32 The control over water is a significant element of Israel's occupation, and the water tank that gradually becomes disconnected from the water source is a telling allegory in this regard. According to Oxfam, Israel controls 80 percent of water resources in the West Bank. Settlers,

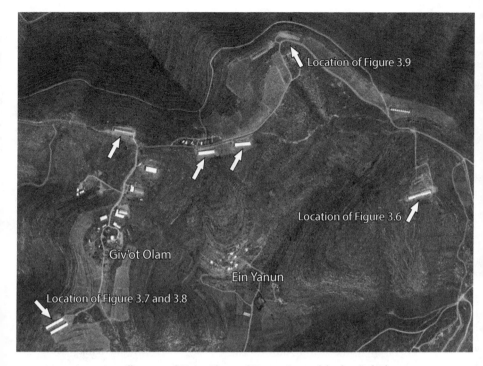

FIGURE 3.4. A satellite map of Giv'ot Olam and Yanun. Some of the farm's chicken coops are marked with arrows. Yanun is composed of two villages: Ein Yanun (or "upper Yanun") is located on the hills, much closer to the farm, whereas lower Yanun (just beyond this map's scope, to the south) is in the valley. The upper part of the village suffered the most from Giv'ot Olam's violence. Note how the spatial work of Golan's chicken coops vis-à-vis the farm replicates the spatial work of the outposts vis-à-vis the original settlement: their location allows Golan's farm to stretch, reach, and spread much beyond its nucleus territory. Access roads and the barriers to Palestinians' movement they create effectively take more land, even if it is not occupied directly.

and pump to begin with. In October 2002, Golan and about fifteen of his people ambushed Marwan, Othman, and Nadia (fictive names), who were picking olives at their plot above Wadi Yanun. The settlers clubbed and shot the three until they fell to the ground unconscious. Othman was shot in the head. Marwan was clubbed with the barrel of an M16 rifle and only

amounting to 12 percent of the West Bank's population, use approximately six times the amount of water used by all Palestinians in the West Bank (Oxfam, "20 Facts: 20 Years since the Oslo Accords," accessed September 2018, https://www.oxfam.org/sites/www.oxfam.org/files/oxfam -oslo-20-factsheet.pdf).

regained consciousness in the hospital. One of his eyes was gouged out, his skull was fractured (causing permanent damage), and both his legs shattered in multiple places. Nadia, a sixty-year-old woman, was slammed in the back with an M16 until her spine and pelvic bones were broken.[33] That same October, Golan and two other workers came to Wadi Yanun, where several Palestinians were picking olives. They drove an all-terrain vehicle and shot sporadically at the grove. Two of the pickers were severely wounded: one was wounded in his arm and regained partial control of it only after being treated in a hospital in Amman. The main leg artery of the second, Hani Beni Maniyeh, was severed. He began running away from the shooting but was shot again and fell to the ground, where he bled to death. He was twenty-four years old. Some witnesses identified Golan as the shooter, but as noted, it seems his name has also become an index of sorts, and may be used to point to someone else. Two IDF jeeps were parked some five hundred meters to the north of the pickers and did not intervene. This is significant, as it presents all this violence as part of a state project and not a private, outlawed enterprise. I will return to this point.

According to one witness, on that day, Golan plowed that particular piece of land for the first time. And even though this testimony was given roughly three years after the event, and even if it may be inaccurate in terms of the actual time it designates, this link between violence and cultivation is crucial.

These are just some of many testimonies. One after the other, the families of Yanun left. The village, which has existed at least since at least 1596 (when it was registered for taxation purposes),[34] has been almost emptied. In October 2002, the last six families of the upper village of Yanun (Ein Yanun; see

---

33 All incidents were documented, assembled, and cross-checked from depositions taken by the organization Yesh Din (I would like to thank Ziv Stahl for her time); an interview with D.N., who participated in the Yanun support group in the period 2002–6 and asked to remain anonymous; and testimonies I collected. Golan was not held accountable for the vast majority of these. Some incidents have been reported in the Israeli media. See, for example, Yifrach, "Meteor of Jewish Settlement in Samaria"; Aviv Lavie, "The Scourge of the Hills" [in Hebrew], Ha'aretz, April 8, 2003, https://www.haaretz.co.il/misc/1.874468. See also testimonials in Thomas Mandal, *Living with Settlers: Interviews with Yanoun Villagers*, n.d., https://docs.google.com/file/d/1TQK20xH76M7koCORQt8v_Xj543Ym6vRp9EZ6kiO3NOAoPLsDeqLb2_Bz_N79/edit. See also Yehezkel Lein, "Foreseen but Not Prevented: The Israeli Law Enforcement Authorities' Handling of Settler Attacks on Olive Harvesters," B'tselem Case Study 16, ed. Yael Stein, trans. Shaul Vardi, Maya Johnston, and Zvi Shulman, November 2002, https://www.btselem.org/download/200211_olive_harvest_eng.pdf.

34 Wolf-Dieter Hütteroth, *Historical Geography of Palestine, Transjordan and Southern Syria in the Late 16th Century* (Erlangen, Germany: Palm und Enke, 1977).

satellite image in figure 3.4) left their homes for the nearby village of A'qraba, after the other twenty families slowly left in previous months, fearing for their lives or unable to make a living after Golan took over their agricultural land. Some returned several years later, with the assistance of several local and international organizations. The exodus from the lower village, which is located farther away from the farm, was less comprehensive. Those who are still there make sure not to go near Golan's territory. If he feels that they come too close, he often appears, they say, and simply stands there, silently (in interviews, he calls this mode of appearance "presence").[35] Ahmad says the "master of all this land" does not need to do anything beyond that.

Violence #2 (Homemaking)

Recall the paddling pool or the fridge brought to the hill, which joined the tent and the car and then the permanent houses. Think of Golan's wife, Sarah (fictive name), bringing Shabbat meals from her home in Itamar to the hill, carrying pots of food for the large family and the workers every Friday until she decides to move with the children and join Golan in the new outpost.[36] Think of the practice of cooking that followed, first in camp-like conditions, with a small fridge operated by a generator, and slowly in a kitchen, which itself becomes larger, until today it can host large groups coming to taste the cheese, eggs, yogurt, and vegetables produced in the farm. Think of Golan and Sarah's ten children having fun in the paddling pool—the children who would grow up, many working in their father's farm and raising children of their own, living in the outposts on the proximate hills. Like Nizri's herbs or his daily practice of making food for his large family, it is through these practices of homemaking that occupation takes place.

These solid links between the political and the domestic transpire not just if we look at the daily practices of homemaking that are inseparable from the act of occupation—a fridge brought to preserve some food, a meal cooked, children in a pool—but also if we look at the inseparability of these practices from the work of the state that eventually provides electricity and water, roads, sewage infrastructure, garbage disposal, and military forces to protect these

35 For example, Sharon, "Avri Ran."
36 See descriptions in Zar, "Price of Freedom"; and in Chen Kotes-Bar, "The Story of Avri Ran, Leader of the Hilltop Youth" [in Hebrew], *Hadrei Hadarim*, September 16, 2005, https://www .bhol.co.il/forums/topic.asp?cat_id=4&topic_id=1572821&forum_id=771.

FIGURE 3.5. A paddling pool outside Itamar, which is an outpost of sorts. On the hill to the left, another outpost can be seen. Photo by author.

homes. The ability to spend hot summer days in a paddling pool is conditioned by these settlers' own individualized violence (which is itself conditioned by the army's tolerance), by the systematic military violence of the state, and by the water pipelines (alongside other layers of infrastructure) laid down by the state, which supply the pool with water.

Feminist scholars of empire have shown for some time now that domesticity and gendered dynamics are not foreign to the entrenchment of colonialism. Women's reproductive labor, as well as their reproductive capacities, has been key to both the symbolic and the material sustainment of colonial powers.[37] The politics of home and homemaking, the politics of care and nurturing, do not necessarily facilitate a politics of nonviolence.[38] *In the act of settlement, the*

---

37 Anne McClintock, *Imperial Leather: Race, Gender, and Sexuality in the Colonial Contest* (New York: Routledge, 1995); Scott Lauria Morgensen, "Theorising Gender, Sexuality and Settler Colonialism: An Introduction," *Settler Colonial Studies* 2, no. 2 (2012): 2–22.

38 This is not a new claim, and the most systematic analyses in this regard have been made in response to Sara Ruddick's seminal *Maternal Thinking: Toward a Politics of Peace* (Boston: Beacon Press, 1989). See, e.g., Frances S. Hasso, "Discursive and Political Deployments by/of the 2002 Palestinian Women Suicide Bombers/Martyrs," *Feminist Review* 81, no. 1 (2005): 23–51; Laleh Khalili, "Gendered Practices of Counterinsurgency," *Review of International Studies* 37, no. 4 (2011):

domestic space is the primary means, technology, and meaning of violence. Golan and Sarah built a home that became a community, a place of refuge for dozens of lost youth (who came to the farm after failing to find a home elsewhere). Indeed, originally, the name *hilltop youth*, which became a name of an entire settlement movement, referred to those young men and women who came to live with and work for Golan. As Akanksha Mehta shows more broadly, the ethics of care, charity, and community building is entangled with the struggle for the land in settler visions (she focuses on women's visions).[39] Similarly to what I will argue about organic agriculture in the epilogue, the language of homeliness, friendship, and kinship employed by many (women) settlers does *not* serve as a euphemism for violence; this language is rather profoundly tinged by a violence that is never hidden. Cruel expropriation works in tandem with the affective relationship to home, land, and other people.

Following Golan, Sarah moved to a hill that became a home—a home that then destroyed an entire village. In some of the couple's own accounts concerning their lives, she is presented not just as a follower but also as a driving power. In other places in the West Bank, particularly in Hebron and East Jerusalem, Jewish families move not to empty hills but to Palestinian homes, and not to depopulated homes, relics, or ruins, but to homes still inhabited by Palestinian families who are forced out. Women are often at the forefront of this particular mode of settlement—the most domestic form of invasion, as it were.

The familial angle pertains also to Golan himself, who has often been described as the "father" of the original hilltop youth and the many youth at risk arriving at his farm.[40] In this familial context, it is telling to see how he maps his own violence: "I think this land is mine," he told a reporter once—referring to the land going far beyond the borders of the state, into Jordan if not further away. "But I do not hate Arabs. Not at all. I am indifferent. It is inconceivable that I will feel some urge to hit an Arab or take pleasure in it. They are irrelevant to me; not part of the game. They are like dust. . . . I am not a violent person. I

1471–91; Laura Sjoberg and Caron E. Gentry, *Mothers, Monsters, Whores: Women's Violence in Global Politics* (New York: Zed Books, 2007).

39 Akanksha Mehta, "Right-Wing Sisterhood: Everyday Politics of Hindu Nationalist Women in India and Zionist Settler Women in Israel-Palestine" (PhD diss., SOAS, University of London, 2017).

40 Lavie, "Scourge of the Hills."

have ten children, and none has ever been hit by me. You can ask my wife, my goats. Am I fierce? Yes. Strong? Yes. But not violent. If there is a war I fight."[41]

Note how violence is tied here to the affective level (pleasure, urge) and is detached from physical power as well as from war. It can be measured or seen within the domain of the family, which importantly contains goats alongside the wife and the children (recall Locke's horse from chapter 1). It is as a "father"— or a husband, or a farmer taking care of goats, and either way as a passionate man—that a man can be violent. According to Golan, he is not. What occurs outside the domestic boundaries is not quite violent in this account, even if it entails the killing or the displacement of others. War and fighting are thereby detached from the affective/domestic and are thus nonviolent; so is the act of cleansing people out, as one cleans dust.

Dust is stubborn. Wiping it is therefore a never-ending commitment of whomever wishes to keep their home clean. A tedious work of expelling it. If in the racial/sexual contract, we see an original act of exclusion (of women or nonwhites) that allows for structuring the democratic sphere of freedom and equality as male and white,[42] here we have a much more quotidian version of it: an ongoing, almost daily cycle in which the home production of Israelis requires the unhoming of Palestinians—in the West Bank, in Gaza, within the borders of the Green Line with the strict limitation on urban development for Palestinians within Israel, with frequent house demolitions of Palestinians' homes throughout these spaces, with making mockery of Palestinian homes by walking through their walls or by making them into Israeli soldiers' residences.[43] And, much like the case of the racial/sexual contract, what makes this duality of home and homelessness possible amid a regime insisting on its democratic nature (though less and less so) is that the Palestinians have to be excluded from the game of homemaking from the outset ("not part of the game," as Golan puts it), outside even the domain of violence.

In a different context, William Walters suggests that *domos* comes from the word *domo*, which is used, alongside other ways, "to speak of the act of conquering or 'subduing men or communities.'" Accordingly, he refers to *domopolitics* as a form of territorial control in which "'warm words' of community, trust,

41 Kotes-Bar, "Story of Avri Ran"; my translation.
42 See Charles W. Mills, *The Racial Contract* (Ithaca, NY: Cornell University Press, 1997); Carole Pateman, *The Sexual Contract* (Stanford, CA: Stanford University Press, 1988).
43 On walking through walls, see Weizman, *Hollow Land*, 185–220. On soldiers' residences, see Ariella Azoulay, "A Sleep in a Sterile Zone," *Refugee Watch Online*, January 29, 2009, http://refugeewatchonline.blogspot.com/2009/01/sleep-in-sterile-zone.html). I am grateful to Laleh Khalili for this thought.

and citizenship are juxtaposed with the sense of insecurity, threat, and radical externality of an 'outside' from which the 'inside' must be kept protected."[44] Similarly, the taking of land takes place here accompanied by "warm" or "soft" words and practices. These include not only the care for kin and communities discussed above, but also the care for the land and the earth, performed through the caring labor of organic agriculture. This brings us to the next section.

Violence #3 (An Ethical Scheme)

When I went to Giv'ot Olam, I did not expect to meet Golan and certainly did not expect that he would engage in a conversation. I went there to try to understand the topography of chicken coops. I went with my father, himself with some expertise in chickens, and my friend and coauthor, Merav Amir, who wanted to join the trip. When Golan saw us, he asked for our identity. Mostly out of concern for our safety (Golan has severely injured several activists who came to his farm, and his violence is quite unpredictable, according to many testimonies), we disclosed very partial information concerning who we were and why we were there. For this reason, we also did not record the conversation. As soon as we left the farm, we parked in a hidden area and reconstructed the conversation to the best of our ability—both separately and then together. In this section, I quote his words only when they were confirmed by all three of us, to ensure their accuracy. Therefore, Golan's name is anonymized here, even though this is a somewhat "flat" anonymization: he is a somewhat public figure and his real identity can easily be tracked, even if only via the footnotes. The Palestinians with whom I talked, however, have given their consent to participate in this research and their details remain secure with me. Golan dominates a reality that is radically and structurally unequal in the distribution of power, risks, and violence. Within such a reality, it seems that some informants need to be better protected than others.[45]

My conversation with Golan was a frantic, broken conversation, in which he kept going away, as if wanting to end the exchange, and then coming back,

44 William Walters, "Secure Borders, Safe Haven, Domopolitics," *Citizenship Studies* 8, no. 3 (2004): 241.
45 For further methodological discussion, see David Mosse, "Anti-Social Anthropology? Objectivity, Objection, and the Ethnography of Public Policy and Professional Communities," *Journal of the Royal Anthropological Institute* 12, no. 4 (December 2006): 935–56.

FIGURE 3.6. A chicken coop northeast of the farm. The Jordan Valley can be seen in the background. In the West Bank, most Jewish-constructed areas are on hilltops: "If, by [the early 1990s], one were to slice the terrain of the West Bank along an invisible horizontal datum line a few hundred meters above sea level, almost all the land over this line was settler territory annexed by the Israeli state." Weizman, *Hollow Land*, 117; photo by author.

as if unable to stop it: getting up to light a cigarette, constantly moving around the room, and jumping between topics. Nevertheless, amid the fragmented claims, there was a systematic worldview. It is reconstructed here. The conversation focused on the ethics of food and organic agriculture. In the epilogue, I return to this subject and expand on organic agriculture as an ethical scheme that can be understood within the paradigm of "washing": much like pinkwashing or greenwashing, organic agriculture in the West Bank will be considered there as a structure in which an ethics of nonviolence (toward animals) "washes" violence (toward Palestinians). Here, I reconstruct and analyze Golan's own account, which is very different from this paradigm. It is one in which the very framework of organic, sustainable agriculture is dependent on a reality of exploitation and violence that *is* part of an ethical existence.

GOLAN SEES EATING as an ethical matter (he is not a vegetarian but would never eat an animal that maintains its form—a whole fish, or even a drumstick, because, he claims, this would be inhumane). He also treats organic agriculture as an ethical practice. He made it clear that, for him, organic agriculture is a form of life that emerges from, manifests itself as, and embodies a love of, if not a mode of symbiosis with, nature.[46] And yet this symbiosis helps him construct a world in which violence is necessary; it can be managed but never cleaned out, and furthermore, any effort to annul it may undercut, rather than support, ethical endeavors. The "washing" paradigm assumes an agonistic relation: one takes something "good" and "washes" something "bad" through it. But in Golan's scheme, there is no tension, contradiction, or opposition between the ethics of care for animals and the violence of occupation, because there is no contradiction or tension between the ethics of care for animals and violence—toward them or at large.

This approach can be illuminated by an anecdote Golan shared with me. Two young reporters from the Israeli daily *Ha'aretz* (which is generally identified with antioccupation politics) came to interview him. He knew who they were, he said, but was still willing to talk to them (perhaps signaling: I know who you are too). They arrived at his farm with a dog, and as they sat down, they tied the dog's leash to one of their chairs' legs. During their conversation, the reporters objected to the fact that Golan raises animals at the farm. They held the view that organic food should be vegan, and that any use of animal products is ultimately violent. Golan, according to his description, decided to play with them. Looking at the dog tied to the chair, he told them how he often ties his goats to poles. Being aware of the fact that they came from a city, he shared a fictive plan to start raising goats on horizontal platforms in order to save space. He also talked about disposing of sick or old chickens, keeping in mind the practice of euthanizing old pets. He told me that the reporters were repelled by his story and failed to see that this is precisely what they do with their dog. The lesson of the tale went beyond the claim that his animals are treated better than urban pets, as beloved as the latter may be. His moral was that the love for the dog—which he did not dismiss—does not prevent the violence inflicted on the dog by those loving it. This violence is a result of this love: the very desire to raise the dog, to share life with it, necessitates the practices of confinement—to legs of chairs or in small apartments—or of taking life.

As a wider worldview, his argument can be outlined as follows: The human race, according to Golan, has two alternatives: a hunter-gatherer model or an agricultural model. The former, he emphasized, is not a romantic model of "returning to nature," as some naïve people or environmental theorists might think, but a complete destruction of nature. To prove this point, he gave the example of oceans, whose spaces are still governed by the hunter-gatherer

---

46 When Golan talks about organic agriculture, it sounds almost as if he quotes, or lives very intimately, IFOAM's principles and ideologies (see note 8). See also Zar, "Price of Freedom."

model. He expressed moral outrage at fish farming,[47] but the alternative (fishing in the open seas) has created a truly violent space in his descriptions: entire species have been exterminated or are close to extinction; the vast majority of fishing methods destroy entire habitats; and even those protesting all this, like Greenpeace, are a violent bunch of criminals, he repeatedly said. Once we understand this, he claimed, we understand that fish farming (agriculture) is, in fact, the better alternative *for the fish themselves, even though it is cruel.*

In agriculture, we again face two alternatives. The first is an agriculture based on using synthetic fertilizers and is unsustainable. The second is an agriculture based on natural fertilizers (that are derived from animals) and a model of crop rotation.[48] It is within the use of natural fertilizers that violence toward animals necessarily resides, and it will continue to be part of any sustainable agriculture, even if the entire world becomes vegan, he claimed. Like the farmed fish, the chickens in his farm are exploited and suffer. Golan did not contend otherwise. Nature is cruel. Mothers constantly abandon some of their offspring, forced to decide who will survive and who will perish. In this regard, what is done in the dairy farm is not merely a duplication of what is done in nature anyway; it is better: "We make sure all the offspring survive," he said several times (it was unclear whether he referred to humans as a species and humans' relation to their offspring, or whether he was talking about the chickens or baby goats on his farm). Although Golan never explicitly made this analogy, his comments in regard to the Palestinians living under occupation were very similar. He acknowledged that their situation is bad and that they suffer from Israel's violence (he did not mention his own), and yet, relying on a classic paradigm of enlightened occupation, he detailed how the alternatives were much worse.[49]

47 We could not reconstruct the exact word he used here and was unsure whether he spoke of it as an act of cruelty or used some softer formulation.

48 Crop rotation is seen by many as essential to sustaining healthy soil. Golan named the Irish famine and the corn crisis in the US as anecdotal proofs of the disasters that can ensue from adhering to a single crop system. Yet it is also a religious command in Judaism. The links between sustainable agriculture and Judaism are often emphasized by organic producers in Israel. Mario Levi, founder of the Israel Bio-Organic Agriculture Association, thus refers to organic agriculture as a "Jewish practice" (quoted in Grosglik, *Organic Food in Israel*, 68).

49 At the outset of the occupation in 1967, Israeli officials, most notably the then security minister Moshe Dayan, formulated a governance doctrine for the Palestinian territories that became known as the *Enlightened Occupation.* The term, mainly employed by critics of the occupation apparatus, sought to capture how Israel rationalized its control over Palestinian lives as a local version of the "white man's burden." This doctrine was based on two assumptions. First, Israeli rule would improve and educate Palestinians, turning them into prosperous individuals by employing minimal forms of coercion and refraining from deploying military might in the

Since violence is a fact of life, those who try to reduce it violate the proper order of the world (i.e., *nature*) and hence may end up generating more violence. Loyal to this thesis, Golan sees Greenpeace or 269Life activists (which started with the Israeli animal rights activists of Anonymous) as criminals or, at best, blind ideologists who have no problem hurting others in the name of justice. Similarly, he blames most of the violent encounters he had with Palestinians on the leftist activists who came to protect them. Those people who endeavor to end violence by making the world more egalitarian are doomed to fail twice: first, because being naïve—perhaps like those who promote a return to the hunter-gatherer model—they are likely to increase violence despite themselves; and second, because they violate the order of the world: Whereas violence is a fact of life as such, the *just* form of violence is a theological fact, a function of the right positioning of different nations and species within the hierarchical theological framework of the chosen people and their chosen land. Those who promote equality would thus merely replace just with unjust violence. The question of violence's visibility resurfaces here with a twist: according to Golan, it is those very organizations and individuals who seek to render violence more visible—those, for example, who arrive at Palestinian villages equipped with cameras and social media accounts to document and make settlers' violence visible—who fail to *see*.[50]

There are many ways in which to refute these claims concerning organic agriculture, and certainly concerning the occupation, but this is not my purpose here. I merely seek to reconstruct a story about rights and wrongs that Golan tells as part of constructing his life within a meaningful frame. This reconstruction is important beyond providing a glimpse into the worldview of an arch-settler. It exposes something essential about the work of ethics

---

territories. Second, Israel would invest a significant amount of human and financial resources in vocational courses, training programs, and different educational programs for the bettering of Palestinian lives. In fact, Israel employed a variety of coercive means from the very first days of the occupation, and the means it introduced to better Palestinians' livelihoods were mainly used to ensure Palestinian communities' compliance with Israel's continuous domination of the territories. See Gordon, *Israel's Occupation*, 48–93. Golan's version emphasized state violence in this context as well, as he repeatedly returned to the (inaccurate) claim that Israel has established police stations in Palestinian villages and towns that provide protection against crime and violence, specifically against women. On this gendered reasoning of colonial control in other contexts, see Lila Abu-Lughod, *Do Muslim Women Need Saving?* (Cambridge, MA: Harvard University Press, 2013); Saba Mahmood, "Feminism, Democracy, and Empire: Islam and the War on Terror," in *Gendering Religion and Politics, Untangling Modernities*, ed. Hanna Herzog and Ann Braude (London: Palgrave Macmillan, 2009), 194–215.

50 See, for example, a report by Sarah, in Zar, "Price of Freedom."

within this context. Contrary to the assumption that ethics is external to violence and always works to limit or restrain it, ethics functions here with and alongside violence, facilitating and supporting it.[51] Accordingly, the ethics of organic agriculture here cannot be seen as a "mask" that "hides" violence, as the paradigm of "washing" proposes, because ethics is itself already embedded in violence; ethics speaks the language of violence and does not mark its ending or threshold. I return to this point in the epilogue.

Violence #4 (Land)

Organic agriculture emerges as tightly linked to violence also if we think of the main form of violence the farm exerts: taking land.

Recently, Israel has adopted new EU regulations that have dramatically improved the spatial conditions of chickens in battery cages. Yet even under these new regulations, organic eggs require roughly seven times more space than eggs produced by chickens grown in battery cages. According to these improved regulations, in battery cages there should be a maximum of nine to twelve chickens per square meter indoors (the exact size changes from country to country) and there is no requirement that chickens are provided with outdoor space to roam. The standard for organic eggs is usually a maximum of six chickens per square meter indoors and a maximum of two chickens per square meter outdoors. That is, the cage itself needs to be twice as large for the same number of chickens, and further space is required for free roaming outside. This, needless to say, requires space, which, conveniently, is much cheaper and more available when it can be taken for free, without any authorization, taxation, or regulation, in the West Bank.

Data concerning the allocation of egg quotas is not public in Israel, perhaps to protect producers behind the Green Line from potential boycotts. After I managed to receive this data,[52] the magnitude of Golan's mini-empire became clear: there are between fourteen and sixteen organic egg producers in Israel (the status of two producers was ambivalent); Golan's yearly egg quota is larger than all other fifteen combined.[53] In fact, his enterprise is so large that he is the fourth-largest

---

51 For a similar, and more systematic analysis of these workings of ethics, see James Eastwood, *Ethics as a Weapon of War: Militarism and Morality in Israel* (Cambridge: Cambridge University Press, 2017); Anat Matar, "What Enables Asa Kasher," *Mita'am* 6 (2006): 121–42.

52 Many thanks to my dad, who has done the work of detection on my behalf.

53 His yearly egg quota (updated to 2016) is 11,568,000 eggs per year. The next-largest producer of organic eggs has a yearly quota of 2,079,000 eggs a year (in the moshav Mle'a, within the 1948 borders), followed by producers with quotas of 1,655,000, 1,493,000, 1,252,000, and then around 500,000 and much lower.

supplier of eggs in Israel (organic and nonorganic), even though the consumption of organic eggs constitutes only 1 percent of all egg consumption in the country.[54] Land grab and organic agriculture thus transpire as part of the same order.

This is, of course, part of a much larger order. In 1979, in the now-famous Ellon Moreh case, the Israeli High Court of Justice ruled that land confiscated for security reasons cannot be used for settlement. With this ruling, a need emerged to find an alternative to the language of security as a justification for state-authorized land confiscation. At that point, agriculture became the main legal means for land grab.[55] The most extensive survey to date of cultivated agricultural land in the West Bank was conducted in 2013 and suggests that agricultural land cultivated by settlers amounts to roughly 25,000 acres, or 140 percent of the constructed area of the settlements. Fifty-two percent of cultivated agricultural land is located *outside* of the official municipal territory of settlements. This becomes even more prevalent during the post-Oslo years: the vast majority (almost 70 percent) of agricultural land that settlers started cultivating after 1997 falls outside these boundaries.[56] According to Dror Etkes, rather than construction (which has been limited, at least somewhat, and which is conditioned on people's willingness to move and live beyond the Green Line), the fastest-growing means of land grabbing in the West Bank today is agriculture.[57] Indeed, if we look at the relations between built areas of settlement (including outposts), and the land effectively annexed to settlements by means of agriculture as well as open territories annexed to either settlements or regional councils, the latter amounts to roughly forty times the former.[58] Patrick

54 The largest producer of eggs in Israel is from Ramot Hashavim, with a quota of 19,524,000 eggs a year (data updated for 2016; The Statutory Authority for Poultry Internal Document, "Eggs Quota, 2016," printed February 10, 2016). Next is a producer in Yarkonawith with 14,007,000 and one in Urim with 12,641,000 eggs a year. Golan follows with 11,568,000. The next three producers have an allocation of 7,400,000, 6,000,000, and 5,500,000 eggs. The vast majority of producers have quotas of less than 500,000 and often closer to 200,000 yearly. Two more producers in the West Bank (in Kedumim and Shilo) have a yearly egg quota of 1,500,000. In terms of organic producers, Golan of course leads; see previous note.

55 Weizman, *Hollow Land*, 116–17.

56 Dror Etkes, "Israeli Settlers' Agriculture as a Means of Land Takeover in the West Bank," trans. Tamar Cohen, *Kerem Navot*, August 2013, https://docs.wixstatic.com/ugd/cdb1a7_370bb4f21ceb4 7adb3ac7556c02b8972.pdf.

57 Etkes, "Israeli Settlers' Agriculture."

58 The built area of the settlements, excluding the neighborhoods in East Jerusalem, occupies roughly 1 percent of the West Bank's territory, which increases to 2 percent if we look at the territory that the settlements de facto occupy (for example, the territory stretching to the security fences surrounding them). It further increases to almost 10 percent (9.73 percent, to be

Wolfe speculates that settler colonialism's expansionist tendencies come from an agricultural need or, better, an economic need addressed through agriculture.[59] But perhaps this works (also) the other way around: agriculture provides a material mechanism for expansion. It is a technology of land theft.

As part of legitimating this technology, the state turned to the Ottoman law in the early 1980s, according to which land that has not been cultivated for more than three consecutive years becomes *makhlul*: the land of the sovereign (the empire, the state).[60] Eyal Weizman shows that within the tax system of the Ottoman Empire, it was in farmers' interests to relinquish land that could not be cultivated to avoid paying tax on unproductive areas. This meant that rocky land, which is common on the hilltops, often became state land. Accordingly, "the borders between cultivated and uncultivated lands often followed a clear topographical logic," with the mountain range—"rocky and windswept"—usually "available" to become state land.[61] Chicken coops, which can be placed on any terrain, are particularly apt for the purpose of occupying such "rocky and windswept" lands. This territorial adaptability, which makes it possible to place such coops on the very top of hills, also means that chicken

---

precise) if we measure the municipal area of the settlements. Yet once we include agricultural areas and the open territories that are annexed to either settlements or regional councils, the total land area under Israeli civic control in area C amounts to 40 percent of the West Bank's territory and 63 percent of area C (Jewish settlers, excluding those in East Jerusalem, amount to 12 percent of the West Bank's population). This means that the area to which access is restricted through unofficial demarcations is more than twenty times larger than the officially demarcated area and forty times larger than the actually built area. These unofficial boundaries, Neve Gordon and Moriel Ram note, "were created to restrict Palestinian movement and undermine their development," and many of them are determined through agricultural practice. Ariel Handel further demonstrates how the road system in the West Bank serves the same purpose. See Neve Gordon and Moriel Ram, "Ethnic Cleansing and the Formation of Settler Colonial Geographies," *Political Geography* 53 (July 2016): 24; Ariel Handel, "Gated/Gating Community: The Settlement Complex in the West Bank," *Transactions of the Institute of British Geographers* 39, no. 4 (2014): 504–17. For data, see Bt'selem, "Settlements: Updated Statistics and Data" [in Hebrew], *B'tselem*, accessed November 2019, https://www.btselem.org/hebrew/settlements; Peace Now, "Land: Updated Statistics and Data" [in Hebrew], Settlements Watch, *Peace Now*, accessed November 2019, http://peacenow.org.il/settlements-watch/matzav/land.

59 Wolfe, "Elimination of the Native," 395.

60 In *Emptied Lands: A Legal Geography of Bedouin Rights in the Negev* (Stanford, CA: Stanford University Press, 2018), Alexandre Kedar, Ahmad Amara, and Oren Yiftachel show how the employment of these elements in the Ottoman law was conveniently partial and was taken out of context in order to justify land taking.

61 Weizman, *Hollow Land*, 116–17.

FIGURES 3.7–3.8. Giv'ot Olam's chicken coops, located on the southwestern edge of the farm, overlooking the agricultural lands of Lower Yanun and A'qraba. Photo by author.

coops can establish visual control over territories they do not occupy directly. Golan's coops are indeed often situated on the hilltop, thereby creating what Weizman refers to as "optical urbanism," in which the homes of chickens replace the homes of settlers as surveillance tools.[62] They also establish a gaze, a look that embodies ownership, a tie, a sense of belonging to and a claim on all the land below.

Chicken coops are an efficient technology of occupying land for other reasons as well. Egg production necessitates less labor compared with other agricultural production processes and hence makes it possible to occupy larger terrains with relatively few people. Perhaps, then, it is not surprising that chicken coops were pioneering tools in the unimpeded movement of the new settlement movement. As briefly mentioned above, Golan's first organic chicken coop in the West Bank was the first act of moving outside of the settlement's fence, and, in a way at least, it was that coop which was the first outpost.

Conclusions: The "New" Settlement Movement and the Old One

One may contend that Golan does not really represent anything. He is considered extreme even by many of his fellow settlers. "Representation" would at any rate be an impossible task, since there is huge diversity among West Bank settlers and they cannot really be captured by a single model.[63] If at all, one may contend that Golan represents a minority among settlers since, as Ariel Handel, Marco Allegra, and Erez Maggor have recently shown, the vast majority of settlements have been completely normalized and function as any other town or village in Israel.[64] But Giv'ot Olam, too, has been normalized. Since 2005, there have been almost no reports of violence by Golan, and the farm is a flourishing business. The reports of violence linked to nearby territories point, more often than not, to violence by IDF soldiers. The army, it seems, took over the task of intimidating the people of Yanun.[65] At the same time, the violence

---

62 Weizman, *Hollow Land*, chapter 4: "Settlements: Optical Urbanism."

63 For diversity in the settlement movement at large, see Susskind et al., "Religious and Ideological Dimensions." For the radical differences between Gush Emunim and the new settlement movement, specifically concerning the relation to land, agriculture, and expansion, see Shimi Friedman, *The Hilltop Youth: A Stage of Resistance and Counter Culture Practice* (Lanham, MD: Lexington Books, 2018).

64 Handel, Allegra, and Maggor, *Normalizing Occupation*.

65 The NGO Yesh Din has documented several such cases (author's field notes, September 17, 2018).

of extreme settlers, which once was captured by Golan's figure as a unique one, is now the new normal in the West Bank.

Many of the descriptions in this chapter fit well into the pattern of a lawless frontier, wherein violence is not merely seen as necessary but is also romanticized. If the frontier provides an "unlimited opportunity for the strong, ambitious, self-reliant individual to thrust his way to the top," as Richard Slotkin argued in relation to the myth of the American frontier, then "the means to that regeneration ultimately became the means of violence, and the myth of regeneration through violence became the structuring metaphor of the American experience."[66] Living such a frontier-like reality, Golan once declared that he is "the sovereign" in his land: "We do not care about the decisions of the [Israeli] government, the US, or the EU. We do not care about anything. . . . We determine where [the army is deployed], and where anyone will settle, and where the borders of this land will be drawn. This is what it is all about."[67] And yet, if we follow Baruch Kimmerling, we see that in the Israeli case the frontier is a *state* project.[68] Kimmerling's observations, published in 1989, should be modified to fit the reality shaped by the new settlement movement, which has rendered the frontier in the West Bank more similar to the lawless, individualized, American frontier. Nevertheless, and while at times they are indeed in confrontation with the state, the individual men and women in the outposts are more often than not supported by state apparatuses. They could not have been there without the backing of state power: a state that builds roads, supplies electricity, shows incredible tolerance for, if not outright protection of, individualized violence and the constant violation of municipal building regulations.

Through this symbiosis of state and individualized violence, the entire C territories are now effectively managed by paramilitary, albeit scattered and often unorganized, groups of settlers, which are nevertheless protected—or actively supported by—the army.[69] As the lawyer Itay Mack observes: "It is not that the soldiers stand by and fail to enforce the law on [violent] settlers; the

---

66 Richard Slotkin, *Regeneration through Violence: The Mythology of the American Frontier, 1600–1860* (Norman: University of Oklahoma Press, [1973] 2000), 5.

67 Sharon, "Avri Ran"; my translation.

68 Baruch Kimmerling, ed., *The Israeli State and Society: Boundaries and Frontiers* (Albany: State University of New York Press, 1989).

69 Michal Peleg, "This Is How the Control of the West Bank Has Shifted to the Settlers' Militias" [in Hebrew], *Sicha Mekomit*, March 9, 2019, https://mekomit.co.il/.

settlers themselves are part of the enforcement system [in the West Bank]. The violent settlers are another layer allowing the state to enforce its rule."[70] As a result of this multilayered regime of violence, Palestinians are rapidly losing access to their agricultural lands, and the route to annexing the C territories—now a declared plan not just of settlers but of governmental officials as well—is more secured than ever. The system of Giv'ot Olam has become central to Israel's modes of operation. Giv'ot Olam, in turn, has been established enough to become a normal, flourishing organic farm.

Further still, the entire project of Giv'ot Olam and the outposts is part of a lineage that has been shaping the Jewish state from its establishment: from the famous system of Tower and Stockade in Mandatory Palestine, to Sharon's plan from the 1970s to turn military outposts into civilian settlements and settlements into a tool of military control,[71] and to the construction of development towns in the periphery in order to secure control and as a way of constructing homes as militarized barriers in case of war. So many homes in Israel are, or have been, military bases to some extent; tools of territorial control.

ACCORDINGLY, WHILE HE LIKES to think of himself as antiestablishment,[72] and in some ways he indeed is, Golan's story cannot be told only as a story of a unique, single individual; it is a story of a state. Golan, too, often describes his work as an integral part of the Zionist story, claiming that he works with the same methods and ideology as those who first came to settle the land.[73] And indeed, even though he is an extreme example, he nonetheless represents an important underlying logic. Slotkin urges us to take a critical look at the American founding fathers: ultimately, they were those who "tore violently a nation from the implacable and opulent

---

70 Cited in Peleg, "This Is How the Control."

71 Eyal Weizman describes in detail this construction of space on the ever-expanding threshold between military violence (war, occupation) and civic settlement (homemaking, occupation) and demonstrates the topological and logical continuums between the Zionist enterprise and the settlement movement. Weizman, *Hollow Land*, 57ff.

72 This information can be found in almost any interview conducted with him. He also emphasized this in the conversation I conducted. See, e.g., Zar, "Price of Freedom."

73 See, for example, Oded Shalom, "A Journey down a Via Dolorosa" [in Hebrew], *Ynet*, June 1, 2017, http://www.yediot.co.il/articles/0,7340,L-4970184,00.html. This is the case for many others among the new—and old—settlement movement. See Harel, "Blessed Deviation," 136.

wilderness—the rogues, adventurers, and land-boomers; the Indian fighters, traders, missionaries, explorers, and hunters who killed and were killed until they had mastered the wilderness."[74] Many of Israel's founding myths can be seen in this light. Perhaps Golan will join such a pantheon one day (I tend to believe that he will not), but even if not, the point is that he fits the pattern.

74 Slotkin, *Regeneration through Violence*, 4.

Epilogue
An Ethic of Violence

ORGANIC WASHING

The ethics of ideological Jewish settlement in the West Bank has many fac-ets.[1] Primarily, it combines two related strata. First, it is founded on a religious belief in the integrity of Eretz Israel (the land of Israel as a theological frame-work) within which the settlement of the land (*yeshuv ha'aretz*) is a binding command. Ultimately, this ethics can be seen as part of a holistic way of being, a unity that can best be captured by the Hebrew term *ahavat hamakom. Makom* in Hebrew means both "the place" (location) and God, and the word that ties them together in this expression—*ahava*—means love. Love for a place that is a love for God, a love for God that assumes a concrete form through loving the land. This layer works in tandem with settlers' firm belief in themselves as the chosen people, which provides a racialized ground on the basis of which violence and dispossession can be justified.[2] Both of these layers are part of the

1 These ideological settlers are distinct from "quality of life" settlers, who came for improved living conditions, as well as from ultra-orthodox settlers, who began migrating to the West Bank because of the limited space in orthodox cities within Israel. See Lee Cahaner, "Between Ghetto-Politics and Geopolitics: Ultraorthodox Settlements in the West Bank," in *Normaliz-ing Occupation: The Politics of Everyday Life in the West Bank Settlements,* ed. Ariel Handel, Marco Allegra, and Erez Maggor (Bloomington: Indiana University Press, 2017), 112–27; Sara Yael Hirschhorn, *City on a Hilltop: American Jews and the Israeli Settler Movement* (Cambridge, MA: Har-vard University Press, 2017).

2 For more on these schemes of justification, see Assaf Harel, "'A Blessed Deviation in Jewish History': On Contemporary Forms of Messianism among Religiously Motivated Settlers in the West Bank," in *Normalizing Occupation,* ed. Handel, Allegra, and Maggor, 128–57; Ian S. Lustick, *For the Land and the Lord: Jewish Fundamentalism in Israel* (New York: Council on Foreign Rela-tions, 1988); Idith Zertal and Akiva Eldar, *Lords of the Land: The War over Israel's Settlements in the Occupied Territories, 1967–2007,* trans. Vivian Eden (New York: Nation Books, 2005).

story of Golan—a religious man who has explicitly talked about violence as a means to assert racial superiority over "Arabs" and to "cleanse" the territory of Palestinians; a man for whom the work of the land is a command ("Each egg I collect, each chicken I care for, and each and every animal that lives in the farm or weed that grows in the yard, is part of my covenant with the land of Israel [Eretz Israel] and the Torah of Israel"),[3] and whose frank racism has become infamous even among other settlers.[4]

Yet at least two elements suggest that this dual framework is not sufficient to explain Golan's ethics of violence. First, his violence does not stop at racial lines. He has threatened, dispossessed, and physically attacked other Jewish settlers, including his neighbors in Itamar. Rabbi Nathan Hai, the chief Rabbi of Itamar, argued that Giv'ot Olam's prosperity was achieved through "stepping on dead bodies," and I presume he did not lament Golan's Palestinian victims.[5] Second, God did not come up even once in the long conversation I had with Golan about the nature of organic agriculture, leftist politics, food ethics, violence, and vegetarianism. This was most likely a choice he made—to speak a language he assumed I would accept, to find a strange, common ground—yet it seems to me that this ability to reconstruct an ethical story without any religious undertone suggests that there is more to the scheme supporting Golan's settlement project.

This brief chapter, then, focuses on organic agriculture as an ethical scheme for violent settlement. Nevertheless, one should bear in mind that the above

---

3 Quoted in Aviv Lavie, "The Scourge of the Hills" [in Hebrew], *Ha'aretz*, April 8, 2003, https://www.haaretz.co.il/misc/1.874468; my translation. The quote from Golan continues: "This land is my flesh and blood, my existence . . . and yes—I would die for this place and am even willing to risk the lives of my loved ones for this place."

4 See Chen Kotes-Bar, "The Arabs Are Scared of Me? They Admire Me!" [in Hebrew], *Maariv-NRG*, September 16, 2005, https://www.makorrishon.co.il/nrg/online/1/ART/983/927.html; Yehuda Yifrach, "The Meteor of Jewish Settlement in Samaria: 'I Am the Sovereign'" [in Hebrew], *NRG*, February 2, 2013, http://www.nrg.co.il/online/1/ART2/433/429.html. As Feige puts it, Golan's "intense hostility towards the Arabs" is not "camouflaged by ideological lingo and not restricted to the Palestinians of the occupied territories." Michael Feige, *Settling in the Hearts: Jewish Fundamentalism in the Occupied Territories* (Detroit: Wayne State University Press, 2009), 237.

5 Quoted in Yehuda Yifrach, "Avri Ran Won the Arbitration," [in Hebrew] *NRG*, April 26, 2013, http://www.nrg.co.il/online/1/ART2/463/901.html. "S.," who has been identified as an important figure in Itamar, told a reporter that the inhabitants of Itamar are scared of Golan. And "this is not a groundless fear," he emphasized, "since [Golan] does hurt people. He has an aura of a fearless man, an audacious man who can enter Palestinian villages on his own and take care of them."

separations are somewhat artificial. These schemes are in fact entangled, as particular modes of agriculture lend themselves to a religious imaginary or ethos.[6] My main argument here will be a critique of the paradigm of "washing" as yet another way of thinking about the politics of visibility and knowledge with which this book has been engaged. But washing will become throughout this chapter a way of violence in and of itself, as fluidity will emerge as one of the most efficient technologies of violence.

IN CRITICAL LITERATURE on the occupation and in activists' struggles against it, Israeli liberal politics are often analyzed through the paradigm of "washing": a form of progressive politics toward x (gay rights, for example) that should divert attention from, if not justify, the occupation. "Washing" is one strategy of normalization; it uses something desirable, beautiful, just, in order to "wash away" all that is wrong with the settlement project and military control. Nizri's story in the interlude was precisely such a story, in which good food served to change the narrative concerning Amona's evacuation and the settlement project at large. Among such analyses, those most closely related to my story here would be Erica Weiss's discussion of "vegan washing," which points to ethical food consumption's distancing itself from the politics of occupation; or Ariel Handel, Galit Rand, and Marco Allegra's work, which coined the term *wine-washing* to refer to the proliferation of boutique wineries and vineyards in the West Bank (many of them organic) as an effort to construct Europe in Israel ("Tuscany ... ten minutes away from your house," as a tourism coordinator of the Samaria Regional Council phrased it).[7] Organic

6 Grosglik shows how in Israel, the ethics of organic food production and consumption is often tightly linked to Jewish traditions and Jewish "roots" (Rafi Grosglik, *Organic Food in Israel: Resistance, Assimilation, and Global Culture* [in Hebrew] [Tel Aviv: Resling Publishing Press, 2017], 68–69). For more about the idea of "working the land" as rooted in a biblical sentiment embedded in Zionism from its outset, see Tamar Novick, "Milk and Honey: Technologies of Plenty in the Making of a Holy Land, 1880–1960" (PhD diss., University of Pennsylvania, 2014). Herding specifically—now the most common agricultural practice in the new outposts—has been considered a way of demonstrating the long duress of Jewish ownership of the land, from early Zionism onward, and a way of reconnecting to presumably biblical modes of living.

7 Erica Weiss showed how ethical veganism in Israel shifted from being "linked to questions of occupation, human rights, and Palestinians" to becoming a "washing" scheme for the violence of occupation. "So far," a vegan activist told her, "a chicken has never tried to blow up a bus." Or, in the words of another: "If animals would organize and teach their children to hate us, and try to kill us, I would feel the same way. But until today, there are no chickens in suicide vests, and

agriculture—clean, sustainable, respectful (of land, animals, and people)—can thus fall under the rubric of "organic washing."

A story of Golan's farm that adheres to this paradigm would join a broader history in which nature has served to "wash" land grab in Israel. From foresting projects that both disguise ruins and create them[8] to the marking of hiking trails or natural reserves[9] and to agricultural work that presumably "made the desert bloom" (Ben Gurion's vision), nature and agriculture beautify and symbolize—quite literally—the creation of roots. These roots—a deepening into the ground, a vertical movement—also need the open horizons of territory. Thus, the vertical movement of putting down roots summons a horizontal movement of expansion. "Expansion" since, as Gadi Algazi observes, these lands, which are often referred to as "open land," are there "not in an ecological sense but in a colonial one: these are lands open to settlement and appropriation."[10] Therefore, "the act of putting down roots is also an ongoing process of uprooting":[11] the uprooting of people who used to live on the land, but also the uprooting of what is being planted—forests, orchards, and groves—since those were planted in order to take space, to maximize territorial control, and may

---

the ones shooting rockets at us from Gaza, they aren't the goats and camels that live over there." Erica Weiss, "'There Are No Chickens in Suicide Vests': The Decoupling of Human Rights and Animal Rights in Israel," *Journal of the Royal Anthropological Institute* 22, no. 3 (September 2016): 691, 700. On wine-washing, see Ariel Handel, Galit Rand, and Marco Allegra, "Wine-Washing: Colonization, Normalization, and the Geopolitics of *Terroir* in the West Bank's Settlements," *Environment and Planning A: Economy and Space* 47, no. 6 (June 2015): 1360.

8 Naama Meishar, "In Search of Meta-Landscape Architecture: The Ethical Experience and Jaffa Slope Park's Design," *Journal of Landscape Architecture* 7, no. 2 (2012): 40–45; Hila Zaban, "Preserving 'the Enemy's' Architecture: Preservation and Gentrification in a Formerly Palestinian Jerusalem Neighbourhood," *International Journal of Heritage Studies* 23, no. 10 (2017): 961–76. Foresting projects were often used not just to cover the traces of destroyed villages, but also to facilitate further destruction or prevent non-Jewish construction.

9 Orit Ben-David, "*Tiyul* (Hike) as an Act of Consecration of Space," in *Grasping Land: Space and Place in Contemporary Israeli Discourse and Experience*, ed. Eyal Ben-Ari and Yoram Bilu (Albany: State University of New York Press, 1997), 129–45.

10 Gadi Algazi, "From Gir Forest to Umm Hiran: Notes on Colonial Nature and Its Keepers" [in Hebrew], *Theory and Critique* 37 (2010): 241; my translation. Indeed, in his research on the debates around the resettlement of those evacuated from Gaza, Liron Shani examines the idea of nature among the settlers. He shows they identified "nature" with "land" and "land" with "settlement" ("Recipe for Nature: The Conflict between Land and Environmentalism: The Struggle to Establish the New Settlement (Mirsham) in Eastern Lachish" [in Hebrew], *Israeli Sociology* 14 [2012]: 57–81).

11 Algazi, "From Gir Forest to Umm Hiran," 250.

become an obstacle to Jewish settlement later on. "There is no such thing as wilderness," Wolfe puts it in one of his definite formulations, "only depopulation."[12] Planting alongside bulldozing, preserving nature alongside displacing people, and hikes on nature trails alongside massive real-estate development are thus not contradictions but duos that complete each other in this scheme. As colonial duos, they have been integral to the Zionist national movement (the rooting of the Jewish people in Eretz Israel) from its outset.[13] Organic agriculture joins this list but entails an additional dimension: its explicit ethical facet makes it possible to anchor settlement in a notion of justice. I will focus here on the treatment of animals, which is essential to this ethics.

Golan's chickens enjoy relatively spacious cages and additional outdoor space where they can roam freely. They are fed organic food grown especially for them on the farm and have the material environment required for any chicken to thrive.[14] This thriving of animals is the pride of the farm and is mentioned by workers, in newspaper articles, and on the farm's website. The entire farm was built, Golan maintains, out of deep respect for nature: "This is the only place in Judea and Samaria [the West Bank] that did not commit a sin toward the landscape, that did not injure the mountain; that did not commit crime against the land. . . . This place is one big act of

---

12 Wolfe, *Traces of History*, 23. Noam Leshem captures this idea through the almost oxymoronic "temporary grove." Temporary groves were planted to disguise the ruins of Palestinian neighborhoods and prevent their repopulation (by Palestinians or unauthorized Jews). Leshem, too, claims: "The temporariness of these groves implies that their presence is not merely an ecological endeavor"; rather, "temporary groves are but one relatively cheap and quick methods [sic] through which the municipality can claim possession of the land" (Leshem, *Life after Ruin*, 43–44). Or, in the words of the Israeli minister of agriculture in 2010: "Wherever we shall plant a forest, we will best preserve national land"; therefore, the more we plant, the better, "even if these [forests] are to be uprooted for other purposes" (quoted in Algazi, "From Gir Forest to Umm Hiran," 244; my translation).

13 This structure—where planting and uprooting, settling and dispossessing, the fostering of nature and the dispossession of people work in tandem with colonial destruction of land and nature—is a common colonial structure. For other contexts, see Seth Garfield, "A Nationalist Environment: Indians, Nature, and the Construction of the Xingu National Park in Brazil," *Luso-Brazilian Review* 41, no. 1 (2004): 139–67; Hamilton Sipho Simelane, "Landlessness and Imperial Response in Swaziland, 1938-1950," *Journal of Southern African Studies* 17, no. 4 (1991): 717–41.

14 As one of Golan's workers stated: "This is a free, and thus happy chicken . . . the egg, which is part of it, is a happy egg, a healthy egg. It has no trace of chemicals, it has no depression." Quoted in Yuval Heiman, "The State of Lettuce in the Territories: The Hills of Judea and Samaria Are an Organic Superpower" [in Hebrew], *Zman Yerushalim*, February 2, 2010, http://www.nrg.co.il /online/54/ART2/048/094.html.

kissing the land."[15] He does not raise animals for meat production ("animals are not being slaughtered here," he told me several times), and when goats are being milked, one of the farm's workers sometimes plays the piano for them to alleviate some of the stress they experience during this act.[16] The flourishing of chickens and goats thus provides an ethical scheme that portrays settlement as an ethical enterprise, dissipating the actual political conditions of violence at the settlement's foundation and normalizing its existence.

It is tempting to compare ethics and occupation on their spatial terms here: the space that the chickens enjoy versus the cramped and shrinking space of Palestinians, the limits set on the latter's freedom of movement or the territorial development of their cities and villages; an ethics of care for animals that generates constant harm to people. Care for "Jewish animals," that is. Golan—who prides himself on strictly following the regulations of organic standards not only out of compliance but also from what seems to be a real concern for nature—has a habit of using fertilizer to poison Palestinian goats and sheep. The use of such fertilizers is prohibited in any form of organic agriculture—not just, needless to say, if used for the wasteful killing of the animals of others. Making use of his topographical advantage, he adds fertilizer into the higher sections of the stream, allowing it to flow downhill to the areas in which Palestinians graze their herds.[17] Omar Jabary Salamanca referred to the "toxic ecologies of settler colonialism" to show the various toxic flows—of sewage, agricultural fertilizers, septic tanks, and more—that subject Palestinians to forms of slow death.[18] Golan's fertilizers, while often killing fast rather than slowly, join this settler toxicity that shapes the environment no less than the sustainable ideology informing his organic practices.

This poison, which travels freely in water, limits the movement—and livelihood, and life—of some, facilitating the ever-expanding movement of others.[19]

---

15 Yifrach, "Avri Ran Won"; my translation.

16 Heiman, "State of Lettuce."

17 Author's field notes, December 31, 2017. Additional testimonies were collected by Yesh Din.

18 Omar Jabary Salamanca, "The Ends of Infrastructure" (paper presented at the Environmental Justice in Israel/Palestine conference, Buffalo, NY, February 6–7, 2019).

19 It may be interesting to note that, as Natalia Gutkowski observes, those who are being enclosed in this scheme are Palestinian animals, often placed in quarantine by Israeli authorities, which thus "performs its increasing control over Area C" by confining animals' bodies and restricting their grazing areas. More often then not, the fences that are erected in the West Bank do not mark the settlement borders, i.e., the territorial claims of the settlers—claims whose horizons

In the Lockean formula, we saw a household that was dependent on the logic of the fence (enclosure) to keep expanding. Territorial units had to be enclosed with fences to create, so I argued, the ontological foundation for unlimited land accumulation. Grazing was an essential element of this territorial expansion: it was for the purpose of grazing that the commons were enclosed and, as Thomas More observed, through sheep that people were dispossessed. With Golan's goats and chickens we have yet another story of homes and territories that are marked between sheep and people. But rather than the fence of the story of enclosure, which protects one's sheep and pushes other people to starvation, Golan had the water tank to mark his terrain. This served simultaneously as a clear enough mark of the border and as an easily movable object, whose constant movement allowed his farm to keep growing. The creek that carries the death of Palestinian sheep and goats, the water tank that keeps moving, itself becoming a fluid border, the mobile homes that keep moving from hill to hill, from morning to evening, or that are established in cars, all compose a home through and in mobility, which destroys as it expands.

Agriculture thus provides a foundation for violence, not just by telling us to look elsewhere (at chickens and their living conditions rather than at Palestinians and their unfreedoms) and thereby somehow blurring the ability to judge, but also by being the very material articulation of violence. In this alternative paradigm—and in the reality of flowing poison—organic agriculture does not wash violence away in the sense of removing it from the territory. Violence itself remains and is even intensified, since—if one is to stick to the parable—it is carried via, rather than washed away by, water.[20]

---

cannot be limited and whose clear demarcation is thus a violation of the project's logic. Rather, most fences in the West Bank mark the confinement of Palestinians. To draw on Handel's terminology, settlements are gating, rather than gated enclaves. Natalia Gutkowski, "Bodies That Count: Multispecies Population Management by the Israeli Administration in the West Bank" (paper presented at the Environmental Justice in Israel/Palestine conference, Buffalo, NY, February 6–7, 2019); Handel, "Gated/Gating Community."

20 Although he did not do so in these terms, Golan explicitly asserted that for him, the poisoning of Palestinian sheep takes precedence over the sustainability of land and water. "The trick isn't to be a person with values, but to preserve your values when they clash with one another. The leading value for me is to do what is necessary. If the Jewish people were extremely ill and a revolution were needed in the consumption of health products, the leading value for me could be to put healthy food in the people's mouths. But I think that today, it's more important to live here." The ethics of occupation thus overcomes the ethics of food. Dafna Arad, "Farming in the West Bank: Organic Paradise, Thorny Reality," Ha'aretz, April 24, 2012, https://www.haaretz.com/1.5216745.

INDEED, FLUIDITY IS ESSENTIAL for this mode of homemaking. Michael Feige identified a shift in the conception and construction of home in the new settlement movement: whereas the establishment of the Gush Emunim settlement made the construction of stable, enduring, entrenched homes part of the ideology of settlement as well as its political technology, the hilltop youth refuse to be "tied down." (Recall the British effort to put "fixed boundaries upon landed property" that led to the Boer War.)[21] Accordingly, "the home that the youth of the hill construct is a mobile one characterized by its fluidity"; home is seen "as a constant struggle, always temporal and constantly moving."[22] In this context, a distinction should be drawn between two types of outposts. Some, like Amona (see interlude for this part), are constructed around the home logic of Gush Emunim (recall how important it was for Nizri to state that he was *not* living in a mobile home and that he had a large kitchen); others physically symbolize and materialize fluidity.[23]

PARTLY, WHAT IS at stake in the paradigm of "washing" is, once again, the validity of the language of violence's invisibility: a question of the possibility to not see as a precondition for the sustainment of violence. Integral to this paradigm is some reference to natural beauty that serves, precisely, to *hide* the political ugliness. In their work on "wine-washing," Handel, Rand, and Allegra highlight the mode of normalization by displacement—rendering the occupied land into a "Tuscany" (as an Israeli TV show that examined the wine industry in the West Bank commented, "wherever you plant a vineyard, the landscape begins to arrange itself like Tuscany").[24] Reemerging as another place, another space, and, significantly, a *beautiful* place, the specific history of violence at the foundation of the land is hidden and control of the disputed territory is maximized. This is no longer an occupied land but an elsewhere,

---

21 Arendt, *Origins*, 196.
22 Feige, *Settling in the Hearts*, 243, 244.
23 Accordingly, Kaniel distinguishes between "outposts" and "hills." Whereas outposts are often very similar to established settlements, distinguished from them only by their status in Israeli law, "hills" comprise unorganized collections of people trying to inhabit or imitate a biblical way of life (Shlomo Kaniel, "The Hilltop Settlers: Are They Biblical Sabras?" [in Hebrew], in *Religious Zionism: The Age of Change* [Jerusalem: Bialik, 2004], 533–58). In this sense, Amona was a classic outpost, whereas Giv'ot Olam is clearly a "hill."
24 Ben Shani, "Vineyards instead of Mobile Homes," November 16, 2009, in Ilana Dayan's *Uvda*, TV show, Keshet TV, https://www.mako.co.il/tv-ilana_dayan/2010-dcc4c8a272df4210/Article-4db3863563df421006.htm; Handel, Rand, and Allegra, "Wine-Washing."

FIGURE 3.9. The foundations for the chicken coop at the Three Seas Lookout. The coop is situated on a high hill overlooking Beit Furik, a Palestinian village at the outskirts of Nablus, seen here in the background. Photo by author.

without a history and actuality of violence woven into it. Beauty ("Tuscany") is essential here since it allows for the fantastical distancing to capture the imagination. Therefore, such strategies of washing or normalization often work through the images of forests, vineyards, and other desired landscapes.[25] But it is not entirely clear to what extent such references properly represent the reality of the farm. Chicken coops are quite ugly after all. And whereas Golan talks about a "big act of kissing the land," he seems to have an inclination to place these coops in some of the most beautiful sites in the area, turning scenic lookouts and picturesque trails into smelly, unattractive, massive coops.[26] The paradigm of "Tuscany" cannot really be carried from the vineyards to the eggs, and this brutality of injuring the landscape is ultimately the aesthetic manifestation of the brutality of houses that become "equals to

25 For another example of such spaces, see Mori Ram, "White but Not Quite: Normalizing Colonial Conquests through Spatial Mimicry," *Antipode* 46, no. 3 (2014): 736–53.
26 Yifrach, "Avri Ran Won."

wiping out . . . Arabs," as in the words of Moshe Zar, the land merchant, with which chapter 3 opened.

GIVEN THE MAGNITUDE of Golan's enterprise, when Irit from chapter 2 goes to the supermarket, she is likely to buy Golan's eggs if she cares about the well-being of chickens. Golan indeed told me that almost all "leftists in Tel Aviv" eat his products without being aware of it. He uses generic brand names (such as those of the main supermarkets) to disguise the origins of his products. He would have preferred, he said, to publicly take pride in his work, in the quality of his products; but he has come to accept the need to disguise their origins. He did not question the ethics of this camouflaging, even though it stands in contradiction to the commitment of organic producers to mark clearly the origin of crops, place of production, and details of the producer, often alongside descriptions of the process of production. But although many of these eggs are differently marked, stories about the origins of free-range eggs are constantly resurfacing in Israeli media, and it is difficult to argue that Irit would not know or could not have known. The daily practices of homemaking are, in this sense too, a form in which so many Israelis are complicit with the ongoing dispossession of Palestinians. And in this sense too, most Israelis end up consuming this dispossession's products, digesting the occupation, as it were. They either do it unknowingly (given the lack of marking) or—as Weiss's work demonstrates clearly—they simply do not care.[27]

27 E. Weiss, "'There Are No Chickens in Suicide Vests.'"

Conclusion

If the question of settler colonialism is a question of violent modes of roots making, if settler landscapes are violent geographies par excellence, my question is about a form of belonging to and in violence without which, I contend, settlement would be impossible. Much more widely, in cases wherein violence is part of the conditions of possibility of one's modes of being—and homemaking is both a concrete example and an emblem in this regard—it becomes, I have argued, tethered to the "I." This is the case when we think of states that were established on the ruins of other states/communities or when we think of an unregulated housing market. It is the case also when we think of the violent access of men to women's bodies that established, as Carole Pateman argued,[1] simultaneously the private sphere and the paradigm of political consent, or when we think of the Freudian model of symbolically killing the head of the household in the process of establishing one's own home and selfhood.[2]

Poststructuralist theory has taught us that structures of desire are formed, mediated through, and shaped by the sociopolitical conditions supporting them. Drawing on this insight, we should at least entertain the possibility that the sociopolitical conditions of settlement are likely to give rise to a particular mode of attachment to violence. This structure is necessary if one is to develop an attachment to a place in which one's presence is conditioned by violence; it is necessary *because* in such contexts one's home, one's presence, always rests on past violence and is often sustained by ongoing, structural violence. And

---

1 Carole Pateman, *The Sexual Contract* (Stanford, CA: Stanford University Press, 1988).
2 See, for example, Sigmund Freud, *Totem and Taboo: Some Points of Agreement Between the Mental Lives of Savages and Neurotics* (New York: W. W. Norton), 1962.

if the object of desire (land, territory, home) in such cases is entangled with violence, then violence itself can—if not must—become woven into desire if the object is to persist. In such cases, violence is not merely a by-product of one's specific mode of existence or a precondition of it; it becomes an essential facet of who one is.

This is not to say that this violence is necessary. As Foucault's genealogical work demonstrates, "who one is" is always contingent and conditioned on a set of social and political orders that are themselves objects of contestation. This is clearly the case when one's identity is a function of a very historically and geographically specific political constellation. Furthermore, this violence is often in conflict with other facets of the self: there are conflicts between self-image and doings, between social positions and political stances, between how we like to think of ourselves and the networks within which we are imbricated. Different people and societies negotiate these intimacies of violence differently; and they do so differently in different times, or when facing changing circumstances (we saw some such negotiations in this book). These conflicts constantly open a path to political change. What I have tried to show here, however, is that when these negotiations fail and one is forced to confront the violent structure subtending their identity, there are good chances that one would resort to violence rather than undertake a radical change of identity.

As part of this claim, I sought to argue that to oppose this violence, it is insufficient to render it more visible or known. As noted in the introduction, this is a claim that seems to me to be much more obvious today, when political violence is increasingly surfacing more shamelessly than when I began writing this book; and nevertheless, I am often finding myself perplexed by how many activists, theorists, and observers of politics still hold on to the hope that making violence more known will lead to its demise. The argument, again, is not that there is no point in struggling against this violence, in endeavoring to move people's ways of being moved—their sentiments, attachments, senses of being just, or entrenchment in a particular mode of being in the land. My argument is that as a precondition for such successful struggles we should understand the schemes of justification of the orders of violence we seek to fracture. The politics of rendering violence visible, of exposing audiences to the sights of wrongdoing or to the facts concerning this violence, rests on two assumptions: first, that these visuals or facts will generate some shock, and second, that the intended recipients of the visuals/facts share the view that violence must be reduced. This is true for 269Life activists taking pictures in slaughterhouses and for antioccupation activists documenting settlers' or military violence. I tried to show that in Golan's case, and in more subtle ways also in the cases of Irit or the many liberal Zionists she represents here, these assumptions fail. In these cases, violence creates neither shock nor moral/political outrage.

This claim is both structural and temporal. I say "temporal" and not "historical" because often the change—the different unfolding of the structure—occurs almost instantly, as part of the internal negotiation of an individual person's encounter with violence and its outcomes. In capturing this point as a means of conclusion, the words of Joseph Weitz can serve as a useful illustration. According to Meron Benvenisti, Weitz was "the man who pushed hardest for Israel to get rid of the Arabs and take possession of their land." Most famously, he initiated the idea of the Transfer Committees (established in 1948). In 1948, he traveled the land and on arriving at the Galilee, previously inhabited by many Palestinians, he encountered the outcome of the war's destruction:

> An empty village: what a terrible thing! Fossilized lives! Lives turned to fossilized whispers in extinguished ovens; a shattered mirror; moldy blocks of dried figs and a scrawny dog, thin-tailed and floppy-eared and dark eyed. At the same time—at the very same moment—a different feeling throbs and rises from the primordial depths, a feeling of victory, of taking control, of revenge, and of casting off suffering. And suddenly the whispers vanish and you see empty houses, good for the settlement of our Jewish brethren who have wandered for generation upon generation, refugees of your people, steeped in suffering and sorrow, as they, at last, find a roof over their heads. And you knew: War! This was our war.[3]

Ruba Salih and Olaf Corry present this quote to show that the "indigenous population's erasure . . . appears in Weitz's affective sensory account as a nonfact."[4] They show how life can quickly enter the settler discourse as fossil, as a "lifeless trace . . . of a past time and people that 'suddenly' vanish."[5] This act of erasure is accompanied by other mechanisms of dissociation, which we encountered in the theoretical overview. Such would be the use of the passive voice—"lives *turned into* fossilized whispers in extinguished ovens"—through which the agents causing wrongdoing disappear. These apparatuses of denial

---

3 Quoted in Meron Benvenisti, *Sacred Landscape: The Buried History of the Holy Land since 1948* (Berkeley: University of California Press, 2000), 155.

4 Ruba Salih and Olaf Corry, "Settler Colonialism, Displacement and the Reordering of Human and Non-Human Life in Palestine," unpublished paper.

5 Salih and Corry, "Settler Colonialism."

and dissociation are at play here as part of an effort to negotiate life with one's own violence. Yet at the same time, there is another "affective sensory account" at operation in these words—and it is this consolidation of sentiments that this book sought to highlight: Weitz reports the eerie feeling of witnessing an empty(ied) village. It is a terrible thing, he says, and nevertheless, "at the same time—at the very same moment," and the conjunction here is crucial—"a different feeling throbs and rises from the primordial depths." This is the feeling of "victory," but also of "revenge" and above all "war"—and not just war but "*our* war." Contrary to the passive voice with which the quote begins and that refuses to take responsibility for the "terrible thing" of emptying a village (the terrible thing whose other name is ethnic cleansing), by the end of these lines, revenge and war are fully acknowledged as "ours" in an almost Nietzschean celebration of destruction.

Within one paragraph, Weitz undergoes the transformation that in chapter 2 took generations.[6] In chapter 2, this generational gap was captured primarily as the distance between the writer S. Yizhar, who witnessed the Nakba, and the fictive figure Irit, who had come to reside in its plunder. Yizhar predicted that in "these bare villages, the day was coming when they would begin to cry out," and it was only later, perhaps by Irit's time, that we find out they never did. Irit lives in these villages (if I may stretch the language here) peacefully. Her walls do not cry out, not even when the violence and injustice they contain are animated by Soraya's knock on the door. In Weitz, the transition from the cry to silence is much swifter. First of all, "his" "bare villages" do not cry but "whisper"—already a reduced presence of the voice of injustice. But even this whisper "suddenly" vanishes. These villages will not come to hound their new inhabitants, as Yizhar assumed; rather, they immediately reveal themselves as "good for the settlement of our Jewish brethren," willing to embrace the newcomers who need them, as if they, too, have forgotten what was so clear in them and through them merely a few sentences before.

IF VIOLENCE IS SO smoothly integrated with identity, what needs to be contended with are the very conditions that render violence intimately linked to the self. Specific to the Israeli/Palestinian context, the question is whether there can be a Jewish presence in the land, and Jewish immigration to the land, that does not take colonial forms. In some sense at least, this is a way of ask-

6 In Shavit's case a decade: between interviewing Said for Ha'aretz in 2003 and his 2013 book.

ing how one can oppose who they are. In asking and also in answering this question, I keep oscillating between two poles. One is the pessimistic answer that, ultimately, one cannot. If one looks at the political map of Israel today, it is naïve to say that most Israelis oppose "the occupation" or the regime of rights deprivation that constitutes so much of what they have. Even if they theoretically support its ending, when one delves into the details it often becomes apparent that they are unwilling to pay the price. Certainly, they are far from being willing to renegotiate with Palestinians the economic and territorial order established after and through the Nakba. On the other hand, a more optimistic approach insists that such social structures are never deterministic and that the contradictions embedded in them allow for subversive desires to emerge. The story has not reached its end, and the outcome is still to be determined. This book is written somewhere between these two poles: it claims that we must understand how deeply people are constituted by their violence in order to begin a new conversation about ending it.

I am often asked what concrete politics I seek to promote here, and the honest answer is that I am not sure. If one needs to nevertheless mark the contours of an answer, one place to begin is the story of Madame Nielsen, which, for me, is the most pessimistic pole of this book. Nielsen is very much aware of the violence present in the infrastructure of her existence in the colony; she tries to inhabit the land in a noncolonial way; she certainly does not desire violence or oppression. And yet her case is also a case in which one's very attachment to the territory, one's networks of belonging and identity, threaten these very attachments, networks, and identity. Similar to Berlant's cruel attachments, what one desires (home) is what destroys her (and destroys so many others, too). One always faces the choice between justice (decolonization) and life, since one's very mode of presence, being (one's home, one's place, one's affiliations), is a form of injustice. Bashir el-Hairi offers, however, a different horizon in his book *Letters to a Lemon Tree*. The book describes a visit to Ramle, the city from which he was deported with his family in 1948. Together with two friends (much like Soraya), he visits the three homes that used to be theirs.[7] Each knock on the door produces a different reaction: one woman shouts at them and tries to push them away; two other women—interestingly it is women who open the doors for the three men in his story—are more welcoming. The woman who resides in el-Hairi's house is so nice and so touched by the encounter that a

---

7 After 1967, many Palestinian refugees were suddenly able to visit their homes located within the 1948 borders. Many Jews living in such depopulated homes were anxious about this moment and anticipated it.

long friendship develops between the two.[8] Unlike Madame Nielsen, this woman, Dalia, does not need to leave or die as part of her contribution to the process of decolonization. She ends up turning the house into a kindergarten for Ramle's Palestinian children as a way to somehow share the house with its original owners.[9] Indeed, this is where this book began—with Edward Said's reminder that justice is possible beyond the option marked by Madame Nielsen's figure: "The last thing I want to do is to perpetuate this process by which one distortion leads to another," he insisted. "I have a horror of that. I saw it happen too many times. I don't want to see more people leave."

One must begin, as with Said's call, with the recognition of Israelis that "their presence in many places in the country entails the loss of a Palestinian family, the demolition of a house, the destruction of a village."[10] Yet this recognition cannot be where politics ends. It cannot be a form of reconciliation in and of itself. And it cannot be a practice in which one pretends they fully understand, or can fully place themself in the position of the others (as we saw with those insisting that they can understand the pain of the Palestinians knocking at their door, because they, too, lost their home). This call, Sara Ahmed clarifies, "is a call not just for an attentive hearing, but for a different kind of inhabitance. It is a call for action, and a demand for collective politics, as a politics based not on the possibility that we might be reconciled, but on learning to live with the impossibility of reconciliation, or learning that we live with and beside each other, and yet we are not as one."[11]

Following this recognition, which is itself a form of action, as Ahmed claims, one must continue by engaging in institutional change, by thinking of material justice, but also by facilitating and taking part in concrete acts of opening the door rather than shutting doors, acts that facilitate forging new friendships and new political alliances. But this, too, may be merely the beginning.

8 Bashir el-Hairi, *Letters to a Lemon Tree*, trans. D. Brafman (Jerusalem: Alternative Information Center, 1997), 22ff.

9 Danna Piroyansky, *Ramle Remade: The Israelization of an Arab Town 1948–1967* (Haifa: Pardes, 2014), 212.

10 Edward W. Said, "Interview with Ari Shavit," *Ha'aretz*, August 18, 2000, republished in *Power, Politics, and Culture: Interviews with Edward W. Said*, by Edward W. Said, ed. Gauri Viswanathan (New York: Vintage Books, 2001).

11 Sara Ahmed, *The Cultural Politics of Emotion*, 2nd ed. (Edinburgh: Edinburgh University Press, 2014), 39.

Bibliography

Abdel-Nour, Farid. "Responsibility and National Memory: Israel and the Palestinian Refugee Problem." *International Journal of Politics, Culture, and Society* 17, no. 3 (March 2004): 339–63.

Abu El-Haj, Nadia. *Facts on the Ground: Archaeological Practice and Territorial Self-Fashioning in Israeli Society.* Chicago: University of Chicago Press, 2001.

Abu-Lughod, Lila. *Do Muslim Women Need Saving?* Cambridge, MA: Harvard University Press, 2013.

Abu-Lughod, Lila. "Return to Half-Ruins: Memory, Postmemory, and Living History in Palestine." In *Nakba: Palestine, 1948, and the Claims of Memory,* edited by Ahmad H. Sa'di and Lila Abu-Lughod, 77–104. New York: Columbia University Press, 2007.

Abu Sitta, Salman H. *The Palestinian Nakba 1948: The Register of Depopulated Localities in Palestine.* London: Palestinian Return Centre, 1998.

Adorno, Theodor W. *Minima Moralia: Reflections on a Damaged Life.* London: Verso Books, 2005.

Adorno, Theodor W., Else Frenkel-Brunswick, and Daniel J. Levinson. *The Authoritarian Personality: Studies in Prejudice.* New York: W. W. Norton, 1982.

Afsai, Shai. "'The Bride Is Beautiful, but She Is Married to Another Man': Historical Fabrication and an Anti-Zionist Myth." *Shofar: An Interdisciplinary Journal of Jewish Studies* 30, no. 3 (spring 2012): 35–61.

Agamben, Giorgio. *Homo Sacer: Sovereign Power and Bare Life.* Translated by Daniel Heller-Roazen. Stanford, CA: Stanford University Press, 1998.

Ahmed, Sara. *The Cultural Politics of Emotion.* 2nd edition. Edinburgh: Edinburgh University Press, 2014.

Ahmed, Sara. "Home and Away: Narratives of Migration and Estrangement." *International Journal of Cultural Studies* 2, no. 3 (December 1999): 329–47.

Ahmed, Sara. "'She'll Wake Up One of These Days and Find She's Turned into a Nigger': Passing through Hybridity." *Theory, Culture and Society* 16, no. 2 (April 1999): 87–106.

al-Barghouti, Mureed. "Songs for a Country No Longer Known." *Journal of Palestine Studies* 27, no. 2 (winter 1998): 59–67.

Aleksandrowicz, Or. "Kurkar, Cement, Arabs, Jews: How to Construct a Hebrew City." [In Hebrew] *Theory and Criticism* 36 (2010): 61–87.

Algazi, Gadi. "From Gir Forest to Umm Hiran: Notes on Colonial Nature and Its Keepers." [In Hebrew] *Theory and Critique* 37 (2010): 233–53.

Algazi, Gadi. "Recipe for Nature: The Conflict between Land and Environmentalism: The Struggle to Establish the New Settlement (Mirsham) in Eastern Lachish." [In Hebrew] *Israeli Sociology* 14 (2012): 57–81.

Alloula, Malek. *The Colonial Harem: Images of Subconscious Eroticism.* Manchester, UK: Manchester University Press, 1986.

Allweil, Yael. *Homeland: Zionism as Housing Regime, 1860–2011.* London: Routledge, 2017.

Aloni, Adam. "Made in Israel: Exploiting Palestinian Land for Treatment of Israeli Waste." *B'tselem.* December 2017. https://www.btselem.org/sites/default/files/publications/201712_made_in_israel_eng.pdf.

Althusser, Louis. "Ideology and Ideological State Apparatuses." In *Essays on Ideology,* 86–98. London: Verso Books, 1984.

Amir, Merav, and Hagar Kotef. "Normal." [In Hebrew] *Mafte'akh* 9 (2015): 111–31.

Anzaldúa, Gloria. *Borderlands/La Frontera: The New Mestiza.* San Francisco: Aunt Lute Books, [1987] 1999.

Appadurai, Arjun. *Fear of Small Numbers: An Essay on the Geography of Anger.* Durham, NC: Duke University Press, 2006.

Appadurai, Arjun. "Spectral Housing and Urban Cleansing: Notes on Millennial Mumbai." *Public Culture* 12, no. 3 (fall 2000): 627–51.

Arendt, Hannah. "The Crisis in Culture." In *Between Past and Future: Eight Exercises in Political Thought,* 194–222. New York: Penguin, [1961] 2006.

Arendt, Hannah. "Culture and Politics." In *Thinking without a Banister: Essays in Understanding, 1953–1975,* edited by Jerome Kohn, 160–84. New York: Schocken Books, 2018.

Arendt, Hannah. *Eichmann in Jerusalem: A Report on the Banality of Evil.* Harmondsworth, UK: Penguin Books, 1992.

Arendt, Hannah. *The Human Condition.* 2nd edition. Chicago: Chicago University Press, 1998.

Arendt, Hannah. *The Origins of Totalitarianism.* 5th edition. New York: Harcourt Brace Jovanovich, 1973.

Arendt, Hannah. *The Promise of Politics.* Edited by Jerome Kohn. New York: Schocken Books, 2009.

Arendt, Hannah. "Some Young People Are Going Home." In *The Jewish Writings,* edited by Jerome Kohn and Ron H. Feldman, 34–37. New York: Schocken Books, 2007.

Arendt, Hannah. "To Save the Jewish Homeland: There Is Still Time" (1948). In *The Jewish Writings,* edited by Jerome Kohn and Ron H. Feldman, 388–401. New York: Schocken Books, 2007.

Arendt, Hannah. "We Refugees." *Menorah Journal* 31 (January 1943): 69–77.

Arendt, Hannah. "What Is Freedom?" In *Between Past and Future: Eight Exercises in Political Thought*, 142–69. New York: Penguin Books, [1961] 2006.

Arendt, Hannah. "Zionism Reconsidered." In *The Jewish Writings*, edited by Jerome Kohn and Ron H. Feldman, 343–74. New York: Schocken Books, 2007.

Aristotle. *The Politics*. Translated by T. A. Sinclair. Harmondsworth, UK: Penguin Classics, 1981.

Armitage, David. *Foundations of Modern International Thought*. Cambridge: Cambridge University Press, 2013.

Armitage, David. "John Locke, Carolina, and the 'Two Treatises of Government.'" *Political Theory* 32, no. 5 (2004): 602–27.

Arneil, Barbara. *John Locke and America: The Defence of English Colonialism*. Oxford: Clarendon Press, 1996.

Arneil, Barbara. "John Locke, Natural Law and Colonialism." *History of Political Thought* 13, no. 4 (1992): 587–603.

Arneil, Barbara. "Liberal Colonialism, Domestic Colonies and Citizenship." *History of Political Thought* 33, no. 2 (2012): 491–523.

Arneil, Barbara. "Trade, Plantations, and Property: John Locke and the Economic Defense of Colonialism." *Journal of the History of Ideas* 55, no. 4 (October 1994): 591–609.

Arneil, Barbara. "The Wild Indian's Venison: Locke's Theory of Property and English Colonialism in America." *Political Studies* 44, no. 1 (March 1996): 60–74.

Arneil, Barbara. "Women as Wives, Servants and Slaves: Rethinking the Public/Private Divide." *Canadian Journal of Political Science/Revue canadienne de science politique* 34, no. 1 (March 2001): 29–54.

Ashcraft, Richard. *Revolutionary Politics and Locke's Two Treatises of Government*. Princeton, NJ: Princeton University Press, 1986.

Atiyah, Patrick S. *The Rise and Fall of Freedom of Contract*. Oxford: Oxford University Press, 1985.

Avieli, Nir. "The Hummus Wars Revisited: Israeli-Arab Food Politics and Gastromediation." *Gastronomica: The Journal of Critical Food Studies* 16, no. 3 (fall 2016): 19–30.

Azoulay, Ariella. "Civil Alliances—Palestine, 1947–1948." *Settler Colonial Studies* 4, no. 4 (2014): 413–33.

Azoulay, Ariella, and Adi Ophir. *The One-State Condition: Occupation and Democracy in Israel/Palestine*. Stanford, CA: Stanford University Press, 2012.

Bakan, Abigail B., and Yasmeen Abu-Laban. "Israel/Palestine, South Africa and the 'One-State Solution': The Case for an Apartheid Analysis." *Politikon* 37, nos. 2–3 (2010): 331–51.

Barnett, Clive, Nick Clarke, Paul Cloke, and Alice Malpass. "The Political Ethics of Consumerism." *Consumer Policy Review* 15, no. 2 (2005): 45–51.

Bassett, William W. "The Myth of the Nomad in Property Law." *Journal of Law and Religion* 4, no. 1 (1986): 133–52.

Baucom, Ian. "Mournful Histories: Narratives of Postimperial Melancholy." *MFS: Modern Fiction Studies* 42, no. 2 (summer 1996): 259–88.

Bauman, Zygmunt. *Modernity and the Holocaust*. Cambridge: Polity Press, 1991.

Bauman, Zygmunt. *Wasted Lives: Modernity and Its Outcasts.* Oxford: Polity, 2004.

Behnegar, Nasser. "Locke and the Sober Spirit of Capitalism." *Society* 49, no. 2 (2012): 131–38.

Beit-Hallahmi, Benjamin. *Original Sins: Reflections on the History of Zionism and Israel.* New York: Palgrave Macmillan, 1992.

Bejan, Teresa. "'The Bond of Civility': Roger Williams on Toleration and Its Limits." *History of European Ideas* 37 (2011): 409–20.

Bejan, Teresa. *Mere Civility: Disagreement and the Limits of Toleration.* Cambridge, MA: Harvard University Press, 2017.

Ben-David, Orit. "*Tiyul* (Hike) as an Act of Consecration of Space." In *Grasping Land: Space and Place in Contemporary Israeli Discourse and Experience*, edited by Eyal Ben-Ari and Yoram Bilu, 129–45. Albany: State University of New York Press, 1997.

Benhabib, Seyla. *The Reluctant Modernism of Hannah Arendt.* Lanham, MD: Rowman and Littlefield, 2000.

Benjamin, Walter. "On the Concept of History." In *Selected Writings*, vol. 4: *1938–1940*, edited by Michael W. Jennings and Howard Eiland, 389–400. Cambridge, MA: Harvard University Press, 2003.

Bennett, Naftali. "No Longer Apologizing" (*Mafsikim Lehitnatzel*). [In Hebrew] December 6, 2014. YouTube video, 2:46. https://www.youtube.com/watch?v=PBNonqQX5xo.

Benvenisti, Meron. "The Hebrew Map." In *Sacred Landscape: The Buried History of the Holy Land since 1948*, 11–54. Berkeley: University of California Press, 2000.

Benvenisti, Meron. *Sacred Landscape: The Buried History of the Holy Land since 1948.* Berkeley: University of California Press, 2000.

Benvenisti, Meron. *The West Bank Data Project: A Survey of Israel's Policies.* Washington, DC: American Enterprise Institute for Public Policy Research, 1986.

Ben-Ze'ev, Efrat. "The Politics of Taste and Smell: Palestinian Rites of Return." In *The Politics of Food*, edited by Marianne E. Lien and Brigitte Nerlich, 141–60. London: Bloomsbury Press, 2004.

Berlant, Lauren. *Cruel Optimism.* Durham, NC: Duke University Press, 2011.

Berman, Marshall. *All That Is Solid Melts into Air: The Experience of Modernity.* New York: Penguin Books, 1982.

Bernasconi, Robert Lambert. "When the Real Crime Began: Hannah Arendt's *The Origins of Totalitarianism* and the Dignity of the Western Philosophical Tradition." In *Hannah Arendt and the Uses of History: Imperialism, Nation, Race, and Genocide*, edited by Richard H. King and Dan Stone, 54–67. New York: Berghahn, 2008.

Bhabha, Homi. "Of Mimicry and Man: The Ambivalence of Colonial Discourse." *October* 28 (spring 1984): 125–33.

Bhandar, Brenna. *Colonial Lives of Property: Law, Land, and Racial Regimes of Ownership.* Durham, NC: Duke University Press, 2018.

Bigon, Liora. *French Colonial Dakar: The Morphogenesis of an African Regional Capital.* Manchester: Manchester University Press, 2016.

Bigon, Liora. "A History of Urban Planning and Infectious Diseases: Colonial Senegal in the Early Twentieth Century." *Urban Studies Research* (2012). https://doi.org /10.1155/2012/589758.

Bigon, Liora, and Amer Dahamshe. "An Anatomy of Symbolic Power: Israeli Road-Sign Policy and the Palestinian Minority." *Environment and Planning D: Society and Space* 32, no. 4 (January 2014): 606–21.

Bishara, Amahl. "House and Homeland: Examining Sentiments about and Claims to Jerusalem and Its Houses." *Social Text* 21, no. 2 (summer 2003): 141–62.

Bishara, Azmi. *Yearning in the Land of Checkpoints*. [In Hebrew] Tel Aviv: Babel Press, 2006.

Blunt, Alison, and Ann Varley. "Introduction: Geographies of Home." *Cultural Geographies* 11, no. 1 (2004): 3–6.

Boryczka, Jocelyn M. "Revolutionary Pasts and Transnational Futures: 'Home Lessons' from US Radical and Third World Feminisms." In *American Political Thought: An Alternative View*, edited by Jonathan Keller and Alex Zamalin, 72–92. New York: Routledge, 2017.

Boyarin, Daniel. *A Traveling Homeland: The Babylonian Talmud as Diaspora*. Philadelphia: University of Pennsylvania Press, 2015.

Brah, Avtar. *Cartographies of Diaspora: Contesting Identities*. London: Routledge, 1996.

Brenner, Yosef Haim. *The Writings of Yosef Haim Brenner*. [In Hebrew] Vol. 4. Tel Aviv: Shtibel, 1937.

Brown, Wendy. *Manhood and Politics: A Feminist Reading in Political Theory*. Totowa, NJ: Rowman and Littlefield, 1988.

Brown, Wendy. *Walled States, Waning Sovereignty*. New York: Zone Books, 2010.

Brown, Wendy. "Wounded Attachments." *Political Theory* 21, no. 3 (August 1993): 390–410.

Brubaker, Stanley C. "Coming into One's Own: John Locke's Theory of Property, God, and Politics." *Review of Politics* 74, no. 2 (spring 2012): 207–32.

Bryant, Rebecca. "History's Remainders: On Time and Objects after Conflict in Cyprus." *American Ethnologist* 41, no. 4 (2014): 681–97.

Bryant, Rebecca. *The Past in Pieces: Belonging in the New Cyprus*. Philadelphia: University of Pennsylvania Press, 2012.

B'tselem. "Access Denied: Israeli Measures to Deny Palestinians Access to Land around Settlements." *B'tselem*. September 2008. https://www.btselem.org/sites /default/files/sites/default/files2/publication/200809_access_denied_eng.pdf.

B'tselem. "50 Days: More Than 50 Children: Facts and Figures on Fatalities in Gaza, Summer 2014." *B'tselem*. Accessed September 13, 2018. https://www.btselem.org /2014_gaza_conflict/en/.

B'tselem. "Settlements: Updated Statistics and Data." [In Hebrew] *B'tselem*. Accessed November 2019. https://www.btselem.org/hebrew/settlements.

B'tselem. "Statistics on Demolition for Alleged Military Purposes." *B'tselem*. Last updated August 7, 2019. https://www.btselem.org/razing/statistics.

B'tselem. "Statistics on Demolition of Houses Built without Permits in the West Bank and East Jerusalem." *B'tselem*. Last modified August 8, 2019. https://www .btselem.org/planning_and_building/east_jerusalem_statistics.

Burton, Antoinette. *Dwelling in the Archive: Women Writing House, Home, and History in Late Colonial India*. Oxford: Oxford University Press, 2003.

Busbridge, Rachel. "Israel-Palestine and the Settler Colonial 'Turn': From Interpretation to Decolonization." *Theory, Culture and Society* 35, no. 1 (January 2018): 91–115.

Butler, Judith. "Bodies in Alliance and the Politics of the Street." *European Institute for Progressive Cultural Policies* 9 (2011). http://www.eipcp.net/transversal/1011/butler/en.

Butler, Judith. *Bodies That Matter: On the Discursive Limits of "Sex."* New York: Routledge, 1993.

Butler, Judith. *The Force of Non-violence*. New York: Verso Books, 2020.

Butler, Judith. *Frames of War: When Is Life Grievable?* London: Verso Books, 2009.

Butler, Judith. *Gender Trouble: Feminism and the Subversion of Identity*. New York: Routledge, 1990.

Butler, Judith. *Parting Ways: Jewishness and the Critique of Zionism*. New York: Columbia University Press, 2013.

Butler, Judith. *Precarious Life: The Powers of Mourning and Violence*. London: Verso Books, 2004.

Butler, Judith. *The Psychic Life of Power: Theories in Subjection*. Stanford, CA: Stanford University Press, 1997.

Butler, Judith. "Remarks on 'Queer Bonds.'" *GLQ* 17, nos. 2–3 (2011): 381–87.

Butler, Judith. "Reply from Judith Butler to Mills and Jenkins." *differences* 18, no. 2 (September 2007): 180–95.

Butler, Judith, and Athena Athanasiou. *Dispossession: The Performative in the Political*. Cambridge: Polity Press, 2013.

Butler, Melissa A. "Early Liberal Roots of Feminism: John Locke and the Attack on Patriarchy." *American Political Science Review* 72, no. 1 (March 1978): 135–50.

Cahaner, Lee. "Between Ghetto-Politics and Geopolitics: Ultraorthodox Settlements in the West Bank." In *Normalizing Occupation: The Politics of Everyday Life in the West Bank Settlements*, edited by Ariel Handel, Marco Allegra, and Erez Maggor, 112–27. Bloomington: Indiana University Press, 2017.

Chafe, William. *The Paradox of Change: American Women in the 20th Century*. Oxford: Oxford University Press, 1991.

Chakrabarty, Dipesh. *Provincializing Europe*. Princeton, NJ: Princeton University Press, 2000.

Clifford, James. "Diasporas." *Cultural Anthropology* 9, no. 3 (August 1994): 302–38.

Cohen, Stanley. *States of Denial: Knowing about Atrocities and Suffering*. Cambridge: Polity Press, 2001.

Cole, Alyson. "All of Us Are Vulnerable, but Some Are More Vulnerable than Others: The Political Ambiguity of Vulnerability Studies, an Ambivalent Critique." *Critical Horizons* 17, no. 2 (2016): 260–77.

Confino, Alon. *The Nation as a Local Metaphor: Wurttemberg, Imperial Germany, and National Memory, 1871–1918*. Chapel Hill: University of North Carolina Press, 1997.

Crais, Clifton C. "The Vacant Land: The Mythology of British Expansion in the Eastern Cape, South Africa." *Journal of Social History* 25, no. 2 (winter 1991): 255–75.

Cresswell, Tim. *On the Move: Mobility in the Modern Western World*. New York: Routledge, 2006.

Dalsheim, Joyce. "Settler Nationalism, Collective Memories of Violence and the 'Uncanny Other.'" *Social Identities* 10, no. 2 (2004): 151–70.

Dayan, Hilla. "Regimes of Separation: Israel/Palestine and the Shadow of Apartheid." In *The Power of Inclusive Exclusion: Anatomy of Israeli Rule in the Occupied Palestinian Territories*, edited by Adi Ophir, Michal Givoni, and Sari Hanafi, 281–322. New York: Zone Books, 2009.

Deleuze, Gilles, and Félix Guattari. *A Thousand Plateaus: Capitalism and Schizophrenia*. Translated by Brian Massumi. London: Continuum, 1987.

Deringil, Selim. "'They Live in a State of Nomadism and Savagery': The Late Ottoman Empire and the Post-Colonial Debate." *Comparative Studies in Society and History* 45, no. 2 (April 2003): 311–42.

Derrida, Jacques. "Plato's Pharmacy." In *Dissemination*, translated by Barbara Johnson, 61–172. Chicago: University of Chicago Press, 1981.

Derrida, Jacques. *The Politics of Friendship*. Translated by George Collins. London: Verso Books, 1997.

Derrida, Jacques. *Rogues: Two Essays on Reason*. Stanford, CA: Stanford University Press, 2005.

de Waal, Alex. *Famine Crimes: Politics and the Disaster Relief Industry in Africa*. Bloomington: Indiana University Press, [1996] 2009.

Dilts, Andrew. "To Kill a Thief: Punishment, Proportionality, and Criminal Subjectivity in Locke's Second Treatise." *Political Theory* 40, no. 1 (February 2012): 58–83.

Disch, Lisa Jane. *Hannah Arendt and the Limits of Philosophy*. Ithaca, NY: Cornell University Press, 1996.

Dossa, Shiraz. "Human Status and Politics: Hannah Arendt on the Holocaust." *Canadian Journal of Political Science/Revue canadienne de science politique* 13, no. 2 (1980): 309–23.

Dunn, John. *The Political Thought of John Locke: An Historical Account of the Argument of the "Two Treatises of Government."* Cambridge: Cambridge University Press, 1969.

Dworkin, Andrea. *Intercourse*. New York: Simon and Schuster, 1997.

Eastwood, James. *Ethics as a Weapon of War: Militarism and Morality in Israel*. Cambridge: Cambridge University Press, 2017.

el-Hairi, Bashir. *Letters to a Lemon Tree*. Translated by D. Brafman. Jerusalem: Alternative Information Center, 1997.

Epstein, Richard A. "Possession as the Root of Title." *Georgia Law Review* 13 (1979): 1221–43.

Eshel, Nimrod. *The Seamen's Strike*. [In Hebrew] Tel Aviv: Am Oved, 1994.

Etkes, Dror. "Israeli Settlers' Agriculture as a Means of Land Takeover in the West Bank." Translated by Tamar Cohen. *Kerem Navot*. August 2013. https://docs .wixstatic.com/ugd/cdb1a7_370bb4f21ceb47adb3ac7556c02b8972.pdf.

Evri, Yuval, and Hagar Kotef. "When Does a Native Become a Settler?" *Constellations* (forthcoming).

Eyal, Gil. *The Disenchantment of the Orient: Expertise in Arab Affairs and the Israeli State.* Stanford, CA: Stanford University Press, 2006.

Falah, Ghazi. "The 1948 Israeli-Palestinian War and Its Aftermath: The Transformation and De-Signification of Palestine's Cultural Landscape." *Annals of the Association of American Geographers* 86 (June 1996): 256–85.

Fanon, Frantz. *Black Skin, White Masks.* New York: Pluto Press, [1967] 1986.

Fanon, Frantz. *The Wretched of the Earth.* Translated by Richard Philcox. New York: Grove Press, [1963] 2004.

Fargeon, Ben, and Michal Rotem. "Enforcing Distress: House Demolition Policy in the Bedouin Community in the Negev." Negev Coexistence Forum for Civil Equality. June 2016. https://www.dukium.org/wp-content/uploads/2016/06/HDR _2016_ENG-1.pdf.

Farr, James. "Locke, Natural Law, and New World Slavery." *Political Theory* 36, no. 4 (August 2008): 495–522.

Farr, James. "'So Vile and Miserable an Estate': The Problem of Slavery in Locke's Political Thought." *Political Theory* 14, no. 2 (May 1986): 263–89.

Feige, Michael. *Settling in the Hearts: Jewish Fundamentalism in the Occupied Territories.* Detroit: Wayne State University Press, 2009.

Feige, Michael. "Soft Power: The Meaning of Home for Gush Emunim Settlers." *Journal of Israeli History* 32, no. 1 (2013): 109–26.

Fenster, Tovi. "Do Palestinians Live across the Road? Address and the Micropolitics of Home in Israeli Contested Urban Spaces." *Environment and Planning A: Economy and Space* 46, no. 10 (2014): 2435–51.

Fenster, Tovi. "Moving between Addresses: Home and Belonging for Jewish Migrant and Indigenous Palestinian Women over Seventy in Israel." *Home Cultures* 10, no. 2 (2013): 159–87.

Fenster, Tovi. "Zikaron, shayachut ve-tichnun merhavi be-yisrael" [Memory, belonging, and spatial planning in Israel]. *Theory and Criticism* 30 (2007): 189–212.

Ferguson, James G. "Of Mimicry and Membership: Africans and the 'New World Society.'" *Cultural Anthropology* 17, no. 4 (November 2002): 551–69.

Fishbein, Einat. "Eviction-Construction: The Story of the Argazim Neighborhood." [In Hebrew] Adva Center. April 2003. http://www.adva.org/UserFiles/File /pinui%20binui%20shhunat%20argazim.pdf.

Fitzmaurice, Andrew. *Sovereignty, Property and Empire, 1500–2000.* Cambridge: Cambridge University Press, 2014.

Forman, Geremy, and Alexandre Kedar. "From Arab Land to 'Israel Lands': The Legal Dispossession of the Palestinians Displaced by Israel in the Wake of 1948." *Environment and Planning D: Society and Space* 22, no. 6 (December 2004): 809–30.

Forty, Adrian. *Concrete and Culture: A Material History.* London: Reaktion Books, 2012.

Foucault, Michel. "Questions of Method." In *The Foucault Effect: Studies in Governmentality,* edited by Graham Burchell, Colin Gordon, and Peter Miller, 73–86. Chicago: University of Chicago Press, 1991.

Foucault, Michel. *Security, Territory, Population: Lectures at the Collège de France, 1977-1978*. Edited by Michel Senellart and Arnold I. Davidson. Translated by Graham Burchell. New York: Palgrave Macmillan, 2007.

Foucault, Michel. *"Society Must Be Defended": Lectures at the Collège de France, 1975-76*. Edited by Mauro Bertani, Alessandro Fontana, and Arnold I. Davidson. Translated by David Macey. New York: Picador, 2003.

Foucault, Michel. "What Is an Author?" In *Aesthetics, Method and Epistemology; Essential Works of Foucault—Vol. II*. Lecture, Collège de France, February 22, 1969. Edited by J. D. Faubion, 205-22. New York: New York University Press, 1998.

Friedman, Shimi. "Hilltop Youth: Political-Anthropological Research in the Hills of Judea and Samaria." *Israel Affairs* 21, no. 3 (2015): 391-407.

Friedman, Shimi. *The Hilltop Youth: A Stage of Resistance and Counter Culture Practice*. Lanham, MD: Lexington Books, 2018.

"From Messiah to Cheese." July 30, 2009. YouTube video, 1:20. https://www.youtube .com/watch?v=WXSjRoApKcQ.

Fromm, Erich. *The Crisis of Psychoanalysis: Essays on Marx, Freud and Social Psychology*. Greenwich, CT: Fawcett Premier Books, 1971.

Fromm, Erich. *The Sane Society*. Greenwich, CT: Fawcett Premier Books, 1955.

Galtung, Johan. "Violence, Peace, and Peace Research." *Journal of Peace Research* 6, no. 3 (1969): 167-91.

Garfield, Seth. "A Nationalist Environment: Indians, Nature, and the Construction of the Xingu National Park in Brazil." *Luso-Brazilian Review* 41, no. 1 (2004): 139-67.

Garnsey, Peter. *Thinking about Property: From Antiquity to the Age of Revolution*. Cambridge: Cambridge University Press, 2007.

Ghanim, Honaida. "Being a Border." In *Displaced at Home: Ethnicity and Gender among Palestinians in Israel*, edited by Rhoda Kanaaneh and Isis Nusair, 109-18. New York: State University of New York Press, 2010.

Ghanim, Honaida. "From Kubaniya to Outpost: A Genealogy of the Palestinian Conceptualization of Jewish Settlement in a Shifting National Context." In *Normalizing Occupation: The Politics of Everyday Life in the West Bank Settlements*, edited by Ariel Handel, Marco Allegra, and Erez Maggor, 244-68. Bloomington: Indiana University Press, 2017.

Ghanim, Honaida. "On Natives, Specters, and Shades of Ruins." [In Hebrew] In *Indigeneity and Exile in Israel/Palestine*, edited by Shaul Seter, 17-24. Tel Aviv: Tel Aviv University Press, 2014.

Ghanim, Honaida. "'Where Is Everyone!' A Dialectics of Erasure and Construction in the Zionist Colonial Project." [In Hebrew] *Zmanim* 138 (2018): 102-15.

Gines, Kathryn T. *Hannah Arendt and the Negro Question*. Bloomington: Indiana University Press, 2014.

Givoni, Michal. "Indifference and Repetition: Occupation Testimonies and Left-Wing Despair." *Cultural Studies* 33, no. 4 (2019): 595-631.

Gobetti, Daniela. "Humankind as a System: Private and Public Agency at the Origins of Modern Liberalism." In *Public and Private in Thought and Practice: Perspec-*

tives on a Grand Dichotomy, edited by Jeff Weintraub and Krishan Kumar, 103–32. Chicago: University of Chicago Press, 1997.

Golan, Arnon. "Jewish Settlement of Former Arab Towns and Their Incorporation into the Israeli Urban System (1948–50)." *Israel Affairs* 9, nos. 1–2 (2002): 149–64.

Golan, Arnon. "The 1948 Wartime Resettlement of Former Arab Areas in West Jerusalem." *Middle Eastern Studies* 51, no. 5 (2015): 804–20.

Golan, Arnon. "The Transformation of Abandoned Arab Rural Areas." *Israel Studies* 2, no. 1 (spring 1997): 94–110.

Gold, David Louis. "Another Look at Israeli Hebrew *Pita* 'Flat Bread': A Borrowing from Judezmo and Yiddish." *Romance Philology* 42, no. 3 (1989): 276–78.

Gordillo, Gastón R. *Rubble: The Afterlife of Destruction*. Durham, NC: Duke University Press, 2014.

Gordon, Neve. "From Colonization to Separation: Exploring the Structure of Israel's Occupation." *Third World Quarterly* 29, no. 1 (2005): 25–44.

Gordon, Neve. *Israel's Occupation*. Berkeley: University of California Press, 2008.

Gordon, Neve, and Moriel Ram. "Ethnic Cleansing and the Formation of Settler Colonial Geographies." *Political Geography* 53 (July 2016): 20–29.

Gregory, Derek. *The Colonial Present: Afghanistan, Palestine, Iraq*. Malden, MA: Blackwell, 2005.

Grosglik, Rafi. "Global Ethical Culinary Fashion and a Local Dish: Organic Hummus in Israel." *Critical Studies in Fashion and Beauty* 2, nos. 1–2 (2011): 165–84.

Grosglik, Rafi. *Organic Food in Israel: Resistance, Assimilation, and Global Culture*. [In Hebrew] Tel Aviv: Resling Publishing Press, 2017.

Grosglik, Rafi. "Organic Hummus in Israel: Global and Local Ingredients and Images." *Sociological Research Online* 16, no. 2 (June 2011): 1–11.

Gross, Aeyal. *The Writing on the Wall: Rethinking the International Law of Occupation*. Cambridge: Cambridge University Press, 2017.

Grotius, Hugo. *The Freedom of the Seas, or the Right Which Belongs to the Dutch to Take Part in the East India Trade*. Translated by Ralph Van Deman Magoffin. New York: Oxford University Press, [1609] 1916.

Gündogdu, Ayten. *Rightlessness in an Age of Rights*. Oxford: Oxford University Press, 2014.

Gutkowski, Natalia. "Bodies That Count: Multispecies Population Management by the Israeli Administration in the West Bank." Paper presented at the Environmental Justice in Israel/Palestine Conference, Buffalo, NY, February 6–7, 2019.

Gvion, Liora. "Cooking, Food, and Masculinity: Palestinian Men in Israeli Society." *Men and Masculinities* 14, no. 4 (October 2011): 408–29.

Hamid, Naved. "Dispossession and Differentiation of the Peasantry in the Punjab during Colonial Rule." *Journal of Peasant Studies* 10, no. 1 (1982): 52–72.

Hanafi, Sari. "Palestinian Refugee Camps in Lebanon as a Space of Exception." *REVUE Asylon(s)* 5 (September 2008). http://www.reseau-terra.eu/article798.html.

Hanafi, Sari. "Spacio-cide and Bio-Politics: The Israeli Colonial Conflict from 1947 to the Wall." In *Against the Wall: Israel's Barrier to Peace*, edited by Michael Sorkin, 251–61. New York: New Press, 2005.

Handel, Ariel. "Gated/Gating Community: The Settlement Complex in the West Bank." *Transactions of the Institute of British Geographers* 39, no. 4 (2014): 504–17.

Handel, Ariel. "Violence." [In Hebrew] *Mafte'akh: Lexical Review of Political Thought* 3 (2011): 53–80.

Handel, Ariel. "Where, Where to and When in the Occupied Palestinian Territories: An Introduction to Geography of Disaster." In *The Power of Inclusive Exclusion: Anatomy of Israeli Rule in the Occupied Palestinian Territories*, edited by Adi Ophir, Michal Givoni, and Sari Hanafi, 179–222. New York: Zone Books, 2009.

Handel, Ariel, Galit Rand, and Marco Allegra. "Wine-Washing: Colonization, Normalization, and the Geopolitics of *Terroir* in the West Bank's Settlements." *Environment and Planning A: Economy and Space* 47, no. 6 (June 2015): 1351–67.

Hansberry, Lorraine. *Les Blancs: The Collected Last Plays: The Drinking Gourd/What Use Are Flowers?* Edited by Robert Nemiroff. New York: Random House, 1994.

Harel, Assaf. "'A Blessed Deviation in Jewish History': On Contemporary Forms of Messianism among Religiously Motivated Settlers in the West Bank." In *Normalizing Occupation: The Politics of Everyday Life in the West Bank Settlements*, edited by Ariel Handel, Marco Allegra, and Erez Maggor, 128–57. Bloomington: Indiana University Press, 2017.

Hareuveni, Eyal. "By Hook and by Crook: Israeli Settlement Policy in the West Bank." *B'tselem*. July 2010. https://www.btselem.org/download/201007_by_hook_and_by_crook_eng.pdf.

Harris, Trudier. *Exorcising Blackness: Historical and Literary Lynching and Burning Rituals.* Bloomington: Indiana University Press, 1984.

Hartman, Saidiya V. *Scenes of Subjection: Terror, Slavery, and Self-Making in Nineteenth-Century America.* Oxford: Oxford University Press, 1997.

Harvey, David. *The Enigma of Capital and the Crises of Capitalism.* Oxford: Oxford University Press, 2010.

Haskell, Thomas L. "Capitalism and the Origins of Humanitarian Sensibility, Part I." *American Historical Review* 90, no. 2 (1985): 339–61.

Hasso, Frances S. "Discursive and Political Deployments by/of the 2002 Palestinian Women Suicide Bombers/Martyrs." *Feminist Review* 81, no. 1 (2005): 23–51.

Herzl, Theodor. *Altneuland* (1902). Translated by D. S. Blondheim. Jewish Virtual Library. Accessed August 2019. https://www.jewishvirtuallibrary.org/quot-altneuland-quot-theodor-herzl.

Herzl, Theodor. *The Jewish State.* New York: Dover Publications, 1989.

Hirsch, Dafna. "'Hummus Is Best When It Is Fresh and Made by Arabs': The Gourmetization of Hummus in Israel and the Return of the Repressed Arab." *American Ethnologist* 38, no. 4 (November 2011): 617–30.

Hirschhorn, Sara Yael. *City on a Hilltop: American Jews and the Israeli Settler Movement.* Cambridge, MA: Harvard University Press, 2017.

Hirschmann, Nancy J. *Gender, Class, and Freedom in Modern Political Theory.* Princeton, NJ: Princeton University Press, 2009.

Hirschmann, Nancy J. "Intersectionality before Intersectionality Was Cool: The Importance of Class to Feminist Interpretations of Locke." In *Feminist Interpretations of John Locke,* edited by Nancy J. Hirschmann and Kirstie M. McClure, 155–86. University Park: Pennsylvania State University Press, 2007.

Hochberg, Gil Z. *Visual Occupation: Violence and Visibility in a Conflict Zone.* Durham, NC: Duke University Press, 2015.

Honig, Bonnie. "Antigone's Two Laws: Greek Tragedy and the Politics of Humanism." *New Literary History* 41, no. 1 (winter 2010): 1–33.

hooks, bell. *Belonging: A Culture of Place.* New York: Routledge, 2004.

hooks, bell. *Yearning: Race, Gender, and Cultural Politics.* Boston: South End Press, 1991.

Hsueh, Vicki. "Cultivating and Challenging the Common: Lockean Property, Indigenous Traditionalisms, and the Problem of Exclusion." *Contemporary Political Theory* 5, no. 2 (May 2006): 193–214.

Hsueh, Vicki. "Unsettling Colonies: Locke, 'Atlantis' and New World Knowledges." *History of Political Thought* 29, no. 2 (2008): 295–319.

Hume, David. *A Treatise of Human Nature.* New York: Mineola Publications, 2003.

Hütteroth, Wolf-Dieter. *Historical Geography of Palestine, Transjordan and Southern Syria in the Late 16th Century.* Erlangen, Germany: Palm und Enke, 1977.

IFOAM. "Principles of Organic Agriculture." IFOAM Organics International. Accessed August 2019. https://www.ifoam.bio/en/organic-landmarks/principles -organic-agriculture.

Ince, Onur Ulas. *Colonial Capitalism and the Dilemmas of Liberalism.* Oxford: Oxford University Press, 2018.

Ince, Onur Ulas. "Enclosing in God's Name, Accumulating for Mankind: Money, Morality, and Accumulation in John Locke's Theory of Property." *Review of Politics* 73, no. 1 (2011): 29–54.

Jacir, Annemarie, dir. *Salt of This Sea.* Augustus Film; Clarity Productions; JBA Production; Louverture Films; Mediapro Philistine Films; Tarantula Thelma Film, 2008.

Jamal, Amal. "The Ambiguities of Minority Patriotism: Love for Homeland versus State among Palestinian Citizens of Israel." *Nationalism and Ethnic Politics* 10, no. 3 (2004): 433–71.

Jamal, Amal. "Beyond 'Ethnic Democracy': State Structure, Multicultural Conflict and Differentiated Citizenship in Israel." *New Political Science* 24, no. 3 (2002): 411–31.

Jamal, Amal. "Place, Home and Being: The Dialectics of the Real and the Imagined in the Conception of Palestinian Domesticity." In *Homeless Home,* edited by Ariella Azoulay, 274–301. Jerusalem: Museum on the Seam, 2010.

Jennings, Francis. *The Invasion of America: Indians, Colonialism, and the Cant of Conquest.* Chapel Hill: University of North Carolina Press, [1975] 2010.

Johnston, Josée, and Kate Cairns. "Eating for Change." In *Commodity Activism: Cultural Resistance in Neoliberal Times,* edited by Roopali Mukherjee and Sarah Banet-Weiser, 219–39. New York: New York University Press, 2012.

Kadman, Noga. *Erased from Space and Consciousness: Israel and the Depopulated Palestinian Villages of 1948.* Bloomington: Indiana University Press, 2015.

Kanaana, Sharif. *Still on Vacation! The Eviction of the Palestinians in 1948.* Jerusalem: Jerusalem International Center for Palestinian Studies, 1992.

Kanafani, Ghassan. "Returning to Haifa." In *Palestine's Children: Returning to Haifa and Other Stories*, 149–96. Boulder, CO: Lynne Rienner, 2000.

Kaniel, Shlomo. "The Hilltop Settlers: Are They Biblical Sabras?" [In Hebrew] In *Religious Zionism: The Age of Change*, 533–58. Jerusalem: Bialik, 2004.

Karmi, Ghada. *Married to Another Man: Israel's Dilemma in Palestine*. Ann Arbor, MI: Pluto Press, 2007.

Karmi, Ghada. *Return: A Palestinian Memoir*. London: Verso Books, 2015.

Karmi, Ram. "Human Values in Urban Architecture." In *New Trends in Urban Planning: Studies in Housing, Urban Design and Planning*, edited by Dan Soen, 159–75. Oxford: Pergamon Press, 1979.

Karmi, Ram. "Merkaz HaNegev: Architecture of Shade." [In Hebrew] *Kav* 3 (1965): 50–63.

Kedar, Alexandre. "The Legal Transformation of Ethnic Geography: Israeli Law and the Palestinian Landholder 1948–1967." *New York University Journal of International Law and Politics* 33, no. 4 (2001): 923–1000.

Kedar, Alexandre, Ahmad Amara, and Oren Yiftachel. *Emptied Lands: A Legal Geography of Bedouin Rights in the Negev*. Stanford, CA: Stanford University Press, 2018.

Khalidi, Walid, ed. *All That Remains: The Palestinian Villages Occupied and Depopulated by Israel in 1948*. Washington, DC: Institute for Palestine Studies, 1992.

Khalili, Laleh. "Gendered Practices of Counterinsurgency." *Review of International Studies* 37, no. 4 (2011): 1471–91.

Kimmerling, Baruch. *Clash of Identities: Explorations in Israeli and Palestinian Societies*. New York: Columbia University Press, 2010.

Kimmerling, Baruch, ed. *The Israeli State and Society: Boundaries and Frontiers*. Albany: State University of New York Press, 1989.

Kimmerling, Baruch. "Sovereignty, Ownership, and 'Presence' in the Jewish-Arab Territorial Conflict: The Case of Bir'im and Ikrit." *Comparative Political Studies* 10, no. 2 (July 1977): 155–76.

Kipling, Rudyard. "The White Man's Burden." In *Kipling: A Selection of His Stories and Poems*, edited by Rudyard Kipling and John Beecroft. Garden City, NY: Doubleday, 1956.

Klausen, Jimmy Casas. "Hannah Arendt's Antiprimitivism." *Political Theory* 38, no. 3 (June 2010): 393–427.

Klein, Melanie. *The Psycho-Analysis of Children*. London: Vintage Books, 1997.

Kotef, Hagar. "Ba'it (Home/Household)." *Mafte'akh: Lexical Review of Political Thought* 1E (2010). http://mafteakh.tau.ac.il/en/2010-01/01/.

Kotef, Hagar. "Little Chinese Feet Encased in Iron Shoes: Freedom, Movement, Gender, and Empire in Western Political Thought." *Political Theory* 43, no. 3 (2015): 334–55.

Kotef, Hagar. *Movement and the Ordering of Freedom: On Liberal Governances of Mobility*. Durham, NC: Duke University Press, 2015.

Kotef, Hagar, and Merav Amir. "Between Imaginary Lines: Violence and Its Justifications at the Military Checkpoints in Occupied Palestine." In *Movement and the Ordering of Freedom: On Liberal Governances of Mobility*, by Hagar Kotef, 27–52. Durham, NC: Duke University Press, 2015.

Kotef, Hagar, and Merav Amir. "(En)Gendering Checkpoints: Checkpoint Watch and the Repercussions of Intervention." *Signs: Journal of Women in Culture and Society* 2, no. 4 (2007): 973–96.

Kramer, Matthew H. *John Locke and the Origins of Private Property: Philosophical Explorations of Individualism, Community, and Equality*. Cambridge: Cambridge University Press, 1997.

Kristeva, Julia. *Powers of Horror: An Essay on Abjection*. New York: Columbia University Press, 1982.

Lanzmann, Claude, dir. *Shoah*. British Broadcasting Corporation (BBC), Historia, Les Films Aleph, Ministère de la Culture de la Republique Française. France, 1985.

Lebovics, Herman. "The Uses of America in Locke's Second Treatise of Government." *Journal of the History of Ideas* 47, no. 4 (October–December 1986): 567–81.

Lee, Daniel. "Sources of Sovereignty: Roman *Imperium* and *Dominium* in Civilian Theories of Sovereignty." *Politica Antica* 1 (2012): 79–80.

Lein, Yehezkel. "Foreseen but Not Prevented: The Israeli Law Enforcement Authorities' Handling of Settler Attacks on Olive Harvesters." Edited by Yael Stein. Translated by Shaul Vardi, Maya Johnston, and Zvi Shulman. B'tselem Case Study 16. November 2002. https://www.btselem.org/download/200211_olive_harvest_eng.pdf.

Lein, Yehezkel. "Thirsty for a Solution: The Water Shortage in the Occupied Territories and Its Solution in the Final Status Agreement." *B'tselem*. July 2000. https://www.btselem.org/publications/summaries/200007_thirsty_for_a_solution.

Leshem, Noam. "Anti-Erasure: The Survival of Space between Salameh and Kfar Shalom." [In Hebrew] In *Place Names and Spatial Identity in Israel-Palestine: Majority-Minority Relations, Obliviating and Memory*, edited by Amer Dahamshe and Yosef Schwartz. Tel Aviv: Tel Aviv University Press, 2018.

Leshem, Noam. *Life after Ruin: The Struggles over Israel's Depopulated Arab Spaces*. Cambridge: Cambridge University Press, 2016.

Levin, Daphna. "Our H'irbe: The Representation of Arab Ruins in Israeli Culture." [In Hebrew] *Yisraelim* 6 (2014): 53–67.

Levine, Philippa. *Prostitution, Race, and Politics: Policing Venereal Disease in the British Empire*. New York: Routledge, 2003.

Linebaugh, Peter, and Marcus Rediker. *The Many-Headed Hydra: The Hidden History of the Revolutionary Atlantic*. Boston: Beacon Press, 2000.

Lloyd, Moya. "The Ethics and Politics of Vulnerable Bodies." In *Butler and Ethics*, edited by M. S. Lloyd, 167–92. Edinburgh: Edinburgh University Press, 2015.

Locke, John. *An Essay Concerning Human Understanding*. Philadelphia: Hayes and Zell, 1854.

Locke, John. "On the Poor Law and Working Schools." In *Locke: Political Essays*, edited by Mark Goldie, 182–200. Cambridge: Cambridge University Press, 1997.

Locke, John. *Two Treatises of Government and a Letter Concerning Toleration*, edited by Ian Shapiro. New Haven, CT: Yale University Press, 2003.

Locke, John. *Some Thoughts Concerning Education*. London: A. and J. Churchill, 1693.

Locke, John. *Two Treatises of Government and a Letter Concerning Toleration*. Edited by Ian Shapiro. New Haven, CT: Yale University Press, 2003.

Lowe, Lisa. *The Intimacies of Four Continents*. Durham, NC: Duke University Press, 2015.

Luck, Chad. *The Body of Property: Antebellum American Fiction and the Phenomenology of Possession*. New York: Fordham University Press, 2014.

Lustick, Ian S. *For the Land and the Lord: Jewish Fundamentalism in Israel*. New York: Council on Foreign Relations, 1988.

MacKinnon, Catharine A. *Toward a Feminist Theory of the State*. Cambridge, MA: Harvard University Press, 1989.

Macpherson, C. B. *The Political Theory of Possessive Individualism: Hobbes to Locke*. Oxford: Oxford University Press, 2011.

Mahmood, Saba. "Feminism, Democracy, and Empire: Islam and the War on Terror." In *Gendering Religion and Politics, Untangling Modernities*, edited by Hanna Herzog and Ann Braude, 194–215. London: Palgrave Macmillan, 2009.

Malkki, Liisa. "National Geographic: The Rooting of Peoples and the Territorialization of National Identity among Scholars and Refugees." *Cultural Anthropology* 7, no. 1 (1992): 24–44.

Mamdani, Mahmood. "Beyond Settler and Native as Political Identities: Overcoming the Political Legacy of Colonialism." *Comparative Studies in Society and History* 43, no. 4 (October 2001): 651–64.

Mamdani, Mahmood. "When Does a Settler Become a Native? Reflections of [sic] the Colonial Roots of Citizenship in Equatorial and South Africa." Inaugural lecture as A. C. Jordan Professor of African Studies, Centre for African Studies, University of Cape Town, May 13, 1998.

Mandal, Thomas. *Living with Settlers: Interviews with Yanoun Villagers*. https://docs .google.com/file/d/1TQK20xH76M7k0CORQt8v_Xj543Ym6vRp9EZ6kiO3NOAo PLsDeqLb2_Bz_N79/edit.

Manning, Erin. *Ephemeral Territories: Representing Nation, Home, and Identity in Canada*. Minneapolis: University of Minnesota Press, 2003.

Marasco, Robyn. *The Highway of Despair: Critical Theory after Hegel*. New York: Columbia University Press, 2015.

Martel, James. *The Misinterpellated Subject*. Durham, NC: Duke University Press, 2017.

Marx, Karl. "On the Jewish Question." In *The Marx-Engels Reader*, edited by Robert Tucker, 26–52. New York: W. W. Norton, 1978.

Masalha, Nur. *The Bible and Zionism: Invented Traditions, Archaeology and Postcolonialism in Israel-Palestine*. London: Zed Books, 2007.

Masalha, Nur. *Expulsion of the Palestinians: The Concept of "Transfer" in Zionist Political Thought, 1882–1948*. Washington, DC: Institute for Palestine Studies, 1992.

Masalha, Nur. *A Land without a People: Israel, Transfer, and the Palestinians 1949–96*. London: Faber, 1997.

Mason, Victoria. "Children of the 'Idea of Palestine': Negotiating Identity, Belonging and Home in the Palestinian Diaspora." *Journal of Intercultural Studies* 28, no. 3 (2007): 271–85.

MasterChef Israel. Keshet (Mako), 2017.

Matalon, Ronit, and Nili Mirski. *Strangers at Home*. [In Hebrew] Tel Aviv: Ha-Ḳibuts Ha-me'uḥad, 1992.

Matar, Anat. "What Enables Asa Kasher." *Mita'am* 6 (2006): 121–42.

Mbembe, Achille. *On the Postcolony*. Oakland: University of California Press, 2001.

McClintock, Anne. *Imperial Leather: Race, Gender, and Sexuality in the Colonial Contest*. New York: Routledge, 1995.

McIntosh, Janet. *Unsettled: Denial and Belonging among White Kenyans*. Oakland: University of California Press, 2016.

McNally, David. "Locke, Levellers and Liberty: Property and Democracy in the Thought of the First Whigs." *History of Political Thought* 10, no. 1 (spring 1989): 17–40.

Meari, Lena. "Colonial Dispossession, Developmental Discourses, and Humanitarian Solidarity in 'Area C': The Case of the Palestinian Yanun Village." *Community Development Journal* 52, no. 3 (July 2017): 506–23.

Mehta, Akanksha. "Right-Wing Sisterhood: Everyday Politics of Hindu Nationalist Women in India and Zionist Settler Women in Israel-Palestine." PhD diss., SOAS, University of London, 2017.

Mehta, Uday Singh. *The Anxiety of Freedom: Imagination and Individuality in Locke's Political Thought*. Ithaca, NY: Cornell University Press, 1992.

Mehta, Uday Singh. *Liberalism and Empire: A Study in Nineteenth-Century British Liberal Thought*. Chicago: University of Chicago Press, 1999.

Meishar, Naama. "In Search of Meta-Landscape Architecture: The Ethical Experience and Jaffa Slope Park's Design." *Journal of Landscape Architecture* 7, no. 2 (2012): 40–45.

Meister, Robert. *After Evil: A Politics of Human Rights*. New York: Columbia University Press, 2012.

Memmi, Albert. *The Colonizer and the Colonized*. London: Souvenir Press, [1974] 2016.

Mendel, Yonatan. *The Creation of Israeli Arabic: Political and Security Considerations in the Making of Arabic Language Studies in Israel*. London: Palgrave Macmillan, 2014.

Mendel, Yonatan, and Ronald Ranta. *From the Arab Other to the Israeli Self: Palestinian Culture in the Making of Israeli National Identity*. London: Ashgate, 2016.

Mills, Charles W. *The Racial Contract*. Ithaca, NY: Cornell University Press, 1997.

Mohanty, Chandra Talpade. *Feminism without Borders: Decolonizing Theory, Practicing Solidarity*. Durham, NC: Duke University Press, 2003.

Monterescu, Daniel. "The Bridled Bride of Palestine: Orientalism, Zionism, and the Troubled Urban Imagination." *Identities: Global Studies in Culture and Power* 16, no. 6 (2009): 643–77.

More, Thomas. *Utopia* (1516). Planet eBook. Accessed August 2019. https://www.planetebook.com/free-ebooks/utopia.pdf.

Morefield, Jeanne. *Empires without Imperialism: Anglo-American Decline and the Politics of Deflection*. Oxford: Oxford University Press, 2014.

Morefield, Jeanne. "World." Lecture, Conceptual Itineraries workshop, SOAS, University of London, June 2017.

Morgan, Jennifer L. *Laboring Women: Reproduction and Gender in New World Slavery.* Philadelphia: University of Pennsylvania Press, 2004.

Morgensen, Scott Lauria. "Theorising Gender, Sexuality and Settler Colonialism: An Introduction." *Settler Colonial Studies* 2, no. 2 (2012): 2–22.

Morris, Benny. *The Birth of the Palestinian Refugee Problem Revisited.* Cambridge: Cambridge University Press, 2004.

Moruzzi, Norma Claire. *Speaking through the Mask: Hannah Arendt and the Politics of Social Identity.* Ithaca, NY: Cornell University Press, 2001.

Mosse, David. "Anti-Social Anthropology? Objectivity, Objection, and the Ethnography of Public Policy and Professional Communities." *Journal of the Royal Anthropological Institute* 12, no. 4 (December 2006): 935–56.

Mossi, Norma. "To View the Landscape, to See a Place and to Name It: On the Tours of *Zochrot.*" [In Hebrew] In *Place Names and Spatial Identity in Israel-Palestine: Majority-Minority Relations, Obliviating and Memory,* edited by Amer Dahamshe and Yosef Schwartz, 167–90. Tel Aviv: Tel Aviv University Press, 2018.

Moulds, Henry. "Private Property in John Locke's State of Nature." *American Journal of Economics and Sociology* 23, no. 2 (1964): 179–88.

Nadan, Amos. "Colonial Misunderstanding of an Efficient Peasant Institution: Land Settlement and Mushāʿ Tenure in Mandate Palestine, 1921–47." *Journal of Economic and Social History of the Orient* 46, no. 3 (2003): 320–54.

Navaro-Yashin, Yael. "Affective Spaces, Melancholic Objects: Ruination and the Production of Anthropological Knowledge." *Journal of the Royal Anthropological Institute* 15, no. 1 (2009): 1–18.

Nemiroff, Robert. "A Critical Background." In *Les Blancs: The Collected Last Plays: The Drinking Gourd/What Use Are Flowers?,* by Lorraine Hansberry, edited by Robert Nemiroff, 32–33. New York: Random House, 1994.

Nichols, Robert. *Theft Is Property! Dispossession and Critical Theory.* Durham, NC: Duke University Press, forthcoming.

Nitzan-Shiftan, Alona. "The Israeli 'Place' in East Jerusalem: How Israeli Architects Appropriated the Palestinian Aesthetic after the '67 War." *Jerusalem Quarterly* 27 (2006): 15–27.

Nitzan-Shiftan, Alona. "Seizing Locality in Jerusalem." In *The End of Tradition?,* edited by Nezar AlSayyad. London: Routledge, 2004.

Nixon, Rob. *Slow Violence and the Environmentalism of the Poor.* Cambridge, MA: Harvard University Press, 2011.

Nocke, Alexandra. *The Place of the Mediterranean in Modern Israeli Identity.* Leiden: Brill, 2009.

Norton, Anne. "Heart of Darkness: Africa and African Americans in the Writings of Hannah Arendt." In *Feminist Interpretations of Hannah Arendt,* edited by Bonnie Honig, 247–61. University Park: Pennsylvania State University Press, 1995.

Novick, Tamar. "Milk and Honey: Technologies of Plenty in the Making of a Holy Land, 1880–1960." PhD diss., University of Pennsylvania, 2014.

Nozick, Robert. *Anarchy, State, and Utopia.* New York: Basic Books, 1974.

Nuriely, Beni. "Strangers in a National Space: Arab-Jews in the Palestinian Ghetto in Lod, 1950–1959." [In Hebrew] *Theory and Criticism* 26 (spring 2005): 13–42.

Ofran, Hagit, and Aharon Shem-Tov. "Unraveling the Mechanism behind Illegal Outposts." Settlement Watch, Peace Now. 2017. Accessed August 2019. http://peacenow.org.il/wp-content/uploads/2017/03/unraveling-the-mechanism-behind-illegal-outpots-full-report-1.pdf.

Olivecrona, Karl. "Locke's Theory of Appropriation." *Philosophical Quarterly* 24, no. 96 (July 1974): 220–34.

Ophir, Adi. "The Semiotics of Power: Reading Michel Foucault's *Discipline and Punish*." *Manuscrito: Revista Internacional de Filosofia* 12, no. 2 (1989): 9–34.

Ophir, Adi. "The Two-State Solution: Providence and Catastrophe." *Theoretical Inquiries in Law* 8, no. 1 (2007): 117–60.

Oxfam. "20 Facts: 20 Years since the Oslo Accords." Oxfam International. Accessed September 2018. https://www.oxfam.org/sites/www.oxfam.org/files/oxfam-oslo-20-factsheet.pdf.

Pagden, Anthony. *Lords of All the World: Ideologies of Empire in Spain, Britain and France c. 1500–c. 1800.* New Haven, CT: Yale University Press, 1998.

Papadakis, Yiannis. *Echoes from the Dead Zone: Across the Cyprus Divide.* New York: Palgrave Macmillan, 2005.

Pappé, Ilan. *The Ethnic Cleansing of Palestine.* London: One World, 2006.

Park, Robert E. "The Mind of the Hobo: Reflections upon the Relation between Mentality and Locomotion." In *The City: Suggestions for Investigation of Human Behavior in the Urban Environment,* edited by Robert E. Park and Ernst W. Burgess, 156–60. 2nd edition. Chicago: Chicago University Press, [1925] 1967.

Pateman, Carole. *The Sexual Contract.* Stanford, CA: Stanford University Press, 1988.

Pateman, Carole. "Women and Consent." *Political Theory* 8, no. 2 (1980): 149–68.

Pateman, Carole, and Charles W. Mills. *Contract and Domination.* Malden, MA: Polity, 2007.

Peace Now. "Land: Updated Statistics and Data." [In Hebrew] Settlements Watch, Peace Now. Accessed November 2019. http://peacenow.org.il/settlements-watch/matzav/land.

Peace Now. "The Outposts System (2018)." [In Hebrew] Peace Now. Last updated March 2018. http://peacenow.org.il/wp-content/uploads/2018/03/OutpostsUpdateMarch2018.pdf.

Peil, T. "Home." In *International Encyclopedia of Human Geography,* edited by Rob Kitchin and Nigel Thrift, 53–57. Amsterdam: Elsevier, 2009.

Piroyansky, Danna. "From Island to Archipelago: The Sakakini House in Qatamon and Its Shifting Ownerships throughout the Twentieth Century." *Middle Eastern Studies* 48, no. 6 (2012): 855–77.

Piroyansky, Danna. *Ramle Remade: The Israelization of an Arab Town 1948–1967.* Haifa: Pardes, 2014.

Prendergast, John. *Frontline Diplomacy: Humanitarian Aid and Conflict in Africa.* Boulder, CO: Lynne Rienner, 1996.

Puar, Jasbir K. *The Right to Maim: Debility, Capacity, Disability*. Durham, NC: Duke University Press, 2017.

Rabinowitz, Dan. "'The Arabs Just Left': Othering and the Construction of Self amongst Jews in Haifa before and after 1948." In *Mixed Towns, Trapped Communities: Historical Narratives, Spatial Dynamics, Gender Relations and Cultural Encounters in Palestinian-Israeli Towns*, edited by Daniel Monterescu and Dan Rabinowitz, 51–64. Aldershot, UK: Ashgate, 2007.

Ram, Mori. "White but Not Quite: Normalizing Colonial Conquests through Spatial Mimicry." *Antipode* 46, no. 3 (2014): 736–53.

Ramadan, Adam. "In the Ruins of Nahr al-Barid: Understanding the Meaning of the Camp." *Journal of Palestine Studies* 40, no. 1 (2010): 49–62.

Rao, Rahul. *Out of Time*. Oxford: Oxford University Press, 2020.

Raz, Avi. *The Bride and the Dowry: Israel, Jordan, and the Palestinians in the Aftermath of the June 1967 War*. New Haven, CT: Yale University Press, 2012.

Razack, Sherene. "How Is White Supremacy Embodied? Sexualized Racial Violence at Abu Ghraib." *Canadian Journal of Women and the Law* 17, no. 2 (2005): 341–63.

Raz-Krakotzkin, Amnon. "Exile and Binationalism: From Gershom Scholem and Hannah Arendt to Edward Said and Mahmoud Darwish." Carl Heinrich Becker Lecture, Fritz Thyssen Stiftung, Berlin Institute for Advanced Study, Berlin, 2012.

Raz-Krakotzkin, Amnon. "Exile, History, and the Nationalization of Jewish Memory: Some Reflections on the Zionist Notion of History and Return." *Journal of Levantine Studies* 3, no. 2 (winter 2013): 37–70.

Raz-Krakotzkin, Amnon. "Zionist Return to the West and the Mizrachi Jewish Perspective." In *Orientalism and the Jews*, edited by Ivan Kalmar and Derek Penslar, 162–81. Waltham, MA: Brandeis University Press, 2005.

Rijke, Alexandra, and Toine van Teeffelen. "To Exist Is to Resist: Sumud, Heroism, and the Everyday." *Jerusalem Quarterly* 59 (2014): 86–99.

Robbins, Bruce. *The Beneficiary*. Durham, NC: Duke University Press, 2017.

Rodinson, Maxime. *Israel: A Colonial-Settler State?* New York: Monad Press, 1973.

Rosen-Zvi, Issachar. *Taking Space Seriously: Law, Space and Society in Contemporary Israel*. Abingdon, VA: Routledge, 2017.

Rotbard, Sharon. *White City, Black City: Architecture and War in Tel Aviv and Jaffa*. Translated by Orit Gat. London: Pluto Press, 2015.

Rothberg, Michael. *The Implicated Subject: Beyond Victims and Perpetrators*. Stanford, CA: Stanford University Press, 2019.

Rousseau, Jean-Jacques. *The Basic Political Writings*. 2nd edition. Translated and edited by Donald A. Cress. Indianapolis, IN: Hackett, 2011.

Ruddick, Sara. *Maternal Thinking: Toward a Politics of Peace*. Boston: Beacon Press, 1989.

Said, Edward W. *Culture and Imperialism*. London: Vintage Books, 1994.

Said, Edward W. *Orientalism: Western Conceptions of the Orient*. London: Routledge, 1978.

Said, Edward W. *The Politics of Dispossession: The Struggle for Palestinian Self-Determination 1969–1994*. New York: Knopf Doubleday, [1995] 2012.

Said, Edward W. *Power, Politics, and Culture: Interviews with Edward W. Said.* Edited by Gauri Viswanathan. New York: Vintage Books, 2001.

Said, Edward W. *The Question of Palestine.* London: Routledge, 1980.

Said, Edward W. *Reflections on Exile and Other Essays.* Cambridge, MA: Harvard University Press, 2000.

Said, Edward W. "Zionism from the Standpoint of Its Victims." *Social Text* 1 (1979): 7–58.

Salamanca, Omar Jabary. "The Ends of Infrastructure." Paper presented at the Environmental Justice in Israel/Palestine Conference, Buffalo, NY, February 6–7, 2019.

Salamanca, Omar, Mezna Qato, Kareem Rabie, and Sobhi Samour. "Past Is Present: Settler Colonialism in Palestine." *Settler Colonial Studies* 2, no. 1 (2012): 1–8.

Salih, Ruba. "'Intellectuals Know, but People Feel': Palestinian Refugees, Gramsci and Cathartic Politics." Lecture, SOAS University of London, London, October 18, 2017.

Salih, Ruba, and Olaf Corry. "Settler Colonialism, Displacement and the Reordering of Human and Non-Human Life in Palestine." Unpublished paper.

Salih, Ruba, and Sophie Richter-Devroe. "Palestine beyond National Frames: Emerging Politics, Cultures, and Claims." *South Atlantic Quarterly* 117, no. 1 (2018): 1–20.

Samnotra, Manu. "'Poor in World': Hannah Arendt's Critique of Imperialism." *Contemporary Political Theory* 18, no. 4 (2018): 562–82.

Sartre, Jean-Paul. *Being and Nothingness: A Phenomenological Essay on Ontology.* New York: Open Road Media, [1943] 2012.

Sartre, Jean-Paul. *Nausea.* Translated by Lloyd Alexander. New York: New Directions, 1964.

Sason, Talya. "Summary of the Opinion Concerning Unauthorized Outposts." Israel Ministry of Foreign Affairs. March 10, 2005. https://mfa.gov.il/mfa/aboutisrael/state/law/pages/summary%20of%20opinion%20concerning%20unauthorized%20outposts%20-%20talya%20sason%20adv.aspx.

Sayigh, Rosemary. "A House Is Not a Home: Permanent Impermanence of Habitat for Palestinian Expellees in Lebanon." *Holy Land Studies* 4, no. 1 (2005): 17–39.

Schmidgen, Wolfram. "The Politics and Philosophy of Mixture: John Locke Recomposed." *Eighteenth Century* 48, no. 3 (fall 2007): 205–23.

Schmitt, Carl. *The Nomos of the Earth in the International Law of the* Jus Publicum Europaeum. Translated by G. L. Ulmen. New York: Telos Press, 2006.

Schroeder, Jonathan D. S. "What Was Black Nostalgia?" *American Literary History* 30, no. 4 (November 2018): 653–76.

Schulz, Helena Lindholm, and Juliane Hammer. *The Palestinian Diaspora: Formation of Identities and Politics of Homeland.* London: Routledge, 2003.

Segev, Tom. *The Seventh Million: The Israelis and the Holocaust.* New York: Hill and Wang, 1993.

Shafir, Gershon. *Land, Labor and the Origins of the Israeli-Palestinian Conflict, 1882–1914.* Cambridge: Cambridge University Press, 1989.

Shafir, Gershon, and Yoav Peled. *Being Israeli: The Dynamics of Multiple Citizenship.* Cambridge: Cambridge University Press, 2002.

Shai, Aron. "The Fate of Abandoned Arab Villages in Israel, 1965–1969." *History and Memory* 18, no. 2 (fall/winter 2006): 86–106.

Shani, Ben. "Vineyards instead of Mobile Homes." *Uvda*, by Ilana Dayan. TV show, Keshet TV. November 16, 2009. https://www.mako.co.il/tv-ilana_dayan/2010-dcc4c8a272df4210/Article-4db3863563df421006.htm.

Shanley, Mary Lyndon. "Marriage Contract and Social Contract in Seventeenth-Century English Political Thought." In *Feminist Interpretations of John Locke*, edited by Nancy J. Hirschmann and Kirstie M. McClure, 17–49. University Park: Pennsylvania State University Press, 2007.

Shapira, Anita. "Hirbet Hizah: Between Remembrance and Forgetting." In *Making Israel*, edited by Benny Morris, 81–123. Ann Arbor: University of Michigan Press, 2007.

Shapira, Anita. *Land and Power: The Zionist Resort to Force, 1881–1948*. Stanford, CA: Stanford University Press, 1999.

Shavit, Ari. *My Promised Land: The Triumph and Tragedy of Israel*. Melbourne: Scribe Publications, 2014.

Shehadeh, Raja. *The Third Way: A Journal of Life in the West Bank*. New York: Quartet Books, 1982.

Shenhav, Yehuda. *Beyond the Two-State Solution*. Cambridge: Polity Press, 2012.

Shklar, Judith N. "The Liberalism of Fear." In *Liberalism and the Moral Life*, edited by Nancy L. Rosenblum, 1–38. Cambridge, MA: Harvard University Press, 1989.

Shohat, Ella. "Sephardim in Israel: Zionism from the Standpoint of Its Jewish Victims." *Social Text* 19/20 (autumn 1988): 1–35.

Shumsky, Dimitry. "'This Ship Is Zion!': Travel, Tourism, and Cultural Zionism in Theodor Herzl's 'Altneuland.'" *Jewish Quarterly Review* 104, no. 3 (summer 2014): 471–93.

Siegert, Bernhard. *Cultural Techniques: Grids, Filters, Doors, and Other Articulations of the Real*. Translated by Geoffrey Winthrop-Young. New York: Fordham University Press, 2015.

Simelane, Hamilton Sipho. "Landlessness and Imperial Response in Swaziland, 1938–1950." *Journal of Southern African Studies* 17, no. 4 (1991): 717–41.

Simmons, A. John. *The Lockean Theory of Rights*. Princeton, NJ: Princeton University Press, 1992.

Simon, Ernst. "What Price Israel's 'Normalcy'? A Young Nation and Its Ideals." *Commentary* 7 (1949). https://www.commentarymagazine.com/articles/ernst-simon/what-price-israels-normalcya-young-nation-and-its-ideals/.

Simonds, Roger T. "John Locke's Use of Classical Legal Theory." *International Journal of the Classical Tradition* 3, no. 4 (spring 1997): 424–32.

Sjoberg, Laura, and Caron E. Gentry. *Mothers, Monsters, Whores: Women's Violence in Global Politics*. New York: Zed Books, 2007.

Slotkin, Richard. *Regeneration through Violence: The Mythology of the American Frontier, 1600–1860*. Norman: University of Oklahoma Press, 2000.

Slyomovics, Susan. *The Object of Memory: Arab and Jew Narrate the Palestinian Village*. Philadelphia: University of Pennsylvania Press, 1998.

Smith, Barbara. Introduction to *Home Girls: A Black Feminist Anthology*. Revised edition. New Brunswick, NJ: Rutgers University Press, [1983] 2000.

Smith, Shawn M. *American Archives: Gender, Race, and Class in Visual Culture*. Princeton, NJ: Princeton University Press, 2000.

Smith, Shawn M. *Photography on the Color Line: W. E. B. Du Bois, Race, and Visual Culture*. Durham, NC: Duke University Press, 2004.

Spivak, Gayatri Chakravorty. "Can the Subaltern Speak?" In *Marxism and the Interpretation of Culture*, edited by Cary Nelson and Lawrence Grossberg, 271–313. Champaign: University of Illinois Press, 1988.

Sreenivasan, Gopal. *The Limits of Lockean Rights in Property*. New York: Oxford University Press, 1995.

Stavig, Ward. "Ambiguous Visions: Nature, Law, and Culture in Indigenous-Spanish Land Relations in Colonial Peru." *Hispanic American Historical Review* 80, no. 1 (February 2000): 77–111.

Stewart, Kathleen. *A Space on the Side of the Road: Cultural Poetics in an "Other" America*. Princeton, NJ: Princeton University Press, 1996.

Stoler, Ann Laura. *Along the Archival Grain: Epistemic Anxieties and Colonial Common Sense*. Princeton, NJ: Princeton University Press, 2009.

Stoler, Ann Laura. *Carnal Knowledge and Imperial Power: Race and the Intimate in Colonial Rule*. Oakland: University of California Press, 2002.

Stoler, Ann Laura. "Colonial Aphasia: Race and Disabled Histories in France." *Public Culture* 23, no. 1 (winter 2011): 121–56.

Stoler, Ann Laura. *Duress: Imperial Durabilities in Our Times*. Durham, NC: Duke University Press, 2016.

Stoler, Ann Laura. *Imperial Debris: On Ruins and Ruination*. Durham, NC: Duke University Press, 2013.

Stoler, Ann Laura. "On Degrees of Imperial Sovereignty." *Public Culture* 18, no. 1 (2006): 125–46.

Stoler, Ann Laura. *Race and the Education of Desire: Foucault's History of Sexuality and the Colonial Order of Things*. Durham, NC: Duke University Press, 1995.

Straumann, Benjamin. *Roman Law in the State of Nature: The Classical Foundations of Hugo Grotius' Natural Law*. Translated by Belinda Cooper. Cambridge: Cambridge University Press, 2015.

Susskind, Lawrence, Hillel Levine, Gideon Aran, Shlomo Kaniel, Yair Sheleg, and Moshe Halbertal. "Religious and Ideological Dimensions of the Israeli Settlements Issue: Reframing the Narrative." *Negotiation Journal* 21, no. 2 (April 2005): 177–91.

Tabachnick, David. "Two Models of Ownership: How Commons Has Co-existed with Private Property." *American Journal of Economics and Sociology* 75, no. 2 (March 2016): 488–563.

Tamari, Salim. "Bourgeois Nostalgia and the Abandoned City." In *Mixed Towns, Trapped Communities: Historical Narratives, Spatial Dynamics, Gender Relations and Cultural Encounters in Palestinian-Israeli Towns*, edited by Daniel Monterescu and Dan Rabinowitz, 35–49. Aldershot, UK: Ashgate, 2007.

Tamari, Salim. *Mountain against Sea: Essays on Palestinian Society and Culture*. Berkeley: University of California Press, 2008.

Tamari, Salim, and Rema Hammami. "Virtual Returns to Jaffa." *Journal of Palestine Studies* 27, no. 4 (summer 1998): 65–79.

Terry, Jennifer. *Attachments to War: Biomedical Logics and Violence in Twenty-First-Century America*. Durham, NC: Duke University Press, 2017.

Tomlins, Christopher. *Freedom Bound: Law, Labor, and Civic Identity in Colonizing English America, 1580–1865*. Cambridge: Cambridge University Press, 2010.

Torpey, John. *The Invention of the Passport: Surveillance, Citizenship and the State*. Cambridge: Cambridge University Press, 2000.

Trigg, Dylan. *The Memory of Place: A Phenomenology of the Uncanny*. Athens: Ohio University Press, 2012.

Trotter, David. "Fanon's Nausea." *Parallax* 5, no. 2 (1999): 32–50.

Tuck, Richard. *Natural Rights Theories: Their Origin and Development*. Cambridge: Cambridge University Press, 1979.

Tully, James. "Aboriginal Property and Western Theory: Recovering a Middle Ground." *Social Philosophy and Policy* 11, no. 2 (summer 1994): 153–80.

Tully, James. *An Approach to Political Philosophy: Locke in Contexts*. Cambridge: Cambridge University Press, 1993.

Tully, James. *A Discourse on Property: John Locke and His Adversaries*. Cambridge: Cambridge University Press, 1980.

Turner, Jack. "John Locke, Christian Mission, and Colonial America." *Modern Intellectual History* 8, no. 2 (2011): 267–97.

Veracini, Lorenzo. "Decolonising Settler Colonialism: Kill the Settler in Him and Save the Man." Lecture, SOAS, University of London, June 5, 2017.

Veracini, Lorenzo. "Introducing: Settler Colonial Studies." *Settler Colonial Studies* 1, no. 1 (2011): 1–12.

Veracini, Lorenzo. "The Other Shift: Settler Colonialism, Israel, and the Occupation." *Journal of Palestine Studies* 42, no. 2 (winter 2013): 26–42.

Veracini, Lorenzo. "Settler Collective, Founding Violence and Disavowal: The Settler Colonial Situation." *Journal of Intercultural Studies* 29, no. 4 (2008): 363–79.

Veracini, Lorenzo. *Settler Colonialism: A Theoretical Overview*. London: Palgrave Macmillan, 2010.

Walcott, Derek. "The Antilles: Fragments of Epic Memory." Nobel lecture, December 7, 1992. http://nobelprize.org/nobel_prizes/literature/laureates/1992/walcott-lecture.htm.

Waldron, Jeremy. *The Right to Private Property*. Oxford: Clarendon Press, 1990.

Walters, William. "Secure Borders, Safe Haven, Domopolitics." *Citizenship Studies* 8, no. 3 (2004): 237–60.

Watson, Alan, ed. *The Digest of Justinian*. Vol. 1. Philadelphia: University of Pennsylvania Press, 1998.

Weheliye, Alexander G. *Habeas Viscus: Racializing Assemblages, Biopolitics, and Black Feminist Theories of the Human*. Durham, NC: Duke University Press, 2014.

Weil, Simone. *The Need for Roots: Prelude to a Declaration of Duties towards Mankind*. Translated by Arthur Wills. London: Routledge, [1949] 2002.

Weiss, Erica. "'There Are No Chickens in Suicide Vests': The Decoupling of Human Rights and Animal Rights in Israel." *Journal of the Royal Anthropological Institute* 22, no. 3 (September 2016): 688–706.

Weiss, Yfaat. *A Confiscated Memory: Wadi Salib and Haifa's Lost Heritage*. Translated by Avner Greenberg. New York: Columbia University Press, 2011.

Weizman, Eyal. *Hollow Land: Israel's Architecture of Occupation*. London: Verso Books, 2007.

Weizman, Eyal. *The Least of All Possible Evils: Humanitarian Violence from Arendt to Gaza*. London: Verso Books, 2011.

Weizman, Eyal, and Fazal Sheikh. *The Conflict Shoreline: Colonization as Climate Change in the Negev Desert*. Göttingen: Steidl, 2015.

Wells, Ida B. *Southern Horrors: Lynch Law in All Its Phases*. Auckland, New Zealand: Floating Press, 2014.

Williams, Raymond. *Marxism and Literature*. Oxford: Oxford University Press, 1977.

Williams, Raymond. "Structures of Feeling." In *Marxism and Literature*, 128–35. Oxford: Oxford University Press, 1977.

Williams, Raymond, and Michael Orrom. *Preface to Film*. London: Film Drama, 1954.

Winter, Yves. "Violence and Visibility." *New Political Science* 34, no. 2 (2012): 195–202.

Yacobi, Haim. "Architecture, Orientalism, Identity: The Politics of the Israeli-Built Environment." *Israel Studies* 13, no. 1 (2008): 94–118.

Yacobi, Haim and Hadas Shadar. "The Arab Village: A Genealogy of (Post)colonial Imagination." *Journal of Architecture* 19, no. 6 (2014): 975–997.

Yifrach, Yehuda. "Avri Ran Won the Arbitration." [In Hebrew] NRG, April 26, 2013, http://www.nrg.co.il/online/1/ART2/463/901.html.

Youngquist, Paul. "Romantic Dietetics! Or, Eating Your Way to a New You." In *Cultures of Taste/Theories of Appetite: Eating Romanticism*, edited by Timothy Morton, 237–55. New York: Palgrave Macmillan, 2004.

Yuval-Davis, Nira. *The Politics of Belonging: Intersectional Contestations*. London: SAGE, 2011.

Zaban, Hila. "Preserving 'the Enemy's' Architecture: Preservation and Gentrification in a Formerly Palestinian Jerusalem Neighbourhood." *International Journal of Heritage Studies* 23, no. 10 (2017): 961–76.

Zambakari, Christopher. "Land Grab and Institutional Legacy of Colonialism: The Case of Sudan." *Consilience: The Journal of Sustainable Development* 18, no. 2 (2017): 193–204.

Zartal, Idit. *Israel's Holocaust and the Politics of Nationhood*. Cambridge: Cambridge University Press, 2005.

Zerilli, Linda M. G. "The Arendtian Body." In *Feminist Interpretations of Hannah Arendt*, edited by Bonnie Honig, 167–94. University Park: Pennsylvania State University Press, 1995.

Zertal, Idith, and Akiva Eldar. *Lords of the Land: The War over Israel's Settlements in the Occupied Territories, 1967–2007.* Translated by Vivian Eden. New York: Nation Books, 2005.

Zinngrebe, Kim Jezabel. "Defying 'the Plan': Intimate Politics among Palestinian Women in Israel." PhD diss., SOAS, University of London, 2017.

Zreik, Raef. "Leumit ve colonialit [National and colonial]." [In Hebrew] *Ha'aretz,* July 21, 2015.

Zreik, Raef. "Theodor Herzl (1860–1904): Sovereignty and the Two Palestines." In *Makers of Jewish Modernity: Thinkers, Artists, Leaders, and the World They Made,* edited by Jacques Picard, Jacques Revel, Michael P. Steinberg, and Idith Zertal, 46–60. Princeton, NJ: Princeton University Press, 2016.

Zreik, Raef. "When Does a Settler Become a Native? (With Apologies to Mamdani)." *Constellations* 23, no. 3 (2016): 351–64.

Index

Abdel-Nour, Farid, 180–81
Absentee's Law, 117n21, 192
Abu-Lughod, Ibrahim, 151–52, 195
Abu-Lughod, Lila, 110n2, 195, 241n49
Abu Sitta, Salman, 38
accumulation: Locke's theory of, 84, 89–90, 99, 102–4, 106, 257; Wolfe on, 215
Adorno, Theodor W., 22
affect: affectual attachment to home, 4n10, 109–10, 196; affectual conditions of settler colonialism, 3–4, 31–32, 132–33; affective perception of destruction, 263–64; cruelty/violence and, 35, 235–36, 239; desire and, 47; ruins and, xi, 172, 174, 188–89, 194
Africa: Arendt on refugees and, 60–61; homemaking and, 61–67, 111; the Jewish question and, 68–70. *See also* Les Blancs; Boers
Agamben, Giorgio, 76, 79n10
agriculture: Boers and, 66–67; ethics of (organic agriculture), 6, 26, 218, 238–42, 252–58, 260; as a means of land grab, 24, 103, 209, 217–19, 227–28, 232, 242–44, 246, 248; Locke and, 87n30, 88–89, 99, 103, 107, 257; the "new Jew" and, 117. *See also* Giv'ot Olam; organic washing
Ahmed, Sara: on exile and privilege, 21–22; on home, 3n10; on home and away, 17n34; on justice and recognition, 266
al-Barghouti, Mureed, 111n5, 196
Aleksandrowicz, Or, 16, 64n29
Allegra, Marco, 246, 258

Althusser, Louis, 33n4
America: as democratized racial society, 133; and its frontier, 247, 248; Locke and, 60–61, 64, 84, 86–89, 92n51, 98–104, 107; lynching in, 36; slavery in, 66; support for Israeli state, 184; wilderness and, 155n32. *See also* Indigenous Americans
Amona, 25, 199, 203–14, 253, 258
animals: as central to occupation of land, 107, 227–30, 257; in domestic sphere, 56, 91; Locke on, 89–91, 95n62, 104; organic washing and, 26, 220, 238–39, 253–56; racialization and, 66n35, 256; violence toward, 236, 238–40, 256–57, 262
Anzaldúa, Gloria, 112–13
A'qraba, 233, 245
architecture: architectonic appropriation, 159–63, 174, 177; of control, 211; Western, as exclusionary, 63–64
Arendt, Hannah: on Africa, 60–63, 65–68, 111; boomerang effect, 106; on compliance with evil, 33n7–8; on domestic and political spheres, 8n19, 56–60, 76–78, 80; on the meaning of home, 2; on refugees and statelessness, 60–61, 71, 111; on stability and place, 56, 58–60, 76–77, 113–14; on unlimited expansion, 83; on Zionism, 68–70. *See also* body, the: Arendtian
Aristotle: on coupling, 106–7; on household/oikos and state/polis, 4, 8n18, 75–79; on politics, 73. *See also* oikos; polis
Armitage, David, 83–84, 87

Arneil, Barbara: on colonies, domestic and otherwise, 64n30; on Locke, 83, 91, 103
Atiyah, Patrick S., 84n23
attachment. *See* affect; wounded attachment
Ayn Hawd/Ein Hod, 6, 162–63, 174, 188
Azoulay, Ariella, 18n38, 120n34, 121n38; on alternative histories, 50n52, 142n12; on the concept of violence, 186, 193–94; on Palestinian houses as soldiers' residences, 236n43; on shock and violence, 40–41

ba'it/beit, 2–3, 109–10
Baucom, Ian, 189–90
Bauman, Zygmunt, 33nn6–7
Bedouin: appropriation and, 175–77; house demolitions and, 121n39, 198–99; state violence and, 81
Behnegar, Nasser, 93, 97n67
Beit Furik, 223, 259
Benhabib, Seyla, 62n24
Benjamin, Walter, 12n28, 106, 195
Benvenisti, Meron, 175n91, 176n94, 211, 263; critiques of, 51n53, 171, 173
Berlant, Lauren: on cruel optimism or attachments, 157, 165, 265; on desire, 9–10, 47–49, 165
Bhabha, Homi K., 176
Bishara, Amahl, 2n3, 139, 152
body, the: Arendtian, 57nn7–8; bodily mimicking, 175–77; as a form of home, 113; injured or assaulted, 34n11, 37, 44, 49, 229; Locke on, 24, 74, 82, 90–100, 107; racial scheme of, 140. *See also* lynching; nausea; vomiting
Boers, 65–68, 70, 258
borders: of the body/self, 97–98, 100; crossing of, 7, 112, 207; defying, 235, 247; fluidity of, 230, 256n19, 257; of the household/domestic sphere, 59, 76, 78, 99; law and, 59; Lockean property as a system of, 82; Palestinian identity and, 112
Brenner, Yosef Haim, 156, 158–59
British Empire, 189–90; in Africa, 65–66; in America, 87, 100–101, 103n85, 258; in Palestine, 50–51, 153
Brit Shalom, 69n44
Bronstein Aparicio, Eitan, ix–x

Brown, Wendy: on action and the body, 57n7; on fences in Locke, 100; on wounded attachments, 25, 142, 165
Bryant, Rebecca, 1, 138n1, 150–51
Butler, Judith: on action and the body, 57n7; on exile, 22; on injury and subjectivity, 32, 45–50; performative politics, 114; on psychic violence, 4n11; on racist violence, 36n17

capitalism: colonialism and, 86n29, 101–4; desire under, 9–10, 47–48; home and, 2n4
Caribbean, 102, 189
Cohen, Stanley, 38–41, 171
compliance (as model of violence), 32–34, 43
construction: colonial administration of, 63–64, 254n8; destruction or ruination as constitutive of, 22, 119, 220; models of home construction in the settlements, 208, 227, 258; of new settlements, 199, 205, 214, 221, 225n23, 227; Zionism and, 11–12, 248. *See also* destruction, constitutive
Corry, Olaf, 263
cruelty: as model of violence, 34–37, 43, 49, 180; torture, 34, 188; toward animals, 240. *See also* animals: violence toward; sadism
Cyprus, 18, 138, 150n25

death: of the author, 191; of the colonized (Palestinians in the West Bank), 39, 220, 232, 256–57; of the colonizer, 129–35; home demolition as technology of, 122; politics/law and, 57n8, 59; settler colonialism/genocide and, 18n37; slavery and, 6n20, 92
decolonization: Fanon on, 176; settler-colonial paradigm and, 19; Said on, 181; the settler's role in, xii, 21, 130–35, 265–66. *See also* Les Blancs
denial (of violence): alternative signification, 39, 41; collective amnesia, 38; colonial aphasia, 40, 153–54, 171; collective blindness, 121; deflection as a form of, 40, 42; dismissal of violence, 35–36; as a framework to explain violence, 14–15, 38, 43, 173; undeniability of violence, 121, 142, 179, 181; visibility and, 167–70, 187. *See also* dissociation; visibility

Derrida, Jacques: on the politics of friendship, 77–78; on violence and signification,
190–92
destruction, constitutive, 10, 12, 22, 119–20,
123, 257
Development Authority, 117n21, 148
diaspora: as an alternative to national politics, 21–22; Jewish, 22, 69–70, 114, 205n6;
Palestinian, 111
digestion: as a mode of colonization or a refusal thereof, 139–40, 260; as manifestation
of complicity, 74; Lockean property and,
95–101, 105–7. See also nausea; vomiting
Dirbas, Sahera. See Stranger in My Home
disengagement from Gaza, 203n1, 205, 220,
224n18, 254n10. See also Gaza
dispossession: colonial construction laws
and, 63, 255n13; diachronic neighbors and,
118–19; expansion as, 103–4, 107; labor as
basis for, 88, 102, 257; limits of the concept
of, 18n37; recognition of, 195n20; ruins as
reliving of, 192, 196; settler's attachment to,
133; subjectivity and, 5–7, 49, 104, 147, 260;
tribal logic and, 70; visibility of, 141, 179,
208. See also house demolitions: of Palestinians; terra nullius
dissociation: as model of explaining violence,
37–43, 45, 48n50, 73, 141n6, 145, 158, 164,
182n111; racial alienation, 140; visibility and,
263–64. See also denial (of violence)
domesticity: colonial violence and, 234–36;
domestic rule in Locke, 82; the occupation
and, 206, 233, 235–36; relation to the political sphere, 56–59, 76–77, 80–81; sexual
contract and, 91; slavery and, 66, 81.
See also Arendt, Hannah: on domestic
and political spheres; domestic violence;
feminist theory; oikos
domestic violence, 74, 235; rape/sexual violence, 9, 81, 91–92. See also feminist theory
domos, 3, 84n24; domopolitics, 236–37
Douglas, Mary, 150n25

Ein Hod. See Ayn Hawd/Ein Hod
Eldar, Akiva, 204n3, 221n13, 222n15, 226n23
el-Hairi, Bashir, 212n19, 265–66
enclosure: bodily borders as, 98, 100; Boers'
refusal of, 65; as foundation of expansion,

107; Locke on, 82, 84n25, 89, 95, 99–101,
103, 257; as necessary for freedom, 76;
nomos and, 59; system of commons and,
84n23; in the West Bank, 256n19, 256.
See also expansion
enlightened occupation, 41, 240
erasure. See destruction, constitutive; denial
(of violence); house demolitions; memory;
visibility
Eretz Israel, 144, 157n37, 175n92, 251–52, 255
ethics: of capitalism in Locke, 90, 103–4; dissociation and, 40–41, 147; as facilitating or
justifying violence, 6, 162n56, 217–18, 235,
238–42, 251–56
Etkes, Dror. See Kerem Navot
Europe: attachments to colonial spaces, 17;
colonial construction and, 63–64; Euro-
peanization of Israel/Palestine, 160–61,
165–66, 178, 253, 258–59; European refugees,
60–61; Locke on European agriculture,
86–89; models of property or home, 23,
65–66, 74, 100; tribal attitude in 70, 67–68;
Zionism as European project, 20n44
Evri, Yuval, 20, 50, 70, 132
exile: in Israeli identity, 12; Palestinian, 111–13,
147, 174; political exile of Israeli Jews, 21–22;
Zionism as negation of, 21, 114
expansion: colonial, 86–87, 89, 254, 257;
corporeal expansion, 98; Locke and, 24,
74–75, 83, 91, 98–100, 103–4, 107; through
mobility, 218, 256–57; racism/tribalism
and, 67–68, 70; self-definition and, 75,
83; of settlements, 223–24, 225n23. See also
agriculture: as a means of land grab
Eyal, Gil, 175–78

Falah, Ghazi, 149
Fanon, Frantz, 135, 140, 176
fascism, 32, 34, 143
Feige, Michael: on home as a political project
in the West Bank, 208nn9–10, 258; on settlers' violence, 252n4
feminist theory: desire and, 31, 44–45, 49;
domestic sphere and, 9, 24, 73–74, 80–82,
107; on women as agents of colonization,
234–35. See also domestic violence
Fenster, Tovi, 150, 154, 158, 197
Fitzmaurice, Andrew, 87n33, 89

ruins: aestheticization of, 145, 162–63, 171, 179, 185–86, 190; attachment to, 162, 174, 177, 185–90, 193, 195; as dispossession relived, 195–96; imperial, 187–90, 197; as signifiers of violence, 190–92; as violence that cannot be erased, 194–95. *See also* house demolitions; rubble; waste

sadism, 34–35, 43, 180. *See also* cruelty
Said, Edward W.: on destruction/displacement, 12, 80, 134; on dissociation, 158; on exile, 21–22, 111; on home, ix, 1, 266; on his home and the right of return, 151–54, 195n20; interview with Ari Shavit, 151–54, 181; on justificatory frames of colonization, 107
Salih, Ruba, 11–12, 111, 114, 263
Salt of This Sea (Jacir), 115n17, 137–42, 144–45, 147, 157–59, 179–81, 195–98, 219, 260, 263–64
Samnotra, Manu, xii, 62
Sartre, Jean-Paul, 138n1, 140
Sason Report, 221n13, 226n23
Sayigh, Rosemary, 111n3, 138
Schmitt, Carl, 59
sedentarism, 23, 55–56, 58, 67, 87n30, 89, 99, 101. *See also* agriculture; terra nullius
Segev, Tom, 147, 151
Seth, Vanita, 98
settlements' evacuation, 199, 203–4, 209–10, 225–26
settlements' regulation, 148, 225; by annexing mundane facets of life, 216–17; official plans to annex West Bank territories, 183–84, 248. *See also* Levy Report; Regulation Law
Shadar, Hadas, 161, 177
Shai, Aron, 120–21, 185
Shapira, Anita, 156, 168n76, 177
Shavit, Arie, 151–54, 158, 181–82, 264n6
Shohat, Ella, 118
Shumsky, Dimitry, 166–67
slavery, 2, 7, 56; Arendt on, 66; Aristotle on, 77, 79–80; imperial ruins and, 189; Locke on, 75n4, 82, 90–92, 104; mobile labor and, 102; nostalgia/pathology and, 6n20; pain and, 35n16; rape and, 81
Slyomovics, Susan, 163n59, 196

Smith, Shawn, 36–37
Spivak, Gayatri, 38n24
stability: 21, 40, 82, 100–101, 110, 114, 258. *See also* Arendt, Hannah: on stability and place; rootedness; sedentarism
statelessness. *See* refugees
Stewart, Kathleen, 194–96
Stoler, Ann Laura: on categories of imperialism, 18; on colonial aphasia/memory, 40, 153–54, 171; on emotional economies, 4, 133; on imperial ruins, 187–90, 193, 195, 197; on knowledge and empire, 29–30; on mobility and empire, 17n34; on sentiment and colonial regimes, 141; on shocked moral outrage, 41n35
Stranger in My Home (Dirbas), 146–48, 158
structural beneficiaries, 27, 37, 44. *See also* implicated subjects; Robbins, Bruce
structures of feelings, 29, 49, 132–33
sumud, 11, 112
Syria, x–xi, 186

Talbieh, 152–53
Tamari, Salim, 137
Tel Aviv, 15–16, 64n29, 116, 182, 260
terrain, 66–67, 214, 228, 244, 246
terra nullius: in Arendt, 61; empty/virgin land, 120–21, 155, 157n37, 165, 171, 176, 217, 263–64; nomadism and, 14n31; Zionism and, 20
Tuck, Richard, 84n24, 85n27
Tully, James, 85n26, 87n32, 88, 96, 102n83
Turner, Jack, 101

Veracini, Lorenzo: on decolonization, 131–33; on disavowal, 41n34; on Israel and settler-colonial paradigm, 19n41; on libidinal economy, 155–56; on settler vs. immigrant, 128n4, 130
visibility: critique as enhancing/politics of, 30, 42–43, 45, 187, 241, 262; denial and, 142, 144–45, 154, 158, 164–71, 263; of destruction and its traces, 121, 141, 170, 174, 179, 188; erasure of traces of violence, 14–15; and invisibility of Palestinians, 40, 211, 212; memory and, 118–19, 173; slow violence and, 193–94; work of rendering visible, ix, 115n16. See also denial (of violence); organic washing

visits: of Palestinians to former homes, 11, 115, 137–39, 141–42, 145–48, 151–52, 196, 265–66; of early Zionists to Palestine, 154, 156n37, 165, 170

vomiting, 74, 101, 107, 138–39, 151, 159, 170, 180. *See also* digestion; nausea

vulnerability: imperial formations and, 187; injury and, 46–47; politics of, 73

Wadi Salib, 117

war: civil war, 18, 205; First World War, 60; integration into Israeli life/identity, 168, 186; second Lebanon War, 26, 121n39; Second World War, 18, 51, 61; and slavery in Locke, 92; 1948 war, 69–70, 116–21; 1967 war, 121, 154, 161. *See also* Gaza; Nakba

waste: as litter (domestic and otherwise), 138, 197, 211n16, 233; waste land, 88. *See also* rubble; terra nullius

water: allocation of in the West Bank, 211n15; as a fluid border, 230

Weber, Max, 8n18

Weil, Simone, 55–56

Weiss, Erica, 253–54, 260

Weiss, Yfat, 118

Weitz, Joseph, 263–64

Weizman, Eyal, 122–23, 160, 211n14, 215, 238, 244, 246, 248n71

Williams, Raymond, 29

Winter, Yves, 164

Wolfe, Patrick: on agriculture as colonial land grab, 103, 215, 217, 229, 244, 255; on colonialism vs. settler colonialism, 17; on elimination, 18n37, 50, 159n44; on Maxime Rodinson, 19n40; on nomadism, 64n32; on settler colonialism, 11, 49, 89, 107, 131–32

wounded attachment, 25, 37, 142, 144, 150, 157, 265

Yacobi, Haim, 117–18, 160–63, 177–78

Yanun, 26, 219–20, 223, 228–32, 245–46. *See also* Giv'ot Olam

Yiftachel, Oren, 19n41, 244n60

Yizhar, S., 157–59, 226n23, 264

Yuval-Davis, Nira, 3n9

Zerilli, Linda, 57n7

Zertal, Idith, 204n3, 221n13, 222n15, 226n23

Zochrot, ix, 115n16

Zreik, Raef: on settler and native, 132–33; on Zionism, 19–20, 143n14, 166–67